M000309770

PENGUIN REFERENCE

Penguin Pocket On This Day

David Crystal was born in 1941 and spent the early years of his life in Holyhead, North Wales. He went to St Mary's College, Liverpool, and University College, London, where he read English and obtained his Ph.D. in 1966. He was a lecturer in linguistics at the universities of Bangor and Reading, becoming Honorary Professor of Linguistics at the University of Wales, Bangor. He is editor of *The Penguin Encyclopedia* and related publications, the former editor of the Cambridge family of general encyclopedias, compiler of several dictionaries, and author of publications on the theory and practice of reference works. He is co-founder of a company which manages a large reference database and which is developing systems for improving document classification and internet search. A past president of the Society of Indexers, in 2001 his book *Words on Words* (co-authored with Hilary Crystal) was awarded the Wheatley Medal for an outstanding index. In 1995 he was awarded the OBE for services to the English language.

PENGUIN POCKET ON THIS DAY

David Crystal

PENGUIN BOOKS

PENGUIN BOOKS

Published by the Penguin Group
Penguin Books Ltd, 80 Strand, London WC2R 0RL, England
Penguin Group (USA) Inc., 375 Hudson Street, New York, New York 10014, USA
Penguin Group (Canada), 90 Eglinton Avenue East, Suite 700, Toronto, Ontario, Canada M4P 2Y3
(a division of Pearson Penguin Canada Inc.)
Penguin Ireland, 25 St Stephen's Green, Dublin 2, Ireland (a division of Penguin Books Ltd)
Penguin Group (Australia), 250 Camberwell Road, Camberwell, Victoria 3124, Australia
(a division of Pearson Australia Group Pty Ltd)
Penguin Books India Pvt Ltd, 11 Community Centre, Panchsheel Park, New Delhi – 110 017, India
Penguin Group (NZ), cnr Airborne and Rosedale Roads, Albany, Auckland 1310, New Zealand
(a division of Pearson New Zealand Ltd)
Penguin Books (South Africa) (Pty) Ltd, 24 Sturdee Avenue, Rosebank, Johannesburg 2196, South Africa

Penguin Books Ltd, Registered Offices: 80 Strand, London WC2R 0RL, England

www.penguin.com

First published 2006
1

Copyright © Crystal Reference Systems Ltd, 2006
All rights reserved

The moral right of the author has been asserted

Set in ITC Stone Sans and ITC Stone Serif
Typeset by Data Standards Ltd, Frome, Somerset
Printed in England by Clays Ltd, St Ives plc

Except in the United States of America, this book is sold subject
to the condition that it shall not, by way of trade or otherwise, be lent,
re-sold, hired out, or otherwise circulated without the publisher's
prior consent in any form of binding or cover other than that in
which it is published and without a similar condition including this
condition being imposed on the subsequent purchaser

ISBN-13: 978-0-141-02715-9
ISBN-10: 0-141-02715-0

Contents

Acknowledgements

Crystal Reference

GENERAL EDITOR
David Crystal

DEVELOPMENT EDITOR
Jan Thomas

EDITORIAL ASSISTANTS
Peter Preston
Todd Warden-Owen

EDITORIAL MANAGER
Hilary Crystal

DATABASE MANAGEMENT
Tony McNicholl

TECHNOLOGY DEVELOPMENT
Philip Johnstone
Dan Wade

CRYSTAL REFERENCE
ADMINISTRATION
Ian Saunders
Rob Phillips

Penguin Books

COMMISSIONING EDITOR
Georgina Laycock

EDITORIAL MANAGERS
Jodie Greenwood
Ellie Smith

PRODUCTION
Kristen Harrison

TEXT DESIGN
Richard Marston

TYPESETTING
Data Standards Ltd

Preface

The frequency with which an 'On This Day' column appears in newspapers or websites illustrates the perennial interest of the genre. There seems to be a universal curiosity to find out about the events that happened throughout history on a significant day, such as one's birthday. The present book provides a fresh selection of these events, international and national.

A collection of this kind also motivates a different kind of interest: the pleasure of coincidence. Everyone is intrigued by coincidences, and especially by events which are time-related, such as when someone is born and dies on the same day.

I have myself been fascinated by some of the events discovered by my editorial team in their trawl through history. I asked them to look out for the more unusual happenings, as well as to note major historical occasions, and they have found them. None, I think, are more unusual than the page representing 30 February.

David Crystal

Abbreviations

ABC	American Broadcasting Company
b.	born
BBC	British Broadcasting Corporation
BC	Before Christ
c	century
c.	circa
CBS	Columbia Broadcasting System
Co	County
d.	died
E	east
EEC	European Economic Community
FA	Football Association
fl.	flourished
fm	frequency modulation
ft	foot/feet
hp	horse power
IRA	Irish Republican Army
ITV	Independent Television
km	kilometre(s)
kph	kilometres per hour
m	metre(s)
ml	millilitre(s)
mph	miles per hour
Mt	Mount
Mts	Mountains
N	north
NASA	National Aeronautics and Space Administration
NBA	National Basketball Association
NBC	National Broadcasting Company
oz	ounce(s)
r.	reigned
R	River
RAF	Royal Air Force
S	south
sq	square

TV	televison
UK	United Kingdom
UN	United Nations
US	United States
USA	United States of America
USSR	Union of Soviet Socialist Republics
W	west
WBA	World Boxing Association
WBC	World Boxing Council

JANUARY

1

New Year's Day.
National Day, Cuba, Haiti, and Sudan.

45 BC The Julian calendar came into effect.

1631 Death of Thomas Hobson (b.1544 in Cambridge, Cambridgeshire), carrier and inn-keeper – the Hobson of the expression 'Hobson's choice'.

1660 Beginning of Samual Pepys' diary, running from 1 January 1660 to 31 May 1669, written in shorthand, and not decoded until 1825.

1729 Birth of Edmund Burke in Dublin, Ireland (d.1797), British statesman and political philosopher, whose *Reflections on the French Revolution* (1790) was influential throughout Europe.

1788 First publication for *The Times*, formerly *The Daily Universal Register*.

1801 Discovery and naming of the first asteroid, Ceres, by Giuseppe Piazzi of the Palermo Observatory, Italy, on the first night of the 19th c.

1861 Slavery in the Confederate states of America was declared unlawful by President Lincoln.

1881 Commencement of the construction of the Panama Canal, by French diplomat and entrepreneur Ferdinand de Lesseps (1805–94).

1892 First use of Ellis Island as the main immigration centre to the USA, with c.2000 immigrants arriving daily in the early 20th c.

1901 Federation of the British colonies of New South Wales, Queensland, Victoria, South Australia, and Western Australia as the Commonwealth of Australia.

1908 A ball was dropped in New York's Times Square, the start of a tradition to mark the New Year.

1921 Introduction of compulsory car tax disc display on car windscreens in Britain.

1947 Nationalization of Britain's coal industry, followed by rail (1948), and steel (1951).

1959 Cuban revolutionary Fidel Castro (b.1927) ousted Cuban dictator Fulgencio Batista (1901–73).

1970 The British half-crown went out of legal tender.

1984 The UK's first mobile telephone call was made by British comedian Ernie Wise (1925–99) from St Katherine's Dock, E London, to Vodafone's headquarters in Newbury, Berkshire.

2002 Introduction of the Euro as the new monetary unit in 12 European nations: Belgium, Germany, Spain, France, Ireland, Italy, Luxembourg, Netherlands, Austria, Portugal, Finland, and Greece.

JANUARY
2

17 Death of Titus Livius, known as Livy (b.59 BC in Patavium, Italy), historian, who traced the history of Rome from its foundation to the death of Drusus.

366 Invasion of the Roman Empire across the frozen R Rhine by the Alemanni, an alliance of war-bands from Germanic tribes.

1492 Recapture of Granada from the Moors by Spain.

1746 Aurora Borealis was visible in Tuam, Ireland, at 4 o'clock in the afternoon.

1757 Capture of Calcutta by British general Robert Clive (1725–74), following its seizure by the Nawab of Bengal.

1788 Georgia became the 4th state of the Union.

1793 Partition of Poland by the invading armies of Prussia and Russia.

1839 First photograph of the Moon taken by French photographic pioneer Louis Daguerre (1789–1851).

1868 British field marshal Sir Robert Napier (1810–90) led an expedition to Ethiopia to release imprisoned members of the British consulate.

1870 Commencement of the construction of the Brooklyn Bridge, New York (completed 24 May 1883).

1879 Death of Fred Spofforth (b.1853 in Balmain, Sydney, Australia), fast bowler, the first man to achieve a hat-trick in Test cricket.

1893 Issue of the USA's first commemorative postage stamps.

1905 Surrender of the Russian fleet at Port Arthur during the Russo–Japanese war.

1920 Birth of Isaac Asimov in Petrovichi, Russia (d.1992), biochemist and science-fiction writer, who added the term *robotics* to the language.

1938 Birth of David Bailey in London, photographer, a specialist in fashion photography.

1947 Replacement of silver coins by cupro-nickel in the UK.

1959 Launch of the unmanned Luna 1 by Russia, the first rocket to pass near the Moon.

1971 Collapse of a barrier at Ibrox Park football stadium, Glasgow, after a Rangers–Celtic match, killing 66.

1981 Murder charges were brought against Peter Sutcliffe (b.1946 in Bingley, West Yorkshire); known as the Yorkshire Ripper, he had killed thirteen women over five years.

2004 Stardust, the US interplanetary spacecraft launched on 7 February 1999, flew by comet Wild 2, collecting dust samples and taking detailed pictures.

JANUARY

3

Feast of St Geneviève (c.422–512), patron saint of Paris.

106 BC Birth of Cicero in Arpinum, Latium (d.43 BC), Roman orator, statesman, and man of letters.

722 Death of Empress Gemmei (b.661), 43rd imperial ruler of Japan, and the fourth woman to hold such a position.

1521 Excommunication of Martin Luther (1483–1546), father of the Protestant Reformation, by Pope Leo X.

1710 Birth of Giovanni Battista Pergolesi in Jesi, Italy (d.1736), composer and musician, whose comic intermezzo *La serva padrona* (1732) influenced the development of *opera buffa*.

1777 Defeat of the British at Princeton, New Jersey, by George Washington, who went on to become the 1st president of the USA.

1795 Death of Josiah Wedgwood (b.1730 in Burslem, Staffordshire), potter, known for his invention of unglazed black basalt and blue jasper ware with raised designs in white.

1888 Patenting of the drinking straw by Marvin C. Stone of Washington, DC.

1892 Birth of J(ohn) R(onald) R(euel) Tolkien in Bloemfontein, South Africa (d.1973), philologist and writer, whose interest in language and saga led to *The Lord of the Rings* (1954–5).

1912 Refusal of Ulster Unionists to recognize the authority of any Irish parliament set up under the Home Rule Bill.

1921 Meeting of the first Indian parliament.

1957 Release of the first battery-powered watch, the Hamilton Electric 500, by the Hamilton Watch Company of Lancaster, Pennsylvania.

1958 New Zealand mountaineer and explorer Sir Edmund Hillary (b.1919) arrived at the South Pole.

1959 Alaska became the 49th state of the Union.

1961 The US government severed all diplomatic relations with Cuba.

1971 Inauguration of the Open University, based in Milton Keynes, Buckinghamshire.

1981 John Lennon's '(Just Like) Starting Over', and the album *Double Fantasy*, reached the top of the US music charts, only weeks after the former Beatle was killed.

1988 Margaret Thatcher, Baroness Thatcher (of Kesteven), became the longest-serving British prime minister of the 20th c.

1990 Surrender of General Noriega in Panama to US authorities; he was taken to Florida to face charges of drug trafficking.

2000 Creation of the last 'Peanuts' comic strip by US cartoonist Charles Schulz (1922–2000).

JANUARY

4

871 The Battle of Reading was fought between King Ethelred (c.837–71) and an invading army of Danes.

1643 [25 December 1642, Old Style calendar] Birth of Sir Isaac Newton in Woolsthorpe, Lincolnshire (d.1727), physicist and mathematician.

1797 Defeat of the Austrians at Rivoli by Napoleon Bonaparte.

1809 Birth of Louis Braille in Coupvray, France (d.1852), blind educationist, who devised a system of raised-point writing which the blind could both read and write.

1847 Samuel Colt (1814–62) sold his first revolvers to the US government.

1884 Foundation of the Fabian society in Britain.

1885 First successful appendix operation, performed by Dr Williams West Grant in Iowa, USA.

1935 Birth of Floyd Patterson in Waco, Texas, boxing champion, who became the youngest world heavyweight title holder in 1956.

1936 Publication of the first pop music chart, based on national sales, in the US magazine *Billboard*.

1951 Capture of Seoul by Chinese and North Korean forces during the Korean War (1950–53).

1958 Re-entry of Sputnik 1 into earth's atmosphere; launched 4 October 1957, it was the first artificial satellite to orbit the earth.

1960 Death of Donald Campbell (b.1921 in Horley, Surrey), land and water speed-record contestant, whose hydroplane *Bluebird* crashed during an attempt to break the world water speed record.

1962 Introduction of the unmanned subway train in New York.

1980 Death of Joy Adamson (b.1910 in Troppau, Austria), naturalist and writer, best known for *Born Free* (1960); she was found murdered at her home in Kenya.

1982 Erika Rowe streaked across the pitch at Twickenham during the England v. Australia rugby match.

1984 Apple Computer Inc. of California won a copyright suit protecting Macintosh and its operating system from duplication.

1986 Death of Christopher Isherwood (b.1904 in Disley, Cheshire), novelist, whose novels *Mr Norris Changes Trains* (1935) and *Goodbye to Berlin* (1939) inspired the musical *Cabaret* (1966).

2000 Safe arrival at the South Pole of Catherine Hartley and Fiona Thornewill, the first British women to walk there across Antarctica.

2004 Landing on Mars of Spirit, the first of two Mars Exploration Rover missions.

JANUARY

5

Wassail Eve: *wassail* was an Old English expression – 'Be in good health'.

1066 Death of Edward the Confessor (b.1042), king of England, the last Anglo-Saxon king before the Conquest.

1787 Birth of John Burke in Co Tipperary, Ireland (d.1848), genealogist, and founder of *Burke's Peerage*, published first in 1826.

1895 French military officer Captain Alfred Dreyfus (1859–1935) was stripped of his rank and sentenced to life imprisonment on Devil's Island.

1896 First demonstration of X-rays by German physicist Wilhelm Konrad von Röntgen (1845–1923).

1902 Birth of Stella Gibbons in London (d.1989), novelist and journalist, best known for her satirical novel *Cold Comfort Farm* (1932).

1919 Formation of the German Workers Party, later to become the Nazi Party, by German politician Anton Drexler (1894–1942).

1922 Death of Sir Ernest Shackleton (b.1874 in Kilkea, Co Kildare, Ireland), Antarctic explorer.

1935 Birth of Umberto Eco in Alessandria, Piedmont, Italy, academic and novelist, whose novels include *The Name of the Rose* (1980).

1940 Demonstration of the first FM (frequency-modulation) radio in the USA by electrical engineer Edwin H. Armstrong (1890–1954).

1941 Death of Amy Johnson (b.1903 in Kingston-upon-Hull), pioneer aviator, who flew solo from England to Australia (1930).

1948 The first colour newsreel was shown by Warner Brothers–Pathé.

1957 Retirement of Jackie (Jack) Roosevelt Robinson (1919–72), the first African-American major-league baseball player of the modern era.

1960 Final journey on the Mumbles Railway from Swansea to Mumbles Head, Wales; it had been in service since 1804.

1964 First automatic ticket barrier introduced in the London Underground, at Stamford Brook.

1979 Sales of the LP featuring the soundtrack of *Saturday Night Fever* reached $25 million.

1984 Development began of the free software operating system GNU (GNU's Not Unix), created by Richard Stallman.

1993 Liberian-registered tanker MV *Braer*, carrying 85,000 tonnes of crude oil, ran aground off the coast of the Shetland Islands, Scotland.

1998 Death of Sonny Bono (b.1935 in Detroit, Michigan), singing partner of Cher; their biggest hit was 'I Got You Babe'.

JANUARY

6

Feast of the Epiphany.

871 Defeat of the Danes at the Battle of Ashdown by Alfred the Great, king of Wessex.

1066 Coronation of Harold II as king of England, succeeding Edward the Confessor.

1412 Birth of Joan of Arc in Domrémy, France (d.1431), patriot and martyr, who halted the English ascendancy in France during the Hundred Years' War.

1540 Marriage of King Henry VIII to Anne of Cleves, his fourth wife.

1745 Birth of Jacques Etienne Mont-golfier in Annonay, France (d.1799), aeronautical inventor, who with his brother Joseph (1740–1810) made the first successful flight in a hot-air balloon.

1822 Birth of Heinrich Schliemann in Neubukow, Germany (d.1890), archaeologist, who discovered and excavated the legendary cities of Troy and Mycenae.

1838 First public demonstration of an electric telegraph system by artist and inventor Samuel Morse (1791–1872), in New Jersey.

1878 Birth of Carl Sandburg in Gales-burg, Illinois (d.1967), poet and biographer, whose books include *Cornhuskers* (1918) and *Good Morning, America* (1928).

1880 Birth of Tom Mix in Mix Run, Pennsylvania (d.1940), actor, who was a popular star of the silent screen, appearing in Westerns.

1884 Death of Gregor Mendel (b.1822 in Heinzendorf, Austria), botanist and biologist, whose laws governing the nature of inheritance became the basis of modern genetics.

1912 New Mexico became the 47th state of the Union.

1919 Death of Theodore Roosevelt (b.1858 in New York), 26th president of the USA.

1931 Opening of London's new Sadler's Wells Theatre.

1938 Arrival of psychoanalyst Sigmund Freud (1856–1939) in London, having fled Vienna and the Gestapo.

1942 Completion of the first commercial round-the-world airline flight, by Pan American Airlines.

1945 Birth of Barry John in Cefneithin, Carmarthenshire, Rugby Union player, Welsh and Lions rugby international.

1955 Birth of Rowan Atkinson in Newcastle-upon-Tyne, Tyne and Wear, comedian and actor, whose television series include *Blackadder* and *Mr Bean*.

1977 EMI fired pop group The Sex Pistols.

JANUARY
7

Christmas Day (Orthodox Church).
Distaff's Day; traditionally the day on which
women resumed work after the Christmas
holidays, which ended on Twelfth Night.

1610 Discovery and naming by Italian astronomer Galileo Galilei (1564–1642) of four satellites of Jupiter: Io, Europa, Ganymede, and Callisto.

1768 Birth of Joseph Bonaparte in Corte, Corsica (d.1844), king of Naples, Sicily, and Spain, and brother of Napoleon.

1785 Hot-air balloon crossing of the Channel from Dover to Calais by Dr John Jeffries (1744–1819) and Jean-Pierre Blanchard (1753–1809).

1789 Election of George Washington as 1st president of the USA, following the first national elections.

1844 Birth of Saint Bernardette of Lourdes, originally Marie-Bernard Soubirous, in Lourdes, France (d.1879); she claimed to have had visions of the Blessed Virgin at the Massabielle Rock.

1857 First day of operation for the London General Omnibus Company.

1899 Birth of François Poulenc in Paris (d.1963), composer and pianist, whose works include the ballet *Les Biches*, produced by Diaghilev in 1924.

1904 Introduction of the distress call CQD (Seek You + D for danger).

1912 Birth of Charles Addams in Westfield, New Jersey (d.1988), cartoonist, best known for the *Addams Family of Ghouls*.

1925 Birth of Gerald Durrell in Jamshedpur, India (d.1995), British author and naturalist, best known for his novel *My Family and Other Animals* (1956).

1927 Founding of The Harlem Globetrotters basketball team by Abraham Sapperstein (1903–66).

1927 Opening of the telephone service between London and New York, with a three-minute call costing £15.

1930 Opening of a picture-by-wire service between Britain and Germany.

1932 Death of André Maginot (b.1877 in Paris), politician, best known for the French defensive fortifications from Belgium to Switzerland, the Maginot Line.

1988 Announcement by Professor Frank Pobell that his team of scientists, at Bayreuth University, West Germany, had cooled metal to the lowest temperature ever achieved in a laboratory.

1989 Death of Showa Tenno Hirohito (b.1901 in Tokyo, Japan), emperor of Japan.

1990 Closure of the leaning tower of Pisa to the public for safety reasons.

JANUARY
8

1642 Death of Galileo Galilei (b.1564 in Pisa, Italy), mathematician and astronomer, who discovered Jupiter's four largest satellites.

1675 The New York Fishing Company became the USA's first chartered corporation.

1713 Death of Arcangelo Corelli (b.1653 in Fusignano, Italy), composer and violinist

1800 Opening of the first soup kitchens for the poor in London.

1824 Birth of William Wilkie Collins in London (d.1889), novelist, best known for *The Woman in White* (1860).

1889 Patenting of an electrically operated computer by Dr Herman Hollerith of New York; his company later became IBM.

1921 Chequers, in Buckinghamshire, UK, became the official country home of British prime ministers, with David Lloyd George taking up residence.

1928 Birth of Ron Moody in London, actor, whose roles include Fagin in the musical *Oliver* (1968).

1935 Birth of Elvis Presley in Tupelo, Mississippi (d.1977), rock singer and actor, who made 45 records that sold in millions.

1937 Birth of Shirley Bassey in Tiger Bay, Cardiff, singer, whose hits include the theme from the Bond film *Goldfinger* (1964).

1940 Introduction of food rationing in Britain.

1942 Birth of Professor Stephen Hawking in Oxford, Oxfordshire, theoretical physicist and cosmologist, best known for his book of popular science, *A Brief History of Time* (1988).

1947 Birth of David Bowie (David Jones) in London, pop singer and actor, known for his range of extreme stage images.

1959 General Charles de Gaulle (1890–1970) became president of the Fifth Republic of France.

1963 Fire broke out on seven floors of the Empire State Building, New York.

1967 The first episode of *The Forsyte Saga*, an adaptation of the novel by John Galsworthy, was televised by the BBC.

1987 For the first time the Dow Jones Industrial Average closed over the 2000 mark.

1989 Crash of a British Midland 737-400 jet on the M1 motorway, killing 47 of the 117 passengers and eight crew.

1990 Death of Terry-Thomas (b.1911 in Finchley, London), actor, best known for his gap-toothed villains and upper-class bounders.

JANUARY

9

1735 Birth of John Jervis in Meaford, Staffordshire, (d.1823), admiral of the fleet, famous for winning a great naval victory at St Vincent (1797).

1788 Connecticut became the 5th state of the Union.

1793 First successful balloon flight in the USA, made by balloonist and inventor of the parachute Jean Pierre François Blanchard (1753–1809).

1799 Imposition of income tax in Britain at a rate of 2 shillings in the pound.

1806 Burial of Viscount Horatio Nelson at St Paul's Cathedral, London.

1848 Death of Caroline Lucretia Herschel (b.1750 in Hanover, Germany), astronomer; while working in Britain she discovered eight comets.

1898 Birth of Gracie Fields, originally Grace Stansfield, in Rochdale, Greater Manchester (d.1979), singer, actress, and comedienne, best known for 'Sally', which became her theme song.

1902 Flirting in public was outlawed in New York State.

1904 [Old Style calendar, New Style 22 January] Birth of George Balanchine in St Petersburg, Russia (d.1983), dancer and choreographer, and co-founder of the New York Ballet.

1909 Explorer Ernest Shackleton's expedition to the South Pole was forced to turn back only 11 miles short of the Pole.

1917 Birth of Herbert Lom in Prague, Czech Republic, actor, best known for his roles in three *Pink Panther* films.

1923 First successful autogyro flight made in Spain by its inventor, Juan de La Cierva (1895–1936).

1929 Bacteriologist Alexander Fleming (1881–1955) discovered penicillin.

1941 Birth of Joan Baez in Staten Island, New York, folk singer, popular with young audiences for her songs and political views.

1951 The first British X certificate was awarded to a film.

1957 Resignation of Sir Anthony Eden after 1 year 279 days as prime minister of Britain, due to ill health.

1969 First trial flight of supersonic aircraft Concorde, at Bristol, Avon.

1972 The *Queen Elizabeth* caught fire and sank in Hong Kong harbour.

1997 Rescue of lone yachtsman Tony Bullimore, five days after his boat capsized in the Southern Ocean.

JANUARY

10

1645 Death of William Laud (b.1573 in Reading, Berkshire), archbishop of Canterbury, beheaded on Tower Hill for treason.

1778 Death of Carl Linnaeus (b.1707 in Råshult, Sweden), botanist, the founder of modern taxonomy.

1839 First sales of Indian tea in Britain.

1840 Introduction of the Penny Post service in Britain.

1862 Death of Samuel Colt (b.1814 in Hartford, Connecticut), gunsmith, and inventor of the automatically revolving breech pistol.

1863 Opening of the London Underground railway.

1903 Birth of Dame Barbara Hepworth in Wakefield, West Yorkshire (d.1975), sculptor, one of the foremost non-figurative sculptors of her time.

1904 Birth of Ray Bolger in Boston, Massachusetts (d.1987), actor and dancer, best known as the Scarecrow in *The Wizard of Oz* (1939).

1910 Birth of Galina Ulanova in St Petersburg, Russia (d.1998), prima ballerina, who became the leading ballerina of the Soviet Union.

1912 Maiden flight of the first flying boat, at Hammondspoint, New York, designed by US aviator and inventor Glenn Curtiss (1878–1930).

1917 Death of Colonel William Cody (b.1846 in Scott Co, Iowa), frontiersman and showman, known as 'Buffalo Bill'.

1920 First meeting of the League of Nations, in Geneva.

1929 First appearance of Hergé's cartoon strip 'Tin-Tin', in the children's supplement of the newspaper *Le Vingtième Siècle*.

1945 Birth of Rod Stewart in London, singer and songwriter, whose hit songs include 'Sailing' (1975).

1949 Production by RCA (Radio Corporation of America) of the new 45 rpm record, which revolutionized the pop music business.

1957 Harold Macmillan (1894–1986) accepted the queen's invitation to become prime minister, following the sudden resignation of Sir Anthony Eden.

1982 Recording of the lowest-ever UK temperature of -27.2°C at Braemar, Aberdeenshire, equalling the record set in the same place on 11 February 1895.

1985 British electronics engineer and inventor Sir Clive Sinclair (b.1940) demonstrated his invention, the C5 car.

2005 Imposition of a smoking ban in Italy, prohibiting tobacco smoking in public places.

JANUARY
11

Feast of Saint Balthasar, patron saint of epileptics, manufacturers of playing cards, and sawyers.

1569 First state lottery held in England.

1762 Death of Louis François Roubillac (b.1702 in Lyon, France), sculptor, who worked in England and is known for his monuments and busts.

1770 Arrival in the USA of the first shipment of rhubarb from London.

1787 Discovery of Titania and Oberon, two moons of Uranus, by German-born British astronomer and composer William Herschel (1738–1822).

1864 Opening of London's Charing Cross railway station.

1878 First deliveries of milk in glass bottles in New York.

1882 Death of Theodor Schwann (b.1810 in Neuss, Germany), physiologist and founder of modern histology, who discovered the enzyme pepsin.

1891 Death of Georges Eugène Haussmann (b.1809 in Paris), financier and town planner, known for improving the design of Paris.

1896 Birth of Sir William Stephenson in Point Douglas, Manitoba (d.1989), head of British intelligence in the USA, a possible inspiration for Ian Fleming's 'M' in the James Bond books.

1903 Birth of Alan Paton in Pietermaritzburg, South Africa (d.1988), writer, best known for his novel *Cry, the Beloved Country* (1948).

1922 First successful treatment of diabetes with insulin.

1928 Death of Thomas Hardy (b.1840 in Upper Bockhampton, Dorset), novelist and poet, whose novels include *Tess of the D'Urbervilles* (1891).

1935 US aviator Amelia Earhart (1897–1937) became the first woman to fly solo from Hawaii to California.

1938 Birth of Arthur Scargill in Leeds, West Yorkshire, trade unionist, who became president of the National Union of Mineworkers in 1982.

1942 Kuala Lumpur was taken by Japan in World War 2.

1962 Thousands died in a landslide in the Peruvian Andes.

1973 The first graduates from Britain's Open University were awarded their degrees after two years studying from home.

1974 Birth of the world's first surviving set of sextuplets, to Susan Rosenkowitz in Cape Town, South Africa.

1985 Completion of the longest and fastest crossing of Antarctica; the three-man British team, led by Sir Ranulph Fiennes (b.1944), reached Scott base after 75 days and 2,500 miles.

JANUARY

12

1580 Birth of Jan Baptista van Helmont in Brussels, Belgium (d.1644), chemist, who invented the word *gas*.

1628 Birth of Charles Perrault in Paris (d.1703), writer and collector of fairy tales, best known for the *Tales of Mother Goose* (1729).

1665 Death of Pierre de Fermat in Beaumont-de-Lomagne, France (d.1601), mathematician, known for his work in number theory and optics.

1729 Birth of Edmund Burke in Dublin, Ireland (d.1797), British statesman and political philosopher.

1822 Birth of Jean Joseph Lenoir in Mussy-la-Ville, Belgium (d.1900), engineer, who invented the first practical internal combustion engine (c.1859), making powered flight possible.

1834 Death of William Wyndham Grenville (b.1759 in Buckinghamshire), British statesman.

1856 Birth of John Singer Sargent in Florence, Italy (d.1925), painter, best known for his high society portraits.

1876 Birth of Jack London in San Francisco, California (d.1916), novelist, known for his adventure novels such as *Call of the Wild* (1903).

1897 Death of Sir Isaac Pitman (b.1813 in Trowbridge, Wiltshire), educationist, who developed the Pitman shorthand system.

1905 Birth of Tex Ritter in Murvaul, Texas (d.1974), singer, known as 'the singing cowboy'; he recorded the title song for the film *High Noon* (1952).

1926 Birth of P(ieter) W(illem) Botha in Paul Roux, Orange Free State, South Africa, first executive state president of South Africa.

1941 Birth of Long John Baldry in Derbyshire (d.2005), blues singer, songwriter, and guitarist, who discovered Elton John and Rod Stewart.

1947 Birth of Joe Frazier in Beaufort, South Carolina, boxer, who became world heavyweight champion (1970).

1948 Opening of Britain's first large supermarket, the Co-op, at London's Manor Park.

1959 Boxer Henry Cooper (b.1934) became British and European heavyweight champion.

1960 Death of Nevil Shute (b.1899 in London), novelist, whose books include *A Town Like Alice* (1949).

1976 Death of Dame Agatha Christie (b.1890 in Torquay, Devon), detective-story writer, best known for her detectives Hercule Poirot and Miss Marple.

2003 Death of Maurice Gibb (b.1949 in Douglas, Isle of Man), Bee Gee band member and singer.

2005 Launch of Deep Impact from Cape Canaveral, a NASA space probe designed to study the composition of the comet Tempel 1.

JANUARY

13

1599 Death of Edmund Spenser (b.1552 in London), poet, best known for his epic poem *The Faerie Queene* (1590–96).

1691 Death of George Fox (b.1624 in Fenny Drayton, Leicestershire), founder of the Society of Friends (Quakers).

1832 Death of Thomas Lord (b.1755 in Thirsk, North Yorkshire), founder of Lord's Cricket Ground.

1854 Patenting of an accordion by Anthony Faas of Philadelphia, Pennsylvania.

1884 Birth of Sophie Tucker in Russia (d.1966), US singer and entertainer, 'The Last of the Red-Hot Mamas'.

1888 Founding of the National Geographic Society in Washington, DC.

1893 Formation of the Independent British Labour Party by British politician Keir Hardie (1856–1915).

1898 Publication of 'J'Accuse', by French author Emile Zola (1840–1902), a letter accusing the French government of a cover-up in the Alfred Dreyfus (1859–1935) treason case.

1910 First radio broadcast of opera, from the Metropolitan Opera House, New York, with Caruso singing Canio in *Pagliacci*.

1915 Death of 29,800 people in an earthquake in Avezzano, Italy.

1921 Cars were fitted with the first windscreen wipers.

1926 Birth of Michael Bond in Newbury, Berkshire, writer, who created the character of Paddington Bear (1958).

1929 Death of Wyatt Earp (b.1848 in Monmouth, Illinois), lawman, best known for his involvement in the gunfight at the OK Corral (1881).

1941 Death of James Joyce (b.1882 in Dublin, Ireland), author, best known for his novel *Ulysses* (1922).

1957 Introduction of the Pluto Platter, by WHAM-O, a flying plastic disc, that would become famous the following year after some remodelling as the 'Frisbee'®.

1974 Opening of the Dallas Fort Worth regional airport (DFW).

1982 Crash of Air Florida Flight 90 during a blizzard into the Potomac R near Washington, DC, killing 78 people.

1989 Infiltration of computers by the Friday the 13th virus.

2003 Death of Harold Shipman (b.1946 in Nottingham, Nottinghamshire), doctor, who was believed to have killed more than 200 people; he was found dead in his prison cell.

JANUARY

14

1741 Birth of Benedict Arnold in Norwich, Connecticut (d.1801), American general and spy, who passed information to the British during the American War of Independence.

1742 Death of Edmond Halley (b.1656 in London), Astronomer Royal, best known for his prediction of the return in 1758 of the comet now named after him.

1814 The last London Frost Fair was held on the frozen R Thames.

1867 Death of Jean Ingres (b.1780 in Montauban, France), painter, a leading exponent of the Classical tradition in France.

1873 Registration as a trademark of celluloid, the invention of John Wesley Hyatt (1837–1920).

1878 Demonstration to Queen Victoria of the telephone, designed by educationist and inventor Alexander Graham Bell (1847–1922).

1886 Birth of Hugh Lofting in Maidenhead, Berkshire (d.1947), author and illustrator, best known for his books about Dr Doolittle (from 1920).

1892 Birth of Hal Roach in Elmira, New York (d.1992), producer and director, who made films with Laurel and Hardy.

1898 Death of Lewis Carroll (b.1832 in Daresbury, Cheshire), author, best known for his novel *Alice's Adventures in Wonderland* (1865).

1904 Birth of Sir Cecil Beaton in London (d.1980), photographer of celebrities, and theatrical designer.

1926 Birth of Warren Mitchell in London, actor, best known for his character Alf Garnett in BBC television's *Till Death Us Do Part* (from 1965).

1934 Birth of Richard Briers in Croydon, London, actor, whose roles include Tom Good in the television series *The Good Life* (1975–8).

1937 Britain's first Gallup opinion poll was conducted by Dr Henry Durant; evolved by George Gallup (1901–84) to test the state of public opinion via representative samples.

1938 First screening of Walt Disney's *Snow White and the Seven Dwarfs*, in the USA.

1940 Birth of Trevor Nunn in Ipswich, Suffolk, artistic director of the Royal Shakespeare Company (1968–87).

1941 Birth of Faye Dunaway in Bascom, Florida, actress, whose films include *Bonnie and Clyde* (1967).

1957 Death of Humphrey Bogart (b.1899 in New York), actor, whose films include *Casablanca* (1942).

1977 Death of Anthony Eden, 1st Earl of Avon (b.1897 at Windlestone Hall, Durham), British prime minister (1955–7).

1986 Permanent enforcement of the law obliging motorists to wear seat belts in the UK.

1990 Death of Gordon Jackson (b.1923 in Glasgow), actor, who became a household name as Hudson in the television series *Upstairs, Downstairs* (1971–5).

JANUARY
15

1559 Coronation of Elizabeth I of England.

1622 Birth of Molière in Paris (d.1673), playwright and actor, whose plays include *Tartuffe* (1664).

1759 Opening of the British Museum in London.

1797 Haberdasher James Hetherington was fined £50 for wearing the first top hat to be seen in London.

1815 Death of Lady Emma Hamilton (b.1765 in Ness, Cheshire), mistress to Lord Nelson.

1878 Degrees were awarded to women for the first time in the UK.

1880 Publication of Britain's first telephone directory, by the London Telephone Company, containing just over 250 names.

1890 The Russian Imperial Ballet gave the first performance of *Sleeping Beauty*, composed by Tchaikovsky and choreographed by Petipa.

1893 Birth of Ivor Novello (David Ivor Davies) in Cardiff (d.1951), composer, actor, and playwright, whose compositions include the First World War song, 'Keep the Home Fires Burning'.

1906 Birth of Aristotle Onassis in Smyrna, Turkey (d.1975), shipowner, and pioneer in supertanker construction, who married Jackie Kennedy.

1909 Birth of Jean Bugatti in Cologne, Germany (d.1939), car designer.

1912 First use of propaganda leaflets dropped by plane; addressed to the Arabs of Tripolitania, during the Italo-Turkish war, they offered a gold medal and a sack of wheat to any man who surrendered.

1913 Introduction in Britain of maternity, sickness, and unemployment benefit of 30 shillings, 10 shillings, and 7 shillings per week respectively.

1918 Birth of General Gamal Abdel Nasser in Alexandria, Egypt (d.1970), first president of Egypt.

1922 The Irish Free State became operative, with Eamon de Valera (1882–1975) as president.

1929 Birth of Martin Luther King in Atlanta, Georgia (d.1968), clergyman and civil rights leader, best known for his famous 'I have a dream' speech (1963) at the Lincoln Memorial.

1943 Completion of the Pentagon near Washington, DC, at the time the world's largest office building.

1964 Death of Jack Teagarden (b.1905 in Vernon, Texas), jazz trombonist and band leader.

1971 Official opening of the Aswan High Dam.

1973 Withdrawal of US forces from Vietnam by President Nixon.

JANUARY

16

Feast of St Honoré (Honoratus), patron saint of bakers.

1547 Coronation of Ivan the Terrible as first tsar of Russia.

1556 Accession to the throne of Philip II, the first official king of Spain.

1794 Death of Edward Gibbon (b.1737 in Putney, Surrey), historian, and author of *The Decline and Fall of the Roman Empire* (1776–88).

1853 Birth of André Michelin in Paris (d.1931), tyre manufacturer, who with his brother Edouard (1859–1940) formed the Michelin tyre company (1888).

1891 Death of Léo Delibes (b.1836 in St Germain du Val, France), composer, whose works include the ballet *Coppélia* (1870).

1909 Nimrod's Northern party, part of Ernest Shackleton's British Antarctic Expedition, reached the Magnetic South Pole.

1909 Birth of Ethel Merman in Astoria, New York (d.1984), singer and actress, who starred in *There's No Business Like Show Business* (1954).

1920 Introduction of Prohibition in the USA, forbidding the sale of intoxicating liquor.

1929 First publication of Britain's *The Listener*.

1937 Patenting of nylon, a 'miracle' fibre made from chemicals, by the Dupont company.

1957 Renaming of the Sadler's Wells Ballet as the Royal Ballet, following a royal charter.

1957 Opening of the Cavern Club in Liverpool, Merseyside.

1969 Death of Jan Palach (b.1948), Czech student, who committed suicide by self-immolation in protest against the Soviet-led invasion of Czechoslovakia in August 1968.

1970 Colonel Gaddafi became prime minister of Libya.

1979 Mohammad Reza Shah Pahlavi, shah of Iran, fled from Iran to Egypt with his family, following months of increasingly violent protests against his regime.

1991 Announcement of Operation Desert Storm during the Gulf War.

2001 Death of Laurent-Désiré Kabila (b.1939 in Jadotville, Katanga province, Congo), president of the Democratic Republic of the Congo, assassinated by one of his own bodyguards.

2005 Adriana Iliescu (b.1938 in Craiova, Romania) became the world's oldest woman to give birth, at age of 66, at the Giulesti Maternity Hospital in Bucharest, Romania.

JANUARY
17

Feast of St Antony, known as Antony the Great, also called Antony of Egypt (c.251–356), patron saint of basket-makers, gravediggers, hermits, monks, and pigs.

1501 Birth of Leonhard Fuchs in Wemding, Germany (d.1566), physician and botanist; the genus *Fuchsia* was named after him.

1706 Birth of Benjamin Franklin in Boston, Massachusetts (d.1790), American statesman, scientist, and inventor, who helped to draft the Declaration of Independence.

1773 British navigator Captain James Cook (1728–79) became the first explorer to cross the Antarctic Circle.

1781 Defeat of a British force by Daniel Morgan at the Battle of Cowpens, South Carolina, during the American War of Independence.

1820 Birth of Anne Brontë in Thornton, West Yorkshire (d.1849), novelist, best known for her book *The Tenant of Wildfell Hall* (1838).

1827 Arthur Wellesley, 1st Duke of Wellington, became chief of the British Army.

1860 [Old Style calendar, New Style 29 January] Birth of Anton Chekhov in Taganrog, Russia (d.1904), playwright and short-story writer, whose plays include *The Seagull* (1896).

1863 Birth of David Lloyd George in Manchester (d.1945), British prime minister (1916–22).

1893 Death of Rutherford Hayes (b.1822 in Delaware, Ohio), 19th president of the USA (1877–81).

1899 Birth of Al Capone in New York (d.1947), racketeer, who achieved worldwide notoriety during the Prohibition era in Chicago.

1912 Formation of the Professional Golfers Association (PGA), the largest working sports organization in the world.

1912 Antarctic explorer Captain Robert Falcon Scott (1868–1912) reached the South Pole, one month after Roald Amundsen (1872–1928).

1926 Birth of Moira Shearer in Dunfermline, Fife, ballerina with the Royal Ballet, best known for her starring role in the film *The Red Shoes* (1948).

1928 Birth of Vidal Sassoon in London, hair stylist, who developed a wide range of hair-care products.

1929 First appearance of Popeye the Sailor Man, created by US strip cartoonist Elzie Segar (1894–1938), in the comic strip 'Thimble Theater'.

1977 Gary Gilmore was the first man to be executed under the newly reintroduced death penalty in the USA.

1983 First broadcast for Britain's breakfast television, BBC Breakfast, presented by Frank Bough and Selina Scott.

1991 Commencement of hostilities during Operation Desert Storm in the Gulf War.

JANUARY
18

1485 Marriage of Henry VII to Elizabeth, daughter of Edward IV, uniting the Houses of Lancaster and York, and ending the Wars of the Roses.

1535 Founding of Lima, capital city of Peru, by conquistador Francisco Pizarro (c.1478–1541).

1778 Discovery of the Sandwich Islands (Hawaii) by Captain James Cook.

1779 Birth of Peter Mark Roget in London (d.1869), doctor and lexicographer, best known for his *Thesaurus* (1852).

1818 Birth of George Palmer (d.1897), biscuit manufacturer, and associate of Huntley, with whom he introduced the biscuit tin.

1879 Publication of the first edition of *Boy's Own Paper*.

1882 Birth of A(lan) A(lexander) Milne in London (d.1956), writer, best known for his books for children, including *Winnie-the-Pooh* (1926).

1884 Birth of Arthur Ransome in Leeds, West Yorkshire (d.1967), author, best known for *Swallows and Amazons* (1930).

1888 Birth of Sir Thomas Sopwith in London (d.1989), aircraft designer, pilot, and sportsman, best known for the Sopwith Camel.

1898 Commencement of strike by cotton-mill workers in New England, USA.

1904 Birth of Cary Grant (Alexander Archibold Leach) in Bristol, Avon (d.1986), actor, who played leading roles in many films, including *North by Northwest* (1959).

1913 Birth of Danny Kaye (David Daniel Kaminsky) in New York (d.1987), comic actor and entertainer, whose films include *Hans Christian Andersen* (1952).

1919 Opening of the Versailles Peace Conference.

1933 Birth of David Bellamy in London, botanist, famous for popularizing ecological issues through his television programmes.

1936 Death of Rudyard Kipling (b.1865 in Mumbai (Bombay), India), British author, best known for the *Jungle Books* (1894–5).

1966 Conviction of Albert DeSalvo (1930–73), the Boston Strangler, for numerous crimes; he was sentenced to life imprisonment.

1977 Death of 83 people in Australia's worst rail disaster, at Granville, Sydney.

1980 Death of Sir Cecil Beaton (b.1904 in London), photographer of celebrities, and theatrical designer.

1993 Official observance of Martin Luther King Day for the first time in all 50 US states, marked by demonstrations for peace, social justice, and racial and class equality.

2005 Unveiling in France of Airbus's 840-passenger A380, the world's biggest passenger jet.

JANUARY
19

Feast of St Knut Sveinnson (Canute), patron saint of Denmark.

1729 Death of William Congreve (b.1670 in Bardsey, West Yorkshire), Restoration playwright and poet, whose plays include *The Way of the World* (1700).

1736 Birth of James Watt in Greenock, Strathclyde (d.1819), inventor, whose name is given to the metric unit of power.

1798 Birth of Auguste Comte in Montpellier, France (d.1857), philosopher and social reformer, the founder of Positivism.

1809 Birth of Edgar Allan Poe in Boston, Massachusetts (d.1849), poet and short-story writer, whose works include *The Pit and the Pendulum* (1843).

1813 Birth of Sir Henry Bessemer in Charlton, Hertfordshire (d.1898), inventor and engineer, who patented the process for turning molten pig-iron into steel (1855–6).

1825 Patenting of a food-canning process by Ezra Daggett and Thomas Kensett.

1839 Birth of Paul Cézanne in Aix-en-Provence, France (d.1906), Post-Impressionist painter, whose paintings include *The Card Players* (1890–92, Musée d'Orsay, Paris).

1881 Death of Auguste Mariette (b.1821 in Boulogne, France), Egyptologist, famous for having excavated the Sphinx.

1915 Patenting of the neon advertising sign by French chemist and physicist Georges Claude (1870–1960).

1915 German Zeppelins raided England for the first time during World War 1.

1942 Birth of Michael Crawford in Salisbury, Wiltshire, actor and singer, best known for his character Frank Spencer in *Some Mothers Do 'Ave 'Em* (1973–8).

1942 Invasion of Burma by Japan.

1943 Birth of Janice Joplin in Port Arthur, Texas (d.1970), blues rock singer; the film *The Rose* (1979) was loosely based on her life.

1946 Birth of Dolly Parton in Locust Ridge, Tennessee, country singer and actress, whose songs include 'Jolene' (1974).

1949 Increase in the US presidential salary from $75,000 to $100,000 a year, with an extra $50,000 expense allowance for each year in office.

1955 Birth of Sir Simon Rattle in Liverpool, conductor, who became chief conductor and artistic director of the Berlin Philharmonic orchestra in 2002.

1966 Indira Gandhi (1917–84) became prime minister of India.

1978 The last Beetle car was produced by the Volkswagen Company, Germany.

JANUARY

20

US president and vice-president terms of office end at noon.

1265 Meeting of the first English parliament at Westminster.

1779 Death of David Garrick (b.1717 in Hereford, Hereford and Worcester), actor, playwright, and theatre manager, who dominated the English stage for 30 years.

1805 Opening of the London docks.

1841 Hong Kong ceded by China to Britain.

1875 Death of Jean François Millet (b.1814 in Gruchy, France), painter, best known for his painting of the rustic life of France.

1892 The first game of basketball was played, in Springfield, Massachusetts.

1896 Birth of George Burns (Nathan Birnbaum) in New York (d.1996), comedian, known for his omnipresent cigar.

1900 Death of John Ruskin (b.1819 in London), art theorist and social critic, who influenced the Arts and Crafts movement.

1907 [Old Style calendar, New Style 2 February] Death of Dmitri Mendeleyev (b.1834 in Tobolsk, Russia), chemist, famous for formulating the periodic table of chemical elements.

1920 Birth of Frederico Fellini in Rimini, Italy (d.1993), director, whose films include *La Dolce Vita* (1960, Cannes Festival prizewinner).

1924 Birth of Slim Whitman in Tampa, Florida, country singer, best known for 'Rose Marie' (1955).

1930 Birth of Dr Edwin 'Buzz' Aldrin in Montclair, New Jersey, astronaut, the second man to walk on the Moon.

1934 Birth of Tom Baker in Liverpool, stage and television actor, best known for his title role in the BBC television series *Dr Who* (1974–81).

1936 Death of King George V of England (b.1865 in London, r.1910–1936).

1964 Release of the first Beatles album, *Meet The Beatles*, in the USA, reaching No. 1 in the charts by 15 February 1964.

1981 Release of 52 American hostages taken at the US embassy in Tehran; they had been held for 444 days.

1984 Death of Johnny Weissmuller (b.1904 in Freidorf, Romania), US Olympic swimming champion, who played Tarzan in the Hollywood films.

1987 Kidnap of Terry Waite (b.1939) in Beirut; he was not released until November 1991.

1988 The remains of a prehistoric mammoth were found in Russia.

JANUARY
21

1793 Execution of King Louis XVI of France for treason.

1813 Birth of John Charles Fremont in Savannah, Georgia (d.1890), US soldier and explorer, who crossed the Rockies and became widely known as 'The Pathfinder'.

1824 Birth of Thomas Jonathan 'Stonewall' Jackson in Clarksburg, Virginia (d.1863), Confederate general in the American Civil War.

1846 First day of publication for the *Daily News*, edited by author Charles Dickens (1812–70).

1901 Death of Elisha Gray (b.1835 in Barnesville, Ohio), inventor and manufacturer of telegraphic apparatus; he claimed invention of the telephone, but lost the patent rights to Alexander Graham Bell.

1905 Birth of Christian Dior in Granville, France (d.1957), couturier, who founded the Dior international fashion house (1945).

1907 Taxi cabs were officially recognized in Britain.

1908 Smoking in public was made illegal for women in New York.

1911 Beginning of the first Monte Carlo car rally.

1924 Birth of Telly Savalas in Long Island, New York (d.1994), Greek-American film and television actor, best known for his role as Kojak the detective.

1924 Death of Vladimir Ilyich Lenin (b.1870 in Simbirsk, Russia), Marxist revolutionary leader, who led the Bolshevik revolution (1917).

1935 Snowdonia, North Wales, became a national park.

1937 Broadcast of the first cookery programme on BBC television, *Cook's Night Out*, presented by the first television cook, Marcel Boulestin.

1940 Birth of Jack Nicklaus in Columbus, Ohio, golfing champion.

1941 Suppression of the British Communist newpaper, the *Daily Worker*, in wartime London.

1950 Death of George Orwell (b.1903 in Motihari, Bengal, India), English novelist, whose books include *Nineteen Eighty-Four* (1949).

1954 Launch of the first nuclear submarine, *Nautilus*, by the USA.

1959 Death of Cecil B(lount) de Mille (b.1881 in Ashfield, Massachusetts), director, producer, and screenwriter, whose films include *The Greatest Show on Earth* (1952).

1972 Denmark, the Irish Republic, and the UK joined the Common Market.

1976 Inaugural flight of BOAC Concorde from Britain to Bahrain.

JANUARY
22

Feast of St Vincent of Zaragoza (?–304), patron saint of Portugal and the wine trade.

1561 Birth of Sir Francis Bacon, Viscount St Albans, in London (d.1626), philosopher, statesman, and writer, famous as a pioneer of scientific thought.

1775 Birth of André-Marie Ampère in Lyon, France (d.1836), mathematician and physicist, who laid the foundation of the science of electrodynamics.

1775 Introduction of the umbrella into Europe, from the Middle East.

1788 Birth of Lord Byron in London (d.1824), Romantic poet, best known for *Don Juan* (1819–24).

1849 Birth of August Strindberg in Stockholm, Sweden (d.1912), playwright, whose plays include *The Father* (1887).

1858 Birth of Beatrice Potter Webb in Standish, Gloucestershire (d.1943), social reformer, who founded the Fabian society with her husband, Sydney Webb (1859–1947).

1879 The Battle of Rorke's Drift was fought in Natal, South Africa; eleven Victoria Crosses were awarded.

1901 Death of Queen Victoria (b.1819 in London), queen of Great Britain (1837–1901) and (from 1876) empress of India.

1904 [9 January, Old Style calendar] Birth of George Balanchine in St Petersburg, Russia (d.1983), dancer, choreographer, and co-founder of the New York Ballet.

1905 Red Sunday: Russian troops fired on protesting workers in St Petersburg.

1924 Ramsay MacDonald (1866–1937) became the first Labour prime minister in Britain.

1931 Sir Isaac Isaacs (1855–1948) became the first Australian-born governor-general of Australia.

1940 Birth of John Hurt in Chesterfield, Derbyshire, actor, whose films include *The Elephant Man* (1978).

1944 Commencement of the Allied landings in Anzio, Italy.

1947 The first commercial television station was broadcast live from a garage in Mississippi, USA.

1952 The first commercial jet plane, BOAC's De Havilland Comet, was put into service.

1973 Death of Lyndon Baines Johnson (b.1908 near Stonewall, Texas), 36th president of the USA (1963–9).

1992 Dr Roberta Bondar (b.1945 in Sault Ste Marie, Ontario) became the first Canadian woman in space.

2005 The Tsunami Relief Concert, a charity music concert held at the Millennium Stadium in Cardiff in aid of the victims of the 2004 Indian Ocean earthquake, raised over £1.25 million.

JANUARY
23

1571 Opening of London's Royal Exchange, built 1566–8 by British financier Sir Thomas Gresham (1519–79).

1806 Death of William Pitt 'the Younger' (b.1759 in Hayes, London), British prime minister (1783–1801, 1804–6).

1832 Birth of Edouard Manet in Paris (d.1883), painter, a forerunner of the Impressionist movement, whose works include *Déjeuner sur l'herbe* (1863).

1849 British-born Elizabeth Blackwell (1821–1910) became the first woman doctor in the USA when she graduated from medical school in Geneva, New York.

1898 Birth of Sergey Eisenstein in Riga, Latvia (d.1948), director, whose films include *Alexander Nevsky* (1938).

1901 Transmission of a radio signal from the Isle of Wight to Cornwall by physicist and inventor Guglielmo Marconi (1874–1937).

1919 Birth of Bob Paisley in Hetton-le-Hole, Durham (d.1996), footballer, trainer, and manager for Liverpool Football Club (1974–83).

1928 Birth of Jeanne Moreau in Paris, actress, whose films include *Jules et Jim* (1961).

1931 Death of Anna Pavlova (b.1881 in St Petersburg, Russia), prima ballerina, whose best-known role was in Fokine's *The Dying Swan* (1905).

1941 First production of nylon in Britain.

1943 Capture of Tripoli by the British, an important Axis base during World War 2.

1944 Death of Edvard Munch (b.1863 in Löten, Norway), painter, best known for *The Scream* (1893).

1947 Death of Pierre Bonnard (b.1867 in Paris), painter and lithographer, known for his painted interiors and landscapes.

1960 World record established when US bathyscaphe *Trieste* descended 10,900 m/35,800 ft into the Marianas Trench of the Pacific Ocean.

1963 Disappearance of British double agent Kim Philby, who moved to Russia.

1976 Death of Paul Robeson (b.1898 in Princeton, New Jersey), actor and singer, who appeared in works ranging from *Show Boat* to *Othello*.

1985 First television broadcast of proceedings from the House of Lords, London.

1989 Death of Salvador Dalí (b.1904 in Figueras, Spain), Surrealist painter and sculptor, whose paintings include *The Persistence of Memory* (1931).

2003 The last radio signal was received by NASA from the Pioneer 10 space probe, the first spacecraft to make direct observations and obtain close-up images of Jupiter.

JANUARY
24

Feast of St Francis of Sales (1567–1622), patron saint of authors, editors, journalists, and writers.

41 Death of Caligula, nickname of Gaius Julius Caesar Germanicus (b.12 in Antium), Roman emperor.

76 Birth of Hadrian (d.138), Roman emperor, known for building Hadrian's Wall along the northern boundary of the then Roman province of Britain.

1670 Birth of William Congreve in Bardsey, West Yorkshire (d.1729), Restoration playwright and poet, whose plays include *The Way of the World* (1700).

1749 Birth of Charles James Fox in London (d.1806), Whig statesman, known for his persuasive role in the abolition of slavery.

1848 First discovery of gold in California.

1888 Jacob L. Wortman of Philadelphia, Pennsylvania, received a patent for his typewriter ribbon.

1895 Death of Lord Randolph Churchill (b.1849 in Blenheim Palace, Oxfordshire), leader of the Conservative Party, and father of Sir Winston Churchill.

1915 Defeat of Germany by Britain at the World War 1 sea battle of Dogger Bank.

1916 Military Service Act passed, introducing conscription in Britain.

1922 Patenting of Eskimo Pie, a chocolate-covered ice-cream, by US schoolteacher and candy-store owner, Christian K. Nelson (1893–1992).

1928 Birth of Desmond Morris in Purton, Wiltshire, zoologist, writer, and artist, best known for his studies of behaviour, including *The Human Ape* (1967) and *Manwatching* (1977).

1935 First sales of canned beer, in Richmond, Virginia, produced by the Krueger Brewing Company.

1941 Birth of Neil Diamond in New York, singer and songwriter, who wrote the hit 'I'm A Believer' (1966) for The Monkees.

1961 Death of Elsa, the lioness made famous in books by Joy Adamson.

1965 Death of Sir Winston Leonard Spencer Churchill (b.1874 in Blenheim Palace, Oxfordshire), British prime minister (1940–45, 1951–5).

1972 Discovery of Shoichi Yokoi (1915–97), Japanese soldier, in a remote section of Guam by two of the island's inhabitants 28 years after the end of World War 2.

1984 The first Apple Macintosh computer went on sale, for $2,495.

1986 The US Voyager 2 space probe passed close to Uranus.

1989 Death of Ted (Theodore Robert) Bundy (b.1946 in Burlington, Vermont), serial killer, executed in Florida by electrocution.

JANUARY
25

Burns night, after Scottish poet Robert Burns (1759–96).

1540 Birth of St Edmund Campion in London (d.1581), scholar and Jesuit martyr, who was hanged, drawn, and quartered for alleged spying.

1627 Birth of Robert Boyle at Lismore Castle, Co Waterford, Ireland (d.1691), physicist and chemist, best known for Boyle's Law.

1759 Birth of Robert Burns in Alloway, South Ayrshire (d.1796), Scotland's national poet.

1855 Death of Dorothy Wordsworth (b.1771 in Cockermouth, Cumbria), sister of poet William Wordsworth, famous for her diaries.

1857 Birth of Lord Lonsdale (Henry Cecil Lowther) (d.1944), English sportsman; as president of the National Sporting Club he founded and presented the *Lonsdale belts* for boxing.

1858 First performance of *The Wedding March*, by Felix Mendelssohn (1809–47), at the marriage of Queen Victoria's daughter to the Crown Prince of Russia.

1874 Birth of W(illiam) Somerset Maugham in Paris (d.1965), English novelist and playwright, whose novels include *Of Human Bondage* (1915).

1882 Birth of Virginia Woolf in London (d.1941), novelist, and member of the Bloomsbury Group, whose novels include *Mrs Dalloway* (1925).

1899 Manufacture of the first radio sets in England.

1917 Purchase of the Danish West Indies by the USA for $25 million, then renamed the Virgin Islands.

1919 Founding of the League of Nations.

1924 The first Winter Olympics took place, at Chamonix in France.

1947 Death of Al(phonse) Capone (b.1899 in New York), racketeer, who achieved worldwide notoriety during the Prohibition era in Chicago.

1949 Presentation of the first Emmy awards, at the Hollywood Athletic Club.

1964 First No. 1 hit in the USA for The Beatles, with their single 'I Want to Hold Your Hand'.

1969 Death of Irene Castle (b.1893 in New Rochelle, New York), exhibition ballroom dancer and teacher with her husband Vernon Castle.

1981 The 'Gang of Four' announced plans to form a Social Democratic Party in the UK.

1989 British actor John Cleese won libel damages when the *Daily Mirror* claimed he had become like his character, Basil Fawlty, in *Fawlty Towers*.

1990 Death of Ava Gardner (b.1922 in Smithfield, North Carolina), actress, whose films include *The Snows of Kilimanjaro* (1952).

JANUARY

26

National Day, India and Australia.

1500 European discovery of Brazil by Vicent Yáñez Pinzón.

1823 Death of Edward Jenner (b.1749 in Berkeley, Gloucestershire), physician, famous for introducing vaccination.

1837 Michigan became the 26th state of the Union.

1871 Formation of the Rugby Football Union in London.

1875 Patenting of the electric dental drill by George F. Green of Kalamazoo, Michigan.

1880 Birth of Douglas MacArthur in Little Rock, Arkansas (d.1964), US general, and supreme commander of the Allied Forces in the Pacific during World War 2.

1885 Death of General Charles George Gordon (b.1833 in Woolwich, London), soldier, and governor of the Sudan, who died of wounds sustained while defending Khartoum.

1905 Discovery of the Cullinan diamond, the largest gem diamond ever found (3255 carats), in the Premier Diamond Mine, Transvaal, South Africa.

1907 Birth of Henry Cotton in Holmes Chapel, Cheshire (d.1987), golfer, three-times winner of the British Open golfing championship.

1908 Birth of Stephane Grappelli in Paris (d.1997), jazz violinist, a principal soloist in the Quintet of the Hot Club of France (1934–9).

1908 Registration of the first Boy Scout group in Britain.

1922 Birth of Michael Bentine in Watford, Hertfordshire (d.1996), actor, comedian, and writer, best known as one of the original members of The Goons.

1925 Birth of Paul Newman in Cleveland, Ohio, actor and director, whose films include *The Sting* (1973).

1939 Barcelona was taken by General Franco in the Spanish Civil War.

1945 Purchase of the New York Yankees baseball team by a syndicate for $3 million.

1950 First insurance policy issued for a baby-sitter, by an American insurance company.

1965 Hindi became the official language of India.

1973 Death of Edward G. Robinson, originally Emanuel Goldenburg (b.1893 in Bucharest, Romania), US actor, famous for playing rogues such as the gangster Rico in *Little Caesar* (1930).

1987 Coca-Cola became the top-selling soft drink in the USA.

JANUARY
27

1186 Marriage of Henry VI (1165–97), Holy Roman emperor (1191–7) and king of Germany (1190–97), to Constance of Sicily (1154–98).

1736 Abdication of Stanislaw Leszczyński from the Polish throne.

1756 Birth of Wolfgang Amadeus Mozart in Salzburg, Austria (d.1791), composer.

1832 Birth of Lewis Carroll (Charles Lutwidge Dodgson) in Daresbury, Cheshire (d.1898), mathematician and author, whose books include *Alice's Adventures in Wonderland* (1865).

1834 [Old Style calendar, New Style 8 February] Birth of Dmitri Mendeleyev in Tobolsk, Russia (d.1907), chemist, famous for formulating the periodic table of chemical elements.

1868 Dr David Livingstone, missionary and explorer in Africa, was reported still alive.

1880 Patenting of the electric lamp, by inventor and physicist Thomas Alva Edison (1847–1931).

1885 Birth of Jerome Kern in New York (d.1945), composer, who wrote a string of successful Broadway shows, such as *Show Boat* (1928).

1901 Death of Giuseppe Verdi (b.1813 in Le Roncole, Italy), composer of dramatic opera, whose works include *Aïda* (1871).

1926 First demonstration of a television image, by British electrical engineer John Logie Baird (1888–1946).

1945 Liberation of prisoners in the Auschwitz and Birkenau Nazi concentration camps in Poland by the Red Army.

1948 The first magnetic tape recorder, the Wireway, with built-in oscillator, went on sale in America for $149.50.

1951 The first atmospheric nuclear test was conducted on the Nevada Test Site.

1967 Death of three astronauts in Apollo 1, when it exploded during a test.

1967 Knighting of Francis Chichester, round-the-world yachtsman, by Queen Elizabeth II.

1968 Release of Otis Redding's record, '(Sittin' on the) Dock of the Bay' in the USA; it reached No. 1 in the US charts on 1 March 1968.

1984 US pop singer Michael Jackson (b.1958) was rushed to hospital with second-degree burns to his head, after an accident involving a firework during the filming of a Pepsi commercial.

1985 Announcement by the Coca-Cola Company of its intentions to sell its products in the Soviet Union.

2004 Keisha Castle-Hughes (b.1990), New Zealand actress, became the youngest person to receive an Oscar nomination for Best Actress, for her role in *Whale Rider*.

JANUARY
28

814 Death of Charlemagne (b.742), king of the Franks and emperor of the West.

1547 Death of Henry VIII (b.1491 in Greenwich, London), king of England.

1596 Death of Sir Francis Drake (b.1540 at Crowndale Farm, near Tavistock, Devon), seaman, best known for his week-long battle against the Spanish Armada (1588).

1807 Pall Mall, London, was the first street lit by gas.

1829 Death of William Burke (b.1792 in Orrery, Ireland), associate of William Hare; they robbed graves to provide bodies for Dr Knox to dissect.

1841 Birth of Sir Henry Morton Stanley in Denbigh, Denbighshire (d.1904), explorer and journalist, best known for being sent to 'find Livingstone' in Africa (1869).

1878 Opening of America's first commercial telephone switchboard exchange in New Haven, Connecticut.

1887 Birth of Artur Rubinstein in Łódź, Poland (d.1982), pianist, who became a US citizen in 1946, making over 200 recordings.

1896 First conviction of a British motorist for speeding; Walter Arnold, driving at 8 mph in a 2 mph zone, was overtaken by a policeman on a bicycle, and a fine of 1 shilling imposed.

1902 A donation of $10 million was made by industrialist and philanthropist Andrew Carnegie (1835–1919) to establish the Carnegie Institution in Washington, DC.

1904 Signing of operatic tenor Enrico Caruso (1873–1943) by Victor Records for his first recording contract, following his Metropolitan Opera debut in New York two months previously.

1912 Birth of Jackson Pollock in Cody, Wyoming (d.1956), Abstract Expressionist painter.

1929 Birth of Acker Bilk in Pensford, Somerset, jazz clarinettist and band leader.

1932 Start of the invasion of China by Japan.

1936 Birth of Alan Alda in New York, actor and director, best known for his role in the anti-war television series *M*A*S*H*.

1939 Death of W(illiam) B(utler) Yeats (b.1865 near Dublin, Ireland), poet and playwright.

1948 Birth of Mikhail Baryshnikov in Riga, Latvia, ballet dancer, who defected to the West in 1974 and joined the American Ballet Theatre.

1956 First television appearance for rock singer Elvis Presley (1935–77), on US national television.

1986 Explosion of US space shuttle Challenger shortly after lift-off at Cape Canaveral.

JANUARY

29

1635 Founding of the Académie Française, for the purpose of maintaining standards of literary taste and to establish the literary language, by Cardinal Richelieu (1585–1642).

1700 Birth of Daniel Bernoulli in Groningen, The Netherlands (d.1782), mathematician, who solved a differential equation now known as *Bernoulli's equation*.

1728 First performance of *The Beggar's Opera* (1685–1732), written by John Gay, at Lincoln's Inn Fields, London.

1737 Birth of Thomas Paine in Thetford, Norfolk (d.1809), social and political philosopher, and author of *The Rights of Man* (1791–2).

1820 Death of George III (b.1738 in London), king of Great Britain and Ireland.

1843 Birth of William McKinley in Niles, Ohio (d.1901), 25th president of the USA (1897–1901).

1845 Publication of 'The Raven' by Edgar Allan Poe (1809–49), under the name 'Quarles', in the *New York Evening Mirror*.

1848 Adoption of Greenwich Mean Time by Scotland.

1850 Birth of Sir Ebenezer Howard in London (d.1928), founder of the garden-city movement.

1861 Kansas became the 24th state of the Union.

1862 Birth of Frederick Delius in Bradford, West Yorkshire (d.1934), composer, whose works include *On Hearing the First Cuckoo in Spring* (1912).

1879 Birth of W. C. Fields (William Claude Dukenfield) in Philadelphia, Pennsylvania (d.1946), actor, famous for his distinctive voice.

1886 Patenting of his motor-driven two-seater tricycle by engineer and car manufacturer Karl Benz (1844–1929).

1935 Approval given to the Green Belt scheme in the UK by London County Council.

1939 Birth of Germaine Greer in Melbourne, Victoria, Australia, feminist writer, best known for her controversial book *The Female Eunuch* (1970).

1941 Birth of Tom Selleck in Detroit, Michigan, actor, whose films include *Magnum, PI* (1980).

1942 First broadcast of the BBC radio programme *Desert Island Discs*.

1980 Death of Jimmy Durante (b.1893 in New York), comedian and entertainer, known as 'Schnozzle' Durante because of his large nose.

2004 A 60-ton sperm whale carcass exploded in downtown Tainan, Taiwan, causing traffic chaos.

JANUARY

30

Feast (Eastern Church) of St Hippolytus, patron saint of horses.

1606 Execution of Thomas Bates, Sir Everard Digby, John Grant, and Thomas Winter for their part in the Gunpowder Plot.

1649 Execution of King Charles I in Whitehall, London.

1790 Launch of the first purpose-built lifeboat, *Original*, at Tynemouth, Tyne and Wear.

1840 Trade with Britain was forbidden by the emperor of China, during the First Opium War (1839–42).

1858 Founding of the Hallé Orchestra by Sir Charles Hallé (1819–95) in Manchester.

1882 Birth of Franklin D. Roosevelt in Hyde Park, New York (d.1945), 32nd president of the USA.

1894 Patenting of the pneumatic hammer by C. B. King of Detroit, Michigan.

1911 Birth of Roy Eldridge in Pittsburgh, Pennsylvania (d.1989), trumpet player and improviser, a featured soloist with many bands.

1928 Birth of Hal Prince in New York, stage director and producer, whose work included several musicals with Stephen Sondheim and Andrew Lloyd Webber.

1937 Birth of Boris Spassky in Leningrad, Russia, chess player and world champion (1969–72).

1948 Death of Mahatma Gandhi (b.1869 in Poorbandar, Kathiawar, India), Indian nationalist leader, assassinated in Delhi by Nathuram Godse, a Hindu fanatic.

1948 Death of Orville Wright (b.1871 in Dayton, Ohio), aviation pioneer, who with his brother, Wilbur (1867–1912), was the first to fly in a heavier-than-air machine (17 December 1903).

1958 Yves St Laurent, fashion designer, held his first major Paris show.

1961 First sales of the contraceptive pill in Britain.

1965 The state funeral of Sir Winston Churchill took place in London.

1969 Last public appearance for the pop group The Beatles in a concert at their Apple studios in London.

1972 Bloody Sunday: British troops opened fire on civilian demonstrators in Londonderry, Northern Ireland, killing 13 people.

1976 Muriel Naughton became the first female jockey to compete under National Hunt rules.

1989 Finding of Pharaonic statues dating back to 1470 BC near the Temple of Luxor, Egypt.

JANUARY
31

Feast of St John Bosco, patron saint of editors, labourers, schoolboys, and youth.

1606 Execution of Guy Fawkes (b.1570 in York, North Yorkshire) for his role as chief conspirator in the Gunpowder Plot.

1747 Opening of the first VD clinic in London.

1788 Death of Charles Edward Stuart (b.1720 in Rome, Italy), claimant to the British crown, known as 'Bonnie Prince Charlie'.

1797 Birth of Franz Schubert in Vienna, Austria (d.1818), composer, whose works include the 'Unfinished' Symphony.

1865 Promotion of Robert Edward Lee (1807–70), Confederate general in the American Civil War, to the position of general-in-chief.

1881 [Old Style calendar, New Style 12 February] Birth of Anna Pavlova in St Petersburg, Russia (d.1931), prima ballerina, whose best known role was in Fokine's *The Dying Swan* (1905).

1910 Dr Hawley Harvey Crippen (1862–1910) poisoned his wife, dissected the body, and interred the remains in his cellar.

1921 Birth of Mario Lanza in Philadelphia, Pennsylvania (d.1959), tenor and actor, who appeared in several musicals, notably *The Great Caruso* (1951).

1923 Birth of Norman Mailer in Long Branch, New Jersey, author, whose novels include *The Naked and the Dead* (1948).

1929 Birth of Jean Simmons in London, actress, whose many films include *The Robe* (1953).

1940 Issue of the first social security check by the US government, for $22.54, to Ida Fuller of Brattlesboro, Vermont.

1946 Promulgation of Yugoslavia's new constitution, establishing six constituent republics: Bosnia-Herzegovina, Croatia, Macedonia, Montenegro, Serbia, and Slovenia.

1951 Birth of Phil Collins in London, singer and drummer, who worked with several groups and also has a successful solo career.

1958 Launch of Explorer I, the first US earth satellite, from Cape Canaveral, Florida.

1961 Ham the Chimp (d.1998) became the first primate astronaut when he was secured in a Project Mercury capsule and launched from Cape Canaveral, Florida, into outer space.

1968 Independence of Nauru, jointly administered by Britain, Australia, and New Zealand since World War 1.

1983 Trial enforcement period for the use of seat belts in cars in Britain.

1990 Opening of the first McDonald's in Moscow, Russia.

FEBRUARY

1

End of the pheasant- and partridge-shooting season in the UK.

Feast of St Bridget (453–523), patron saint of blacksmiths, dairymaids, healers, and poets. Feast of St Severus, patron saint of drapers, silk and wool manufacturers, and weavers.

1650 Death of René Descartes (b.1596 in La Haye, France), philosopher and mathematician, famous for the phrase 'I think, therefore I am'.

1811 The Bell Rock lighthouse came into operation.

1851 Death of Mary Shelley (b.1797 in London), writer, best known for her novel *Frankenstein, or the Modern Prometheus* (1818).

1884 Publication of the first volume, *A–Ant*, of the *Oxford English Dictionary*.

1893 Opening of the first film studio, in New Jersey, by US inventor Thomas Edison (1847–1931).

1895 Birth of John Ford in Cape Elizabeth, Maine (d.1973), director, whose films include *Stage Coach* (1939).

1901 Birth of Clark Gable in Cadiz, Ohio (d.1960), actor, best known for his role of Rhett Butler in *Gone With the Wind* (1939).

1910 Opening of the first labour exchanges in Britain.

1915 Introduction of passport photographs in Britain.

1915 Birth of Sir Stanley Matthews in Hanley, Staffordshire (d.2000), footballer, the first to be knighted.

1930 First publication of *The Times* crossword.

1931 Birth of Boris Yeltsin in Bukta, Russia, the first Russian president to be freely elected (1991–9).

1941 Formation of the junior branch of Britain's Royal Air Force, the Air Training Corps (ATC).

1966 Death of Buster Keaton (b.1895 in Piqua, Kansas), film comedian, famous for his deadpan expression, who starred and directed such classics as *The General* (1926).

1971 Launch of Apollo 14 on the Moon mission from Cape Kennedy, now Cape Canaveral, Florida.

1977 Opening of the Centre National d'Art et de Culture, or Pompidou Centre, on the Plateau Beaubourg in Paris.

1979 Return from exile of the Ayatollah Khomeini (1900–1989), to become leader of Iran.

1983 First broadcast of TV-am, British Independent Television's breakfast-time station.

FEBRUARY
2

Groundhog Day.
Feast of Candlemas.
Feast of the Purification of the Virgin Mary.

1536 Founding of Buenos Aires by Pedro de Mendoza.

1594 Death of Giovanni Pierluigi da Palestrina (b.1525 in Palestrina, Italy), Renaissance composer.

1650 Birth of Nell Gwyn in London (d.1686), orange seller, who became the mistress of King Charles II.

1709 Rescue of sailor Alexander Selkirk (1676–1721), said to have inspired Defoe's *Robinson Crusoe*, after five years alone on an island.

1801 First meeting of the parliament of the United Kingdom of Great Britain and Ireland.

1852 Opening of the first 'gents' public lavatory, in London's Fleet Street.

1878 Greece declared war on Turkey.

1880 First imports of frozen meat to Britain, from Sydney, Australia.

1882 Birth of James Joyce in Dublin, Ireland (d.1941), writer, best known for his novel *Ulysses* (1922), published in Paris, but banned in the UK and USA until 1934.

1917 Introduction of bread rationing in Britain.

1934 Birth of Les Dawson in Manchester (d.1993), comedian, known for his mother-in-law jokes and playing the piano out of tune.

1940 Birth of Sir David Jason in Edmonton, London, actor, best known for his character Del Boy in *Only Fools and Horses* (1981–2003).

1970 Death of Bertrand Russell (b.1872 in Trelleck, Monmouthshire), philosopher, known for his influence on 20th-c analytic philosophy.

1971 Ugandan soldier Idi Amin (c.1925–2003) declared himself absolute ruler in Uganda.

1979 Death of Sid Vicious, originally John Ritchie (b.1957 in London), member of the punk rock band The Sex Pistols.

1987 Death of Alistair Maclean (b.1922 in Glasgow), best-selling novelist, whose books include *The Guns of Navarone* (1957) and *Where Eagles Dare* (1967).

1995 Death of Fred Perry (b.1909 in Stockport, Greater Manchester), tennis player, the last British male to win the singles title at Wimbledon (1934–6).

1996 Death of Gene Kelly (b.1912 in Pittsburgh, Pennsylvania), modern dancer and actor, whose films include *Singin' in the Rain* (1952).

FEBRUARY

3

Feast of Saint Anskar, patron saint of Denmark.

Feast (Western Church) of St Blaise (?–c.316), patron saint of builders, sick cattle, stonecutters, throat sufferers, wool-combers, and wool-weavers.

1399 Death of John of Gaunt (b.1340 in Ghent, Belgium), fourth son of Edward III, influential during the reign of Richard II.

1488 Arrival of Portuguese explorer Bartolomeu Diaz (c.1450–1500) in Africa, the first European to land there.

1651 Surrender of Hume Castle, Berwickshire, to Colonel Fenwick of Oliver Cromwell's army.

1762 Death of Richard 'Beau' Nash (b.1674 in Swansea), dandy and gambler, known for his reforms in manners and his leadership in fashion.

1809 Birth of Felix Mendelssohn in Hamburg, Germany (d.1847), composer, whose works include the oratorio *Elijah* (1846).

1811 Birth of Horace Greely in Amherst, New Hampshire (d.1872), founder of the daily *New York Tribune* (1841).

1821 Birth of Elizabeth Blackwell in Bristol, Avon (d.1910), English-American physician, who became the first female doctor in the USA.

1830 Independence of Greece, under the protection of Britain, France, and Russia.

1830 Birth of Robert Cecil, 3rd Mar-

quess of Salisbury, in Hatfield, Hertfordshire (d.1903), British prime minister (1885–6, 1886–92, 1895–1902).

1913 Ratification of the Sixteenth Amendment to the US Constitution, allowing the imposition and collection of income tax.

1919 First meeting of the League of Nations, at the Paris Peace Conference.

1924 Death of Thomas Woodrow Wilson (b.1856 in Staunton, Virginia), 28th president of the USA.

1945 Daylight bombing of Berlin by the Allies, using over 1000 planes.

1954 Queen Elizabeth II made the first visit to Australia by a reigning British monarch.

1959 Death of Buddy Holly in a plane crash (b.1936 in Lubbock, Texas), rock singer, songwriter, and guitarist, who became a cult figure following his death.

1960 Harold Macmillan, British prime minister 1957–63, made his 'Wind of Change' speech in Cape Town, South Africa.

1966 Arrival of Soviet spacecraft Luna 9 on the Moon, where it began sending back television images of the surface.

1969 Death of Boris Karloff (b.1887 in London), US film star, who made his name as the monster in *Frankenstein* (1931).

1994 End of the US economic embargo against Vietnam.

FEBRUARY

4

1615 Death of Giambattista della Porta (b.1535 in Naples, Campania, Italy), scientist, writer, and inventor of the camera obscura.

1861 Formation of the Confederate States of America; the secession took place in Montgomery, Alabama.

1881 Death of Thomas Carlyle (b.1795 in Ecclefechan, Dumfries and Galloway), writer, whose works include *Sartor Resartus* (1833–4).

1902 Birth of Charles A. Lindbergh in Detroit, Michigan (d.1974), pilot, who made the first non-stop solo transatlantic flight (1927) from New York to Paris.

1912 Birth of Byron Nelson in Fort Worth, Texas, golfing champion, who won the US Open (1939), and the US Masters (1937, 1942).

1915 Birth of Sir Norman Wisdom in London, comedian, best known for his appearances in variety and film (beginning with *Trouble in Store* (1953)).

1927 British land and water speed-record contestant Sir Malcolm Campbell (1885–1948) broke the land speed record in his car *Bluebird*, driving at over 174 mph.

1932 Opening of the 3rd Winter Olympic Games, in Lake Placid, New York.

1938 German dictator Adolf Hitler (1889–1945) assumed command of the German Army.

1945 Beginning of the Yalta Conference in the Crimea, with the meeting of Churchill, Roosevelt, and Stalin.

1948 Birth of Alice Cooper (Vincent Damon Furnier) in Detroit, Michigan, rock singer, known for his deliberate attempts to shock audiences.

1948 Independence of Ceylon, later known as Sri Lanka.

1953 Ending of sweet rationing in Britain.

1962 Publication of the first colour supplement, by *The Sunday Times*.

1971 Bankruptcy announcement by Rolls-Royce, manufacturer of luxury cars.

1974 The Symbionese Liberation Army kidnapped heiress Patty Hearst in California.

1976 Opening of the 12th Winter Olympic Games, in Innsbruck, Austria.

1983 Death of Karen Carpenter (b.1950 in New Haven, Connecticut), singer, who performed in the vocal duo The Carpenters with her brother Richard (b.1946).

1987 Death of Liberace (b.1919 in Milwaukee, Wisconsin), entertainer, who performed popular piano classics with a lavish sense of showmanship.

1997 American football player O(renthal) J(ames) Simpson (b.1947) was found responsible for the deaths of his ex-wife and her male friend by a civil trial jury.

36

FEBRUARY

5

Feast of St Agatha (?–251), patron saint of bell-founders, Catania (Sicily), and firefighters.

1782 Capture of Minorca by Spanish and French forces, when British forces were defeated during the American Revolution.

1788 Birth of Sir Robert Peel near Bury, Lancashire (d.1850), British prime minister (1834–5, 1841–6), and founder of the Metropolitan Police.

1811 The Prince of Wales was declared Prince Regent, later becoming King George IV.

1840 Birth of John Boyd Dunlop in Dreghorn, Strathclyde (d.1921), inventor, who patented the pneumatic tyre.

1840 Birth of Sir Hiram Maxim in Sangerville, Maine (d.1916), inventor and engineer, who perfected the Maxim machine-gun (1883).

1893 Birth of Captain W(illiam) E(arl) Johns in Hertford, Hertfordshire (d.1968), pilot and author, best known as the creator of Biggles.

1914 Birth of William Burroughs in St Louis, Missouri (d.1997), novelist, whose works include *Naked Lunch* (1959).

1919 Formation of the first independent film corporation, United Artists, in Hollywood, California, led by Charlie Chaplin, Douglas Fairbanks, Mary Pickford, and D. W. Griffith; the head of Metro Pictures, Richard A. Rowland, remarked that 'the inmates are taking over the asylum'.

1920 Founding of the Royal Air Force College at Cranwell, Lincolnshire.

1922 First publication of New York magazine *Reader's Digest*.

1924 First broadcast of the Greenwich Observatory time signal via the BBC 'pips'.

1945 Birth of Bob Marley near Kingston, Jamaica (d.1981), singer, guitarist, and composer of reggae music, whose songs include 'No Woman, No Cry'.

1953 Release of Walt Disney's cartoon *Peter Pan*.

1958 The Tybee hydrogen bomb was lost by the US Air Force off the coast of Savannah, Georgia, and never recovered.

1958 Beginning of a trial period for parking meters, in Mayfair, London.

1961 Apollo 14, the eighth manned mission in the Apollo programme, became the third to land on the Moon.

1961 First publication of Britain's *Sunday Telegraph*.

1982 Collapse of Laker Airways 'Skytrain' project, with debts of well over £2 million.

1988 First Comic Relief Red Nose Day, raising £15 million for charity.

FEBRUARY
6

National Day, New Zealand.
Feast of St Amand, patron saint of brewers, hotelkeepers, inn-keepers, and wine merchants.
Feast of St Dorothy, patron saint of florists and gardeners.

1564 Birth of Christopher Marlowe in Canterbury, Kent (d.1593), playwright and poet, whose works include *The Tragical History of Dr Faustus* (c.1592).

1665 Birth of Anne in London (d.1714), queen of Great Britain and Ireland (1702–14).

1685 Death of Charles II (b.1630 in London), king of Britain and Ireland (1660–85).

1783 Death of Lancelot Brown, known as Capability Brown (b.1715 in Kirkharle, Northumberland), landscape gardener, whose designs included the gardens at Blenheim and Kew.

1788 Massachusetts became the 6th state of the Union.

1802 Birth of Sir Charles Wheatstone in Gloucester, Gloucestershire (d.1875), physicist, known for his experiments in sound.

1819 Treaty between Sultan Hussein Mohamed Shah of Johor and Sir Thomas Stamford Bingley Raffles (1781–1826), founding modern Singapore.

1840 Signing of the Treaty of Waitangi in New Zealand by Great Britain and Maori chiefs.

1911 Birth of Ronald Reagan in Tampico, Illinois (d.2004), 40th president of the USA (1981–9).

1918 Introduction of £150 deposit from prospective parliamentary candidates in Britain.

1918 Women over 30 in Britain were given the right to vote by an Act of Parliament.

1952 Succession of Queen Elizabeth II to the British throne on the death of her father, King George VI.

1958 Seven members of Britain's Manchester United football team were among 21 killed in a plane crash in Munich.

1959 Patenting of an integrated circuit by US electrical engineer Jack St Clair Kilby (1923–2005) of Texas Instruments.

1964 Agreement of Channel Tunnel plans by Britain and France, at a proposed cost of £160 million.

1971 US astronaut Alan Shepard, Jr (1923–98) became the first man to hit a golf ball on the Moon, during a Moon walk from Apollo 14.

2005 Jerrick De Leon, born 13 weeks premature, became the smallest infant to survive an arterial switch, an open-heart procedure.

FEBRUARY

7

1301 King Edward I (1239–1307) of England revived the title Prince of Wales, and bestowed it on his son, later Edward II.

1700 Birth of Philippe Buache in Paris (d.1773), geographer and cartographer, who devised contour lines for maps and charts.

1812 Birth of Charles Dickens in Landport, Hampshire (d.1870), novelist.

1837 Birth of Sir James (Augustus Henry) Murray in Denholm, Scottish Borders (d.1915), lexicographer, whose life's work was the editing of the *New English Dictionary* (begun 1879, completed 1928).

1886 Discovery of gold in the Transvaal, South Africa, by Englishman George Walker.

1894 Death of Adolf Sax (b.1814 in Dinant, Belgium), musician and inventor, best known for his invention of the saxophone.

1935 The board game 'Monopoly' was first marketed by Charles Darrow.

1940 US premiere of Walt Disney's animated film *Pinocchio*.

1959 Death of Daniel Malan (b.1874 in Riebeek West, South Africa), prime minister of South Africa (1948–54), who introduced the apartheid policy (1948).

1964 Beatlemania hit the States, as the Fab Four arrived in New York for their first US tour.

1968 Agreement by all 10 provincial premiers of Canada to draft a new constitution giving French equal status with English.

1971 Swiss men voted in favour of women being allowed to vote in federal elections and to stand for parliament.

1974 Independence within the Commonwealth of Granada, West Indies.

1984 US astronauts Bruce McCandless II (b.1937) and Robert L. Stewart (b.1942) made the first untethered space walk, using the Manned Maneuvering Unit.

1985 The song 'New York, New York', made famous by Frank Sinatra (1915–98), became the official anthem of New York.

1989 Raining of sardines over Ipswich, Australia, thirty miles from the Brisbane coast; the cause was freak storm conditions.

1992 Signing of the Maastricht Treaty of European Union by European Community ministers.

1996 Supersonic airliner Concorde made a record crossing of the Atlantic between New York and London (2 hours, 52 minutes, 59 seconds).

2005 British sailor Dame Ellen MacArthur (b.1976) set a new record for the fastest round-the-world solo sail, completing the 27,354-mile journey in 71 days, 14 hours, 18 minutes, 33 seconds.

FEBRUARY
8

Feast of St Jerome Emiliani, patron saint of orphans and abandoned children.

1587 Execution of Mary, Queen of Scots (b.1542 in Linlithgow Palace, West Lothian), beheaded for treason at Fotheringay Castle, Northamptonshire.

1693 Granting of a charter for the College of William and Mary in Williamsburg, Virginia, making it the second institution of higher learning in the American colonies.

1819 Birth of John Ruskin in London (d.1900), art theorist and social critic, who influenced the Arts and Crafts movement.

1828 Birth of Jules Verne in Nantes, France (d.1905), science-fiction writer, whose works include *Around the World in Eighty Days* (1873).

1861 Jefferson Davis (1808–89) was chosen provisional president of the Confederate States of America.

1888 Birth of Dame Edith (Mary) Evans, born in London (d.1976), actress, whose famous roles included Lady Bracknell in Oscar Wilde's *The Importance of Being Earnest*.

1904 Beginning of the Russo–Japanese war, when Japan launched a surprise torpedo attack against the Russian fleet at Port Arthur, China.

1910 Founding of the Boy Scouts of America movement in the District of Columbia.

1924 First use of the gas chamber as a method of execution in the USA, when gangster Gee Jon was put to death at the Nevada State Prison, Carson City.

1931 Birth of James (Byron) Dean in Marion, Indiana (d.1955), actor and teenage icon, whose best-known film is *Rebel Without a Cause* (1955).

1952 HRH Princess Elizabeth (b.1926) was formally proclaimed queen of England, following the death of her father, King George VI, on 6 February.

1967 Death of Sir Victor Gollancz (b.1893 in London), publisher, writer, and philanthropist.

1974 Return to Earth for the crew of the first US space station, Skylab, after a record-breaking 84 days in space.

1983 Kidnapping of the Derby-winning racehorse Shergar in Ireland, held for a ransom of £2 million; he was not seen again.

1984 Opening of the 14th Winter Olympic Games, in Sarajevo, Bosnia and Herzegovina.

2005 Cuba banned tobacco smoking in public places.

FEBRUARY
9

Feast of St Apollonia, patron saint of dentists and toothache sufferers.

474 Coronation of Imperator Caesar Flavius Zeno Augustus (c.425–91) as co-emperor of the Byzantine Empire.

1404 Birth of Constantine XI Dragases in Constantinople (d.1453), the last Byzantine emperor.

1540 The first recorded horse-race meeting in Britain was held at Chester, Cheshire.

1773 Birth of William Henry Harrison in Charles City Co, Virginia (d.1841), 9th president of the USA (1841).

1811 Death of Nevil Maskelyne (b.1732 in London), Astronomer Royal, known for his work on methods and instruments of observation.

1822 Invasion of the Dominican Republic by Haiti.

1830 Discovery of the termination of the Murray River, Australia, by explorer Charles Sturt (1795–1869).

1881 [28 January, Old Style calendar] Death of Fyodor (Mikhaylovich) Dostoevsky (b.1821 in Moscow), novelist, whose works include *Crime and Punishment* (1866).

1895 Invention of volleyball, originally called *mintonette*, by William G. Morgan (1870–1942).

1916 Enforcement of the Military Service Act, introducing conscription in Britain.

1922 Birth of Jim Laker in Bradford, West Yorkshire (d.1986), cricketer and broadcaster, who made Test cricket history at Old Trafford in 1956 when he took 19 Australian wickets for 90 runs.

1942 Introduction of soap rationing in Britain.

1950 More than 200 staff in the State Department were accused of being members of the Communist Party by US Senator Joe McCarthy (1908–57).

1960 US actress Joanne Woodward (b.1930) became the first actress to receive a star on the Hollywood Walk of Fame.

1969 First test flight of a Boeing 747 Jumbo Jet.

1971 Return to Earth of Apollo 14, after the third manned Moon landing.

1979 Britain's first £1m football transfer, when Nottingham Forest football club secured the deal for England forward Trevor Francis (b.1954).

1981 Death of Bill Haley (b.1927 in Highland Park, Michigan), singer and musician, who popularized rock-and-roll in the 1950s.

2001 The submarine USS *Greeneville* accidentally collided with and sank the *Ehime-Maru*, a Japanese training vessel, drowning nine crew members including four high-school students.

FEBRUARY
10

Feast of St Scholastica, patron saint of Benedictine nuns.

1098 Crusaders of the First Crusade defeated Prince Redwan of Aleppo (d.1113), capturing Antioch and most of Syria.

1763 The Treaty of Paris ended the Franco–Indian War; France ceded Canada to England, and gave up all her territories in the New World except New Orleans and a few scattered islands.

1824 Birth of Samuel Plimsoll in Bristol (d.1898), social reformer and MP, whose Merchant Shipping Act (1876) caused the *Plimsoll line* to be marked on all ships.

1837 [29 January, Old Style calendar] Death of Alexander Pushkin (b.1799 in Moscow), poet and novelist, killed in a duel.

1840 Marriage of Queen Victoria to Prince Albert of Saxe-Coburg-Gotha.

1863 Marriage of world-famous dwarfs General Tom Thumb (1838–83) and Lavinia Warren (1841–1919) in New York.

1894 Birth of Harold Macmillan, 1st Earl of Stockton, in London (d.1986), British prime minister (1957–63).

1902 Birth of Walter Houser Brattain in Amoy, China (d.1987), US physicist, who shared the 1956 Nobel Prize for Physics for his role in the development of the point contact transistor.

1910 Birth of Joyce Grenfell in London (d.1979), writer and entertainer, famous for her comic monologues and songs.

1912 Death of Joseph Lister (b.1827 in Upton, Essex), surgeon, who introduced the use of antiseptic conditions during surgery.

1931 Delhi became the capital of India.

1940 Cinematic debut of cartoon characters Tom and Jerry in *Puss Gets the Boot* (1940), directed by Bill Hanna and Joe Barbera.

1942 US trombonist and bandleader Glenn Miller (1904–44) received the first actual golden disc for recording sales, for 'Chattanooga Choo Choo'.

1944 Introduction of the Pay As You Earn tax system (PAYE) in Britain, replacing annual or biannual collections.

1949 Opening of *Death of a Salesman* by Arthur Miller (1915–2005) at the Morocco Theatre, New York.

1962 Captured American U-2 pilot Francis Gary Powers (1929–77) was exchanged by the Soviet Union for Rudolph Abel (1903–71), a Soviet spy held by the USA.

1996 World chess champion Gary Kasparov (b.1963) was beaten by a computer named 'Deep Blue'.

FEBRUARY
11

Feast (Eastern Church) of St Blaise (?–c.316), patron saint of builders, sick cattle, stone-cutters, throat sufferers, wool-combers, and wool-weavers.

Feast of St Caedmon (?–c.680), patron saint of singers.

660 BC Date of the ascension of Japan's first emperor, Jimmu Tenno (711–585 BC according to legend).

1812 Signing of a law by Elbridge Gerry, 5th vice-president of the USA, in Massachusetts, changing the state's boundaries to ensure a Republican majority; the move gave rise to the term 'gerrymandering'.

1847 Birth of Thomas Alva Edison in Milan, Ohio (d.1931), physicist, whose inventions included the phonograph (1877) and the light bulb (1879).

1858 Saint Bernadette (1844–79) received her first vision of the Virgin Mary at Lourdes, France.

1868 Death of Jean Foucault (b.1819 in Paris), physicist; from Foucault's pendulum could be deduced the rotation of the Earth.

1878 Issue of the first weekly weather report by the British Meteorological Office.

1908 Birth of Sir Vivian Fuchs in Freshwater, Isle of Wight (d.1999), explorer and geologist, who led the Commonwealth Trans-Antarctic Expedition (1955–8).

1928 Opening of the 2nd Winter Olympic Games, in St Moritz, Switzerland.

1929 The Lateran Treaty made the Vatican City an independent Papal sovereign state in Rome.

1934 Birth of Mary Quant in London, fashion designer, whose designs and colours were a feature of the 'swinging Britain' of the 1960s.

1945 Ending of the Yalta Conference, a meeting between leaders Winston Churchill, Josef Stalin, and Franklin D. Roosevelt, with agreement on the founding of the United Nations.

1961 Start of the trial of Adolf Eichmann (1906–62), high-ranking official in Nazi Germany, responsible for the extermination of millions during the Holocaust.

1975 Election of Margaret Thatcher (b.1925) as leader of the Conservative Party, the first woman party leader in British politics.

1976 Ice skater John Curry (1949–94) won Britain's first Olympic gold for figure-skating.

1989 Reverend Barbara C. Harris (b.1931) became the first woman in America to be consecrated as a bishop in the Episcopal Church.

1990 Release of Nelson Mandela (b.1918) after 27 years in jail in South Africa.

FEBRUARY
12

Feast of St Julian the Hospitaller, patron saint of clowns, fiddlers, hoteliers, sailors, and travellers.

1554 Death of Lady Jane Grey (b.1537), queen of England for nine days, executed for high treason on Tower Green, London.

1733 Founding of Savannah, Georgia, by English colonists led by James Edward Oglethorpe (1696–1785).

1804 Death of Immanuel Kant (b.1724 in Königsberg, Germany, now Kaliningrad, Russia), philosopher, whose main work is the *Critique of Pure Reason* (translated 1781).

1809 Birth of Abraham Lincoln in Hodgenville, Kentucky (d.1865), 16th president of the USA (1861–5), best known for his role in the freeing of slaves and his Gettysburg Address.

1809 Birth of Charles Darwin in Shrewsbury, Shropshire (d.1882), naturalist, whose major work was *On the Origin of Species by Means of Natural Selection* (1859).

1851 Gold prospector Edward Hammond Hargraves (1816–91) found gold in Summer Hill Creek, Australia, starting the Australian gold rush.

1877 Demonstration between Boston and Salem of the telephone developed by educationist and inventor Alexander Graham Bell (1847–1922).

1898 Death of Henry Lindfield of Brighton, first British motorist killed in a car accident.

1912 Abdication of Puyi (1906–67), 10th and last emperor of the Manchu Qing Dynasty to rule over China.

1924 Premiere of George Gershwin's *Rhapsody in Blue* in New York.

1935 Death of Auguste Escoffier (b.c.1847 in Villeneuve-Loubet, France), chef, the inventor of *Pêche Melba* and *Tournedos Rossini* for the singer and composer respectively.

1941 The first human test subject was injected with penicillin by biochemist Ernst Boris Chain (1906–79) and pathologist Howard Walter Florey (1898–1968), who developed this antibiotic.

1956 Britain's first double yellow 'no parking' lines were painted in Slough, Berkshire.

1994 Theft of Edvard Munch's painting *The Scream* by two art thieves from the Norwegian National Gallery in Oslo, Norway.

1994 A charity walk through the Channel Tunnel took place, the first time the trip from Britain to France had been possible on foot since the ice age.

2000 Death of Charles (Monroe) Schulz (b.1922 in Minneapolis, Minnesota); strip cartoonist and the creator of 'Peanuts'.

2002 Commencement of the trial of Slobodan Milošević (1941–2006), former president of Yugoslavia, at the UN war crimes tribunal in The Hague.

FEBRUARY
13

Feast of St Modomnoc, patron saint of bee-keepers.

1542 Death of Catherine Howard, fifth wife of King Henry VIII, executed for adultery.

1635 Founding of the oldest public school in the USA, the Boston Public Latin School.

1689 William of Orange (1650–1702) and his wife Mary (1662–94) were declared joint sovereigns of Great Britain and Ireland.

1858 British explorers Sir Richard Burton (1821–90) and Captain John Speke (1827–64) became the first Europeans to discover Lake Tanganyika in East Africa.

1866 Wild West outlaw Jesse James (1847–82) and his gang stole $60,000 from a bank in Missouri, USA.

1923 Birth of Brigadier General Charles Elwood (Chuck) Yeager in Myra, Lincoln Co, West Virginia, World War 2 ace and test pilot, the first human to travel faster than sound.

1935 German carpenter Bruno Hauptmann (1899–1936) was found guilty of the 1932 kidnapping and murder of aviator Charles Lindbergh's infant son.

1943 Establishment of the Nuffield Foundation in London by motor magnate and philanthropist William Richard Morris (1877–1963), 1st Viscount Nuffield.

1958 Death of Dame Christabel Pankhurst (b.1880 in Manchester), suffragette, who founded, with her mother Emmeline Pankhurst (1858–1928), the Women's Social and Political Union (1903).

1960 France carried out its first atomic-bomb test at Reggane Proving Grounds, Algeria.

1969 Fertilization of the first human eggs 'in vitro'.

1974 Birth of Robert Peter (Robbie) Williams in Burslem, Stoke-on-Trent, Staffordshire, pop singer, whose hits include 'Angels' (1997) and 'Rock DJ' (2001).

1980 Opening of the 13th Winter Olympic Games in Lake Placid, New York.

1988 Opening of the 15th Winter Olympic Games, in Calgary, Alberta.

1996 Beginning of the Nepal Civil War, a conflict between Maoist rebels and the Nepalese government.

2000 The final 'Peanuts' strip, by US cartoonist Charles M. Schulz (1922–2000), ran in Sunday newspapers the day after his death.

2005 Death of Lucia de Jesus dos Santos (b.1907 in Aljustrel, Portugal), Carmelite nun, and last of the three children to whom the Virgin Mary is said to have appeared at Fatima, Portugal in 1917.

FEBRUARY
14

Old Candlemas.
Feast (Western Church) of St Valentine (?–c.269), patron saint of lovers.
Feast (Western Church) of St Cyril (c.827–69) and St Methodius (c.825–85), patron saints of ecumenists.

1477 The world's first known valentine was sent to John Paston from Margery Brews, addressed 'To my ryght welbelovyd Voluntyne'.

1779 Death of Captain James Cook (b.1728 in Marton, North Yorkshire), navigator, killed during a dispute with tribesmen in Hawaii.

1819 Birth of Christopher Latham Sholes near Mooresburg, Pennsylvania (d.1890), inventor of the typewriter along with colleagues Carlos Glidden and Samuel Soulé.

1845 Birth of Quintin Hogg in London (d.1903), philanthropist, who opened Regent Street Polytechnic (1882) for the teaching of various trades.

1852 Elizabeth Armstrong was the first patient to be admitted to the Great Ormond Street Children's Hospital in London.

1858 Oregon became the 33rd state of the Union.

1895 Opening of *The Importance of Being Earnest*, Oscar Wilde's final play, at St James's Theatre, London.

1912 Arizona became the 48th state of the Union.

1929 St Valentine's Day Massacre: seven members of Bugsy Moran's gang were gunned down in a Chicago warehouse; the Al Capone gang were suspected.

1933 France's first telephone speaking-clock began operating, in Paris.

1944 Birth of Alan Parker in London, director, whose films include *Bugsy Malone* (1976).

1946 Unveiling of ENIAC (Electronic Numerical Integrator and Computer), the first general-purpose electronic computer, at the University of Pennsylvania.

1952 Opening of the 6th Winter Olympic Games, in Oslo, Norway.

1975 Death of Sir P(elham) G(renville) Wodehouse (b.1881 in Guildford, Surrey), novelist, best known as the creator of Bertie Wooster and Jeeves.

1984 British figure-skating couple Jayne Torvill (b.1957) and Christopher Dean (b.1958) won a gold medal at the Sarajevo Winter Olympics after their performance to Ravel's *Boléro*.

2003 Death of Dolly the sheep, the first mammal cloned from an adult, put to sleep because she was affected by premature aging and disease.

2005 Death of Rafiq al-Hariri (b.1944 in Sidon, Lebanon), fomer prime minister of Lebanon, killed by a car bomb in central Beirut.

FEBRUARY

15

1386 Introduction of Christianity as the official religion of Lithuania by Grand Duke Jogaila (c.1351–1434).

1564 Birth of Galileo Galilei in Pisa, Italy (d.1642), mathematician and astronomer, who discovered the four largest satellites of Jupiter.

1748 Birth of Jeremy Bentham in London (d.1832), philosopher, who founded utilitarianism, and believed legislation should allow 'the greatest happiness of the greatest number'.

1763 Signing of the Treaty of Hubertusburg, ending hostilities between Austria, Saxony, and Prussia in the Seven Years' War.

1820 Birth of Susan B(rownell) Anthony in Adams, Massachusetts (d.1906), social reformer, who co-founded the National American Woman Suffrage Association (1869).

1834 Birth of Sir William Henry Preece in Bryn Helen, Gwynedd (d.1913), pioneer of wireless telegraphy and telephony, who introduced Britain's first telephones.

1844 Death of Henry Addington, 1st Viscount of Sidmouth (b.1757 in London), British prime minister (1801–4).

1874 Birth of Sir Ernest Shackleton in Kilkea, Co Kildare, Ireland (d.1922), Antarctic explorer.

1887 [Old Style calendar; New Style 27 February] Death of Alexander Porfiryevich Borodin (b.1833 in St Petersburg, Russia), composer and chemist, best known for his unfinished opera, *Prince Igor* (1869–87).

1928 Death of Herbert Henry Asquith, 1st Earl of Oxford (b.1852 in Morley, West Yorkshire), British prime minister (1908–16).

1933 An assassination attempt on Franklin D(elano) Roosevelt (1882–1945) failed when Giuseppe Zangara (1900–33) instead shot the mayor of Chicago, Illinois, who died of his wounds.

1942 The fall of Singapore: British general Arthur Percival (1887–1966) surrendered following an assault by Japanese forces.

1965 Canada adopted the Red Maple Leaf as its new national flag, replacing the Canadian Red Ensign and the Union Jack.

1965 Death of Nat King Cole (b.1919 in Montgomery, Alabama), jazz pianist and singer, whose hits include 'Unforgettable'.

1971 After 1200 years, Britain abandoned the shilling and pence system for a decimal currency.

1978 In Wellington, New Zealand beat England at cricket for the first time.

2003 Protests against the Iraq war took place in over 600 cities worldwide, with an estimated 10–15 million people, making this the largest day of protest in history.

FEBRUARY
16

Feast (Greek Orthodox Church) of St Valentine (?–c.269), patron saint of lovers.

1222 Birth of Nichiren in Kominato, Awa province, Japan (d.1282), Buddhist monk, the founder of Nichiren Buddhism.

1497 Birth of Philipp Melanchthon in Bretten, near Karlsruhe, Germany (d.1560), theologian, writer, and Protestant Reformer.

1659 This date is written on the first cheque known to have been presented at a British bank.

1923 Opening of Tutankhamun's burial chamber by British archaeologist and Egyptologist Howard Carter (1874–1939).

1935 Birth of Sonny Bono in Detroit, Michigan (d.1998), songwriter and singing partner of Cher; their biggest hit was 'I Got You Babe'.

1943 Birth of Sir Anthony Dowell in London, ballet dancer, who joined the Royal Ballet company (1961) and became artistic director (1986–2001).

1945 Venezuela declared war on Germany and Japan.

1957 Death of Baron Leslie Hore-Belisha (b.1893 in Devonport, Devon), British statesman, who drafted a highway code, inaugurated driving tests, and gave his name to *Belisha beacons*.

1958 Birth of Tracy Morrow, better known as Ice-T or Ice T, in Newark, New Jersey, rapper, singer, and actor.

1959 Birth of John McEnroe in Wiesbaden, Germany, international tennis champion, well known for his temperamental behaviour on court.

1959 Fidel Castro became prime minister of Cuba.

1960 First underwater round-the-world trip by a nuclear submarine, the USS *Triton*.

1968 British pop group The Beatles went to India to meet Maharishi Mahesh Yogi.

1973 Birth of Cathy Freeman in Mackay, Queensland, Australia, athlete, who won a gold medal in the 400 m event at the Sydney 2000 Olympics.

1978 Leon Spinks (b.1953) beat Muhammad Ali (b.1942), winning the world heavyweight boxing championship in Las Vegas, Nevada.

2005 The Kyoto Protocol, an international treaty on climate change, came into force following its ratification by Russia.

2005 Cancellation of the entire 2004–5 regular season and playoffs by the US National Hockey League due to a labour dispute.

FEBRUARY
17

1673 Death of Molière (b.1622 in Paris), playwright and actor, who died on stage during a performance of *Le Malade imaginaire* (1673).

1766 Birth of Thomas Robert Malthus near Dorking, Surrey (d.1834), economist, and author of *Essay on the Principle of Population* (1798), advocating control of the birth rate.

1818 Patenting of the draisine, a predecessor of the bicycle, by Baron Karl von Drais de Sauerbrun.

1883 Patenting of the first vacant/ engaged signs for use in public conveniences.

1890 Death of Christopher Latham Sholes (b.1819 near Mooresburg, Pennsylvania), inventor of the typewriter along with colleagues Carlos Glidden and Samuel Soulé.

1904 First production of Puccini's *Madame Butterfly*, in Milan.

1909 Death of Geronimo (b.1829 along the Gila R in present-day Arizona), Chiricahua Apache war chief.

1933 First publication of the weekly US news magazine *Newsweek*.

1933 Issue of the Blaine Act, ending Prohibition in the USA.

1934 Birth of Barry Humphries in Kew, Melbourne, Australia, actor and comedian, best known for his alter egos Dame Edna Everage and Sir Les Patterson.

1958 Pope Pius XII declared Saint Clare of Assisi (1193–1253), patron saint of television.

1959 Launch of Vanguard 2, the first earth-orbiting weather satellite, designed to measure cloud-cover distribution over the daylight portion of its orbit.

1968 Death of Sir Donald Wolfit (b.1902 in Newark, Nottinghamshire), actor-manager, who formed his own company in 1937 and became known for his Shakespeare performances.

1972 The Volkswagen Beetle became the most successful production model, with sales of over 15 million.

1975 Art by Cézanne, Gauguin, Renoir, and van Gogh, valued at over £2.5 million, was stolen from the Municipal Museum in Milan.

1979 Beginning of the Sino–Vietnamese or Third Indochina War.

1980 Death of Graham Sutherland (b.1903 in London), artist, who produced several memorable portraits, including Sir Winston Churchill (1955).

1992 US serial killer Jeffrey Lionel Dahmer (1960–94) was sentenced to fifteen consecutive life sentences – a minimum of 936 years' imprisonment.

FEBRUARY
18

National Day, Gambia and Nepal.
Feast of St Bernadette of Lourdes (1844–79), patron saint of shepherds.

1229 During the Sixth Crusade, Frederick II (1194–1250), Holy Roman Emperor, signed a ten-year truce with al-Kamil, regaining Jerusalem, Nazareth, and Bethlehem.

1478 Death of George, Duke of Clarence (b.1449 in Dublin, Ireland), drowned in a butt of Malmsey wine in the Tower of London on the orders of his brother Richard, Duke of Gloucester.

1546 Death of Martin Luther (b.1483 in Eisleben, Germany), religious reformer and Bible translator.

1564 Death of Michelangelo (b.1475 in Caprese, Italy), sculptor, painter, and poet, whose works include the painting of the ceiling of the Sistine Chapel, Rome.

1678 Publication of John Bunyan's *Pilgrim's Progress*.

1735 First performance of *Flora*, the first opera staged in America, in Charleston, South Carolina.

1745 Birth of Alessandro Volta in Como, Italy (d.1827), physicist, who developed the first electric battery (1800).

1795 Birth of George Peabody in Peabody, Massachusetts (d.1869), philanthropist, whose endowments include the Peabody Museums at Yale and Harvard.

1876 Opening of the direct telegraph link between London and New Zealand.

1885 First publication of *The Adventures of Huckleberry Finn* by US author Mark Twain (1835–1910).

1930 Elm Farm Ollie, known in Missouri as 'Nelly-J', became the first cow to fly – and to be milked – in an aeroplane.

1930 Discovery of Pluto by astronomer Clyde Tombaugh (1906–97) at the Lowell Observatory, Arizona.

1954 Birth of John Travolta in Englewood, New Jersey, actor and singer, whose films include *Saturday Night Fever* (1977).

1965 Independence of the Gambia from the UK.

2004 Scientists at NASA and the European Space Agency witnessed a supermassive black hole in galaxy RXJ1242-11 graze, partially consume, and tear apart a star, the first time such a phenomenon had been observed.

2005 The Hunting Act, banning hunting with dogs in England and Wales, came into force.

FEBRUARY
19

1473 Birth of Nicolas Copernicus in Toruń, Poland (d.1543), astronomer, the first to put forward the heliocentric theory of the solar system.

1647 Signing of the Treaty of Westminster, ending the third Anglo–Dutch War; under its terms, New Netherlands (New York) became British.

1717 Birth of David Garrick in Hereford, Hereford and Worcester (d.1779), actor, theatre manager, and playwright, who dominated the English stage for 30 years.

1736 Premiere of George Frideric Handel's *Alexander's Feast*.

1819 Discovery of the South Shetland Islands by British sea captain William Smith (b.c.1775).

1855 Bread riots broke out in Liverpool.

1861 Abolition of serfdom in Russia by Tsar Alexander II (1818–81).

1878 Patenting of the phonograph by US inventor and physicist Thomas Alva Edison (1847–1931).

1881 Kansas became the first US state to prohibit all alcoholic beverages.

1897 Death of Charles Blondin (b.1824 in St Omer, France), tight-rope walker and acrobat, famous for his crossing of the Niagara Falls.

1897 Founding of the Women's Institute, by Adelaide Hoodless of Ontario, Canada; the first meeting in Britain was held in Llanfairpwll, Anglesey (1915).

1906 Forming of the Battle Creek Toasted Corn Flake Company, later renamed W. K. Kellogg Company, by US cereal manufacturer and philanthropist W(illie) K(eith) Kellogg (1852–1943).

1916 First sales of National Savings Certificates in Britain.

1942 Invasion of Bali by Japanese forces.

1960 Birth of Prince Andrew, Duke of York, in Buckingham Palace, London, the second son of Queen Elizabeth II.

1976 Iceland broke off diplomatic relations with Britain, during the third 'Cod War'.

1985 The first episode of *EastEnders* was broadcast by the BBC.

1986 Launch of the Russian space station Mir (Russian for 'Peace').

1997 Death of Deng Xiaoping (b.1904 in Sichuan province, China), ruler of the People's Republic of China from the late 1970s to the early 1990s.

2005 The $3.2 billion USS *Jimmy Carter* entered the US Navy's fleet as the most heavily armed submarine ever built.

FEBRUARY

20

1547 Coronation of Edward VI (1537–53), son and heir of Henry VIII, as king of England at Westminster Abbey.

1791 Birth of Karl Czerny in Vienna, Austria (d.1857), pianist and composer, whose piano exercises and studies are still widely used.

1816 The opening night of Rossini's *The Barber of Seville* in Rome was a fiasco; one performer sang with a bleeding nose after tripping on a trapdoor, and a cat attacked another during the first act finale.

1835 Concepción, Chile, was destroyed by an earthquake.

1861 Fierce storms hit England, damaging London's Crystal Palace, and blowing the steeple off Chichester Cathedral.

1888 Birth of Marie Rambert in Warsaw, Poland (d.1982), ballet dancer and teacher, who founded the Ballet Rambert in Britain.

1898 Birth of Enzo Ferrari in Modena, Italy (d.1988), racing-car designer, who founded the Ferrari company in 1929.

1913 Australian politician King O'Malley (1858–1953) drove in the first survey peg to mark the start of work on Canberra, Australia's new capital.

1920 Death of Robert Peary (b.1856 in Cresson Springs, Pennsylvania), naval commander and explorer, who on 6 April 1909 was in the first team to reach the North Pole.

1939 Nylon stockings first shown at the San Francisco Exposition.

1940 Birth of Jimmy Greaves in London, footballer and television commentator, who played for Chelsea, Tottenham Hotspur, and West Ham United.

1947 Appointment of Louis Mountbatten, 1st Earl Mountbatten of Burma (1900–1979), as last viceroy of India.

1957 Emmett L. Ashford (1914–80) became the first African-American umpire in organized baseball, as a substitute umpire in the Southwestern International League.

1962 John Glenn (b.1921) became the first US astronaut to orbit the Earth, making a three-orbit flight in the Friendship 7 space capsule.

1985 First legal sales of contraceptives in Ireland.

1992 Formation of Britain's FA Premier League, replacing the former Football League Division One from the 1992–3 season.

2005 Death of Hunter S(tockton) Thompson (b.1937 in Louisville, Kentucky), author and journalist, whose work includes *Fear and Loathing in Las Vegas* (1971).

2005 Spain became the first country to vote in a referendum on the proposed Constitution of the European Union, passing it by a substantial margin.

FEBRUARY
21

1595 Death of Robert Southwell (b.1561 in Horsham, Norfolk), poet and martyr, who was hanged, drawn, and quartered at Tyburn, London.

1741 Death of Jethro Tull (b.1674 in Basildon, Berkshire), agriculturalist and pioneer of farming methods, who invented a seed drill (1701) which planted seeds in rows.

1836 Birth of Léo Delibes in St Germain du Val, France (d.1891), composer and musician, whose works include the ballet *Coppélia* (1870).

1848 Publication of *The Communist Manifesto* by Karl Marx (1818–83) and Friedrich Engels (1820–95), social philosophers and founders of international Communism.

1875 Birth of Jeanne Calment in Arles, France, supercentenarian, who died in 1997 aged 122 years 164 days, the longest-living human being in history.

1907 Birth of W(ystan) H(ugh) Auden in York, North Yorkshire (d.1973), poet and essayist, whose works include *Homage to Clio* (1960).

1910 Birth of Sir Douglas Bader in London (d.1982), aviator, who overcame the loss of both legs in a flying accident to become an RAF hero during World War 2.

1916 Beginning of the Battle of Verdun, during World War 1.

1925 Publication of the first issue of the *New Yorker*.

1937 Birth of Jilly Cooper in Hornchurch, London, novelist and journalist, whose best-selling novels include *Appassionata* (1996).

1941 Death of Sir Frederick Banting (b.1891 in Alliston, Ontario), physiologist, who won the 1923 Nobel Prize for Physiology or Medicine for the discovery of insulin.

1946 Birth of Alan Rickman in London, actor, whose films include *Truly, Madly, Deeply* (1991).

1952 Identity cards were no longer legally required in Britain.

1965 Death of Malcolm X (b.1925 in Omaha, Nebraska), African-American activist, assassinated in New York by members of the Nation of Islam.

1970 US president Richard Nixon visited the People's Republic of China.

1972 Landing of unmanned Soviet spaceship Luna 20 on the Moon.

1995 Landing of US adventurer Steve Fossett (b.1944) in Leader, Saskatchewan, the first to make a solo flight across the Pacific Ocean in a balloon.

2003 US basketball player Michael Jordan (b.1963) made NBA history when he scored 43 points for the Washington Wizards, the first player over 40 to score 40 or more points in a game.

FEBRUARY
22

Feast of St Margaret of Cortona, patron saint of repentant prostitutes.

896 Coronation as emperor of Arnulf of Carinthia (850–99), one of the last ruling members of the Carolingian house.

1512 Death of Amerigo Vespucci (b.1454 in Florence, Italy), merchant, cartographer, and explorer, famous for his discovery of the Americas (1499–1504).

1732 [11 February, Old Style calendar] Birth of George Washington in Westmoreland Co, Virginia (d.1799), army leader during the American Revolution, and 1st president of the USA (1789–97).

1744 The naval Battle of Toulon took place between the blockaded Spanish–French fleet and the British fleet.

1788 Birth of Arthur Schopenhauer in Gdańsk, Poland (d.1860), philosopher, and a major influence on existentialism.

1819 Purchase of E Florida from Spain by the USA.

1879 Opening of the first 'nothing over five cents' store by Frank W. Woolworth (1852–1919) in Utica, New York, the start of the Woolworth chain of stores.

1889 US president Stephen Cleveland (1837–1908) signed a bill admitting North Dakota, South Dakota, Montana, and Washington as US states.

1908 Birth of Sir John Mills in Felixstowe, Suffolk (d.2005), actor and director, whose roles include the village idiot in *Ryan's Daughter* (1970, Oscar).

1924 John Calvin Coolidge (1872–1933) became the first US president to deliver a radio broadcast from the White House; the speech was broadcast on 42 stations.

1926 Birth of Kenneth Williams in London (d.1987), comedy actor, who appeared in 22 of the *Carry On* films.

1950 Birth of Julie Walters in Birmingham, West Midlands, actress, whose films include *Educating Rita* (1983).

1956 The first floodlit football league game was played, between Portsmouth and Newcastle United (Newcastle won 2–0).

1959 The first ever Daytona 500 race was won by US stock-car driver Lee Petty (1913–2000).

1979 Independence of the Caribbean island of Saint Lucia from the UK.

1980 Defeat of the Soviet Union ice hockey team by the USA at the 1980 Winter Olympic Games in an upset dubbed the 'Miracle on Ice'.

1987 Death of Andy Warhol (b.1927 in Pittsburgh, Pennsylvania), pop artist and film maker.

1997 Announcement by scientists in Roslin, Scotland, that an adult sheep named Dolly had been successfully cloned.

FEBRUARY
23

1633 Birth of Samuel Pepys in London (d.1703), naval administrator, who kept a diary from 1 January 1660 to 31 May 1669.

1684 Birth of George Frideric Handel in Halle, Germany (d.1759), composer, best known for his oratorio *Messiah* (1742).

1743 Birth of Meyer Rothschild in Frankfurt, Germany (d.1812), financier, the founder of a banking dynasty.

1820 Exposure of a plot to murder all the British cabinet ministers, known as the Cato Street Conspiracy.

1821 Death of John Keats (b.1795 in London), poet, one of the principal figures of the Romantic movement.

1836 Start of the battle of the Alamo, a fort held by 180 Texans for 13 days against Mexican troops during the Texan War of Independence.

1848 Death of John Quincy Adams (b.1767 in Braintree, later Quincy, Massachusetts), 6th president of the USA (1825–9).

1874 Patenting of sphairistike, a game introduced by Major Walter Clopton Wingfield at a Christmas party in Nantclwyd, Wales, in 1873; it later became known as lawn tennis.

1905 Founding of the Rotary Club for business and professional men by US lawyer Paul Harris (1868–1947); women were admitted for the first time in 1987.

1919 Founding of the Fascist Party in Italy by Benito Mussolini.

1944 Death of Leo Baekeland (b.1863 in Ghent, Belgium), chemist, who discovered the first synthetic phenolic resin (Bakelite) and was a founder of the plastics industry.

1945 During the Battle of Iwo Jima, the 28th regiment of the 5th Marine Division reached the top of Mt Surabachi and were photographed raising the American flag; the picture later won a Pulitzer Prize.

1947 Founding of the International Organization for Standardization (ISO).

1950 First TV broadcast of election returns in Britain.

1970 Guyana, formerly British Guiana, became an independent republic within the Commonwealth.

1970 Opening of the passenger railway service linking Perth, Western Australia, with Sydney, New South Wales (3,961 km/2,461 miles).

1997 Fire broke out aboard the Mir space station.

2004 Launch of a massive immunization campaign by the World Health Organization, targeting 63 million children in 10 African countries following a polio outbreak.

FEBRUARY
24

1389 Defeat and capture of King Albert of Sweden by the Danes at the Battle of Falköping.

1582 Pope Gregory XIII announced the introduction of the new Gregorian Calendar.

1723 Death of Sir Christopher Wren (b.1632 in East Knoyle, Wiltshire), architect, who designed the new St Paul's Cathedral.

1786 Birth of Wilhelm Grimm (d.1859) in Hanau, Germany, folklorist and philologist, best known for *Grimm's Fairy Tales*, which he wrote with his brother Jacob (1785–1863).

1810 Death of Henry Cavendish (b.1731 in Nice, France), physicist and chemist, who discovered hydrogen.

1821 Mexico declared its independence from Spain.

1822 Death of Thomas Coutts (b.1735 in Edinburgh), banker, who founded the London banking-house of Coutts & Co with his brother, James.

1841 Birth of Pierre Auguste Renoir in Limoges, France (d.1919), Impressionist artist.

1885 Birth of Chester Nimitz in Fredericksburg, Texas (d.1966), US admiral who commanded US naval forces in the Pacific during World War 2.

1887 Opening of the telephone link between Paris and Brussels, the first two capitals to be so connected.

1925 Death of Joseph Rowntree (b.1836 in York, North Yorkshire), Quaker industrialist and reformer, and partner in Rowntree's cocoa-manufacturing firm in York.

1938 Production of the first commercially made nylon products – toothbrush bristles – in Arlington, New Jersey.

1946 Election of Juan Perón (1895–1974) as president of Argentina.

1955 Birth of Alain Prost in St Chamond, France, motor-racing driver, the first Frenchman to win the Formula 1 world title.

1981 Announcement of the engagement of Charles, Prince of Wales (b.1948), and Lady Diana Spencer (1961–97).

1987 Appearance of the first supernova since 1604 near enough to be seen with the naked eye.

1987 First day of publication for the *London Daily News* and *Evening News*.

1992 Marriage of Kurt Cobain (1967–94), lead singer of the rock band Nirvana, to singer and actress Courtney Love (b.1964).

2006 Death of Dennis Weaver (b.1924 in Joplin, Missouri), actor, who played the title role in the long-running television series *McCloud* (1970–77).

FEBRUARY
25

National Day, Kuwait.

1308 Coronation of Edward II (1284–1327) as king of England.

1570 Excommunication of Queen Elizabeth I by Pope Pius V.

1836 Patenting of the first revolving barrel multishot firearm by US gunsmith Samuel Colt (1814–62).

1862 Issue of the American bank notes known as 'greenbacks' by President Abraham Lincoln (1809–65).

1890 Birth of Dame Myra Hess in London (d.1965), concert pianist, who wrote an arrangement of the Bach chorale *Jesu, Joy of Man's Desiring.*

1913 Federal income tax became law in the USA.

1937 Birth of Tom Courtenay in Kingston-upon-Hull, actor, whose films include *Billy Liar* (1963).

1939 Building of the first Anderson bomb shelter, in a garden in Islington, London.

1943 Birth of George Harrison in Liverpool (d.2001), musician, who played lead guitar and sang with The Beatles.

1946 Britain received the first delivery of bananas after the war.

1955 Completion of Britain's aircraft carrier, HMS *Ark Royal.*

1964 Cassius Clay (b.1942, now Muhammad Ali) beat Sonny Liston (1917–70) to become world heavyweight boxing champion.

1972 Landing of unmanned space capsule Luna 20 in the Soviet Union, after a mission to the Moon to collect lunar samples.

1983 Ruling by the European Court of Human Rights that corporal punishment in Britain's schools is a violation of the Human Rights Convention.

1983 Death of Tennessee Williams (b.1911 in Columbus, Mississippi), playwright, whose many plays include *Cat on a Hot Tin Roof* (1955).

1986 Ferdinand Marcos (1917–89), 10th president of the Philippines, was ousted from power and fled the country with his wife Imelda.

1994 Dr Baruch Goldstein, Jewish American-Israeli physician and militant, killed 29 Muslims and injured approximately 100 in a shooting attack in the Cave of the Patriarchs in Hebron, Israel.

2001 Death of Don Bradman (b.1908 in Cootamundra, New South Wales, Australia), cricketer, whose batting records include the highest score (452 not out).

FEBRUARY
26

1361 Birth of Wenceslaus, king of Bohemia (d.1419).

1797 Issue of the first £1 notes, by the Bank of England.

1802 Birth of Victor Hugo in Besançon, France (d.1885), writer, whose major works include the novel *Les Misérables* (1862).

1815 Escape of Emperor Napoleon from Elba, where he had been exiled since 4 May 1814.

1829 Birth of Levi Strauss in Franconia, Germany (d.1902), US clothing manufacturer.

1839 The first 'Grand National' horse race was run at Aintree, Liverpool.

1846 Birth of Colonel William Cody in Scott Co, Iowa (d.1917), frontiersman and showman, known as 'Buffalo Bill'.

1908 Birth of Tex Avery in Taylor, Texas (d.1980), film cartoon director, and creator of Bugs Bunny, Daffy Duck, and Droopy.

1909 An audience at London's Palace Theatre saw the first colour film, in *Kinemacolor*.

1928 Birth of Fats Domino in New Orleans, Louisiana, rhythm-and-blues and rock-and-roll singer, songwriter, and pianist, whose first hit record was 'Ain't That a Shame' (1955).

1932 Birth of Johnny Cash in Kingsland, Arkansas (d.2003), country-music singer, songwriter, and guitarist, whose dark clothing earned him the nickname 'the man in black'.

1935 Demonstration of his system for the radio location of aircraft, radar (RAdio Detection And Ranging), by physicist Sir Robert Alexander Watson-Watt (1892–1973).

1936 Opening of the first factory for the production of the Volkswagen, the 'People's Car', in Saxony, Germany, by Adolf Hitler.

1984 The last US marines in the multinational peacekeeping force in Lebanon left Beirut.

1987 The Church of England's General Synod voted by a huge majority in favour of the ordination of women priests.

2004 Opening by Russian president Vladimir Putin of the 10,000-km/6200-mile Moscow to Vladivostok highway, making it possible to travel by road to Asia.

2005 Death of Jef Raskin (b.1943 in New York), human–computer interface expert, best known for starting the Macintosh project for Apple Computers in the late 1970s.

FEBRUARY

27

1594 Coronation of Henry IV (1553–1610) as king of France at Chartres, the first of the Bourbon kings of France.

1700 Discovery of New Britain, largest island in the Bismarck Archipelago of Papua New Guinea, by English navigator and buccaneer William Dampier (1652–1715).

1807 Birth of Henry Wadsworth Longfellow in Portland, Maine (d.1882), poet, whose works include 'The Song of Hiawatha' (1855).

1887 [15 February, Old Style calendar] Death of Alexander Porfiryevich Borodin (b.1833 in St Petersburg, Russia), composer and chemist, whose works include the unfinished opera *Prince Igor* (1869–87).

1897 The USA Postal Act provided an indemnity for loss of registered mail of up to $10 for each registered item.

1899 Birth of Charles H. Best in West Pembroke, Maine (d.1978), physiologist, who helped Sir Frederick Grant Banting (1891–1941) to isolate insulin (1921).

1900 Founding of the British Labour Party, with Ramsay MacDonald (1866–1937) as secretary.

1902 Birth of John Steinbeck in Salinas, California (d.1968), novelist, who won the 1962 Nobel Prize for Literature.

1907 Opening of the Old Bailey, London's Central Criminal Court.

1928 Birth of Ariel Sharon in Kfar Malal, pre-state Israel, prime minister of Israel (2001–6).

1932 Birth of Elizabeth Taylor in London, US film star, whose films include *Cleopatra* (1962).

1933 Destruction of the Reichstag, the German parliament building, by fire; Dutchman Marius van der Lubbe was executed for starting the blaze.

1936 Death of Ivan Petrovich Pavlov (b.1849 in Ryazan, Russia), physiologist, who is best known for his studies of animal behaviour, *Pavlovian conditioning*.

1939 Destruction by fire, under mysterious circumstances, of Borley Rectory, Essex, Britain's most haunted house.

1941 Birth of Paddy Ashdown in New Delhi, India, British politician, and leader of the Liberal Democrats (1988–99).

1976 Independence of the former Spanish territory of Western Sahara as the Sahrawi Arab Democratic Republic.

1993 Death of Lillian Gish (b.1893 in Springfield, Ohio), actress, who became known as the 'First Lady of the Silent Screen'.

1996 Death of Pat(ricia) Smythe (b.1928 in East Sheen, London), show jumper, the first female winner of the Hickstead Derby.

FEBRUARY
28

1683 Birth of René Antoine Ferchault de Réaumur in La Rochelle, France (d.1757), polymath, who invented the thermometer that bears his name.

1784 Signing of the deed of declaration of the Weslyan faith by John Wesley (1703–91).

1820 Birth of Sir John Tenniel in London (d.1914), artist, who illustrated *Alice's Adventures in Wonderland* (1865).

1890 Birth of Nijinsky in Kiev, Ukraine (d.1950), ballet dancer, a member of Diaghilev's Ballets Russes, famous for *L'Après-midi d'un faune* (1912, Afternoon of a Fawn).

1900 Lifting of the 118-day siege of Ladysmith in the Second Boer War.

1901 Birth of Professor Linus Pauling in Portland, Oregon (d.1994), chemist and physicist, the first person to be awarded two Nobel Prizes.

1910 Birth of Vincente Minnelli in Chicago, Illinois (d.1986), director, whose films include *Gigi* (1958).

1916 Death of Henry James (b.1843 in New York), novelist, whose works include *The Portrait of a Lady* (1881).

1922 Declaration of the termination of the British protectorate in Egypt, and the commencement of Egyptian independence under the new king, Fuad I (1868–1936).

1933 Issue of the Reichstag Fire Decree, by request of Adolf Hitler, suspending most human rights provided for by the 1919 constitution of the Weimar Republic.

1936 Discovery of the fictitious word 'Dord' (originally the alphabet heading 'D or d') in the second edition of Webster's New International Dictionary, prompting an investigation.

1940 The first televised basketball match was from Madison Square Garden; Fordham University played the University of Pittsburgh.

1946 Birth of Robin Cook in Bellshill, North Lanarkshire (d.2005), secretary of state for Foreign and Commonwealth Affairs (1997–2001).

1975 A London Underground train crashed at Moorgate, killing the driver and at least 29 passengers.

1986 Broadcast of the final episode of *M*A*S*H* in the USA.

1991 Ending of the Gulf War.

1995 The *Independent* published the first column of 'The Diary of Bridget Jones' by Helen Fielding.

2000 Sir Alex Ferguson received the freedom of the city of Manchester in recognition of his achievements with football team Manchester United.

FEBRUARY

29

Leap Year.
Bachelors' Day, alternative name for Leap Day; traditionally the day on which women may propose marriage to men, following an older tradition that such proposals may occur on any day during a leap year.

1528 Death of Patrick Hamilton (b.1503 in Glasgow), protomartyr of the Scottish Reformation, burned before St Salvator's College on a charge of heresy.

1620 Death of Thomas Campion (b.1567 in Witham, Essex), physician, poet, and composer.

1720 Abdication of Queen Ulrika Eleonora of Sweden in favour of her husband, who became King Frederick I.

1792 Birth of Gioacchino Rossini in Pesaro, Italy (d.1868), composer, whose works include *Il Barbiere di Siviglia* (1816, The Barber of Seville).

1812 Birth of Augustus Pugin in London (d.1852), architect, who did much to revive Gothic architecture in Britain.

1840 Birth of John Holland in Liscannor, Co Clare, Ireland (d.1914), inventor, who designed and built the modern submarine.

1909 Birth of David Niven in Kirriemuir, Angus (d.1983), actor, whose films include *Around the World in 80 Days* (1956).

1940 Hattie McDaniel (1895–1952) became the first African-American woman to receive an Academy Award, Best Supporting Actress, for her role in *Gone with the Wind* (1939).

1956 Birth of Aileen Wournos in Rochester, Michigan (d.2002), serial killer, executed in Florida State Prison by lethal injection.

1960 Opening of the first Playboy nightclub in Chicago, Illinois, by Hugh Hefner (b.1926).

1960 Death of 12,000 people in an earthquake in Agadir, Morocco.

1964 Birth of James Ogilvy in Surrey, son of Princess Alexandra of Kent.

1968 The discovery of the first pulsar was announced by radio astronomer Dr Jocelyn Bell Burnell (b.1943) of Cambridge, Cambridgeshire.

2004 The film *The Lord of the Rings: The Return of the King* won a record-equalling 11 Academy Awards, including best picture.

2004 Resignation of Jean-Bertrand Aristide, president of Haiti.

FEBRUARY
30

1712 Two leap days were added to
Sweden's Julian calendar to resolve
dating discrepancies, thus giving
the country a February 30th.

MARCH

1

Feast of St David (Dewi) (?–601), patron saint of Wales and of poets.

1711 First publication of the British magazine, *The Spectator*.

1803 Ohio became the 17th state of the Union.

1810 Birth of Frédéric (François) Chopin in Zelazowa Wola, Poland (d.1849), composer and pianist.

1867 Nebraska became the 37th state of the Union.

1904 Birth of Glenn Miller in Clarinda, Iowa (d.1944), trombonist and bandleader, famous for his distinctive sound with a saxophone–clarinet combination.

1912 Death of George Grossmith (b.1847 in London), comedian and entertainer; with his brother, Weedon, he wrote 'Diary of a Nobody' in *Punch* (1892).

1922 Birth of Itzhak Rabin in Jerusalem (d.1995), Israeli soldier, statesman, and prime minister, who headed the armed forces during the Six-Day War (1967).

1932 Kidnapping of the infant son of aviator Charles Lindbergh from the family home near Hopewell, New Jersey.

1945 Birth of Roger Daltry in Hammersmith, London, singer and actor, lead singer with rock group The Who.

1947 International Monetary Fund began operations, formed in 1945 to promote international monetary co-operation, trade, and exchange-rate stability, and to give financial assistance to states in need.

1952 Testing of the first hydrogen bomb, in the Pacific, by the USA.

1966 Soviet space probe Venera 3 crashed on to Venus, becoming the first spacecraft to arrive on another planet.

1969 Retirement of New York Yankees baseball legend Mickey (Charles) Mantle (1931–95), who took his number 7 with him.

1978 The coffin of US movie star Charlie Chaplin (1889–1977) was stolen from a Swiss cemetery.

1980 Death of Dixie Dean (b.1907 in Birkenhead, Merseyside), footballer, who died shortly after watching his former team Everton lose 2–1 at home to Liverpool in the Merseyside derby.

1983 Swiss watchmakers Swatch introduced their first timepieces.

1990 End of daily rum tots for sailors aboard New Zealand Navy ships.

1998 Britain's old-style 50p coins went out of circulation.

2002 The peseta ceased to be legal tender in Spain.

MARCH
2

1545 Birth of Sir Thomas Bodley in Exeter, Devon (d.1613), scholar and diplomat, who funded the extension of Oxford University library, then renamed the Bodleian (opened 1602).

1725 Premiere in London of George Frideric Handel's opera, *Giulio Cesare in Egitto* (Julius Caesar in Egypt).

1791 Death of John Wesley (b.1703 in Epworth, Lincolnshire), evangelist and founder of Methodism.

1877 Republican Rutherford Hayes was declared winner of the 1876 US presidential election over Democrat Samuel J. Tilden, even though Tilden won the popular vote.

1882 An assassination attempt was made on Queen Victoria (1819–1901), the eighth since her accession to the British throne.

1904 Birth of Dr Seuss in Springfield, Massachusetts (d.1991), writer and illustrator of children's books, such as *The Cat in the Hat* (1957).

1930 Death of D(avid) H(erbert) Richard) Lawrence (b.1885 in Eastwood, Nottinghamshire), poet and novelist, whose books include *Sons and Lovers* (1913).

1931 Birth of Mikhail Sergeyevich Gorbachev in Privolnoye, Russia, Soviet president (1988–91), who launched a programme of reform (*perestroika*) and civil liberty (*glasnost*).

1933 Premiere of the film *King Kong* in New York.

1946 Election of Ho Chi Minh (1890–1969) as president of North Vietnam.

1949 Birth of Dame Naomi James in New Zealand, yachtswoman and author, who sailed single-handed around the world, and was the first woman solo round Cape Horn.

1956 Independence of Morocco from France.

1958 Completion of the first crossing of the Antarctic, from Shackleton Base via the South Pole to Scott Base, by Sir Vivian Fuchs leading a British team, taking 99 days for the journey of 3,500 km/2,000 miles.

1969 Maiden flight of supersonic aeroplane Concorde.

1972 Launch of NASA's Pioneer 10 space probe from Cape Canaveral, Florida, the first spacecraft to travel through Jupiter's asteroid belt and obtain close-up images of the planet.

2000 The British government returned Chilean dictator Augusto Pinochet (b.1915) to his home country, where he would face charges of human rights abuses.

2005 US Microsoft founder Bill Gates (b.1955) received an honorary knighthood for his contribution to enterprise in the UK and his efforts to reduce poverty around the world.

MARCH

3

National Day, Morocco.
Feast of St Ailred of Rievaulx (1109–66).

1706 Death of Johann Pachelbel (b.c.1653 in Nuremberg, Germany), composer and organist, best known for his Canon in D.

1831 Birth of George Pullman in Brocton, New York (d.1897), inventor, businessman, and cabinet maker, who designed the Pullman railroad sleeping car (1865).

1845 Florida became the 27th state of the Union.

1847 Birth of Alexander Graham Bell in Edinburgh (d.1922), educationist and inventor, who produced the first intelligible telephonic transmission (10 March 1876).

1855 US Congress appropriated $30,000 for the creation of the US Camel Corps, to be used in the American Southwest, where the arid conditions and harsh terrain made the use of horses impractical.

1869 Birth of Sir Henry Joseph Wood in London (d.1944), conductor, who co-founded the Promenade Concerts held annually at London's Albert Hall.

1875 First performance of Bizet's opera *Carmen*, in Paris.

1911 Birth of Jean Harlow in Kansas City, Missouri (d.1937), actress, whose roles in such films as *Hell's Angels* (1930) made her the sex symbol of the 1930s.

1923 First publication of *Time* magazine.

1931 Adoption of 'The Star Spangled Banner' by the US Congress as the US national anthem.

1969 Launch of Apollo 9 with three crew members, James McDivitt, David Scott, and Russell Schwickart.

1974 A Turkish Airlines DC10 crashed into the forest of Ermenonville near Paris, killing all 345 people on board.

1985 British coal miners voted to return to work after a year's strike.

1987 Opening of the largest arts centre in western Europe, the Barbican Centre for Arts and Conferences, London, by Queen Elizabeth II.

1987 Death of Danny Kaye (b.1913 in Brooklyn, New York), comic actor and entertainer, whose films include *Hans Christian Andersen* (1952).

1997 Opening of the Sky Tower in Auckland, New Zealand, the tallest free-standing structure in the Southern Hemisphere, 328 m/1076 ft high.

2005 US adventurer Steve Fossett (b.1944) became the first person to fly an aeroplane solo around the world without any stops and without refuelling, a journey of 40,234 km/25,000 miles completed in 67 hours, 2 minutes.

MARCH

4

Feast of St Casimir, patron saint of Poland.

1152 Election of Frederick I Barbarossa (1122–90) as king of Germany, succeeding his uncle Conrad III (1093–1152).

1193 Death of Saladin (b.1193 in Tekrit, Mesopotamia), sultan of Egypt and Syria, leader of the Muslims against the crusaders in Palestine.

1471 Death of Sir Thomas Malory (b.1400 probably in Warwickshire), writer, known for his work *Le Morte Darthur* (1469–70, The Death of Arthur).

1678 Birth of Antonio (Lucio) Vivaldi in Venice, Italy (d.1741), composer and violinist, best known for *The Four Seasons* (1725).

1791 Vermont became the 14th state of the Union.

1824 Sir William Hillery (1771–1847) founded the Royal National Institution for the Preservation of Life from Shipwreck, which changed its name in 1854 to the Royal National Lifeboat Institution.

1832 Death of Jean-François Champollion (b.1790 in Figeac, France), Egyptologist, who used the Rosetta Stone to decipher Egyptian hieroglyphics.

1873 Printing of the first illustrated daily newspaper in New York, the *New York Daily Graphic*.

1877 Invention of the microphone by German inventor Emile Berliner (1851–1929).

1882 Electric trams first ran in London.

1890 Official opening of the Forth Bridge, Scotland.

1917 Jeannette Rankin (1880–1973) became the first woman elected to the US House of Representatives, and the first female member of Congress.

1928 Birth of Alan Sillitoe in Nottingham, Nottinghamshire, novelist, whose novels include *Saturday Night and Sunday Morning* (1958).

1933 Franklin D. Roosevelt (1882–1945) was sworn in as 32nd president of the USA, the first to be elected for a third and fourth term.

1966 During an interview John Lennon said, 'The Beatles are more popular than Jesus', causing great controversy in the USA.

1967 Britain's first North Sea gas was piped ashore, near Durham, Tyne and Wear.

1977 An earthquake in Bucharest, magnitude 7.4, killed around 1570 people and injured more than 11,000.

1994 Death of John Candy (b.1950 in Newmarket, Ontario), actor and comedian, while filming *Wagons East* (1994).

MARCH

5

1558 Introduction of tobacco smoking to Europe by Francisco Fernandes, governor of São Tomé and Príncipe.

1751 [Old Style calendar, New Style 16 March] Birth of James Madison in Port Conway, Virginia (d.1836), 4th president of the USA (1809–17).

1770 Boston Massacre: British troops opened fire on a crowd in Boston, Massachusetts, killing five people, the first bloodshed of the American Revolution.

1790 Death of Flora Macdonald (b.1722 in South Uist, Western Isles), who helped the Young Pretender, Charles Edward Stuart, to safety in Skye.

1849 Inauguration of Zachary Taylor (1784–1850) as 12th president of the USA; he was the second president to die in office.

1850 Opening of the Menai Bridge, designed by civil engineer Robert Stephenson (1803–59), a tubular bridge joining Anglesey to mainland Wales.

1856 London's Covent Garden theatre was destroyed by fire.

1879 Birth of Sir William Henry Beveridge in Rangpur, India (d.1963), economist, a leading authority on unemployment insurance.

1908 Birth of Sir Rex Harrison in Huyton-with-Roby, Lancashire (d.1990), actor, whose film appearances include *My Fair Lady* (1964, Oscar).

1912 Italian armed forces were the first to employ airships for military purposes, using them for reconnaissance behind Turkish lines.

1918 Moscow replaced St Petersburg as the new capital city of Russia.

1936 First showing of the new Spitfire fighter plane.

1946 Winston Churchill, British prime minister (1940–45, 1951–5), delivered his 'Iron Curtain' speech at Westminster College in Fulton, Missouri.

1953 Death of Josef Stalin (b.1879 in Gori, Georgia), Marxist revolutionary and dictator of the Soviet Union (1928–53).

1956 Britain's telephone weather-forecast service commenced operation.

1966 A BOAC Boeing 707 crashed into Mt Fuji in Japan 25 minutes after take-off, killing all 124 people on board.

1979 The US Voyager 1 space probe passed close to Jupiter.

1982 Death of John Belushi (b.1949 in Chicago, Illinois), comedian and actor, known for his roles in such films as *The Blues Brothers* (1980).

MARCH
6

National Day, Ghana.

1521 Discovery of Guam by Portuguese explorer Ferdinand Magellan (1480–1521) during his round-the-world voyage.

1619 Birth of Cyrano de Bergerac in Paris (d.1655), satirist and playwright, whose life was the subject of the play by Edmond Rostand (1897).

1754 Death of Henry Pelham (b.1696 in London), British prime minister (1743–54).

1836 Ending of the battle of the Alamo, a fort held by 180 Texans for 13 days against Mexican troops during the Texan War of Independence; among those killed were Jim Bowie (b.1796) and Davy Crockett (b.1786).

1844 [Old Style calendar, New Style 18 March] Birth of Nikolai (Andreyevich) Rimsky-Korsakov in Tikhvin, Russia (d.1908), composer, best known for *Scheherazade* (1887–8).

1853 First performance of Verdi's opera *La Traviata*, in Venice.

1857 Judge Roger Taney delivered the US Supreme Court's Dred Scott decision, that a slave could not sue for freedom in a federal court.

1869 Frenchman Ernest Michaux won the first international cycle race, held at Crystal Palace, London.

1888 Death of Louisa May Alcott (b.1832 in Germantown, Pennsylvania), novelist, best known for her children's classics such as *Little Women* (1868).

1899 Patenting of aspirin by German chemist Felix Hoffmann (1868–1946).

1900 Death of Gottlieb Daimler (b.1834 in Schorndorf, Germany), engineer, who patented a high-speed internal combustion engine (1885), and founded the Daimler Automobile Company (1890).

1902 British soldiers were allowed to wear spectacles both on and off duty.

1930 First sales of frozen foods in the USA, a process developed by US businessman and inventor Clarence Birdseye (1886–1956).

1946 Signing of an agreement between Vietnam and France, recognizing Vietnam as an autonomous state in the Indochinese Federation and the French Union.

1947 Birth of Dick Fosbury in Portland, Oregon, athlete, who pioneered a new technique in high jumping, the *Fosbury Flop*.

1961 Minicabs first ran in London.

1987 Death of 193 people when the ferry *Herald of Free Enterprise* foundered as she left Zeebrugge harbour with her main car deck doors open to the sea.

2003 Election of Fidel Castro (b.1926) unopposed to a sixth term as president of Cuba.

MARCH

7

Feast of St Thomas Aquinas (1225–74), patron saint of philosophers, scholars, students, and theologians.

1802 Birth of Sir Edwin Landseer in London (d.1873), artist, whose sculptures include the bronze lions in Trafalgar Square (1867).

1804 Founding of the Royal Horticultural Society by botanist Sir Joseph Banks (1743–1820) and John Wedgwood (1766–1844), with five other members.

1875 Birth of Maurice Ravel in Ciboure, France (d.1937), composer, best known for his work *Boléro* (1928).

1876 Patenting of the first telephone by British educationist and inventor Alexander Graham Bell (1847–1922).

1912 Announcement by Norwegian polar explorer Roald Amundsen (1872–1928) that his expedition had reached the South Pole; his group actually arrived there on 14 December 1911.

1917 Release of the world's first jazz record, 'The Dixie Jazz Band One Step', recorded by Nick LaRocca's Original Dixieland Jazz Band, by RCA Victor in Camden, New Jersey.

1918 The Bolsheviks became the Russian Communist Party.

1932 Death of Aristide Briand (b.1862 in Nantes, France), prime minister of France (1909–11, 1913, 1915–17, 1921–2, 1925–6, 1929).

1936 German chancellor Adolf Hitler broke the Treaty of Versailles and the Locarno Pact when he ordered troops to march into the Rhineland.

1944 Birth of Sir Ranulph (Twisleton-Wykeham-) Fiennes in Windsor, Berkshire, explorer and expedition leader; with Michael Stroud he completed the first unsupported crossing on foot of the Antarctic in 1993.

1945 Capture of the key bridge over the Rhine at Remagen, Germany, by US forces, instrumental in shortening World War 2.

1960 Birth of Ivan Lendl in Ostrava, Czech Republic, tennis player, who dominated male tennis in the 1980s, and won 94 singles titles.

1969 Opening of London Underground's Victoria Line.

1987 Indian cricketer Sunil Gavaskar (b.1949) became the first batsman to score 10,000 runs in Test matches.

1999 Death of Stanley Kubrick (b.1928 in New York), screenwriter, producer, and director, whose films include *2001: A Space Odyssey* (1965).

2002 At Glasgow Sheriff's Court the gay father (sperm donor) of a lesbian couple's baby won 'full parental rights and responsibilities'.

2005 Sir Howard Stringer (b.1942 in Cardiff) became Sony's first non-Japanese chairman and CEO.

MARCH
8

Feast of St John of God, patron saint of booksellers, hospitals, nurses, printers, and the sick.

1702 [Old Style calendar, New Style 19 March] Death of William III (b.1650 in The Hague, The Netherlands), king of Great Britain (1689–1702).

1717 Death of Abraham Darby (b.c.1678 near Dudley, West Midlands), ironmaster, the first to use coke successfully in the smelting of iron (1709).

1859 Birth of Kenneth Grahame in Edinburgh (d.1932), writer, best known for *The Wind in the Willows* (1908).

1869 Death of (Louis-)Hector Berlioz (b.1803 in La Côte-Saint-André, France), composer, whose works include the *Symphonie Fantastique* (1830).

1874 Death of Millard Fillmore (b.1800 in Summerhill, Cayuga Co, New York), 13th president of the USA (1850–53).

1917 Beginning of the February Revolution, so called because of the Old Style calendar used by the Russians at the time.

1918 Beginning of the Spanish flu pandemic, a deadly strain of avian influenza that killed 50–100 million people worldwide (1918–19).

1921 French troops occupied Düsseldorf and other towns in the Ruhr, following Germany's failure to pay reparations from World War 1.

1930 Death of William Howard Taft (b.1857 in Cincinnati, Ohio), 27th president of the USA (1909–13).

1939 Birth of Lynn Seymour in Wainwright, Alberta, ballet dancer, best known for her passionate interpretations of the choreography of MacMillan and Ashton.

1943 Birth of Lynn Redgrave in London, actress, whose films include *Georgy Girl* (1966).

1952 First use of an artificial heart.

1965 Around 3,500 US marines landed in Da Nang, South Vietnam.

1978 Transmission of the first radio episode of *The Hitch-hiker's Guide to the Galaxy*, by Douglas Adams, on BBC Radio 4.

1999 Death of Joe DiMaggio (b.1914 in Martinez, California), baseball player, who spent his entire career as an outfielder for the New York Yankees (1936–51).

2001 Raising of *Bluebird*, the boat in which land and water speed-record contestant Donald Campbell died (1967), from Coniston Water in Cumbria.

2003 Malta was the first of 10 countries to vote on joining the European Union; the referendum was approved with a majority of 53.65 per cent in favour.

MARCH

9

Feast of St Catherine of Bologna, patron saint of painters.
Feast of St Frances of Rome, patron saint of motorists.

1454 Birth of Amerigo Vespucci in Florence, Italy (d.1512), explorer, whose name was given to America through an inaccurate account of his travels published in Lorraine (1507).

1562 In Naples, kissing in public was banned and made punishable by death.

1796 Marriage of Napoleon Bonaparte (1769–1821) to Josephine Beauharnais.

1831 Founding of the French Foreign Legion.

1842 Premiere of Giuseppe Verdi's third opera, *Nabucco*, in Milan, his first major success.

1846 The First Sikh War ended when Kashmir was ceded to the British East India Company by the Treaty of Lahore.

1862 The ironclads (floating gun platforms) USS *Monitor* and CSS *Virginia* clashed for five hours at Hampton Roads, Virginia.

1881 Birth of Ernest Bevin in Winsford, Somerset (d.1951), statesman, who built up the National Transport and General Workers' Union, and became its general secretary (1921–40).

1932 Eamon de Valera (1882–1975) became prime minister of the Irish Free State.

1934 Birth of Yuri Gagarin in Gagarin (formerly Gzhatsk), Russia (d.1968), cosmonaut, who in 1961 became the first human to travel into space.

1962 Birth of John Lyon in St Helens, Merseyside, boxer, who won the 1986 Commonwealth Games flyweight title.

1964 Production of the first Ford Mustang sports car, in Dearborne, Michigan; a white convertible with a black interior.

1967 Defection to the USA of Svetlana Alliluyeva (b.1926), daughter of Soviet leader Josef Stalin (1878–1953).

1974 End of the three-day working week in Britain, which began on 31 December 1973.

1990 Puerto-Rican born Dr Antonia Novello (b.1944) was sworn in as US surgeon-general, becoming the first woman and the first Hispanic to hold the position.

1995 Research in California showed that in Los Angeles nine times more pollution was produced by fast-food hamburger restaurants than by buses.

1996 Death of George Burns (b.1896 in New York), actor and comedian, whose films include *Oh God!* (1977).

2001 Fiftieth anniversary of the first appearance of Anthony Wedgwood Benn on *Any Questions* (1951), Radio 4.

MARCH
10

1528 Death of Balthasar Hübmaier (b.1481 in Friedburg, Bavaria, Germany), a leader of the Austrian Anabaptists, burned at the stake as a heretic.

1535 Discovery of the Galapagos Islands by Tomás de Berlanga (1486–1551), bishop of Panama (1534–7).

1628 Birth of Macello Malpighi near Bologna, Italy (d.1694), anatomist and founder of microscopic anatomy, who described the major types of plant and animal structures.

1788 Birth of Edward Hodges Baily in Bristol, Avon (d.1867), sculptor, best known for his statue of Lord Nelson in Trafalgar Square, London.

1848 Birth of Wyatt Earp in Monmouth, Illinois (d.1929), gambler, gunfighter, and lawman, who, with his brothers, fought the Clanton gang in the gunfight at the OK Corral (1881).

1863 Marriage of Albert Edward, Prince of Wales (later King Edward VII) to Princess Alexandra of Denmark at St George's Chapel, Windsor.

1876 British educationist and inventor Alexander Graham Bell (1847–1922) made his first telephone call, to his assistant Thomas Watson.

1885 Birth of Tamara Karsavina in St Petersburg, Russia (d.1978), ballet dancer, one of the original members of Diaghilev's Ballets Russes in Paris.

1886 Cruft's dog show was held in London for the first time.

1903 Birth of (Leon) Bix Beiderbecke in Davenport, Iowa (d.1931), cornettist and composer, who was a celebrated jazz performer of the 1920s.

1906 Opening of London Underground's Bakerloo Line.

1914 Suffragette Mary Richardson (1889–1961) damaged *The Rokeby Venus*, a painting by Velazquez in London's National Gallery, in protest against the UK government's treatment of Emmeline Pankhurst.

1948 Herbert H. Hoover became the first civilian pilot to exceed the speed of sound, flying a research aircraft at Edwards Air Force Base, California.

1964 Birth of Prince Edward, Earl of Wessex and Viscount Severn, third son of Queen Elizabeth II.

1969 James Earl Ray (1928–98) pleaded guilty to the murder of Martin Luther King, and was sentenced to 99 years in jail.

1982 All nine planets in the Solar System were in alignment, an astronomical situation known as syzygy.

1998 Death of Lloyd Bridges (b.1913 in San Leandro, California), actor, whose films include *The Rainmaker* (1956).

MARCH

11

105 Invention of paper, made in China by Cài Lún (50–121), from pulped rags or plant fibres.

1669 Eruption of Mt Etna in Sicily, killing 15,000 people.

1682 Founding of the Chelsea Hospital for old soldiers, in London.

1702 First publication of the single-sheet *Daily Courant*, the first successful English daily newspaper.

1811 Beginning of the Luddite riots, with the destruction by British craftsmen of stocking-manufacturing frames, machinery which was threatening their livelihood.

1819 Birth of Sir Henry Tate in Chorley, Lancashire (d.1899), sugar magnate, art patron, and philanthropist, who founded the Tate Gallery.

1851 Verdi's *Rigoletto* was first performed in Venice.

1916 Birth of Harold Wilson in Huddersfield, West Yorkshire (d.1995), British prime minister (1964–70, 1974–6).

1931 Birth of Rupert Murdoch in Melbourne, Australia, media proprietor, who built a substantial newspaper and magazine publishing empire in Australia, the USA, Hong Kong, and the UK.

1938 The German Army marched into Austria.

1940 Introduction of meat rationing in Britain.

1941 Agreement of the Lend-Lease Bill by the US Congress, which allowed Britain to borrow money for extra food and arms during World War 2.

1952 Birth of Douglas Adams in Cambridge, Cambridgeshire (d.2001), writer, best known for his novel *The Hitch-hiker's Guide to the Galaxy* (1979).

1955 Death of Sir Alexander Fleming (b.1881 near Darvel, East Ayrshire), bacteriologist, who shared the 1945 Nobel Prize for Physiology or Medicine for his discovery of penicillin.

1981 Death of Sir Maurice Oldfield (b.1915 in England), British intelligence chief, a possible inspiration for Ian Fleming's 'M' in the James Bond series of spy novels.

1988 Last day of legal tender for Britain's £1 note.

1990 Lithuania declared independence from the USSR, not recognized by the USSR until the following year.

2001 The longest spacewalk in the 20-year history of the space-shuttle programme took place, lasting 8 hours 56 minutes.

2004 Terrorist bombings at railway stations in Madrid, Spain, killed at least 200 people and injured more than 1400.

2005 Former world chess champion Garry Kasparov (b.1963) announced his retirement from competitive chess.

MARCH
12

1789 Founding of the USA Post Office.

1832 Birth of Charles Cunningham Boycott in Burgh St Peter, Norfolk (d.1897), estate manager, source of the verb 'to boycott' when he was shunned by his tenants on trying to evict them in 1880.

1838 Birth of Sir William Henry Perkins in London (d.1907), chemist, who discovered a mauve substance with dying properties (1856), which led to the foundation of the aniline dye industry.

1858 Birth of Adolph Simon Ochs in Cincinnati, Ohio (d.1935), publisher, who bought the *New York Times* (1896), lifting it from bankruptcy to become a leading US newspaper.

1889 Test cricket was first played in South Africa.

1904 Britain's first main-line electric train ran, from Liverpool to Southport.

1912 Juliette Gordon Low (1860–1927) founded the Girl Scouts of America movement.

1924 Death of Hilaire Berignaud, comte de Chardonnet (b.1839 in Besançon, France), chemist, a pioneer in the artificial silk (rayon) industry.

1930 Mahatma Gandhi led an attack on Britain's punitive salt taxes with a 200-mile march to the sea to collect salt.

1933 Franklin D. Roosevelt, US president (1933–45), gave the first of his nationwide radio 'fireside chats' during the Great Depression.

1935 Imposition of the 30 mph speed limit for driving in Britain's towns and built-up areas.

1938 Invasion of Austria by Germany, after the Austrian Nazi Party invited German troops into Austria.

1945 Death of Anne Frank (b.1929 in Frankfurt, Germany), Jewish diarist, who kept a diary during two years of concealment from the Nazis, and died in Belsen concentration camp.

1947 Establishment of the Truman Doctrine, giving military and economic aid to countries threatened by Communist interference.

1969 Marriage of Beatle Paul McCartney to Linda Eastman in London.

1991 Wendy Toms became the first women to officiate at a Football League game.

1994 Ordination of the first women priests by the Church of England.

1999 Death of Yehudi Menuhin (b.1916 in New York), child prodigy and violinist, who founded a school near London for musically gifted children.

MARCH
13

1470 Defeat of the Lancastrians by the Yorkists at the Battle of Stamford.

1733 Birth of Joseph Priestley in Fieldhead, Cumbria (d.1804), chemist and clergyman, who discovered oxygen.

1764 Birth of Charles Grey, 2nd Earl Grey, in Fallodon, Northumberland (d.1845), British prime minister (1830–34).

1781 Discovery of the planet Uranus by Sir William Herschel (1738–1822).

1855 Birth of Percival Lowell in Boston, Massachusetts (d.1916), astronomer, famous for his prediction of the existence of the planet Pluto.

1868 Beginning of the impeachment trial of President Andrew Johnson in the US Senate.

1884 Establishment of standard time by the USA.

1894 Staging of the first professional striptease at a music hall in Paris.

1901 Death of Benjamin Harrison (b.1833 in North Bend, Ohio), 23rd president of the USA (1889–93).

1906 Death of Susan B. Anthony (b.1820 in Adams, Massachusetts), social reformer and women's suffrage leader.

1927 The lance ceased to be an official weapon of the British army.

1928 Over 450 people drowned after the St Francis Dam burst in California; it was breached at three minutes to midnight on the night of the 12th.

1939 Birth of Neil Sedaka in New York, singer and songwriter, whose hit songs include 'Breaking Up Is Hard to Do' (1962).

1961 Withdrawal from circulation of Bank of England black-and-white £5 notes in Britain.

1967 Death of Sir Frank Worrell (b.1924 in Bridgetown, Barbados), cricketer, the first non-Caucasian West Indian Test captain.

1969 Release of *The Love Bug*, first film in the series about a Volkswagen Beetle car named Herbie; it was followed by three sequels (1974, 1977, 1980).

1992 Final day of publication for *Pravda*.

1994 Closure of Heathrow airport for two hours after the third IRA mortar attack in five days.

1996 Gunman Thomas Hamilton killed 16 children, a teacher, and himself in a primary school in Dunblane, Perthshire.

MARCH
14

Feast (Eastern Church) of St Benedict of Nursia (c.480–c.547), patron saint of Europe, monks, and speleologists.

1790 British naval officer William Bligh (1754–1817) arrived in Portsmouth with news of the mutiny on HMS *Bounty*.

1794 Patenting of the cotton gin, a machine that removes the seeds from cotton fibre, by US inventor Eli Whitney (1765–1825).

1811 Death of Augustus Henry Fitzroy, 3rd Duke of Grafton (b.1735), British prime minister (1768–70).

1836 Birth of Isabella Mary Beeton, known as Mrs Beeton, in London (d.1865), writer on cookery and household management.

1879 Birth of Albert Einstein in Ulm, Germany (d.1955), mathematical physicist, who was awarded the 1921 Nobel Prize for Physics for his special (1905) and general (1916) theories of relativity.

1884 Death of Karl Marx (b.1818 in Trier, Germany), political and social philosopher and founder of modern international Communism, who wrote *Das Kapital* (1867).

1885 Gilbert and Sullivan's *The Mikado* was performed for the first time at the Savoy Theatre, London.

1918 Launch of the SS *Faith*, the first concrete ship to cross the Atlantic, at Redwood City, California.

1925 First transatlantic broadcast.

1932 Death of George Eastman (b.1854 in Waterville, New York), inventor and philanthropist, who manufactured the transparent celluloid film which eventually made possible the moving-picture industry.

1933 Birth of Sir Michael Caine (Maurice Micklewhite) in London, actor, whose many films include *The Ipcress File* (1965).

1936 First flight of the London to Hong Kong air service.

1945 The heaviest bomb of World War 2, the 22,000 pound 'Grand Slam', was dropped by the RAF Dambuster Squadron on the Bielefeld railway viaduct in Germany.

1951 Recapture of Seoul by UN forces during the Korean War.

1976 Death of Busby Berkeley (b.1895 in Los Angeles, California), choreographer and director, who became one of the cinema's most innovative choreographers.

1983 OPEC (the Organization of the Petroleum Exporting Countries) agreed to cut its oil prices by 15 per cent for the first time in its 23-year history.

1995 Astronaut Norman Thagard (b.1943) became the first American to enter space in a Russian rocket, travelling with two cosmonauts from Baikonur Cosmodrome to Mir space station.

MARCH

15

The Ides of March, as mentioned in Shakespeare's *Julius Caesar*.

44 BC Death of Julius Caesar (b.101 BC), Roman general, statesman, and dictator.

1341 Signing of an alliance between Louis IV, Holy Roman emperor, and Philip VI of France, at Vincennes during the Hundred Years' War.

1767 Birth of Andrew Jackson in Waxhaw, South Carolina (d.1845), 7th president of the USA (1829–37).

1779 Birth of William Lamb, 2nd Viscount Melbourne, in London (d.1848), British prime minister (1834, 1835–41).

1781 Defeat of US forces by the British at the Battle of Guilford Courthouse, Connecticut, during the American Revolution.

1820 Maine became the 23rd state of the Union.

1869 Cincinnati Red Stockings became the first professional baseball team.

1877 The first Test cricket match between Australia and England was played in Melbourne; Australia won by 45 runs.

1892 Patenting of the first escalator, the Reno Inclined Elevator, by Jesse Reno.

1898 Death of Sir Henry Bessemer (b.1813 in Charlton, Hertfordshire), inventor and engineer, who patented an economical process for converting pig-iron to steel.

1909 Opening of Selfridge's department store, London.

1933 German dictator Adolf Hitler (1889–1945) proclaimed his vision for an enlarged Germany, the Third Reich.

1949 Ending of clothes rationing in Britain.

1964 Marriage of actors Elizabeth Taylor (b.1932) and Richard Burton (1925–84) for the first time; it was her fifth marriage and his second.

1965 Opening of the first TGI Friday restaurant, in New York.

1975 Death of Aristotle Onassis (b.1906 in Smyrna, Turkey), millionaire ship-owner, who made a fortune in tobacco.

1984 Death of Tommy Cooper (b.1922 in Caerphilly, Wales), comedian and magician, who wore a red fez and used the catch phrase 'Just like that'.

1999 Induction of musicians Dusty Springfield (1939–99), Paul McCartney (b.1942), Bruce Springsteen (b.1949), and Billy Joel (b.1949) into the Rock and Roll Hall of Fame.

2004 Discovery of Sedna, a planet-like body c.8 billion miles from Earth, and the most distant known object in the solar system.

MARCH
16

1521 Discovery of the San Lazaro archipelago, later renamed the Philippines, by Portuguese explorer Ferdinand Magellan (c.1480–1521).

1751 [5 March, Old Style calendar] Birth of James Madison in Port Conway, Virginia (d.1836), 4th president of the USA (1809–17).

1787 Birth of George Simon Ohm in Erlangen, Bavaria, Germany (d.1854), physicist, whose research in electricity resulted in *Ohm's law* (1827).

1792 Shooting of Gustavus III (b.1746), king of Sweden, during a masked ball; he died on 29 March.

1802 Authorization by US Congress of the establishment of a Military Academy at West Point, New York.

1823 Birth of William Henry Monk in London (d.1889), organist and composer, the first editor of *Hymns Ancient and Modern*.

1872 The first English FA Cup final was played at the Oval, London: Wanderers beat Royal Engineers 1–0.

1878 Death of William Banting (b.1797 in England), undertaker and slimming pioneer, who to reduce his own weight devised a diet that cut down the intake of sugars, starches, and fats.

1898 Death of Aubrey Beardsley (b.1872 in Brighton, East Sussex), illustrator, who became famous for his black-and-white illustrations for *Morte Darthur* (1893) and other books.

1904 Issue of Britain's first books of stamps (24 at 1d), by the General Post Office.

1909 The Port of London Authority held its first meeting.

1926 Launch of the first liquid-fuel rocket, by Robert Goddard (1882–1945) at Auburn, Massachusetts; it travelled 56 m/184 ft in 2.5 seconds.

1953 Arrival of Marshal Tito (1892–1980), president of Yugoslavia, in Britain, the first Communist head of state to visit the country.

1966 Launch of Gemini 8, with Neil Armstrong and David Scott.

1973 Opening of the second London Bridge by Queen Elizabeth II.

1976 Resignation of British prime minister Harold Wilson (1916–95).

1978 The *Amoco Cadiz* ran aground off the coast of Brittany, polluting 240 miles of coastline with 223,000 tons of crude oil.

1988 Death of over 5000 people in the Kurdish town of Halabja, when chemical weapons were dropped by Iraqi jets during the Iran–Iraq war.

MARCH

17

Feast of St Gertrude of Nivelles (626–59), patron saint of cats.

Feast (Western Church) of St Joseph of Arimathea (1st c), patron saint of gravediggers and funeral directors.

Feast of St Patrick (c.385–461), patron saint of Ireland.

1337 Edward the Black Prince (1330–76) was given England's first dukedom, the duchy of Cornwall, a title now held by Charles, Prince of Wales.

1649 English soldier and statesman Oliver Cromwell (1599–1658) declared England a Commonwealth.

1762 The first St Patrick's Day parade was held in New York.

1766 Repeal of the British Stamp Act of 1765, which levied direct tax on papers required in official business in the American colonies.

1789 Birth of Edmund Kean in London (d.1833), tragic actor, known for his naturalistic performances.

1834 Birth of Gottlieb Daimler in Schorndorf, Germany (d.1900), engineer, who patented a high-speed internal combustion engine (1885) and founded the Daimler Automobile Company (1890).

1845 Patenting of the first rubber bands made of vulcanized rubber by Stephen Perry of Perry and Co, Rubber Manufacturers, London.

1846 Birth of Kate Greenaway in London (d.1901), artist and book-illustrator, well known in the 1880s for her portrayals of child life.

1899 The first 'mayday' distress call was sent, by a merchant ship aground off the English coast.

1905 Marriage of Franklin D. Roosevelt (1882–1945), future president of the USA (1933–45), to his distant cousin, Eleanor Roosevelt (1884–1962).

1912 Lawrence Oates, team member of Scott's weatherbound South Pole expedition, left the tent saying, 'I am just going outside, I may be some time.'

1921 Opening of Marie Stopes' first birth control clinic in London.

1938 Birth of Rudolf Nureyev in Irkutsk, Russia (d.1993), ballet dancer.

1948 Signing of the Treaty of Brussels by Britain, France, Luxembourg, and The Netherlands.

1950 Creation of a new radioactive element, californium, announced by scientists at the University of California at Berkeley.

1983 Sale of a copy of Admiral Horatio Nelson's orders to the fleet before the battle of Trafalgar for £6000.

2003 The Netherlands became the first country to allow pharmacies to prescribe marijuana in the same way as other prescription drugs.

MARCH
18

1229 During the Sixth Crusade, Frederick II (1194–1250), Holy Roman emperor, crowned himself king of Jerusalem.

1745 Death of Sir Robert Walpole, 1st Earl of Orford (b.1676 in Houghton, Norfolk), statesman, and leading minister (1721–42) of George I and George II.

1768 Death of Laurence Sterne (b.1713 in Clonmel, Co Tipperary, Ireland), author and clergyman, best known for his comic novel *The Life and Opinions of Tristram Shandy* (1760–67).

1834 Six Dorset farm labourers were transported for forming a trade union, and became known as the 'Tolpuddle Martyrs'.

1837 Birth of (Stephen) Grover Cleveland in Caldwell, New Jersey (d.1908), 22nd and 24th president of the USA (1885–9, 1893–7).

1844 [6 March, Old Style calendar] Birth of Nikolai (Andreyevich) Rimsky-Korsakov in Tikhvin, Russia (d.1908), composer, whose works include *Scheherazade* (1887–8).

1850 Formation of the American Express by Henry Wells (1805–78) and William Fargo (1818–81) in Buffalo, New York.

1858 Birth of Rudolph Diesel in Paris (d.1913), engineer, who in 1892 patented his design for a 'rational heat motor', demonstrating the first compression-ignition engine (1897).

1869 Birth of Arthur Neville Chamberlain in Birmingham, West Midlands (d.1940), British prime minister (1937–40).

1891 Official opening of the London–Paris telephone system.

1893 Birth of Wilfred Owen at Plas Wilmot, near Oswestry, Shropshire (d.1918), poet, who became a leading poet of World War 1.

1905 Birth of Robert Donat in Manchester (d.1958), actor, whose films include *Goodbye, Mr Chips* (1939, Oscar).

1910 Magician and escape artist Harry Houdini (1874–1926) made the first successful powered flight in Australia.

1916 Beginning of the Battle of Naroch Lake, an attempt by Russia to divert German forces from the Western front during World War 1.

1949 Formation of NATO, the North Atlantic Treaty Organization.

1965 Astronaut Alexei Leonov made the first walk in space, from the Soviet spaceship Voskhod 2.

1967 Wreck of the oil tanker *Torrey Canyon* off the Cornish coast in Britain.

1988 Death of Percy Thrower (b.1913 in Winslow, Buckinghamshire), horticulturist and broadcaster.

1993 A hijacked Ethiopian airliner was attacked by security forces in Dire Dawa after a six-day stand-off; two of the four hijackers were killed.

2004 An asteroid measuring 100 ft passed within 26,500 miles of Earth, the closest-ever recorded approach.

MARCH
19

Feast (Western Church) of St Joseph (1st c BC), patron saint of Belgium, bursars, cabinet makers, Canada, carpenters, fathers, and manual workers.

721 BC The Babylonians observed the first eclipse to be recorded.

1563 Ending of the First War of Religion with the Peace of Amboise, granting the Huguenots limited tolerance.

1616 Release of Sir Walter Raleigh (1552–1618) from the Tower of London; he had been charged with treason by James I.

1702 [8 March, Old Style calendar] Death of William III (b.1650 in The Hague, The Netherlands), king of Great Britain (1689–1702).

1813 Birth of Dr David Livingstone in Blantyre, South Lanarkshire (d.1873), missionary and explorer, the first European to discover the Victoria Falls.

1821 Birth of Sir Richard Burton in Torquay, Devon (d.1890), explorer, who set out with John Speke (1827–64) on the journey which led to the European discovery of Lake Tanganyika.

1859 Premiere of *Faust*, an opera by Charles Gounod (1818–93), at the Théâtre-Lyrique, Paris.

1891 Birth of Earl Warren in Los Angeles, California (d.1974), Republican politician and judge, responsible for outlawing school segregation.

1920 Rejection of the Treaty of Versailles by the US Senate for a second time by a vote of 49–35, falling short of the two-thirds majority needed for approval.

1930 Death of Arthur James Balfour, 1st Earl Balfour (b.1848 in Whittinghame, East Lothian), statesman and philosopher.

1932 Opening of Sydney Harbour Bridge, Australia, with a span of 503 m/1650 ft.

1950 Death of Edgar Rice Burroughs (b.1875 in Chicago, Illinois), novelist, best known for his Tarzan adventure stories.

1953 First televising of the Academy Awards ceremony, with US comedian Bob Hope (1903–2003) as host.

1970 First meeting of Willi Stoph (1914–99), prime minister of East Germany, and Willy Brandt (1913–92), chancellor of West Germany, since the division of Germany in 1949.

1982 Raising of the Argentinian flag on South Georgia, Falkland Islands, by Argentinian scrap-metal merchants, which led eventually to the Falklands War.

1986 Announcement by Buckingham Palace of the engagement of Prince Andrew and Sarah Ferguson.

1996 Nelson Mandela (b.1918), South African statesman and president (1994–9), divorced Winnie Mandela (b.1936) after 38 years of marriage.

MARCH
20

43 BC Birth of Publius Ovidius Naso, known as Ovid, in Sulmo, Italy (d.AD 17), Latin poet, whose works include the *Ars amatoria* and *Metamorphoses*.

1602 Founding of the Dutch East India Company, to protect trade in the Indian Ocean, Indonesia, Japan, and other parts of the East, and to assist in the war against Spain.

1727 Death of Sir Isaac Newton (b.1642 in Woolsthorpe, Lincolnshire), physicist and mathematician, who stated the law of gravitation.

1806 Laying of the foundation stone of Dartmoor prison, in Princetown, Devon.

1815 Return to Paris of Emperor Napoleon Bonaparte (1769–1821) from banishment on the island of Elba.

1852 *Uncle Tom's Cabin*, by US author Harriet Beecher Stowe (1811–96), was first published in book form.

1899 Martha Place, of Brooklyn, New York, was the first woman to face execution in the electric chair.

1908 Birth of Sir Michael Redgrave in Bristol, Avon (d.1985), actor, whose notable stage roles included Richard II (1951) and Uncle Vanya (1962).

1917 Birth of Dame Vera Lynn, originally Vera Welch, in London, singer and entertainer, who became known as 'The Forces' Sweetheart'.

1933 Opening of the first Nazi concentration camp at Dachau, near Munich.

1944 Eruption of Italy's Mt Vesuvius volcano.

1966 Theft of football's World Cup while being exhibited at Central Hall in Westminster, London.

1969 Marriage of Beatle John Lennon to multimedia artist Yoko Ono.

1980 End of sixteen years of illegal broadcasting from Radio Caroline, British pop pirate radio station, when its ship, *Mi Amigo*, ran aground and sank.

1990 Independence of Namibia after 75 years of South African rule.

1995 Release of the poisonous gas sarin on Tokyo's subways by the Aum Shinri Kyo cult, killing 12 people, and affecting more than 5500 others.

1996 The British government admitted that 'mad cow' disease could probably be transmitted to humans.

1999 Bertrand Piccard (b.1958) from Switzerland and Brian Jones (b.1947) from England became the first to fly a hot-air balloon nonstop around the world.

2003 Ground troops entered Iraq and a second round of air strikes was launched against Baghdad during the second Iraq war.

MARCH
21

Spring Equinox (northern hemisphere).

1556 Death of Thomas Cranmer (b.1489 in Aslockton, Nottinghamshire), first Protestant archbishop of Canterbury, burned at the stake as a heretic.

1685 Birth of Johann Sebastian Bach in Eisenach, Germany (d.1750), composer, known to his contemporaries mainly as an organist.

1857 Around 107,000 people died in an earthquake in Tokyo, Japan.

1871 Beginning of the expedition to Africa by journalist Henry Stanley (1841–1904) to find missing Scottish missionary David Livingstone (1813–73).

1925 Birth of Peter Brook in London, director, whose films include *Lord of the Flies* (1962).

1925 Approval of a statute in Tennessee forbidding the teaching of Charles Darwin's theory of evolution in state schools.

1944 Birth of Timothy Dalton in Colwyn Bay, Conwy, actor, who became the fourth James Bond, starring in *The Living Daylights* (1987).

1952 Election of Kwame Nkrumah (1909–72) as prime minister of the Gold Coast (later Ghana), first African prime minister south of the Sahara.

1958 Opening of the London Planetarium, Britain's first planetarium.

1960 Police opened fire on a peaceful demonstration in Sharpeville, Transvaal, South Africa, killing nearly 70 people and wounding over 180.

1961 British boxer Henry Cooper (b.1934) won his first Lonsdale belt when he beat Joe Erskine.

1962 A female black bear was the first living creature to survive a parachute jump from an aeroplane flying faster than sound, when she was ejected in a special capsule from a bomber flying at 850 mph.

1963 Closure of Alcatraz, maximum security federal prison in San Francisco Bay.

1965 Martin Luther King (1929–68) led the beginning of a 4000-strong civil rights march in Alabama, from Selma to Montgomery.

1999 Death of Ernie Wise (b.1925 in Leeds, West Yorkshire), comedian, who teamed up in 1943 with fellow entertainer Eric Morecambe to form Britain's leading comedy double-act.

2000 Beginning of the first official visit to Israel by a Roman Catholic pontiff, when Pope John Paul II arrived in Tel Aviv.

2004 British architect Zaha Hadid (b.1950 in Baghdad, Iraq) became the first woman to win the Pritzker Architecture Prize in its 25-year history.

MARCH
22

Feast of St Katarina of Sweden, patron saint of women in danger of miscarrying.
Feast of St Turibius de Mogrovejo, patron saint of missionary bishops.
World Day for Water, following the adoption of a resolution made in December 1992 by the UN General Assembly.

1312 Suppression of the Order of The Templars by Pope Clement V.

1599 Birth of Sir Anthony van Dyck in Antwerp, Belgium (d.1641), Flemish artist, and court painter to King Charles I.

1765 Introduction of the British Stamp Act, which levied direct tax on papers required in official business in the American colonies.

1859 Founding of the Political Labour League of Victoria in Melbourne, Australia, the first political party for the working classes.

1888 Founding of the English Football League.

1895 Chemists Auguste Lumière (1862–1954) and Louis Lumière (1864–1948) gave the first demonstration of motion pictures using film projection.

1896 Death of Johann Wolfgang von Goethe (b.1749 in Frankfurt, Germany), poet, novelist, playwright, and scientist.

1906 England won the first rugby international against France, 35–8.

1907 London cabs started to use meters.

1910 Birth of Nicholas Monsarrat in Liverpool (d.1979), novelist, whose books include *The Cruel Sea* (1951).

1923 Birth of Marcel Marceau in Strasbourg, France, mime artist, best known for his white-faced character, Bip, based on the 19th-c French Pierrot.

1930 Birth of Stephen Sondheim in New York, composer and lyricist, whose successful musicals contributed greatly to the revival of the musical in the USA.

1931 Birth of William Shatner in Montreal, Quebec, film and television actor, best known for his role as Captain James T. Kirk in *Star Trek* (from 1966).

1945 Founding of the Arab League by Egypt, Iraq, Saudi Arabia, Transjordan, Lebanon, Yemen, and Syria, with the aim of encouraging inter-Arab cooperation.

1948 Birth of Sir Andrew Lloyd Webber in London, popular composer, whose musicals include *The Phantom of the Opera* (1986).

1997 The Andrew Lloyd Webber musical *Sunset Boulevard* closed on Broadway after $2\frac{1}{2}$ years and 977 performances.

MARCH

23

1369 Death of Pedro 'the cruel' (b.1334 in Burgos, Castile, Spain), king of Castille and Leon, murdered by his brother Henry.

1743 King George II stood at the start of the Hallelujah chorus in the first performance in London of Handel's oratorio, *Messiah*; the audience followed suit, and established the continuing tradition.

1752 Publication of Canada's first newspaper, the *Halifax Gazette*.

1858 Patenting of the cable street-car by Eleazer A. Gardener of Philadelphia, Pennsylvania.

1887 Birth of Roscoe 'Fatty' Arbuckle in Smith Centre, Kansas (d.1933), silent film comedian, who was a Keystone Kop.

1912 Birth of Werner von Braun in Wirsitz, Germany (d.1977), rocket pioneer, who was chiefly responsible for the launching of the first US artificial Earth satellite, Explorer 1 (1958).

1919 Founding of *Fasci di Combattimento*, the Fascist political movement, in Milan, Italy.

1921 Birth of E(rnest) W(illiam) Hornung (b.1866 in Middlesbrough), novelist, who created Raffles, the gentleman thief.

1929 Birth of Sir Roger Bannister in Harrow, London, athlete and neurologist, who became the first man to run the mile in under 4 minutes (3 minutes, 59.4 seconds), on 6 May 1954.

1933 Adolf Hitler (1889–1945) became dictator of Germany.

1956 Pakistan became an independent Islamic republic within the British Commonwealth, with Iskander Mirza as president (1956–8).

1964 Death of Peter Lorre (b.1904 in Rosenberg, Hungary), actor, whose films include *Casablanca* (1942).

1965 Launch of Gemini from Cape Kennedy (now Cape Canaveral), with astronauts Virgil I. Grisson and John W. Young aboard.

1966 First meeting in 400 years for the heads of the Anglican and Roman Catholic Churches, when Archbishop of Canterbury Michael Ramsey met Pope Paul VI in Rome.

1970 Banning of South Africa from the Davis Cup tennis tournament, because of its apartheid policies.

1983 Announcement by US president Ronald Reagan of plans for a space-based defence against enemy nuclear missiles.

1998 The film *Titanic* (1997) matched *Ben-Hur* (1959) when it won 11 Academy Awards.

2001 Space station Mir burnt up as it entered Earth's atmosphere over Nadir, Fiji.

MARCH
24

Feast (Western Church) of St Gabriel (also 29 September), patron saint of broadcasters, diplomats, messengers, and postal, radio, and television workers.

1603 Death of Queen Elizabeth I (b.1533 in Greenwich, London), queen of England and Ireland (1558–1603).

1765 Issue of a decree to establish a School for Healing Animal Diseases by Empress Maria Theresa of Austria.

1776 Death of John Harrison (b.1693 in Foulby, West Yorkshire), inventor and horologist, who developed the marine chronometer.

1834 Birth of William Morris in Walthamstow, London (d.1896), craftsman, poet, and political activist, whose work revolutionized house decoration and furniture design.

1837 In Canada, African Canadians were given the right to vote.

1882 Announcement by German bacteriologist Robert Koch (1843–1910) that he had discovered the tuberculosis bacillus.

1905 Death of Jules Verne (b.1828 in Nantes, France), science-fiction writer, whose novels include *Journey to the Centre of the Earth* (1864).

1926 The first Safeway supermarket was started by Marian B. Skaggs, in Maryland.

1930 Birth of (Terence) Steve(n) McQueen in Beech Grove, Indiana (d.1980), actor and rebel, both on and off the screen, whose films include *Bullitt* (1968).

1942 Introduction of the national loaf in Britain.

1949 Walter Huston and his son John won Oscars for the film *The Treasure of the Sierra Madre* (1948), the first father and son to win Oscars at the same time.

1953 The body of Mrs Ethel Christie was found in a concealed cupboard at 10 Rillington Place, Notting Hill Gate, London.

1958 Rock singer Elvis Presley (1935–77) finished filming *King Creole* and joined the Army.

1960 Birth of Kelly LeBrock in New York, actress and model, whose films include *The Woman in Red* (1984).

1964 Selection of a provisional site, Stansted, for London's third airport.

1965 US space probe Ranger 9 broadcast images live on television as it descended from 2,363 km/1,468 miles to crash-land on the Moon's surface.

1980 Death of Oscar Romero (b.1917 in Ciudad Barrios), Roman Catholic archbishop, shot by gunmen while celebrating Mass in San Salvador.

1989 Supertanker *Exxon Valdez* ran aground on an Alaskan reef, spilling 45,000 tonnes of oil into the fishing waters of Prince William Sound.

MARCH
25

Feast of St Dismas, patron saint of prisoners, thieves, and undertakers.

1306 Coronation of Robert the Bruce as king of the Scots at Scone.

1409 First meeting of the Council of Pisa, formed to resolve the schism in the Catholic Church between Popes Gregory XII and Benedict XIII.

1634 Founding of Maryland by English colonists, sent by Cecil Baltimore (c.1605–75).

1655 Discovery of Titan, Saturn's largest satellite, by Dutch scientist Christiaan Huygens (1629–95).

1669 Eruption of Mt Etna in Sicily, destroying Nicolosi and killing 20,000 people.

1807 Abolition of the slave trade in England.

1843 Opening of the Thames Tunnel, linking Wapping with Rotherhithe.

1908 Birth of Sir David Lean in Croydon, London (d.1991), director, whose films include *Lawrence of Arabia* (1962, Oscar).

1918 Death of Claude Debussy (b.1862 in St Germain-en-Laye, France), composer, whose works include *La Mer* (1905).

1918 Birth of Howard Cosell in Winston-Salem, North Carolina (d.1995), sports broadcaster, known for ABC's *Monday Night Football*.

1920 Birth of Patrick Troughton in Mill Hill, London (d.1987), actor, best known for his role as Doctor Who (1966–9).

1947 Birth of Sir Elton John, originally Reginald Kenneth Dwight, in Pinner, Middlesex, musician and pop singer, whose songs include 'Candle In the Wind' (1974).

1949 *Hamlet*, directed by and starring Lawrence Olivier, won the first British Oscar for film.

1957 The Treaties of Rome paved the way for the formation in 1958 of the EEC, a common market with the removal of barriers to trade among members.

1975 Death of King Faisal of Saudi Arabia (b.1904 in Riyadh, Saudi Arabia), assassinated by Prince Museid, his nephew.

1978 During the Oxford and Cambridge University boat race, the Cambridge boat sank.

1980 Reverend Robert Runcie (1921–2000) was installed as 102nd archbishop of Canterbury.

2004 US Congress passed the Unborn Victims of Violence Act, making the harming of a foetus during violent federal crime a separate offence.

MARCH
26

Feast (Eastern Church) of St Gabriel, patron saint of broadcasters, diplomats, messengers, and postal, radio, and television workers.

1827 Death of Ludwig van Beethoven (b.1770 in Bonn, Germany), composer.

1863 The first steeplechase under National Hunt rules was won by Socks, ridden by Mr Goodman at Market Harborough, Leicestershire.

1885 The first cremation in Britain took place at Woking Crematorium in Surrey.

1892 Death of Walt Whitman (b.1819 in Huntington, Long Island, New York), poet and essayist, a proponent of free verse, whose major poetic work was *Leaves of Grass* (1855).

1902 Death of Cecil Rhodes (b.1853 in Bishop's Stortford, Hertfordshire), statesman and financier, who founded scholarships at Oxford for Americans, Germans, and colonials ('Rhodes scholars').

1911 Birth of Tennessee Williams in Columbus, Mississippi (d.1983), playwright, whose plays include *A Streetcar Named Desire* (1947).

1923 Transmission of the first daily weather forecast by the BBC.

1934 Road Traffic Act made driving tests compulsory for British motorists.

1944 Birth of Diana Ross in Detroit, Michigan, singer, formerly of The Supremes, now a solo performer, whose hits include 'Reach Out and Touch' (1970).

1945 Death of David Lloyd-George (b.1863 in Manchester), British prime minister (1916–22).

1954 Explosion of an H-bomb by the US on Bikini Island, Marshall Islands, contaminating nearby Rongelap Island and other atolls.

1973 Admittance of the first woman to the floor of the London Stock Exchange.

1979 Signing of the Camp David Peace Treaty.

1980 British rock group The Police performed in Mumbai (Bombay), India, the first rock concert there for 10 years, raising £5000 for charity.

1981 Launch of Britain's Social Democratic Party by the 'Gang of Four': Roy Jenkins (1920–2003), David Owen (b.1938), William Rodgers (b.1928), and Shirley Williams (b.1930).

1985 British actor Ben Kingsley (b.1943) won a Best Actor Oscar for his role in the film *Gandhi* (1980).

2000 Election of Vladimir Putin (b.1952), former KGB operative, as second post-Communist president of Russia.

MARCH
27

1350 Death of Alfonso XI (b.1312 in Salamanca, Spain), king of Castile, who died from the Black Death while besieging Gibraltar.

1513 Spanish explorer Juan Ponce de León (1460–1521) sighted the coast of Florida.

1625 Death of James I (b.1566 in Edinburgh), first Stuart king of England (1603–25), also king of Scotland (1567–1625) as James VI.

1794 Creation of the US Navy.

1836 Dedication of the first Mormon temple, in Kirtland, Ohio.

1845 Birth of Wilhelm Konrad von Röntgen in Lennep, Germany (d.1923), physicist, who discovered the electromagnetic rays which he called *X-rays*, for which he received the first Nobel Prize for Physics in 1901.

1855 Patenting of kerosene by Canadian physician and geologist Abraham Gesner (1797–1864).

1860 Patenting of the corkscrew by M. L. Byrn of New York.

1871 The first rugby international was played in Edinburgh; Scotland defeated England.

1899 Birth of Gloria Swanson in Chicago, Illinois (d.1983), star of the silent screen, whose films include *Sadie Thompson* (1928).

1899 Italian physicist and inventor Guglielmo Marconi (1874–1937) transmitted the first radio signals across the English Channel.

1912 Birth of James Callaghan in Portsmouth, Hampshire, British prime minister (1976–9).

1914 The first successful non-direct blood transfusion, using sodium citrate as an anticoagulant, was given by Belgian doctor Albert Hustin in Brussels.

1942 Birth of Michael York in Fulmer, Buckinghamshire, actor, whose films include *Cabaret* (1971).

1964 The Great Train Robbers received jail sentences totalling 307 years.

1964 A four-minute earthquake registering 8.4 hit Valdez, Alaska, the strongest ever recorded in North America, killing 114 people.

1968 Death of Yuri Gagarin (b.1934 in Gagarin (formerly Gzhatsk), Russia), cosmonaut, the first human to fly in space; he was killed in a plane accident while training.

1977 A KLM Boeing 747 crashed into a Pan Am 747 on take-off at Tenerife airport, killing 583 people; there were 54 survivors.

MARCH
28

1592 Birth of John Amos Comenius in Moravia, Slovak Republic (d.1670), educational reformer, who composed *Orbis sensualium pictus* (1658, The Visible World in Pictures), the first picture-book for children.

1819 Birth of Sir Joseph William Bazalgette in Enfield, London (d.1891), engineer, a pioneer of public health engineering.

1834 US Senate voted to censure Andrew Jackson (1767–1845), US president, for removing federal deposits from the Bank of the United States.

1854 Beginning of the Crimean War, when Britain declared war on Russia.

1868 Death of James Thomas Brudenell, 7th Earl of Cardigan (b.1797 in Hambleden, Buckinghamshire), general who led the charge of the Light Brigade at Balaclava (1854); the woollen *cardigan* is named after him.

1879 Defeat of British troops by the 22,000-strong Zulu army on Mt Hlobane, the worst British cavalry rout, and the last Zulu victory.

1902 Birth of Dame Flora Robson in South Shields, Durham (d.1984), actress, famous for her historical roles in plays and films.

1910 A seaplane made the first successful take-off from water in Martiniques, France, flown by its French inventor, Henri Fabre (1882–1984).

1917 Founding of the Women's Army Auxiliary Corps in Britain.

1921 Birth of Dirk Bogarde (Derek Van Den Bogarde) in London (d.1999), actor and novelist, whose films include *The Servant* (1963).

1930 The Turkish cities of Constantinople and Angora changed their names to Istanbul and Ankara.

1935 Birth of Michael Parkinson in Barnsley, South Yorkshire, journalist and television chat-show host.

1939 Ending of the Spanish Civil War, as Madrid fell to General Franco (1892–1975), who became dictator of Spain.

1964 Radio Caroline, Britain's first pirate radio station, began broadcasting off the Essex coast.

1977 Beginning of experimental breakfast television broadcasts in Britain, on Yorkshire TV.

1979 Radiation leak at Three Mile Island nuclear station, Pennsylvania.

1985 Death of Marc Chagall (b.1887 in Vitebsk, Belarus), painter, whose work was described as Surrealist.

2005 A law outlawed English on road signs and official maps on much of Ireland's west coast, where many people are Gaelic-speaking.

MARCH

29

1461 The Battle of Towton was fought in North Yorkshire during the Wars of the Roses, the bloodiest battle on British soil.

1751 Death of Thomas Coram (b.c.1668 in Lyme Regis, Dorset), philanthropist, who planned and founded the Foundling Hospital in London (1741).

1799 Birth of Edward Geoffrey Smith Stanley, 14th Earl of Derby, at Knowsley Hall, Lancashire (d.1869), British prime minister (1852, 1858–9, 1866–8).

1853 Birth of Elihu Thomson in Manchester (d.1937), electrical engineer, who patented over 700 electrical inventions.

1869 Birth of Sir Edwin Landseer Lutyens in London (d.1944), architect, whose projects include the Cenotaph in Whitehall, London, and the laying out of New Delhi, India.

1871 Opening of the Royal Albert Hall, Kensington, London, by Queen Victoria; it was built in memory of her husband, Prince Albert.

1879 Premiere of Tchaikovsky's opera *Eugene Onegin* in Moscow.

1886 Invention of Coca-Cola by Dr John Pemberton, Atlanta, Georgia.

1901 Tasmania, New South Wales, Victoria, and Western Australia voted in the first election for the first Australian parliament.

1912 The last entry in the diary of Antarctic explorer Captain Robert Falcon Scott: 'It seems a pity, but I do not think I can write any more.'

1940 Introduction of metal strips into British £1 notes, in an attempt to prevent forgery.

1943 Birth of Eric Idle in South Shields, Tyne and Wear, writer, comedian, and member of the Monty Python team.

1951 Alleged US spies Julius Rosenberg (1918–53) and Ethel Rosenberg (1915–53) were convicted of passing on atomic secrets through an intermediary to the Soviet vice-consul.

1967 Launch of France's first nuclear submarine, *La Redoutable*.

1972 Death of Baron J. Arthur Rank (b.1888 in Kingston-upon-Hull), film magnate, and owner of a chain of 600 cinemas.

1974 US spacecraft Mariner 10 took the first close-up pictures of Mercury.

1981 The first London Marathon was run.

2004 Smoking was outlawed in workplaces in Ireland, in the strictest anti-tobacco measure taken by any country.

MARCH

30

1406 Capture and imprisonment of James I of Scotland by Henry IV of England.

1840 Death of George Bryan Brummell, known as Beau Brummell (b.1778 in London), dandy, and an arbiter of elegancies.

1842 Ether was used for the first time as an anaesthetic, by Dr Crawford Lang, in Jefferson, Georgia.

1858 Patenting of the combined pencil and eraser by Hymen L. Lipman of Philadelphia.

1867 Purchase of Alaska from Russia by America, for $7·2 million (around 2 cents per acre).

1870 Readmission of Texas to the Union, after it joined the Confederate States in 1861.

1870 The 15th Amendment to the US Constitution came into effect, guaranteeing US citizens the right to vote regardless of race.

1909 Birth of Sir Ernst Gombrich in Vienna, Austria (d.2001), art historian, whose books include *The Story of Art* (1950).

1909 Opening of the Queensboro Bridge, New York, to the public.

1928 Birth of Tom Sharpe in London, novelist, whose works include *Porterhouse Blue* (1974).

1929 Inauguration of Imperial Airways, the first commercial airline between London and Karachi.

1930 Birth of Rolf Harris in Bassendean, Western Australia, painter, and popular stage and television performer.

1945 Birth of Eric Clapton in Ripley, Surrey, rock guitarist and singer.

1945 Capture of Danzig (Gdańsk), Baltic Sea port, by the Russians.

1979 Death of Airey Neave (b.1916), Conservative MP and shadow Northern Ireland Secretary, killed by a bomb attached to his car in the House of Commons car park.

1980 Death of Mantovani (b.1905 in Venice, Italy), violinist, composer, and conductor of popular light music.

1980 US president Ronald Reagan was shot and wounded by John W. Hinckley (b.1955) outside a hotel in Washington, DC.

1987 Death of Maria von Trapp (b.1905 in Vienna); Maria and her family were the inspiration for the film *The Sound of Music* (1965).

1987 Sale of Vincent van Gogh's *Sunflowers* for £24,750,000, by Christie's of London.

2002 Death of Elizabeth Bowes-Lyon, HM Queen Elizabeth, the Queen Mother (b.1900 in St Paul's Waldenbury, Hertfordshire).

MARCH
31

1084 Coronation of Henry IV as Holy Roman emperor by antipope Clement III.

1492 Issue of an edict by Ferdinand (1452–1516) and Isabella (1451–1504) of Spain, expelling from Spain all Jews except those willing to convert to Christianity.

1596 Birth of René Descartes in La Haye, France (d.1650), philosopher and mathematician, famous for the phrase 'I think, therefore I am'.

1631 Death of John Donne (b.1572 in London), poet and priest, whose works include *Songs and Sonnets*.

1693 Birth of John Harrison in Foulby, West Yorkshire (d.1776), inventor and horologist, who developed the marine chronometer.

1732 Birth of Franz Joseph Haydn in Rohrau, Austria (d.1809), composer, whose innovations include the four-movement string quartet and the 'classical' symphony.

1811 Birth of Robert Wilhelm Bunsen in Göttingen, Germany (d.1899), chemist and physicist, whose inventions included the Bunsen burner.

1837 Death of John Constable (b.1776 in East Bergholt, Suffolk), landscape painter, whose works include *The Hay Wain* (1821).

1854 Signing of the Treaty of Kanagawa by Japan and the USA, Japan's first treaty with a Western nation, opening up Shimoda and Hakodate ports to US traders.

1855 Death of Charlotte Brontë (b.1816 in Thornton, West Yorkshire), novelist and poet, whose works include *Jane Eyre* (1847).

1889 Opening of the Eiffel Tower in Paris, at that time the world's tallest building.

1897 Patenting of the zip fastener by its inventor, Whitcomb Judson.

1918 First implementation of Daylight Saving Time in the USA.

1923 Alma Cummings (b.1891) won the first US dance marathon, held in New York, with a world record of 27 hours.

1934 US bank robber John Dillinger (1903–34) escaped from police custody, and was later shot dead by FBI agents.

1943 Opening of *Oklahoma!*, the Rodgers and Hammerstein musical, on Broadway.

1959 The Dalai Lama left Tibet for India to avoid the occupying Chinese forces.

1986 Abolition of the Greater London Council, largest local government in the world.

1990 An anti-poll-tax rally in central London led to the worst riots in the city for a century.

1998 Purchase of luxury British car firm Rolls-Royce by German firm BMW, for £340 million.

APRIL

1

Feast (Eastern Church) of St Mary of Egypt, patron saint of repentant prostitutes.

1578 Birth of William Harvey in Folkestone, Kent (d.1657), physician, who first described the circulation of the blood.

1786 Birth of William Mulready in Ennis, Co Clare, Ireland (d.1863), painter, who designed the first penny-postage envelope (1840).

1795 Declaration of martial law in France, following riots about food shortages.

1826 Patenting of the internal combustion engine by US inventor Samuel Morey (1762–1843).

1875 *The Times* newspaper printed the first daily weather chart.

1883 Birth of Lon Chaney in Colorado Springs, Colorado (d.1930), actor, whose films include *The Hunchback of Notre Dame* (1924).

1891 Opening of the London–Paris telephone link for the general public.

1918 Establishment of the Royal Air Force in Britain by amalgamating the Royal Flying Corps and the Royal Naval Air Service; the Women's Royal Air Force (WRAF) was established on the same day.

1924 Launch of the first automatic gramophone, by HMV.

1930 Premiere of the film *Blue Angel* in Berlin, starring Marlene Dietrich (1904–92) and Emil Jannings (1884–1950).

1946 More than 170 died when tidal waves struck the Hawaiian Islands.

1957 Birth of David Gower in Tunbridge Wells, Kent, cricketer, who was captain of England (1984–6, 1989).

1960 Launch of TIROS-1, the first US weather satellite, from Cape Canaveral.

1976 Founding of Apple Computer, by US computer inventors Stephen Wozniak (b.1950) and Steven Jobs (b.1955).

1983 Thousands of anti-nuclear demonstrators formed a 14-mile human chain, covering three defence installations in England.

1984 Death of Marvin Gaye (b.1939 in Washington, DC), soul singer and composer, best known for 'I Heard It Through the Grapevine' (1968); he was shot dead by his father during a row.

2001 The world's first legal gay marriage took place in Holland.

2001 Arrest of Slobodan Milošević (1941–2006), former president of Serbia, on corruption charges.

APRIL

2

Feast (Western Church) of St Mary of Egypt, patron saint of repentant prostitutes.
Feast of St Francis of Paola (1416–1507), patron saint of sailors.

1743 [Old Style calendar, New Style 13 April] Birth of Thomas Jefferson in Albermarle Co, Virginia (d.1826), 3rd president of the USA (1801–9), who drafted the Declaration of Independence (1776).

1792 America struck the first silver dollar in its new currency.

1827 Birth of William Holman Hunt in London (d.1910), painter, and founder member of the Pre-Raphaelite Brotherhood, whose works include *The Light of the World* (1854).

1872 Death of Samuel Morse (b.1791 in Charlestown, Massachusetts), painter, and inventor of the Morse code.

1873 Britain's trains were fitted with toilets, but only in sleeping carriages.

1875 Birth of Walter Chrysler, born in Wamego, Kansas (d.1940), automobile manufacturer, who introduced the Plymouth motorcar and designed the first high-compression engine.

1889 Patenting of aluminium by US chemist Charles Hall (1863–1914).

1902 Opening of the first motion-picture theatre, in Los Angeles; the cost to see one hour's programme was one dime.

1913 Suffragette leader Emmeline Pankhurst (1858–1928) was sentenced to three years' penal servitude.

1914 Birth of Sir Alec Guinness in London (d.2000), actor, whose films include *The Bridge on the River Kwai* (1957, Oscar).

1917 The USA declared war against Germany and joined with the Allies in World War 1.

1966 Death of C(ecil) S(cott) Forester (b.1899 in Cairo), British writer and novelist, known for his creation of Horatio Hornblower.

1974 San Francisco art gallery owner Robert Opel (1941–79) streaked naked across the stage during the 46th Academy Awards ceremony.

1977 Red Rum won his third Grand National steeplechase, the first racehorse ever to do so.

1977 Charlotte Brew became the first woman to ride in a Grand National steeplechase.

1982 Invasion of the Falkland Islands by Argentina; troops stormed the capital, Port Stanley.

1992 US Mafia boss John Gotti (1940–2002) was convicted in New York for five murders and racketeering.

1998 Police in Northern Ireland intercepted a 980-pound bomb at Dublin ferry port.

2005 Death of Pope John Paul II (b.1920 in Wadowice, Poland), the first non-Italian pope in 430 years.

APRIL

3

Feast of St Richard of Chichester, patron saint of coachmen.

1042 Coronation of Edward the Confessor (1003–66) as king of England.

1366 Birth of Henry Bolingbroke in Lincolnshire (d.1413), king of England as Henry IV (1399–1413).

1559 Signing of the Treaty of Cateau-Cambresis, ending the long-standing war between Spain and France.

1721 Appointment of Sir Robert Walpole (1676–1745) as first lord of the treasury and chancellor of the exchequer, widely recognized as Britain's first prime minister.

1860 The first Pony Express crossed from St Joseph, Missouri, to Sacramento, California.

1882 Death of Jesse James (b.1847 in Centerville, Missouri), Wild West outlaw, killed by Robert Ford, a member of his gang, for $5000 reward.

1898 Birth of Henry Luce in Shandong, China (d.1967), US magazine publisher and editor, who launched the business magazine *Fortune* (1929) and the picture magazine *Life* (1936).

1901 Death of Richard D'Oyly Carte (b.1844 in London), theatrical impresario, who built the Savoy Theatre in London, and was the first producer of the Gilbert and Sullivan operas.

1920 Marriage of F. Scott Fitzgerald (1896–1940), US author, to aspiring writer Zelda Sayre (1900–48) at St Patrick's Cathedral, New York.

1924 Birth of Marlon Brando in Omaha, Nebraska, actor, whose films include *Last Tango in Paris* (1972).

1930 Haile Selassie was proclaimed emperor of Ethiopia.

1933 Completion of the first aerial photographic survey of Mt Everest, by RAF officer David McIntyre.

1947 Formation of BUPA, private health care service, in the UK.

1954 The 100th Oxford and Cambridge University Boat Race, held annually on the R Thames, was won by Oxford.

1961 Birth of Eddie Murphy in New York, comic actor, whose films include *Beverly Hills Cop* (1984; sequel, 1987).

1981 Beginning of the Brixton riots, London.

1987 A sale of jewellery belonging to the late duchess of Windsor fetched £31 million/$50 million, six times more than expected.

1993 The Grand National horse race was abandoned, after two false starts.

2004 Five Madrid railway bombing suspects blew themselves up in a building outside Madrid, Spain.

APRIL

4

National Day, Hungary.
Feast of St Isidore of Seville (c.560–636),
patron saint of farmers.

1460 Founding of the University of Basel, Switzerland.

1541 Theologian Ignatius of Loyola (c.1491–1556) became the first superior-general of the Jesuits.

1581 Queen Elizabeth I knighted Francis Drake (c.1540–96) on the completion of his circumnavigation of the world.

1774 Death of Oliver Goldsmith (b.1728 in Kildare, Ireland), novelist, poet, and playwright, whose works include *She Stoops to Conquer* (1773).

1818 US Congress agreed the US flag would have 13 red-and-white stripes and 20 stars, with a new star added for each new state of the Union.

1821 Birth of Linus Yale in Salisbury, New York (d.1868), lock manufacturer and inventor of the Yale lock.

1823 Birth of Sir William Siemens in Lenthe, Germany (d.1883), electrical engineer, responsible for the development of the first telegraph cable from Britain to America.

1896 Announcement that gold had been discovered in the Yukon, Canada, precipitating the Gold Rush.

1929 Death of Karl (Friedrich) Benz (b.1844 in Karlsruhe, Germany), engineer, the founder of Benz & Co car manufacturers, which merged with Daimler in 1926 to form Daimler-Benz & Co.

1932 Birth of Anthony Perkins in New York (d.1992), actor, best known as Norman Bates from the Hitchcock thriller *Psycho* (1960).

1932 Isolation of vitamin C by C. C. King at the University of Pittsburgh, Pennsylvania.

1934 First use of reflective cat's-eyes on the road, in Yorkshire.

1945 Liberation of the Ohrdruf death camp from Nazi occupation.

1968 James Earl Ray shot civil rights leader Martin Luther King (b.1929) in Memphis, Tennessee.

1981 Election of Henry Cisneros (b.1947) as mayor of San Antonio, Texas, first elected Mexican-American mayor of a major US city.

1983 Launch of space shuttle Challenger on its maiden voyage, with crew members including Sally Ride (b.1951), the first female US astronaut in space.

2003 Saddam international airport, near Baghdad, was seized by US forces.

APRIL

5

Feast of St Vincent Ferrer, patron saint of brick and tile makers, and plumbers.

1614 Marriage of American-Indian princess Pocahontas (1595–1617) to English Jamestown colonist John Rolfe.

1722 Discovery of Easter Island by Dutch explorer Jacob Roggeveen (1659–1729).

1725 Birth of Giacomo Casanova in Venice, Italy (d.1798), adventurer and spy, best known as one of the world's great lovers.

1794 Death of Georges Danton (b.1759 in Arcis-sur-Aube, France), French revolutionary leader, who lost his leadership to Robespierre and was guillotined.

1815 Eruption of Mt Tambora on Sumbawa Island, Indonesia; a third of the 13,000-ft volcano was blasted into the air, killing thousands.

1827 Birth of Joseph Lister in Upton, Essex (d.1912), surgeon, who introduced antiseptic conditions during surgery (1865).

1895 Irish playwright Oscar Wilde (1854–1900) lost his criminal libel case against Sir John Sholto Douglas, Marquess of Queensberry, who had accused him of homosexual practices.

1902 The stand at Ibrox Park football stadium in Glasgow collapsed for the first time during an England v. Scotland match; it collapsed a second time 69 years later (2 January 1971).

1910 France banned kissing on French railways, in case it caused delays.

1929 Birth of Sir Nigel Hawthorne in Coventry, West Midlands (d.2001), actor, whose films include *The Madness of King George* (1994).

1955 Resignation of Sir Winston Churchill (1874–1965) as British prime minister.

1971 Eruption of Mt Etna, Europe's largest active volcano, situated in Catania province, Sicily, Italy.

1971 Canadian Fran Phipps became the first woman to reach the North Pole.

1976 Death of Howard Hughes (b.1905 in Houston, Texas), millionaire businessman, film producer and director, and aviator.

1984 US basketball player Kareem Abdul-Jabbar (b.1947) became the highest-scoring player in NBA history, with 31,421 career points.

1989 Death of Sir Arthur Travers Harris (b.1892 in Cheltenham, Gloucestershire), British airman, nicknamed 'Bomber Harris', commander-in-chief of Bomber Command during World War 2.

1999 Surrender by Libya to a UN representative of two suspects in the 1988 bombing of Pan Am Flight 103 over Lockerbie, Scotland.

APRIL

6

1199 Death of Richard I, king of England, known as Richard the Lionheart (b.1157 in Oxford, Oxfordshire), killed while besieging the castle of Châlus, Aquitaine.

1520 Death of Raphael (b.1483 in Urbino, Italy), Renaissance painter.

1580 An earth tremor badly damaged St Paul's Cathedral and other churches in London.

1722 Ending of a tax on beards, imposed in Russia in 1698 by Peter the Great (1672–1725).

1758 Birth of Maximilien Robespierre in Arras, France (d.1794), French revolutionary leader, who is identified with the Reign of Terror.

1830 Foundation of the Mormons by Joseph Smith as the 'Church of Jesus Christ of Latter-day Saints' at Fayette, New York.

1850 Arrival of the Koh-i-noor diamond from India, to form part of the British Crown Jewels.

1860 Birth of René Lalique in Ay, France (d.1945), founder of the Lalique jewellery firm (1885), whose glass designs were an important contribution to the Art Nouveau and Art Deco movements.

1890 Birth of Anthony Herman Gerard Fokker in Kediri, Java (d.1939), aircraft engineer, who developed the first effective way of firing a machine-gun through a turning propeller.

1896 Inauguration of the first modern Olympic Games in Athens.

1909 US Naval commander Robert Peary (1856–1920), with explorer Matthew Henson (1866–1955) and four Inuit, became the first man to reach the North Pole.

1944 Introduction of the P(ay) A(s) Y(ou) E(arn) income-tax system in Britain.

1965 Launch in the USA of Early Bird, the first commercial communications satellite.

1971 Death of Igor (Fyodorovich) Stravinsky (b.1882 near St Petersburg, Russia), composer, known for his music for the Diaghilev ballets, such as *The Firebird* (1910).

1980 Introduction of Post-It notes in the USA.

1992 Death of Isaac Asimov (b.1920 in Petrovichi, Russia), novelist, critic, and popular scientist, whose science fiction includes *The Naked Sun* (1957).

1994 The presidents of Rwanda and Burundi died in a plane crash near Kigali, Rwanda.

1998 Pakistan conducted successful tests on a medium-range missile capable of reaching neighbouring India.

2000 The Zimbabwe ruling party approved a bill allowing the government to seize white-owned land without compensation.

APRIL

7

Feast of St Jean-Baptiste de la Salle, patron saint of teachers.

1521 Portuguese navigator Ferdinand Magellan (c.1480–1521) landed on Cebu Island in the Philippines.

1724 Premiere of Johann Sebastian Bach's *St John Passion* in Leipzig, Germany.

1739 Death by hanging of Dick Turpin (b.1705 in Hempstead, Essex), butcher's apprentice, robber, smuggler, housebreaker, highwayman and horse-thief, hanged for murder.

1795 The French National Assembly established the metre as the official unit for measurement of length.

1827 'Congreves', the first friction matches, were made by British chemist and inventor John Walker (c.1781–1859).

1832 Farmer Joseph Thompson sold his wife for twenty shillings and a Newfoundland dog in Carlisle.

1862 The Union army won the Battle of Shiloh, SW Tennessee, the second major engagement of the American Civil War.

1902 Founding of the Texas Fuel Company, which later changed its name to the Texas Company and, eventually, Texaco.

1906 Eruption of Mt Vesuvius, an active volcano situated in Campania, SW Italy.

1924 The first brain tumour operation carried out under local anaesthetic was performed at Beth Israel Hospital, New York, by Dr K. Winfield Ney.

1927 A speech made in Washington by US secretary of commerce Herbert Hoover was broadcast in New York, in the first long-distance television transmission.

1945 Sinking of Japanese battleship *Yamato*, the world's largest battleship, during the battle for Okinawa.

1948 Founding of the World Health Organization, a specialized agency formed within the UN to advance international cooperation for the improvement of health.

1949 Opening of Rodgers and Hammerstein's musical, *South Pacific*, Broadway, New York.

1968 Death of Jim Clark (b.1936 in Kilmany, Fife), British motor-racing champion, killed during a Formula 2 race at the Hockenheim circuit, Germany.

1986 British electronic engineer and inventor Sir Clive Sinclair (b.1940) sold the marketing and merchandising rights to his inventions for £5 million to rival company Amstrad.

APRIL

8

First day of the Hindu New Year.

217 Death of Caracalla (b.188 in Lugdunum), Roman emperor, assassinated while preparing for war against the Parthians.

1513 Discovery of Florida by Spanish explorer Juan Ponce de Léon (1460–1521).

1838 Maiden voyage of the steamship *Great Western*, designed by Isambard Kingdom Brunel (1806–59), from Bristol to New York.

1861 Death of Elisha Otis (b.1811 in Halifax, Vermont), inventor, who designed the elevator.

1893 Birth of Mary Pickford in Toronto, Ontario (d.1979), actress, who co-founded United Artists Film Corporation (1919).

1904 Signing of the Anglo-French agreement, the 'Entente Cordiale'.

1929 Birth of Jacques Brel in Schaerbeek, Belgium (d.1978), writer, composer, and performer, whose songs include 'Ne me quitte pas'.

1931 Birth of Dame Dorothy Tutin in London (d.2001), actress.

1953 Kenya's British rulers convicted Jomo Kenyatta (1891–1978) for leading the Mau Mau Rebellion against white settlers in Kenya.

1963 Birth of Julian Lennon, singer, first son of Beatles pop group member John Lennon (1940–80).

1968 The Beatles received a gold disc for sales of their record 'Lady Madonna'.

1973 Death of Pablo Picasso (b.1881 in Málaga, Spain), painter, whose works include *Guernica* (1937).

1974 US baseball player Hank Aaron (b.1934) hit his 715th home run, breaking Babe Ruth's record.

1986 Election of Clint Eastwood (b.1930), US film star and director, as mayor of Carmel, California.

1986 Jennifer Guinness, of the Guinness Brewery family in Ireland, was kidnapped for a £2 million ransom.

1992 Announcement by US tennis player Arthur Ashe (1943–93) at a news conference that he had AIDS.

1994 Death of Kurt Cobain (b.1967 in Hoquaim, Seattle), lead singer and guitarist for grunge band Nirvana, from an apparently self-inflicted gunshot wound.

1996 Signing of a treaty between Yugoslavia and Macedonia to normalize relations.

2002 Suzan-Lori Parks became the first female African-American Pulitzer Prize drama winner for her play *Topdog/Underdog*.

APRIL

9

1241 Mongol armies defeated the Poles and Germans in the battle of Liegnitz, Silesia, then invaded Poland and Hungary.

1667 The first public art exhibition was held at the Palais-Royale in Paris.

1682 French explorer Rene Robert Cavelier (1643–87) claimed for France the lower Mississippi R and all lands that touched it.

1770 Discovery of Botany Bay by British navigator James Cook (1728–79).

1806 Birth of Isambard Kingdom Brunel in Portsmouth, Hampshire (d.1859), bridge-builder, and engineer to the Great Western Railway.

1838 Opening of the National Gallery in London.

1865 Surrender of General Robert E. Lee to General Ulysses S. Grant at Appomattox, so ending the American Civil War.

1882 Death of Dante Gabriel Rossetti (b.1828 in London), poet and painter, a founder member of the Pre-Raphaelite Brotherhood.

1914 The first full-colour film, *World, Flesh and Devil*, was shown in London.

1926 Birth of Hugh Hefner in Chicago, Illinois, editor and publisher of *Playboy* magazine.

1940 Invasion of Denmark and Norway by German forces during World War 2.

1957 Birth of Sevvy Ballesteros in Pedreña, Spain, golfer, the first man to win 50 European golf tournaments.

1969 Maiden test flight for British-built supersonic aircraft Concorde, flying from Filton, near Bristol, to Fairford, Gloucestershire.

1970 Issue of a High Court writ by Paul McCartney (b.1942), terminating his business partnership with The Beatles.

1977 Swedish pop group Abba reached No. 1 in the US pop charts with 'Dancing Queen'.

1992 The Tories were returned for a fourth term at the General Election.

1992 Former ruler of Panama Manuel Noriega (b.1932) was convicted on eight drug and racketeering charges in Miami, Florida.

1994 Launch of US space shuttle Endeavour on an 11-day mission, which included three-dimensional mapping of the Earth's surface.

2001 Tiger Woods (b.1976) became the only golfer in history to hold the four major championship titles at the same time.

2003 US military commanders declared the end of Saddam Hussein's rule over Baghdad.

APRIL

.10

1633 First sales of bananas in London shops.

1710 The Copyright Act (1709) came into effect in Britain, allowing authors exclusive rights to their own work for up to 50 years after their death.

1829 Birth of William Booth in Nottingham, Nottinghamshire (d.1912), founder and general of the Salvation Army.

1841 First publication of the *New York Tribune*, with editor Horace Greeley (1811–72).

1847 Birth of Joseph Pulitzer in Makó, Hungary (d.1911), newspaper proprietor, whose will established annual Pulitzer Prizes for literature, drama, music, and journalism.

1849 Patenting of the safety pin by Walter Hunt of New York; he later sold the rights for £250.

1864 Coronation of Archduke Maximilian of Austria (1832–67) as emperor of Mexico.

1866 The ASPCA (American Society for the Prevention of Cruelty to Animals) was chartered.

1870 [Old Style calendar, New Style 22 April] Birth of Vladimir Ilyich Lenin in Simbirsk, Russia (d.1924), Marxist revolutionary leader, who led the Bolshevik revolution (1917) and became head of the first Soviet government.

1912 Start of the maiden – and final – voyage for the liner *Titanic*.

1919 Death of Emiliano Zapata (b.1871 in Anencuilo, Mexico), revolutionary, who was ambushed and killed by government troops in Mexico.

1925 Publication of F. Scott Fitzgerald's novel, *The Great Gatsby*, by Scribner's of New York.

1930 Production of the first synthetic rubber, neoprene, by the Dupont company.

1932 Birth of Omar Sharif in Alexandria, Egypt, actor, whose films include *Lawrence of Arabia* (1962).

1963 The *Thresher* disaster: US Navy atomic submarine *Thresher* sank off Cape Cod.

1966 Death of Evelyn Waugh (b.1903 in London), novelist, whose works include *Brideshead Revisited* (1945).

1988 The largest single transaction in the history of Wall Street was made on the New York Stock Exchange, when 48 million shares changed hands.

1989 Nick Faldo (b.1957) became the first Englishman to win the US Masters golf tournament.

2001 Mercy killings and assisted suicide for people with unbearable terminal illness were legalized in The Netherlands.

APRIL
11

Feast of St Stanislaus, patron saint of Poland.

1142 Death of Abelard (b.1079 near Nantes, France), theologian, and famous lover of Héloïse.

1512 Defeat of the Holy League by the French at the Battle of Ravenna.

1689 Coronation of William III (1650–1702) and Mary II (1662–94) as joint sovereigns of Britain.

1814 Abdication of Napoleon, who was then exiled to the island of Elba.

1819 Birth of Sir Charles Hallé in Hagen, Germany (d.1895), pianist and conductor, who founded the Hallé Orchestra in Manchester.

1855 Erection of the first six pillar boxes in London, painted green.

1914 Opening of George Bernard Shaw's *Pygmalion* in London.

1930 The *Daily Express* was the first British newspaper to publish details of television programmes.

1935 Crops were destroyed and many made homeless when severe dust storms hit the US prairie states from Kansas to Texas.

1945 Liberation of the Buchenwald concentration camp in Germany by the USA.

1951 The Stone of Scone was found at an abbey in Forfar, Scotland, having been stolen by Scottish nationalists from Westminster Abbey in London.

1957 The Ryan X-13 Vertijet was the first jet to take off and land vertically, making aeronautical history.

1960 Death of Sir Archibald McIndoe (b.1900 in Dunedin, New Zealand), plastic surgeon, who became known for his work on the faces and limbs of severely injured airmen during World War 2.

1968 US president Lyndon B. Johnson made law the Civil Rights Act of 1968, a week after the assassination of Martin Luther King Jr (1929–68).

1970 Launch of Apollo 13, with James Lovell, Fred Haise, and John Swigert on board.

1979 Rebels and exiles backed by Tanzanian forces seized control in Uganda, deposing Idi Amin (c.1925–2003) as president.

1983 British film *Gandhi* (1982) won eight Oscars during the 55th Academy Awards.

1997 Fire damaged the 500-year-old San Giovanni Cathedral in Italy, home of the Turin Shroud.

2001 Death of Sir Harry Secombe (b.1921 in Swansea, West Glamorgan), comedian, singer, and media personality.

APRIL

12

Feast of St Zeno, patron saint of fishers.

65 Death of Lucius Annaeus Seneca (b.5 BC in Córdoba, Spain), Roman philosopher, statesman, and writer, put to death by Nero.

1204 The Fourth Crusade, led by Boniface of Montferrat (c.1150–1207), sacked the Byzantine Christian capital of Constantinople.

1545 Francis I (1494–1547), king of France, ordered the murder of the Protestants of Vaudois.

1606 Adoption of the Union Flag – the Union Jack – by England.

1709 First day of publication for the *Tatler*.

1782 Britain won its only naval engagement in the American Revolutionary war, at the Battle of Les Saintes in the West Indies.

1861 Beginning of the American Civil War, when the Confederate Army bombarded Fort Sumter in South Carolina.

1924 Birth of Raymond Barre in St Denis, Réunion, French prime minister (1976–81), who made his reputation as an influential neo-liberal economist at the Sorbonne.

1941 Birth of Bobby Moore in London (d.1993), footballer, who captained the victorious England side in the 1966 World Cup.

1945 Death of Franklin D. Roosevelt (b.1882 in Hyde Park, New York), 32nd president of the USA (1933–45).

1949 Birth of Sir Alan Ayckbourn in London, playwright, whose plays include *The Norman Conquests* (1974).

1954 Popular US singer and musician Bill Haley (1927–81) recorded the best-selling pop record 'Rock Around the Clock'.

1955 The polio vaccine developed by virologist Jonas E. Salk (1914–95) was declared 'safe, effective and potent'.

1961 Russian cosmonaut Yuri Gagarin (1934–68) became the first man to travel in space, completing a circuit of the Earth in the Vostok spaceship.

1981 Launch of the first space shuttle, Columbia, by the USA.

1985 Launch of US space shuttle Discovery with Jake Garn (b.1932) on board, US senator.

1992 Opening of Euro Disneyland in Marne-La-Vallée, France.

1993 Enforcement by NATO warplanes of a UN no-fly zone over Bosnia-Herzegovina.

2003 Marriage of Prince Laurent of Belgium (b.1963) to British-born commoner Claire Coombs (b.1974).

APRIL

13

First day of the Sikh New Year (Baisakhi Mela).

1598 Issue of the Edict of Nantes by Henry IV, king of France, granting religious and civil liberties to his Protestant Huguenot subjects at the end of the Wars of Religion.

1668 Appointment of John Dryden (1631–1700) as first poet laureate.

1732 Birth of Frederick North, 8th Baron North, in London (d.1792), British prime minister (1770–82).

1742 Handel's oratorio *Messiah* was first performed in Dublin, Ireland.

1748 Birth of Joseph Bramah in Stainborough, South Yorkshire (d.1814), inventor, whose work included a hydraulic press (1795) and a machine for printing bank notes (1806).

1771 Birth of Richard Trevithick in Illogan, Cornwall (d.1833), engineer and inventor, who designed a steam carriage.

1796 Arrival of the first elephant brought to America, from Bengal, India.

1829 The British parliament passed the Catholic Emancipation Act, giving freedom of religion to Catholics.

1902 Opening of US retailer JC Penney's first store, in Kemmerer, Wyoming.

1906 Birth of Samuel Beckett in Dublin, Ireland (d.1989), playwright and writer, whose plays include *Waiting for Godot* (1954).

1919 Massacre at Amritsar, Punjab, when troops opened fire on an unarmed crowd.

1935 Inauguration of the London to Australia airline service.

1943 Dedication of the Jefferson Memorial in Washington, DC, by US president Franklin Roosevelt (1882–1945).

1964 Ian Smith (b.1919) became prime minister of Southern Rhodesia.

1964 Sidney Poitier (b.1924) became the first African-American actor to win an Oscar, for his role in *Lilies of the Field*.

1970 Apollo 13 astronaut Jack Swigert said, 'Hey, we've got a problem here … Houston, we've had a problem', after a liquid oxygen tank burst on the way to the Moon.

1975 Beginning of a 15-year civil war in the Lebanon, when the Christian Falange group killed 27 Palestinians in retaliation for the murder of three Christians.

1980 Closure of the US musical *Grease* at Broadhurst Theater, New York, after 3388 performances.

1997 US golfer Tiger Woods (b.1976) became the first African-American and youngest person to win the US Masters tournament.

APRIL

14

1471 Defeat of the Lancastrians led by the Earl of Warwick, and death of Warwick (b.1428), at the battle of Barnet during the Wars of the Roses.

1629 Birth of Christiaan Huygens in The Hague, The Netherlands (d.1695), physicist and astronomer, who made the first pendulum clock (1655).

1738 Birth of William Henry Cavendish, 3rd Duke of Portland, in Bulstrode, Buckinghamshire (d.1809), British prime minister (1783, 1807–9).

1775 Founding of the Society for the Relief of Free Negroes Unlawfully Held in Bondage, by Benjamin Franklin and Benjamin Rush in Philadelphia, Pennsylvania, the first American society for the abolition of slavery.

1828 Publication of the *American Dictionary of the English Language*, compiled by Noah Webster (1758–1843).

1894 Opening of the first kinetoscope cinema in New York.

1900 Opening of the Paris International Exhibition, covering 547 acres and the biggest of its kind in European history.

1904 Birth of Sir John Gielgud in London (d.2000), leading Shakespearian actor and director, whose films include *Arthur* (1970, Oscar).

1917 Death of Ludwig Zamenhof (b.1859 in Białystok, Poland), oculist, philologist, and inventor of Esperanto.

1931 Issue of the *Highway Code* by Britain's Ministry of Transport.

1931 Proclamation of the Spanish Republic, with the overthrow and exile of King Alfonso XIII of Spain.

1950 Frank Hampson's comic strip hero 'Dan Dare, Pilot of the Future' appeared in the first edition of the *Eagle*.

1951 Death of Ernest Bevin (b.1881 in Winsford, Somerset), statesman and trade union leader, who built up the National Transport and General Workers' Union.

1956 Demonstration of the first videotape, in Chicago.

1969 Katherine Hepburn (1907–2003) and Barbra Streisand (b.1942) shared the Best Actress Oscar, with Hepburn becoming the first to win three Best Actress Oscars.

1981 Landing of US space shuttle Columbia after her maiden flight, the first reusable spacecraft.

1983 Introduction of the first cordless telephone in Britain.

1990 Nelson Mandela (b.1918) was guest of honour at a concert at Wembley Stadium, and thanked the world for his freedom after 26 years' imprisonment.

1991 Release of the 'Birmingham Six', convicted in 1975 for IRA pub bombings in Birmingham, UK.

APRIL

15

1452 Birth of Leonardo da Vinci at Vinci, Italy (d.1519), painter, architect, musician, engineer, and sculptor, whose most celebrated painting is the *Mona Lisa* (completed c.1504).

1755 Publication of the *Dictionary of the English Language* by Samuel Johnson (1709–84).

1793 Issue of the first £5 notes by the Bank of England.

1800 Birth of Sir James Clark Ross in London (d.1862), polar explorer; the *Ross Barrier*, *Sea*, and *Island* are named after him.

1817 Opening of the first American school for the deaf, in Hartford, Connecticut.

1843 Birth of Henry James in New York (d.1916), novelist, whose works include *The Portrait of a Lady* (1881).

1865 Death of Abraham Lincoln (b.1809 near Hodgenville, Kentucky), 16th president of the USA, from wounds received when he was shot the previous evening by John Wilkes Booth at Ford's Theatre, Washington, DC.

1912 The liner *Titanic* hit an iceberg in the N Atlantic and sank during her maiden voyage.

1925 Sir James Barrie donated the copyright fee for *Peter Pan* to Great Ormond Street Children's Hospital in London.

1940 Birth of Jeffrey Archer in Weston-Super-Mare, Somerset, writer and former parliamentarian.

1942 The George Cross was awarded to the Island of Malta.

1945 Liberation of the Nazi concentration camp at Bergen-Belsen by British and Canadian troops.

1955 Opening of the first McDonald's hamburger restaurant, in San Bernadino, California.

1959 Birth of Emma Thompson in London, actress, whose film credits include *Howards End* (1992, Oscar).

1970 Production of the first pocket calculator, by Canon.

1983 Opening of Tokyo Disneyland to the public.

1985 End of military rule in Brazil.

1989 Hillsborough Stadium, Sheffield, was the scene of the worst disaster in British sporting history, when 95 Liverpool fans died and 400 people were injured in a crush at the FA Cup semi-final match between Liverpool and Nottingham Forest.

1990 Mikhail Gorbachev was sworn in as the first (and last) executive president of USSR.

1994 Death of John Curry (b.1949 in Birmingham, West Midlands), figure-skating champion, gold medal winner at the 1976 winter Olympic Games.

APRIL

16

Feast of St Benedict Joseph Labre, patron saint of the homeless, tramps, and beggars.

1529 Death of Louis de Berquin (b.1485), French humanist, reformer, and heretic, burned at the stake.

1661 Birth of Charles Montagu, 1st Earl of Halifax, in Horton, Northamptonshire (d.1715), English Whig statesman, who established the National Debt and the Bank of England (1694).

1705 English physicist and mathematician Isaac Newton (1642–1727) was knighted by Queen Anne at Trinity College, London.

1746 Defeat of Charles Stuart, known as 'the Young Pretender' and 'Bonnie Prince Charlie' (1720–88), at the Battle of Culloden.

1800 Birth of William Chambers in Peebles, Borders (d.1883), publisher and writer, who founded the publishing firm of W. & R. Chambers with his brother, Robert (1802–71).

1850 Death of Marie Tussaud (b.1761 in Strasbourg, France), modeller in wax, who set up a permanent exhibition in Baker Street, London (1835), resited in Marylebone Road (1928) after a fire.

1854 Destruction of San Salvador, capital city of El Salvador, by an earthquake.

1856 Abolition of privateering with the signing of the Declaration of Paris.

1889 Birth of Charlie Chaplin in London (d.1977), actor and director, best known for his character with bowler hat, out-turned feet, moustache, and walking-cane.

1900 Issue of the world's first book of stamps.

1904 Death of Samuel Smiles (b.1812 in Haddington, Lothian), writer and social reformer, and editor of the *Leeds Times* (1838–42).

1912 US aviator Harriet Quimby (1875–1912) became the first woman to fly across the English Channel.

1918 Birth of Spike Milligan in Ahmadnagar, India (d.2002), British humorist, founder member of The Goons and a major influence on British humour.

1953 Launch of the Royal Yacht *Britannia*.

1964 Sentence was passed on the members of the gang who committed the 'Great Train Robbery'.

1972 Launch of Apollo 16 to make the fifth manned Moon landing.

1975 Seizure of Cambodian capital Phnom Penh by the Khmer Rouge, led by Pol Pot.

1988 Death of Khalil el-Wazir, also known as Abu Jihad (b.1935), Palestinian commando chief, assassinated in Tunis.

APRIL
17

National Day, Syria.

1421 The sea broke through dykes at Dort in The Netherlands, drowning more than 100,000 people.

1524 Discovery of New York Bay and the mouth of the Hudson River (present-day New York harbour) by Italian explorer Giovanni da Verrazano (1485–1528).

1895 The Treaty of Shimonoseki ended the Sino-Japanese war: China and Japan recognized the independence of Korea, and China ceded Formosa to Japan.

1897 Birth of Thornton Wilder in Madison, Wisconsin (d.1975), writer, whose works include the Pulitzer Prize-winning play *Our Town* (1938).

1930 Birth of Chris Barber in Welwyn Garden City, Hertfordshire, jazz musician, trombonist, and vocalist, who established the Chris Barber Jazz Band.

1937 Debut of cartoon characters Daffy Duck, Elmer J. Fudd, and Petunia Pig in the film *Porky's Duck Hunt*.

1941 The first successful helicopter flight was made by Igor Sikorsky (1889–1972).

1956 Introduction of Premium Savings Bonds in Britain.

1961 Attempted invasion of Cuba by Cuban exiles, at the Bay of Pigs.

1964 US aviator Geraldine Mock (b.1925) became the first woman to fly solo around the world.

1964 Introduction of the Ford Motor Company's new Mustang, with a base price of $2368.

1969 Representation of the People Act received the royal assent, enabling Britons over the age of 18 to receive the vote (previously age 22).

1969 Sirhan B. Sirhan (b.c.1943 in Palestine) was found guilty of the assassination of Senator Robert Kennedy in June 1968.

1969 Election of Bernadette Devlin (b.1947) as an Independent Unity candidate in Northern Ireland, becoming at 21 the youngest MP in the House of Commons since William Pitt.

1970 Apollo 13 landed safely after an oxygen tank exploded, causing a serious emergency; James Lovell, Fred Haise, and John Swigert were on board.

1977 Women in Liechtenstein were granted the right to vote.

1984 Death of WPC Yvonne Fletcher (b.1959 in Wiltshire), shot dead by gunmen from inside the Libyan embassy, London.

APRIL
18

Feast (Coptic Church) of St George (early 4th c), patron saint of archers, armourers, England, farmers, knights, plague, leprosy and syphilis sufferers, Portugal, scouts, and soldiers.

1775 US patriot Paul Revere (1735–1818) rode from Charlestown to Lexington to warn colonists of the arrival of British troops at the start of the American Revolution.

1881 Opening of the Natural History Museum in South Kensington, London.

1882 Birth of Leopold Stokowski in London (d.1977), conductor and composer, known for his role in Walt Disney's *Fantasia* (1940).

1906 A major earthquake in San Francisco at 5.13 a.m. killed around 3000 and caused tremendous damage.

1923 The first baseball game was played at the Yankee Stadium: the New York Yankees beat the Boston Red Sox 4–1.

1932 Introduction of business reply-paid envelopes in Britain by the G(eneral) P(ost) O(ffice).

1934 Opening of the world's first launderette in Fort Worth, Texas.

1945 Death of Sir John Ambrose Fleming (b.1849 in Lancaster, Lancashire), physicist, who invented the thermionic valve, and pioneered the application of electricity on a large scale.

1946 Formal dissolution of the League of Nations; its assets were handed over to the United Nations.

1949 Beginning of the first Scout 'bob-a-job' week in Britain.

1949 The Republic of Ireland Act came into force, making Eire a republic.

1955 Death of Albert Einstein (b.1879 in Ulm, Germany), mathematical physicist, who was awarded the 1921 Nobel Prize for Physics for his special (1905) and general (1916) theories of relativity.

1968 Purchase of London Bridge by Lake Havasu City, Arizona, for £1 million; it was dismantled, and eventually rebuilt there.

1978 Vote by the US Senate to give control over the Panama Canal to Panama on 31 December 1999.

1980 Independence of Zimbabwe, formerly Southern Rhodesia, from Britain.

1982 Salisbury, the capital of Zimbabwe, was renamed Harare.

1989 Storming of the Beijing Communist Party headquarters by thousands of Chinese students demanding democracy.

APRIL

19

1529 The Lutheran minority at the Diet of Speyer protested against restrictions on their teachings, and were first called 'Protestants'.

1587 Sir Francis Drake (c.1540–96) sank the Spanish fleet in the harbour of Cadiz.

1661 Introduction of postmarks in Britain by the Post Office.

1775 The Battle of Lexington and Concord was fought in Massachusetts, the first armed conflict of the American War of Independence.

1881 Death of Benjamin Disraeli, 1st Earl of Beaconsfield (b.1804 in London), British prime minister (1868, 1874–80).

1882 Death of Charles Darwin (b.1809 in Shrewsbury, Shropshire), naturalist, and pioneer in the field of evolutionary biology.

1897 John J. McDermott won the first Boston Marathon, in 2 hours, 55 minutes, 10 seconds.

1906 Death of Pierre Curie (b.1859 in Paris), physicist, and husband of Marie Curie, both sharing the 1903 Nobel Prize for Physics with Antoine Henri Becquerel for the discovery of radioactivity.

1935 Birth of Dudley Moore in London (d.2002), actor, comedian, and musician, whose films include *Arthur* (1981).

1943 Beginning of the Warsaw Ghetto uprising, a reaction to the daily transportation of Jews from the ghetto to the extermination camp at Treblinka.

1951 The first Miss World contest took place in London.

1954 Birth of Trevor Francis in Plymouth, Devon, soccer player, the first to be the subject of a £1 million transfer deal.

1956 Marriage of US actress Grace Kelly (1929–82) to Prince Rainier III of Monaco (1923–2005).

1958 Bobby Charlton (b.1937) played his first football game for England, against Scotland.

1965 The trial of Myra Hindley and Ian Brady for the 'Moors Murders' began.

1971 The Soviet Union launched the first manned spacelab, Salyut 1.

1992 Death of Frankie Howerd (b.1922 in London), comedian, his best-known role being that of a Roman slave in *Up Pompeii* (1970–71).

1993 Ending of the 51-day siege at the Branch Davidian compound near Waco, Texas, destroyed by fire; dozens of people died, including leader David Koresh (b.1960).

1997 More than 50,000 residents abandoned Grand Forks, North Dakota, when the Red River flooded.

APRIL

20

1657 The English navy destroyed the Spanish fleet in Santa Cruz harbour, Tenerife, and then the city.

1768 Death of Canaletto (b.1697 in Venice, Italy), painter, who produced popular series of views of London and elsewhere (1746–56).

1770 British navigator Captain James Cook (1728–79) reached New South Wales, Australia.

1792 France declared war on Austria, Prussia, and Sardinia, the start of the French Revolutionary wars.

1841 Publication of Edgar Allen Poe's first detective story, 'Murders in the Rue Morgue'.

1889 Birth of Adolf Hitler in Braunau, Upper Austria (d.1945), German dictator and Nazi leader.

1893 Birth of Harold Lloyd in Burchard, Nebraska (d.1971), film comedian, who became one of America's most popular daredevils in films such as *High and Dizzy* (1920).

1912 Death of Bram Stoker (b.1847 in Dublin, Ireland), novelist, and creator of *Dracula*.

1930 US aviators Charles (1902–74) and Anne (1906–2001) Lindbergh flew from Los Angeles to New York in 14 hours and 45 minutes, setting a transcontinental speed record.

1949 The first three-day Badminton horse trials were held at Badminton House, Gloucestershire, the seat of the Duke of Beaufort.

1949 Birth of Jessica Lange in Cloquet, Minnesota, actress, whose films include *Tootsie* (1982, Oscar).

1961 Birth of Nicholas Lyndhurst in Emsworth, Hampshire, actor, best known for his role as Rodney in *Only Fools and Horses* (1981–2003).

1968 Pierre Trudeau (1919–2000) was sworn in as prime minister of Canada.

1970 US president Richard Nixon announced the withdrawal of 150,000 troops from Vietnam.

1981 British snooker player Steve Davis (b.1957) won his first world title.

1984 Britain announced that Hong Kong would be returned to China in 1997.

1987 *Starlight Express* by Andrew Lloyd Webber (b.1948) broke the record for the most takings in a week in the history of Broadway, earning $606,081.

1992 Death of Benny Hill (b.1925 in Southampton, Hampshire), comedian and entertainer, best known for his own television show *The Benny Hill Show* (1955–68).

APRIL
21

Feast of St Beuno, patron saint of sick animals and sick children.

753 BC Traditionally, the founding of the city of Rome.

1649 The Maryland Assembly, Maryland, passed the Maryland Toleration Act, providing freedom of worship for all Christians.

1789 John Adams (1735–1826) was sworn in as 1st vice-president of the USA.

1816 Birth of Charlotte Brontë in Thornton, West Yorkshire (d.1855), whose masterpiece was *Jane Eyre* (1847).

1836 Defeat of the Mexicans by Texans, led by US soldier Sam Houston (1793–1863), on the San Jacinto, achieving independence for Texas.

1894 Premiere in London of *Arms and the Man*, a play by George Bernard Shaw (1856–1950).

1918 Death of Baron von Richthofen, the Red Baron (b.1882 in Wrocław, Poland), German World War 1 flying ace, who was killed over France.

1926 Birth of Princess Elizabeth Alexandra Mary in London, queen of the United Kingdom (from 1952).

1946 Death of John Maynard Keynes, 1st Baron Keynes (b.1883 in Cambridge, Cambridgeshire), economist, who advised the Treasury during both world wars.

1960 Inauguration of Brasilia as the new capital of Brazil, transferring the seat of national government from Rio de Janeiro.

1964 A new television channel, BBC 2, began broadcasting in Britain; the first programme broadcast was *Playschool*.

1972 Apollo 16 landed on a previously unexplored part of the Moon, the fifth mission by NASA to land men on the Moon; astronauts John Young and Charles Duke landed in the Descartes crater region.

1975 Resignation of Nguyen Van Thieu, president of South Vietnam.

1977 Opening of the musical *Annie* on Broadway, New York.

1983 New pound coins introduced in England and Wales.

1997 Gene Roddenberry, creator of *Star Trek*, and 23 others were the first to receive a space funeral, blasted into orbit from a Pegasus rocket.

APRIL

22

First Day of the Passover.

1370 The first stone of the Bastille, the French fortress in Paris, was laid by order of King Charles V.

1500 Discovery of Brazil by explorer Pedro Cabral (c.1467–c.1520).

1662 Death of John Tradescant (b.1608 in Meopham, Kent), gardener, who bequeathed his father's Musaeum Tradescantianum, Lambeth, to Elia Ashmole (1617–92).

1662 Incorporation of the Royal Society, a prestigious scientific institution in the UK.

1707 Birth of Henry Fielding at Sharpham Park, Glastonbury, Somerset (d.1754), novelist, whose works include *The History of Tom Jones, A Foundling* (1749).

1724 Birth of Immanuel Kant in Königsberg, Germany (d.1804), philosopher, whose main work is the *Critique of Pure Reason* (translated 1781).

1778 Death of James Hargreaves (b.c.1720, probably in Blackburn, Lancashire), illiterate weaver and carpenter, who invented the spinning jenny (c.1764), named after his daughter.

1833 Death of Richard Trevithick (b.1771 in Illogan, Cornwall), engineer, and pioneer of the steam engine.

1838 British vessel *Sirius* was the first steamship to cross the Atlantic.

1864 US Congress authorized the use of the phrase 'In God We Trust' on a 2-cent coin.

1908 Death of Sir Henry Campbell-Bannerman (b.1836 in Glasgow), British prime minister (1905–8).

1915 Germany used poison gas for the first time, at the second Battle of Ypres, during World War 1.

1916 Birth of Yehudi Menuhin in New York (d.1999), child prodigy and violinist, who founded near London a school for musically gifted children.

1933 Death of Sir Henry Royce (b.1863 in Alwalton, Cambridgeshire), engineer, who founded the firm of Royce Ltd in Manchester (1884) and Rolls-Royce Ltd (1906) with C. S. Rolls.

1964 Opening of the New York World's Fair.

1984 Britain broke off diplomatic relations with Libya, and ordered all Libyan embassy staff to leave Britain within seven days.

1993 Dedication of the US Holocaust Memorial Museum in Washington, DC.

1994 Death of Richard Nixon (b.1913 in Yorba Linda, California), 37th president of the USA; facing impeachment, in the Watergate scandal, he was the first US president to resign.

APRIL

23

Feast (Western Church) of St George (early 4th c), patron saint of archers, armourers, England, farmers, knights, plague, leprosy and syphilis sufferers, Portugal, scouts, and soldiers.

1564 Birth of William Shakespeare in Stratford-upon-Avon, Warwickshire (died on the same date in 1616), playwright, actor, and poet.

1804 Birth of Marie Taglioni in Stockholm, Sweden (d.1884), Italian ballet dancer, one of the first women to dance on pointes – the extreme tips of the toes.

1850 Death of William Wordsworth (b.1770 in Cockermouth, Cumbria), Romantic poet, whose works include *The Prelude* (1805); he became poet laureate in 1843.

1858 Birth of Max Planck in Kiel, Germany (d.1947), physicist, who introduced quantum theory (1900), for which he was awarded the 1918 Nobel Prize for Physics.

1867 Dismissal of plans for a Channel Tunnel by Emperor Napoleon III of France and Queen Victoria of Great Britain.

1893 Birth of Billy Smart in London (d.1966), circus proprietor.

1915 Death of Rupert Brooke (b.1887 in Rugby, Warwickshire), poet, who wrote *1914 and Other Poems* (1915).

1928 Birth of Shirley Temple Black in Santa Monica, California, actress and diplomatic official, whose films include *Curly Top* (1935).

1932 Opening of the Shakespeare Memorial Theatre at Stratford-upon-Avon, Warwickshire.

1962 Racing driver Stirling Moss was injured in a 110 mph crash at Goodwood, ending his career.

1965 Opening of the 270-mile-long Pennine Way in Britain, stretching from Edale in Derbyshire to Kirk Yetholm in Roxburghshire.

1967 Russian cosmonaut Vladimir Komarov (1927–67) became the first man to make two space flights.

1968 Britain's first decimal coins (5p and 10p) went into circulation, but were used as one-shilling and two-shilling pieces until decimalization (15 February 1971).

1982 Declaration by Key West, Florida, of its secession from the USA, taking the name the Conch Republic.

1985 Announcement by the Coca-Cola Company of a change in its formula, and introduction of New Coke.

1992 Opening of McDonald's first fast-food restaurant in Beijing, China.

1998 Death of James Earl Ray (b.1928 in Alton, Illinois), assassin, who shot and killed Martin Luther King Jr in 1968, and the following year was sentenced to 99 years in prison.

APRIL

24

1547 Defeat of the Protestant League of Schmalkalden by Holy Roman Emperor Charles V at the battle of Mühlberg.

1558 Marriage of Mary, Queen of Scots, to the Dauphin, later Francis II of France.

1731 Death of Daniel Defoe (b.1660 in London), writer, whose works include *Robinson Crusoe* (1719–20).

1743 Birth of Edmund Cartwright in Marnham, Nottingham (d.1823), inventor of the power loom (1785–90) and of a wool-combing machine (1790).

1800 Approval by US Congress of a bill establishing the Library of Congress in Washington, DC, with a $5000 allocation for the purchase of books.

1815 Birth of Anthony Trollope in London (d.1882), novelist, who began writing when he became postal surveyor in Ireland (1841).

1866 Planning of the first official branch of the Ku Klux Klan in the USA to oppose Reconstruction and the new rights being granted to blacks after the Civil War.

1900 First publication of the *Daily Express*, in London.

1915 Deportation of Armenians during World War 1 by the Ottoman Turkish Empire, leading to the massacre of between 600,000 and 1.5 million Armenians.

1916 Beginning of the Easter Rising in Dublin.

1924 Greece was proclaimed a Republic.

1942 Birth of Barbra Streisand in New York, singer, actress, and director, who has maintained parallel careers as a recording artist and film actress.

1949 End of sweet and chocolate rationing in Britain.

1953 Winston Churchill (1874–1965) was knighted by Queen Elizabeth II at Buckingham Palace, London.

1967 Death of Vladimir Komarov (b.1927 in Moscow), cosmonaut, who died when Soyuz 1 crashed to Earth.

1970 The People's Republic of China launched its first space satellite.

1986 Death of Wallis Simpson (b.1896 in Blue Ridge Summit, Pennsylvania), duchess of Windsor, the wife of Edward VIII, who abdicated in order to marry her.

1990 Launch of NASA's space shuttle Discovery carrying the Hubble space telescope into orbit 611.5 km/380 miles above the Earth.

1993 Explosion of an IRA truck bomb in London's financial district, killing one person and injuring 44.

APRIL

25

Anzac Day.
Feast of St Mark (fl.1st c), patron saint of glaziers, lawyers, and secretaries.

1599 Birth of Oliver Cromwell in Huntingdon, Cambridgeshire (d.1658), soldier and statesman, who became Lord Protector of England.

1684 Patenting of the thimble.

1769 Birth of Sir Marc Isambard Brunel in Hacqueville, France (d.1849), engineer, who built the 460-m/503-yd Thames Tunnel from Rotherhithe to Wapping.

1792 Death of Nicolas Jacques Pelletier, highwayman, first person under French law to be executed by guillotine.

1840 [Old Style calendar, New Style 7 May] Birth of Piotr Ilyich Tchaikovsky in Kamsko-Votkinsk, Russia (d.1893), composer, whose works include the ballet *Swan Lake* (1876–7).

1859 Construction work began on the Suez Canal, linking the Mediterranean and Red Seas.

1874 Birth of Guglielmo Marconi in Bologna, Italy (d.1937), physicist and inventor, whose successful experiments in wireless telegraphy led him to form the Marconi Telegraph Company in London (1899).

1917 Birth of Ella Fitzgerald in Newport News, Virginia (d.1996), jazz singer, often referred to as 'the first lady of song'.

1926 Premiere of Puccini's opera *Turandot* at La Scala, Milan, conducted by Arturo Toscanini (1867–1957).

1950 Chuck Cooper (b.1926) became the first African-American to play basketball in the NBA.

1959 Opening of the St Lawrence Seaway, a navigable channel from the Atlantic and the Gulf of St Lawrence to the Great Lakes, 143 km/89 miles long.

1961 Patenting of an integrated circuit by US electrical engineer Robert Noyce (1927–90).

1964 The head of Copenhagen's 'Little Mermaid' was stolen.

1969 Final episode of the British radio soap *The Dales*, also known as *Mrs Dale's Diary*, after 21 years and more than 5400 episodes.

1992 Islamic forces in Afghanistan took control of most of the capital of Kabul, following the collapse of the Communist government.

1995 Death of Ginger Rogers (b.1911 in Independence, Missouri), actress and dancer, whose films include *Top Hat* (1935).

2003 Vote by the Georgia legislature to remove the Confederate flag design from its state flag.

APRIL
26

121 Birth of Marcus Aurelius in Rome, Italy (d.180), Roman emperor.

1798 Birth of Eugène Delacroix in Charenton, France (d.1863), painter, a leader of the Romantic movement.

1828 Russia declared war on Turkey in support of Greece's fight for independence.

1865 Death of John Wilkes Booth (b.1839 near Bel Air, Maryland), assassin of US president Abraham Lincoln, killed in a shootout with Federal troops 11 days after Lincoln's death.

1880 Birth of Michel Fokine in St Petersburg, Russia, (d.1942), US choreographer, and pioneer of modern ballet.

1900 Birth of Charles Richter near Hamilton, Ohio (d.1985), seismologist, who devised with Beno Gutenberg the scale of earthquake strength which now bears his name.

1923 Marriage of King George VI, Duke of York, to Elizabeth Bowes-Lyon.

1928 Reopening of Madame Tussaud's in Marylebone Road, London, following the fire which destroyed the original Baker Street exhibition.

1937 Guernica, Northern Spain, was bombed and destroyed by German aircraft.

1945 Arrest of Henri Philippe Pétain (1856–1951), leader of France's collaboration with Germany during World War 2, on charges of treason.

1957 First broadcast of the BBC television programme *The Sky at Night*, presented by British astronomer Patrick Moore.

1959 Invasion of Panama by Cuba.

1964 Merger of the African nations of Tanganyika and Zanzibar to form Tanzania.

1986 An accident at a Soviet power station in Chernobyl, Kiev, resulted in the world's largest known nuclear disaster.

1989 Death of Lucille Ball (b.1911 in Celaron, New York), comedienne, known for her television shows such as *I Love Lucy* (1951–5).

1992 Celebration of Orthodox Easter by thousands of Russians for the first time since Bolshevik leaders vowed to crush Christianity.

1994 The first all-race elections for the national assembly and provincial parliaments took place in South Africa.

1999 Death of Jill Dando (b.1961 in Weston-Super-Mare, Avon), television newscaster, who co-presented BBC's *Crimewatch*, shot on her doorstep.

2001 The rules of table tennis underwent the most radical change in its 90-year history, the winner of a game now being the first to 11 points, not 21.

APRIL

27

Feast of St Zita, patron saint of bakers, housewives, and servants.

1296 Defeat of a Scottish army by the English under Edward I at the battle of Dunbar.

1521 Death of Ferdinand Magellan (b.c.1480 in Sabrosa or Porto, Portugal), navigator, killed by natives on the Philippine island of Mactan.

1737 Birth of Edward Gibbon in Putney, Surrey (d.1794), historian, whose major work was *The History of the Decline and Fall of the Roman Empire* (5 vols., 1776–88).

1759 Birth of Mary Wollstonecraft, married name Godwin, in London (d.1797), feminist, who wrote *Vindication of the Rights of Woman* (1792), advocating equality of the sexes.

1791 Birth of Samuel Morse in Charlestown, Massachusetts (d.1872), painter, and inventor of the Morse code.

1822 Birth of Ulysses S. Grant in Point Pleasant, Ohio (d.1885), 18th president of the USA (1869–77).

1828 Opening of the Zoological Gardens in Regent's Park, London.

1880 Patenting of the electrical hearing aid by Francis Clarke and M. G. Foster.

1904 Birth of C(ecil) Day-Lewis in Ballintubber, Co Kildare, Ireland (d.1972), poet and novelist, who became poet laureate in 1968.

1908 London hosted the Olympic Games for the first time.

1932 Inauguration of the London to Cape Town air service.

1946 First day of service for the first commercial carrier ship to be equipped with radar, the SS *African Star*.

1961 Independence of Sierra Leone after more than 150 years of British colonial rule.

1981 Marriage of former Beatle Ringo Starr (b.1940) to Barbara Bach at London's Marylebone Register Office.

1992 Betty Boothroyd was elected speaker of the House of Commons, London, the first woman to take up the position.

1993 Independence of Eritrea from Ethiopia following a UN-monitored referendum, after 30 years of civil war.

1997 Opening of the Tsing Ma Bridge, one of the longest road-and-rail suspension bridges in the world, connecting mainland Hong Kong with the islet of Chek Lap Kok.

2002 Completion of a 229 miles hike between Machynlleth and Cardiff by England cricketer Ian Botham, raising c.£900,000 for an appeal to build Wales' first children's hospital.

2005 The world's largest passenger plane, Airbus A380, completed its maiden flight.

APRIL

28

Feast of St Peter Martyr, patron saint of the Inquisition.

1220 The foundation stone of Salisbury Cathedral was laid.

1758 Birth of James Monroe in Westmoreland Co, Virginia (d.1831), 5th president of the USA (1817–25).

1788 Maryland became the 7th state of the Union.

1789 British seaman Fletcher Christian led the crew of the HMS *Bounty* in mutiny.

1801 Birth of Anthony Ashley Cooper, 7th Earl of Shaftesbury, in London (d.1885), factory reformer and philanthropist.

1878 Birth of Lionel Barrymore in Philadelphia, Pennsylvania (d.1954), actor, whose film roles include *Free Soul* (1931, Oscar).

1913 Patenting of the modern-day zip fastener, by electrical engineer Gideon Sundback, working for the Universal Fastener Company, USA.

1916 Birth of Ferruccio Lamborghini in Renazzo, Italy (d.1993), car designer and manufacturer.

1919 Imposition of the Treaty of Versailles by the Allies, causing Germany to make large reparations after World War 1.

1930 Opening of the telephone link between Britain and Australia.

1936 Farouk became the last reigning king of Egypt (1936–52).

1937 Birth of Jack Nicholson in Neptune, New Jersey, actor, whose films include *The Shining* (1980).

1945 Death of Benito Mussolini (b.1883 in Predappio, Romagna), Italian dictator (1922–43), executed by partisans.

1947 Anthropologist Thor Heyerdahl (1914–2002) and five others set off from South America to Polynesia on the *Kon-Tiki*, a balsa-wood raft, to prove his theories on the migration of early man.

1948 Birth of Terry Pratchett in Beaconsfield, Buckinghamshire, author and journalist, whose works include the series of fantasy novels, Discworld (from 1983).

1967 US heavyweight boxing champion Muhammad Ali (b.1942) refused to be inducted into the US Army and was stripped of his boxing title.

1969 Resignation of Charles de Gaulle (1890–1970) from the presidency of France.

1990 Closure of the musical *A Chorus Line* after 6137 performances and fifteen years on Broadway.

2001 US businessman Dennis Tito made history as the world's first 'space tourist', paying a reputed $20 million for his 6-day stay aboard the international space station.

APRIL
29

Feast of St Catherine of Siena (1347–80), patron saint of Dominicans.

1289 Capture of Tripoli by Qala'un, sultan of Egypt.

1429 Joan of Arc (c.1412–31) entered the besieged town of Orléans, France, and defeated the English.

1624 Appointment of Cardinal Richelieu (1585–1642) to the post of chief minister of the Royal Council by Louis XIII of France.

1863 Birth of William Randolph Hearst in San Francisco, California (d.1951), newspaper publisher and politician, whose life inspired the film *Citizen Kane* (1941).

1879 Birth of Sir Thomas Beecham in St Helens, Merseyside (d.1961), conductor, and founder of the Royal Philharmonic Orchestra.

1885 Women were permitted to sit examinations at Oxford University for the first time.

1899 Birth of Duke Ellington in Washington, DC (d.1974), composer, arranger, bandleader, and pianist.

1916 Collapse of the Easter Rising in Dublin, as Irish nationalists surrendered to British authorities.

1933 First use of numbered shirts to identify players in a British FA Cup final.

1936 Birth of Zubin Mehta in Mumbai (Bombay), India, conductor, who became musical director and conductor of many prestigious orchestras.

1937 Death of Wallace Carothers (b.1896 in Burlington, Iowa), industrial chemist, who developed nylon.

1943 Arrest of German theologian Dietrich Bonhoeffer (1906–1945) by the Nazis for his pro-Jewish activities.

1945 Allied forces reached Dachau concentration camp.

1945 Unconditional surrender of the German army in Italy to the Allies.

1958 Birth of Daniel Day-Lewis in London, actor, whose films include *My Left Foot* (1989, Oscar).

1968 Opening on Broadway of the musical *Hair*.

1980 Death of Sir Alfred Hitchcock (b.1899 in London), director, whose films include *Psycho* (1960).

1992 Rioting in Los Angeles followed the acquittal of four white police officers accused of beating African-American motorist Rodney King.

1997 US astronaut Jerry Linenger and Russian cosmonaut Vasily Tsibliyev made the first US–Russian space walk, from space station Mir.

APRIL

30

Feast (Eastern Church) of St James (the Great) (1st c), patron saint of pilgrims, Spain, knights, labourers, rheumatism sufferers, and soldiers.

311 Roman emperor Galerius Valerius Maximianus (c.250–311) issued an edict by which Christians were legally recognized in the Roman Empire.

1789 Inauguration of George Washington (1732–99) as the 1st president of the USA.

1803 America bought Louisiana and New Orleans from France, for around 3 cents per acre.

1812 Louisiana became the 18th state of the Union.

1883 Death of Edouard Manet (b.1832 in Paris), painter, a forerunner of the Impressionist movement, whose works include *Déjeuner sur l'herbe* (1863).

1900 Death of Casey Jones (b.1863 in Missouri), railroader and folk hero, who died in a crash involving the Cannonball Express.

1904 Opening of the World Fair in St Louis, Missouri.

1936 Death of A(lfred) E(dward) Housman (b.1859 near Bromsgrove, Hereford and Worcester), poet and scholar, whose work includes *A Shropshire Lad* (1896).

1945 Death by suicide of German dictator Adolf Hitler (b.1889) and Eva Braun, to whom he had been married for one day.

1958 *My Fair Lady* was staged in London.

1972 The Brighton Belle train made its final run from Victoria Station in London to Brighton.

1975 Saigon fell to Communist North Vietnamese forces.

1979 Opening of London's Jubilee underground line, running from Charing Cross to Stanmore.

1980 The Iranian embassy in London was seized by terrorists.

1983 Death of George Balanchine (b.1904 in St Petersburg, Russia), dancer and choreographer, who co-founded the New York Ballet.

1993 Tennis player Monica Seles (b.1973) was stabbed by a deranged fan of Steffi Graf during a match in Hamburg, Germany.

2002 The 42-year-old burgundy vintage MKII Jaguar, driven by John Thaw as Inspector Morse in all 33 episodes of the television drama series, was sold for £53,000 at auction.

2003 Announcement by Libyan foreign minister Abdel Rahman Shalgam that his government accepted responsibility for the 1998 bombing of Pan Am Flight 103 over Lockerbie, Scotland.

MAY
1

May Day. Labour Day.

1672 Birth of Joseph Addison in Milston, Wiltshire (d.1719), essayist and politician, who co-founded *The Spectator* (1711) with Sir Richard Steele.

1707 Union of the parliaments of England and Scotland.

1769 Birth of Arthur Wellesley, 1st Duke of Wellington in Dublin, Ireland (d.1852), British general and prime minister (1828–30).

1851 Opening of the Great Exhibition in the Crystal Palace in Hyde Park, London, by Queen Victoria; conceived by Prince Albert, the palace was designed by Joseph Paxton, the head gardener at Chatsworth, and contained over 300,000 panes of glass.

1873 First day of issue of postcards in the USA.

1904 The first football international outside Britain was played at Uccle, near Brussels; Belgium and France drew 3–3.

1927 The first hot in-flight meals were served by Imperial Airways on a flight from London to Paris.

1931 Completion of New York's Empire State Building, 449 m/1472 ft high with 102 floors.

1933 Inauguration of the Britain–India telephone system.

1941 Premiere of Orson Welles' film *Citizen Kane* in New York.

1949 Nationalization of the British gas industry.

1961 Opening of the first betting shops in Britain.

1963 James Whittaker of Redmond, Washington, was the first American to reach the summit of Everest.

1967 Rock singer Elvis Presley married Priscilla Beaulieu in Las Vegas, Nevada.

1968 Opening of the Legoland Family Park at Billund in Denmark, the first of four parks; the others are in Germany, the USA (California), and the UK (Windsor).

1977 Release of the film *Star Wars*, directed by George Lucas, and the first encounter with the tagline 'A long time ago in a galaxy far, far away …'

1978 Britain first celebrated the May Day holiday.

1994 Death of Ayrton Senna (b.1960 in São Paulo, Brazil), three times World Formula 1 racing champion, killed during the San Marino Grand Prix.

1997 Return of the Labour Party to power in Britain.

MAY

2

1519 Death of Leonardo da Vinci (b.1452 in Vinci, Florence), painter, architect, musician, engineer, and sculptor.

1670 The Hudson Bay Company was given a monopoly on trade into Hudson Bay, Canada.

1859 Birth of Jerome K. Jerome in Walsall, Staffordshire (d.1927), novelist and playwright, whose novels include *Three Men in a Boat* (1889).

1860 Birth of William Bayliss in Wolverhampton, West Midlands (d.1924), physiologist, who discovered secretin, the first known hormone.

1903 Birth of Dr Benjamin Spock in New Haven, Connecticut (d.1998), paediatrician, best known for *The Common Sense Book of Baby and Child Care* (1946).

1904 Birth of Bing Crosby in Tacoma, Washington (d.1977), singer and film star, whose recordings include 'White Christmas'.

1923 BBC radio broadcast the first *Woman's Hour* programme.

1936 Abyssinian emperor Haile Selassie and his family fled Addis Ababa, three days before its capture by Italy.

1939 US baseball player Lou Gehrig (1903–41) played his 2130th consecutive game, setting a new major-league baseball record.

1945 Surrender of Berlin to the 1st White Russian and 1st Ukrainian Armies during World War 2.

1949 Birth of Alan Titchmarsh in Ilkley, West Yorkshire, gardener and writer, presenter of television's *Ground Force* (1998–2002).

1952 Inauguration of the first turbo-jet airline service, with the flight of a British DH Comet from London to Johannesburg.

1959 Opening of Chapelcross, Scotland's first nuclear power station.

1965 First transmission of television programmes to 24 countries through the operation of the 'Early Bird' communications satellite.

1969 Maiden voyage of the British passenger liner *Queen Elizabeth II*.

1972 Death of J. Edgar Hoover (b.1895 in Washington, DC), director of the FBI from 1924.

1975 Birth of David Beckham in London, footballer, and husband of Victoria Adams (Posh Spice).

1982 Sinking of the Argentinian battleship *General Belgrano* by British submarine HMS *Conqueror* during the Falklands conflict.

1994 Nelson Mandela beat President F. W. de Klerk in South Africa's historic first all-race elections.

MAY

3

1469 Birth of Niccolò Machiavelli in Florence, Italy (d.1527), Italian statesman, writer, and political theorist, whose *Il Principe* (1532, The Prince) gave rise to the adjective *machiavellian*.

1747 Defeat of France by Britain at the first battle of Cape Finisterre in the War of Austrian Succession.

1810 Lord Byron swam the Hellespont (Dardanelles), Turkey.

1841 New Zealand was formally proclaimed a British colony.

1903 The first electrically powered train travelled through the Mersey Railway tunnel between Liverpool and Birkenhead.

1919 Birth of Pete Seeger in New York, folk singer and songwriter, whose songs include 'Where Have All the Flowers Gone?'.

1921 Birth of Sugar Ray Robinson in Detroit, Michigan (d.1989), professional boxer, who held the world welterweight (1946–51) and middleweight (1950–51) titles.

1928 Birth of James Brown in Barnwell, South Carolina, pop singer, songwriter, and producer, who by 1962 had become America's leading rhythm and blues star.

1934 Birth of Sir Henry Cooper in Bellingham, Kent, heavyweight boxer, who was the only man to win the Lonsdale belt outright on three occasions.

1936 US baseball player Joe DiMaggio (1914–99) made his major-league debut with the New York Yankees.

1937 US author Margaret Mitchell (1900–1949) won the Pulitzer Prize in fiction for *Gone With the Wind* (1936).

1944 Production of synthetic quinine by Dr R. B. Woodward and Dr William Doering at Harvard University.

1951 Opening of the Festival of Britain in London by King George VI.

1952 Landing of the first aeroplane, a ski-modified US Air Force C-47, at the geographic North Pole.

1956 British television station Granada made its first broadcast.

1959 Birth of Ben Elton in Catford, London, stand-up comedian, actor, writer, and novelist.

1968 The first heart-transplant operation in Britain was carried out by Dr Donald Ross at the National Heart Hospital, London.

1999 More than 55 tornadoes hit Kansas and Oklahoma, including one measuring F5 on the Fujita scale.

2001 The USA lost its seat on the UN Human Rights Commission for the first time since the formation of the commission in 1947.

MAY

4

Feast of St Florian, patron saint of firemen.

1471 The Yorkists defeated the Lancastrians at the Battle of Tewkesbury in the Wars of the Roses.

1493 Pope Alexander VI issued three papal bulls dividing discoveries made by explorer Christopher Columbus between Spain and Portugal.

1626 Dutch explorer Peter Minuit (c.1580–1638) landed on what is now Manhattan Island.

1655 Birth of Bartolommeo Cristofori in Padua, Italy (d.1731), harpsichord maker, usually credited with the invention of the pianoforte (c.1710).

1780 The first Derby: the name of the race was decided at the toss of a coin between the 12th Earl of Derby and Sir Charles Bunbury; Bunbury's horse Diomed won the race.

1820 Birth of Joseph Whitaker in London (d.1895), publisher, who established *Whitaker's Almanack* (1868).

1827 Birth of John Hanning Speke in Bideford, Devon (d.1864), explorer, who was the first European to see Lake Victoria.

1896 Founding of the British newspaper *Daily Mail*, by journalist and newspaper magnate Alfred Harmsworth (1865–1922), 1st Viscount Northcliffe.

1923 Birth of Eric Sykes in Oldham, Lancashire, comedy writer and performer.

1926 Beginning of the General Strike in Britain, organized by the Trades Union Congress (TUC) in support of the miners' campaign to resist wage cuts.

1932 US Mafia boss Al Capone (1899–1947), who became USA's Public Enemy Number One, started a prison sentence for tax evasion.

1973 The tallest office building in the world, the Sears Tower in Chicago, Illinois, was 'topped out' with the completion of the 110th storey (443 m/1454 ft).

1979 Britain's first female prime minister, Margaret Thatcher (b.1925), took office.

1982 Sinking of the British destroyer HMS *Sheffield* by an Exocet missile during the Falklands War.

1994 Signing of an accord on Palestinian autonomy by Yitzhak Rabin and Yasser Arafat, Israeli and Palestinian leaders, granting self-rule in the Gaza Strip and Jericho.

1998 US Unabomber (UNiversities and Airlines) Ted Kaczynski (b.1942) was given four life sentences plus 30 years, in a plea bargain that spared him the death penalty.

2005 A record bid for sculpture at auction was made when Brancusi's *Bird in Space* sold for $27,456,000 at Christies' of London.

MAY
5

1646 Surrender of Charles I to a Scottish army at Newark, following his defeat at the battle of Naseby in the English Civil War.

1760 The first hanging took place at Tyburn, London.

1818 Birth of Karl Marx in Trier, Germany (d.1883), social philosopher, the founder of international Communism.

1821 Death of Emperor Napoleon I (b.1769 in Ajaccio, Corsica), in exile on the Isle of St Helena.

1830 Birth of John Batterson Stetson in Orange, New Jersey (d.1906), hat manufacturer, whose name was given to the wide-brimmed cowboy hat.

1835 The first train ran on Belgium's national railway, from Brussels to Malines.

1865 The first train robbery took place at South Bend, Ohio.

1914 Birth of Tyrone Power in Cincinnati, Ohio (d.1958), actor, whose films include *Jesse James* (1939).

1930 British pioneer aviator Amy Johnson (1903–41) left Croydon, near London, on her solo flight to Australia.

1943 Birth of Michael Palin in Sheffield, South Yorkshire, scriptwriter, actor, and novelist, best known as a member of the Monty Python team and for his television travel programmes.

1952 Queen Elizabeth II moved into Buckingham Palace, London.

1961 Astronaut Alan Shepard (1923–98) became the first American in space, in the capsule Freedom 7.

1963 Launch of the first all-British satellite, Ariel 3, from the USA.

1975 Publication of the *Scottish Daily News*, the first workers cooperative national newspaper.

1980 SAS commandos stormed the Iranian Embassy, London, killing four of five gunmen and freeing 19 hostages.

1981 Death of Bobby Sands (b.1954 in Belfast), Irish revolutionary, who went on hunger-strike in protest against the authorities' refusal to treat himself and his fellow IRA prisoners as 'political'.

2000 Grand conjunction of the Sun, Moon, Mercury, Venus, Mars, Jupiter, and Saturn.

2004 A record $104 million was paid for a painting when Sotheby's, New York, sold Picasso's *Garçon à la pipe* (1905, Boy with a Pipe).

2005 Election of Tony Blair (b.1953) to a third term as British prime minister.

MAY
6

Feast (Western Church) of St John the Apostle, patron saint of publishers, writers, and theologians.

1626 Purchase of Manhattan Island from local Indians for goods to the value of $24 by colonist Peter Minuit (?1580–1638).

1835 First publication of the *New York Herald*.

1840 Issue of the penny black and the twopenny blue, the first adhesive British stamps, by the General Post Office.

1851 Patenting of the Yale lock by US lock manufacturer and inventor Linus Yale (1821–68).

1856 Birth of Robert Peary in Cresson Springs, Pennsylvania (d.1920), naval commander and explorer, who on 6 April 1909 was in the first team to reach the North Pole.

1856 Birth of Sigmund Freud in Freiburg, Moravia, now Príbor, Czech Republic (d.1939), founder of psychoanalysis.

1868 [Old Style calendar, New Style 18 May] Birth of Nicholas II near St Petersburg, Russia (d.1918), last tsar of Russia (1895–1917), shot with his family at Yekaterinburg.

1882 The Phoenix Park murders, Dublin, were carried out by 'The Invincibles', a terrorist nationalist group.

1889 Opening of the Universal Exposition in Paris, to mark the dedication of the recently completed Eiffel Tower.

1895 Birth of Rudolf Valentino (Rodolpho Guglielmi) in Castellaneta, Italy (d.1926), actor, the leading 'screen lover' of the 1920s.

1910 Death of Edward VII (b.1841 in London), king of the United Kingdom (1901–10).

1915 Birth of Orson Welles in Kenosha, Wisconsin (d.1985), director, producer, writer, and actor, whose *Citizen Kane* (1941) was a landmark in cinema.

1937 The German airship *Hindenburg* burst into flames as it was landing in New Jersey.

1954 British athlete and neurologist Roger Bannister (b.1929) became the first man to run the mile in under 4 minutes (3 minutes 59·4 seconds).

1959 Sale of a painting of a Dutch girl by Picasso (1881–1973) in London for $154,000, setting the record for the highest price paid for a painting by a living artist.

1961 Tottenham Hotspur became the first football team to achieve the double; already League champions, they won the FA Cup.

1966 Sentencing of Myra Hindley (1942–2002) and Ian Brady (b.1938) for the 'Moors Murders'.

1994 Official opening of the Channel Tunnel, linking Britain and France.

MAY

7

1274 Opening of the second Council of Lyon in France, to regulate the election of the pope.

1663 Opening of the Theatre Royal, Drury Lane, London.

1765 Launch of British battleship HMS *Victory*, Nelson's flagship at the Battle of Trafalgar (1805), at Chatham.

1812 Birth of Robert Browning in London (d.1889), poet, the husband of Elizabeth Barrett Browning.

1833 Birth of Johannes Brahms in Hamburg, Germany (d.1897), composer.

1847 Birth of Archibald Philip Primrose, 5th Earl of Rosebery, in London (d.1929), British prime minister (1894–5).

1876 Birth of Samuel Courtauld in Braintree, Essex (d.1947), industrialist, who promoted the British rayon and nylon industry, and was patron of art and music.

1888 Inventor and philanthropist George Eastman (1854–1932) began sales of his Kodak camera in America.

1907 The first Isle of Man T(ourist) T(rophy) motorcycle race was held.

1909 Birth of Edwin Land in Bridgeport, Connecticut (d.1991), inventor of the instant camera, and producer of the light-polarizing filter material 'Polaroid'.

1915 Sinking of the Cunard passenger liner *Lusitania* by a German U-boat in the Irish Sea, with great loss of life.

1928 The voting age for women in Britain was reduced from 30 to 21 years.

1941 Glenn Miller and his Orchestra recorded 'Chattanooga Choo Choo', said to be the first gold record when it sold over 1 million copies.

1945 Unconditional surrender of Germany to the Allies at Reims.

1954 Surrender of the French forces, ending the Viet Minh siege at Dien Bien Phu, North Vietnam.

1976 Italy's worst earthquake to date, measuring 6.5 on the Richter scale, killed over 550 people and left 80,000 homeless.

1994 Recovery of Norway's most famous painting, Edvard Munch's *The Scream* (1893), nearly three months after its theft from an Oslo museum.

1998 Agreement between Daimler-Benz and Chrysler for the purchase of Chrysler Corporation for more than $37 billion.

1999 Start of a three-day visit by Pope John Paul II (1920–2005) to Romania; his first visit to a country with an Orthodox Christian majority.

2000 Inauguration of Vladimir Putin (b.1952) as president of Russia.

MAY
8

1541 Discovery of the Mississippi R by Spanish explorer Hernando de Soto (1496–1542); he called it Rio de Espiritu Santo.

1559 The Act of Supremacy made Queen Elizabeth I Supreme Governor of the Church of England.

1660 Restoration of the monarchy in Britain.

1828 Birth of Henri Dunant in Geneva, Switzerland (d.1910), philanthropist, influential in the founding of the International Red Cross and the emergence of the Geneva Convention.

1880 Death of Gustave Flaubert (b.1821 in Rouen, France), novelist, best known for his masterpiece *Madame Bovary* (1857).

1884 Birth of Harry S. Truman in Lamar, Missouri (d.1972), 33rd president for the USA.

1886 First production of Coca-Cola by Dr John Pemberton at Jacob's Pharmacy in Atlanta, Georgia.

1903 Death of Paul Gauguin (b.1848 in Paris), Post-Impressionist painter, whose works include *The Vision After the Sermon* (1888).

1926 Birth of Sir David Attenborough in London, naturalist and broadcaster, whose documentaries include *Planet Earth* (2006).

1935 Birth of Jack Charlton in Ashington, Northumberland, footballer, who played for Leeds United, and also for England, later becoming manager of the Republic of Ireland.

1940 Birth of Peter Benchley in New York, author, best known for his novel *Jaws* (1974).

1945 VE (Victory in Europe) Day, celebrating the end of the war with Germany.

1956 First performance of John Osborne's play *Look Back in Anger* at the Royal Court Theatre, London.

1962 The last trolley buses ran in London.

1980 Announcement by the World Health Organization that 'smallpox is eradicated throughout the world'.

1981 Britain's 100th FA Cup took place: Manchester City 1, Tottenham Hotspur 1 (see 14 May).

1983 Opening of the Thames Barrier in London, a tidal barrier built across the Thames' approach to London to reduce risk of floods.

2000 Announcement by scientists in Japan and Germany that they had mapped chromosome 21, associated with Down's syndrome, epilepsy, Lou Gehrig's disease, and Alzheimer's disease.

MAY
9

1502 Christopher Columbus (1451–1506) left Cadiz, Spain, on his fourth and final voyage.

1671 Disguised as a clergyman, Irish adventurer Thomas Blood (c.1618–80) attempted to steal the Crown Jewels from the Tower of London.

1785 Patenting of a beer-pump handle, by British inventor Joseph Bramah (1748–1814).

1800 Birth of John Brown in Torrington, Connecticut (d.1859), abolitionist; the song 'John Brown's Body' commemorates the Harper's Ferry raid for which he was hanged.

1860 Birth of Sir J. M. Barrie in Kirriemuir, Angus (d.1937), novelist and playwright, whose works include *Peter Pan* (1904).

1874 Birth of Howard Carter in Swaffham, Norfolk (d.1939), archaeologist, who discovered the tomb of Tutankhamun (1922).

1920 Birth of Richard Adams in Newbury, Berkshire, novelist, whose works include *Watership Down* (1972).

1927 At the first world professional snooker championship, held in Birmingham, UK, Joe Davis beat Tom Dennis 20–11; the prize money was 10s 6d (just over 50 pence).

1927 Canberra replaced Melbourne as the capital of Australia.

1931 Death of Albert Michelson (b.1852 in Strzelno, Poland), US physicist, who recognized the speed of light as a fundamental constant.

1934 Birth of Alan Bennett in Leeds, West Yorkshire, writer, whose work includes *Talking Heads* (1987).

1936 Birth of Glenda Jackson in Birkenhead, Merseyside, actress and politician, a leading member of the Royal Shakespeare Company, who became a Labour MP in 1992.

1936 Birth of Albert Finney in Salford, Greater Manchester, actor, whose performance in *Saturday Night and Sunday Morning* (1960) established him as a star.

1949 Opening of Britain's first self-service launderette in Queensway, London.

1962 Pop group The Beatles signed their first recording contract, with EMI Parlophone.

1972 Twelve Israeli soldiers disguised as maintenance staff stormed a hijacked aeroplane at Lod airport, Tel Aviv, releasing the 100 hostages on board.

1986 Death of Tenzing Norgay (b.1914 in Tsa-chu, near Makalu, Nepal), Sherpa, who succeeded in reaching the summit of Everest with Sir Edmund Hillary (b.1919).

1994 Quarantine of Kinshasa, capital of Zaire, after an outbreak of the Ebola virus.

1994 The newly elected parliament of South Africa chose Nelson Mandela (b.1918) to be the country's first black president.

MAY

10

Feast (Eastern Church) of St Simon, patron saint of fishers.

1566 Death of Leonhard Fuchs (b.1501 in Wemding, Germany), physician and botanist; the genus Fuchsia was named after him.

1788 Birth of Augustin Jean Fresnel in Broglie, France (d.1827), physicist, known for the development of the *Fresnel lens*.

1850 Birth of Sir Thomas Johnstone Lipton, in Glasgow, Strathclyde (d.1931), businessman and philanthropist, who opened the first of his many grocery shops in 1870.

1857 Beginning of the Indian Mutiny, an uprising against British rule in India.

1869 Completion of the US transcontinental railroad, linking the Union Pacific and Central Pacific railways.

1886 The British FA approved the giving of caps to players appearing in international matches.

1899 Birth of Fred Astaire in Omaha, Nebraska (d.1987), actor and dancer, who with Ginger Rogers (1911–95) revolutionized the film musical with his original tap-dance routines.

1907 First celebration of Mother's Day, founded by Anna Jarvis, in Philadelphia, Pennsylvania.

1920 Death of John Wesley Hyatt (b.1837 in Starkey, New York), inventor, whose products included celluloid, the first synthetic plastic.

1924 Appointment of J. Edgar Hoover (1895–1972) as head of the USA's Federal Bureau of Investigation.

1937 Frozen asparagus was sold by Smedley's of Wisbech, Cambridgeshire – Britain's first frozen food.

1940 Winston Churchill took over as British prime minister after the resignation of Neville Chamberlain.

1946 Birth of Maureen Lipman in Kingston-upon-Hull, actress and writer, whose books include *How Was It for You?* (1985).

1957 Birth of Sid Vicious (John Ritchie) in London (d.1979), member of the punk rock band The Sex Pistols.

1963 The British pop group The Rolling Stones made their first recordings.

1973 The Irish Republic voted to join the EEC.

2003 Re-election of David Oddsson (b.1948) as prime minister of Iceland, Europe's longest-serving prime minister (1991–2004).

MAY
11

Feast (Eastern Church) of Sts Cyril (c.827–69) and Methodius (c.825–85), patron saints of ecumenists.

330 Dedication of Constantinople, named after Emperor Constantine, as the new capital of the Roman Empire.

1573 Henry III (1551–89) became the first elected king of Poland.

1788 Death of William Pitt, 1st Earl of Chatham (b.1708 in Hayes, London), statesman, who formed a new ministry in 1766, but ill health contributed to his resignation in 1768.

1811 Birth of the original Siamese twins, Chang and Eng Bunker, in Siam; they were joined at the chest.

1854 Birth of Ottmar Mergenthaler in Hachtel, Germany (d.1899), inventor of the Linotype typesetting machine.

1858 Minnesota became the 32nd state of the Union.

1888 Birth of Irving Berlin in Temun, Russia (d.1989), composer, whose works include the musical *Annie Get Your Gun* (1946).

1889 Birth of Paul Nash in London (d.1946), landscape painter, and official war artist in both World Wars.

1904 Birth of Salvador Dalí in Figueras, Spain (d.1989), artist, a principal figure of the Surrealist movement.

1908 Laying of the foundation stone for the Royal Liver Building, Liverpool.

1927 Founding of the Academy of Motion Picture Arts and Sciences, widely known for its annual awards for creative merit and craftsmanship in film production.

1950 Birth of Jeremy Paxman in Leeds, West Yorkshire, television presenter, journalist, and writer.

1964 Opening of Sir Terence Conran's first Habitat shop in London.

1981 Death of Bob Marley (b.1945 in St Ann's, near Kingston, Jamaica), singer, guitarist, and composer of reggae music, whose songs include 'No Woman, No Cry'.

1981 First performance of Sir Andrew Lloyd Webber's *Cats* in London.

1985 A wooden stand at Bradford City Football Club caught fire, killing 56 people.

1987 Commencement of the trial of former Nazi Gestapo chief Klaus Barbie (1913–91), known as the Butcher of Lyon.

1998 India exploded three atomic bombs underground at a desert site near the Pakistan border, its first nuclear tests in 24 years.

1999 The solar wind died away almost completely for 24 hours, allowing the Earth's magnetic field to reach as far as the Moon, in the longest-lasting decrease ever observed.

MAY

12

Feast of St Pancras of Rome (?–304), patron saint of children.

1191 Marriage of King Richard the Lionheart (1157–99) and Berengaria of Navarre (c.1163–1230).

1792 Patenting of a regularly self-flushing toilet by John Ashley.

1812 Birth of Edward Lear in London (d.1888), artist and writer, remembered for his illustrated books of travels, and for his books of nonsense verse.

1820 Birth of Florence Nightingale, known as the Lady of the Lamp, in Florence, Italy (d.1910), hospital reformer, who led a team of nurses at Scutari during the Crimean War.

1828 Birth of Dante Gabriel Rossetti in London (d.1882), poet and painter, a founder member of the Pre-Raphaelite Brotherhood.

1870 Purchase of Manitoba by Canada from the Hudson's Bay Company.

1910 Birth of Dorothy Mary Hodgkin in Cairo, Egypt (d.1994), British biochemist, who won the 1964 Nobel Prize for Chemistry.

1926 First performance of Shostakovich's First Symphony.

1926 Ending of a nine-day national strike in Britain, organized by the TUC (Trades Union Congress) in support of the miners' campaign to resist wage cuts.

1932 The body of the kidnapped son of Charles (1902–74) and Anne (1907–2001) Lindbergh was found in woods in Hopewell, New Jersey.

1935 Founding of the self-help organization Alcoholics Anonymous in Akron, Ohio, by William Griffith Wilson, known as Bill W (1895–1951).

1937 Transmission of the BBC's first outside broadcast, the coronation of King George VI.

1942 Birth of Susan Hampshire in London, actress, whose TV credits include *Monarch of the Glen* (2000–2005).

1943 Surrender of General von Arnim, German commander in North Africa, and the ending of organized Axis resistance in Tunisia during World War 2.

1951 The first H-bomb test took place on Enewetak Atoll in the mid-Pacific.

1971 Marriage of Rolling Stones rock star Mick Jagger (b.1943) to Bianca de Macias.

1981 Riots took place in Belfast, following the deaths of hunger strikers.

2002 Arrival of former US president Jimmy Carter in Cuba, the first current or former president of the USA to visit since Fidel Castro's rise to power in 1959.

MAY
13

1568 Defeat of Mary, Queen of Scots (1542–87), at the Battle of Langside in Glasgow.

1787 The first fleet of convict ships left England, carrying the prisoners to a new penal colony in Australia.

1835 Death of John Nash (b.1752 in London), architect and city planner, responsible for the design of many areas of central London.

1842 Birth of Sir Arthur Sullivan in London (d.1900), composer, known for his collaboration with W. S. Gilbert (from 1871) in their series of comic operas.

1846 US Congress formally declared war on Mexico over California, although fighting had begun days earlier.

1873 Patenting of the sewing machine lamp-holder by Ludwig Wolf of Avon, Connecticut.

1884 Death of Cyrus McCormick (b.1809 in Rockbridge Co, Virginia), inventor of the reaper (1831), whose company manufactured over 6 million machines during his lifetime.

1906 Appointment of Polish physicist Marie Curie (1867–1934) as professor at the Sorbonne, Paris.

1907 Birth of Daphne du Maurier in London (d.1989), novelist, whose works include *Rebecca* (1938).

1914 Birth of Joe Louis in Lafayette, Alabama (d.1981), boxer, who held the world heavyweight title for a record 12 years.

1918 First day of issue for airmail postage stamps in the USA, available in denominations of 6, 16, and 24 cents.

1927 Black Friday: start of the collapse of the economic system in Germany.

1937 Birth of Trevor Baylis in Kilburn, London, engineer and inventor, best known for his 'wind-up' radio.

1941 Martin Bormann (1900–?1945) became deputy leader of Germany's Nazi party.

1950 Birth of Stevie Wonder in Saginaw, Michigan, blind soul singer, songwriter, and instrumentalist.

1961 Death of Gary Cooper (b.1901 in Helena, Montana), actor, the archetypal hero of many Westerns, notably *High Noon* (1952).

1981 Pope John Paul II (1920–2005) was shot and wounded in St Peter's Square by Mehmet Ali Agca.

1992 Three astronauts walked in space together for the first time, repairing the Intelsat-6 satellite from the US Endeavour in a walk lasting 8 hours, 29 minutes.

1995 British mountaineer Alison Hargreaves (1963–95) became the first woman, and the second person, in history to climb Everest without oxygen or the help of Sherpas.

MAY

14

1686 Birth of Gabriel Fahrenheit in Gdańsk, Poland (d.1736), inventor of the alcohol thermometer (1709) and the mercury thermometer (1714).

1796 British physician Edward Jenner (1749–1823) innoculated James Phipps in the first public trial of vaccination.

1804 US explorers Meriwether Lewis (1774–1809) and William Clark (1770–1838) left St Louis to explore the Louisiana Territory.

1904 Opening of the first Olympic Games to be held in the USA, in St Louis, Missouri.

1913 Establishment of the Rockefeller Foundation by industrialist and philanthropist John D. Rockefeller (1839–1937) with $1000 million, the largest gift of money to date.

1918 Death of James Gordon Bennett (b.1841 in New York), newspaper proprietor, who sent Stanley to find Livingstone in 1870.

1919 Death of H. J. Heinz (b.1844 in Pittsburgh, Pennsylvania), food manufacturer, who co-founded the '57 varieties' company.

1926 Birth of Eric Morecambe (Eric Bartholomew), in Morecambe, Lancashire (d.1984), comedian, who teamed up with Ernie Wise to form Britain's leading comedy double-act.

1940 Formation of the Local Defence Volunteers, later called the Home Guard, in Britain.

1944 Birth of George Lucas in Modesto, California, director, the creator of *Star Wars*.

1948 Creation of the independent state of Israel, with David Ben-Gurion (1886–1973) as first prime minister.

1955 Signing of the Warsaw Pact by representatives from the Soviet Union, Albania, Bulgaria, Czechoslovakia, East Germany, Hungary, Poland, and Romania.

1964 Egypt diverted the course of the R Nile to make way for the Aswan High Dam.

1973 Launch of US Skylab 1, which orbited the earth 34,981 times before its return on 11 July 1979.

1981 Replay of the 100th British FA Cup: Manchester City 2, Tottenham Hotspur 3.

1987 Death of Rita Hayworth (b.1918 in New York), actress, who partnered both Fred Astaire and Gene Kelly in musicals of the 1940s.

1998 Death of Frank Sinatra (b.1915 in Hoboken, New Jersey), singer and actor, whose films include *From Here to Eternity* (1953, Oscar).

2004 Australian Mary Donaldson (b.1972 in Tasmania) married Danish Crown Prince Frederik (b.1968 in Copenhagen), becoming Crown Princess Mary.

MAY
15

Feast of St Dympna (9th c), patron saint of epileptics and the mentally ill.

1567 Birth of Claudio Monteverdi in Cremona, Italy (d.1643), composer and violist, whose works contained tone colours and harmonies well in advance of their time.

1718 Patenting of the world's first machine-gun by its British designer, James Puckle.

1848 Birth of Carl Wernicke in Tarnowitz, Germany (d.1905), neurologist, who studied brain damage leading to loss of language ability.

1860 Defeat of the superior Neapolitan army at the Battle of Calatafimi by Italian patriot Garibaldi (1807–82), with 1000 volunteers.

1863 Birth of Frank Hornby in Liverpool (d.1936), inventor of Meccano, who produced the Hornby model railway in 1920.

1895 Death of Joseph Whitaker (b.1820 in London), publisher, the founder of *Whitaker's Almanack*.

1909 Birth of James Mason in Huddersfield, West Yorkshire (d.1984), actor, whose films include *The Verdict* (1982).

1918 Inauguration of the first regular air-mail service between New York and Washington, operated by the US Navy.

1928 Dr Vincent Welsh was the first doctor in the new flying-doctor service, inaugurated in Cloncurry, Queensland, Australia.

1930 Ellen Church became the world's first air hostess; the flight was Boeing 80A from Oakland, California to Cheyenne, Wyoming.

1940 First sales of nylon stockings in the USA.

1941 First flight of Britain's first jet-propelled aircraft, designed by aviator and inventor Sir Frank Whittle (1907–96), at Cranwell.

1957 Britain's first H-bomb was dropped at a nuclear testing site in the Pacific Ocean.

1963 US astronaut L. Gordon Cooper (1927–2004) began the final mission of the Project Mercury space programme in Faith 7, orbiting Earth 22 times and becoming the first man to sleep in space.

1972 George Wallace (1919–98), governor of Alabama, was shot and crippled in an assassination attempt during his US presidency campaign.

1988 Withdrawal of Soviet troops from Afghanistan, more than eight years after entering the country.

2001 An empty runaway freight train travelled c.70 miles through Ohio before a railway employee jumped on board and brought it to a halt.

MAY
16

Feast of St Brendan the Navigator (484–577), patron saint of sailors.

1763 First meeting of Dr Johnson and James Boswell, in Tom Davie's bookshop, Russell Street, London.

1770 Marriage of the future Louis XVI to Marie Antoinette, daughter of Empress Maria Theresa of Austria.

1831 Birth of David Hughes in London (d.1900), inventor, whose products include a telegraph typewriter (1855) and a carbon microphone (1878).

1888 Demonstration of the first gramophone by inventor Emile Berliner (1851–1929) in Philadelphia, Pennsylvania.

1905 Birth of Henry Fonda in Grand Island, Nebraska (d.1982), actor, whose films include *On Golden Pond* (1981, Oscar).

1913 Birth of Woody Herman in Milwaukee, Wisconsin (d.1987), bandleader, alto saxophonist, and clarinettist, a leader of the swing era of the 1930s and 1940s.

1920 Canonization of Joan of Arc (c.1412–31).

1929 Presentation of the first Academy Awards in Hollywood.

1938 Britain's WVS (Women's Voluntary Service) was begun by the Marchioness of Reading; it became 'Royal' in 1966.

1943 Breaching of the Mohne, Eder, and Sorpe dams in Germany by 19 Lancaster bombers of 617 squadron, led by Guy Gibson, using special 'bouncing bombs' invented by Sir Barnes Wallis.

1946 Opening of the musical *Annie Get Your Gun* on Broadway at the Imperial Theatre, starring Ethel Merman (1908–84).

1952 Birth of Pierce Brosnan in Co Meath, Ireland, actor, best known for his role as James Bond, first played in *Goldeneye* (1995).

1969 Touch-down of Soviet spacecraft Venera 5 on Venus.

1983 Introduction of wheel clamps in London for illegally parked vehicles.

1985 Announcement by scientists at the British Antarctic Survey that they had found a hole in the ozone layer in Antarctica.

1990 Death of Sammy Davis Jr (b.1925 in New York), singer, actor, and dancer, whose films include *Porgy and Bess* (1959).

1990 Death of Jim Henson (b.1936 in Greenville, Mississippi), puppeteer, the creator of the Muppets.

1999 Picasso's painting *Woman Nude Before Garden* (1956) was damaged by a mental patient in Amsterdam's Stedelijk Museum.

MAY
17

1642 French colonial administrator Paul de Chomedy de Maisonneuve (1612–76) landed on Montreal Island, and founded the town Ville-Marie.

1749 Birth of Edward Jenner in Berkeley, Gloucestershire (d.1823), physician, famous for introducing vaccination.

1792 Twenty-four US brokers fixed commission rates on stocks and bonds, in an agreement which formed the basis of the New York Stock Exchange.

1861 A six-day trip from London Bridge to Paris, arranged by railway excursion and tourist pioneer Thomas Cook (1808–92), became the first 'package holiday'.

1875 The first Kentucky Derby horse race was held at Churchill Downs, in Louisville, Kentucky.

1883 Premiere of Buffalo Bill Cody's first wild-west show, in Omaha, Nebraska.

1890 Issue of the first comic paper in London, *Comic Cuts*.

1899 Queen Victoria (1819–1901) laid the foundation stone of the Victoria and Albert Museum, London.

1900 Relief of Mafeking; Colonel Robert Baden-Powell and a detachment of British troops had been besieged by the Boers since October 1899.

1916 The Daylight Saving Act ('Summer Time') was passed in Britain.

1935 Birth of Dennis Potter in the Forest of Dean, Gloucestershire (d.1994), playwright and screenwriter, whose works include *Pennies from Heaven* (1978).

1939 Sweden, Norway, and Finland rejected Germany's non-aggression pact.

1954 The US Supreme Court ruled against segregation in schools.

1956 Birth of Sugar Ray Leonard in Wilmington, Delaware, boxing champion, the only boxer to have been world champion at five weights.

1965 Transmission of the first transatlantic colour programme by the Early Bird satellite.

1970 Thor Heyerdahl (1914–2002) set sail on his expedition with *Ra II*, a papyrus boat, from Morocco to the West Indies.

1973 Start of the investigation into the Watergate political scandal.

1975 US television company NBC paid $5 million to broadcast *Gone With the Wind* once.

1987 An Iraqi fighter fired two Exocet missiles at USS *Stark*, on patrol in the Gulf, killing 37 and injuring 62.

2000 Royal Marine commandos Alan Chambers (b.1968) and Charlie Paton (b.1970) became the first Britons to reach the geographical North Pole without outside backup.

MAY
18

Feast of St Erik (12th c), patron saint of Sweden.

1152 Marriage of Eleanor, Duchess of Aquitaine, recently divorced from King Louis VII of France, to Henry Plantagenet, later Henry II of England.

1619 Dutch jurist and humanist Hugo Grotius (1583–1645) was sentenced to life in prison for religious and political conflicts.

1804 Napoleon was proclaimed emperor of France.

1872 Birth of Bertrand Russell in Trelleck, Monmouthshire (d.1970), philosopher, known for his influence on analytic philosophy.

1883 Birth of Walter Gropius in Berlin, Germany (d.1969), architect, director of the Grand Ducal group of schools of art in Weimar, which he reorganized to form the Bauhaus.

1897 Birth of Frank Capra in Palermo, Italy (d.1991), director, whose films include *Arsenic and Old Lace* (1942).

1901 Opening of Alexandra Palace, London, to the public.

1919 Birth of Margot Fonteyn, originally Margaret Hookham, in Reigate, Surrey (d.1991), ballerina, who joined the Sadler's Wells Ballet in 1934.

1920 Birth of John Paul II, originally Karol Jozef Wojtyła, in Wadowice, Poland (d.2005), the first non-Italian pope in 430 years.

1953 US aviator Jacqueline Cochran (1910–80) became the first woman to fly faster than the speed of sound.

1954 Enforcement of the European Convention on Human Rights.

1969 Launch of Apollo 10, with Thomas Stafford, John Young, and Eugene Cernan on board.

1974 Explosion of India's first nuclear bomb.

1977 Signing of a UN pact by the USA, the Soviet Union, and 29 other nations, banning use of the weather as a weapon, and agreeing never to attack with artificially triggered storms, earthquakes, or tsunamis.

1979 Five years after her death American nuclear plant worker Karen Silkwood (1946–74) won $10.5 million for suffering nuclear contamination.

1980 Eruption of Mt St Helens, a volcano in SW Washington, in the Cascade Range, causing damage amounting to $2,500 million.

1991 Helen Sharman (b.1963) became Britain's first astronaut, on an 8-day mission aboard a Soviet Soyuz spacecraft with two cosmonauts.

MAY
19

Feast of St Dunstan (c.909–88), patron saint of blacksmiths, the blind, goldsmiths, jewellers, and locksmiths.
Feast of St Ivo, patron saint of lawyers and orphans.

1536 Execution of Ann Boleyn, second wife to Henry VIII, on Tower Green, London.

1635 Cardinal Richelieu (1585–1642) of France declared war on the Habsburgs in Spain during the Thirty Years' War.

1802 Napoleon I created the 'Légion d'Honneur', the French order of distinction for civil or military service.

1848 Birth of Dame Nellie Melba in Melbourne, Victoria, Australia, operatic soprano, for whom 'Peach Melba' and 'Melba toast' is named.

1849 Arrest of Irishman William Hamilton for firing blank shots at Queen Victoria in London.

1898 Death of W(illiam) E(wart) Gladstone (b.1809 in Liverpool), British prime minister (1868–74, 1880–85, 1886, 1892–4).

1906 Official opening of the Simplon rail tunnel between Italy and Switzerland, length 20 km/12 miles.

1912 Introduction of Aeroplane International Registration numbers.

1929 Opening of the World's Fair in Barcelona, Spain.

1935 Death of T(homas) E(dward) Lawrence (b.1888 in Tremadoc, Gwynedd), soldier, Arabist, and writer, best known as Lawrence of Arabia.

1945 Birth of Pete Townshend in London, guitarist and singer with The Who, notorious for smashing guitars as part of his stage performance.

1953 Birth of Victoria Wood in Prestwich, Lancashire, comedienne, whose television career includes *An Audience With Victoria Wood* (1988, BAFTA).

1962 Actress Marilyn Monroe (1926–62) sang 'Happy Birthday' for US president John F. Kennedy during a fund-raising event at Madison Square Garden, New York.

1974 Election of Valéry Giscard d'Estaing (b.1926) as president of France.

1984 Death of Sir John Betjeman (b.1906 in London), poet, broadcaster, and writer on architecture, who became poet laureate in 1972.

1994 Death of Jacqueline Kennedy Onassis, née Jacqueline Lee Bouvier, popularly known as Jackie Kennedy (b.1929 in Southampton, New York), former US first lady.

1995 Medical student Balamurali Ambati (b.1977) became the youngest doctor in history on his graduation from Mount Sinai School of Medicine, New York, aged 17.

MAY

20

Feast of St Bernardino of Siena (1380–1444), patron saint of advertisers, preachers, and weavers.

1303 Restoration of Gascony to Britain by the Treaty of Paris in the Hundred Years' War.

1498 Arrival in India of Portuguese explorer Vasco da Gama (c.1469–1525).

1501 Discovery of the Ascension Islands by Spanish explorer João da Nova Castell (c.1460–1509).

1506 Death of Christopher Columbus (b.1451 in Genoa, Italy), European discoverer of the New World, who died penniless in Spain.

1806 Birth of John Stuart Mill in London (d.1873), empiricist philosopher and social reformer, who helped form the Utilitarian Society.

1830 Patenting of the fountain pen by H. D. Hyde of Reading, Pennsylvania.

1867 The foundation stone of the Royal Albert Hall, London, was laid by Queen Victoria.

1873 Patenting of miner's work trousers with rivet-reinforced pockets by US clothing manufacturer Levi Strauss (1829–1902) and tailor Jacob Davis (1834–1908).

1875 Foundation of the International Bureau of Weights and Measures at Sèvres, near Paris.

1908 Birth of James Stewart in Indiana, Pennsylvania (d.1997), actor, whose films include *Rear Window* (1954).

1910 Halley's Comet passed at its closest point to Earth.

1913 Opening of the first Chelsea Flower Show in London.

1939 Beginning of the first US transatlantic air-mail service, from Port Washington, New York, to Marseilles, France.

1946 Birth of Cherilyn 'Cher' Sarkisian LaPierre in El Centro, California, singer and actress.

1959 Arrest of Frenchman Guy Trebert, the first person to be identified through an identikit picture.

1977 Last journey of the Orient Express train, from Paris to Istanbul.

1985 For the first time the Dow Jones Industrial Average closed over the 1300 mark, at 1304.88.

1996 Death of John Pertwee (b.1919 in Chelsea, London), actor, best known as the third Dr Who and Worzel Gummidge.

2000 Birth of Leo Blair in London, son of Tony Blair and his wife, Cherie, first child to be born to a serving British prime minister for over 150 years.

MAY
21

1471 Birth of Albrecht Dürer in Nuremberg, Germany (d.1528), painter and engraver, who in 1498 published his first great series of designs on wood, the illustrations of the Apocalypse.

1535 Capture and imprisonment of William Tyndale (c.1496–1536) in Antwerp, for heresy over his translation of the Bible into English.

1542 Death of Hernando de Soto (b.1496 in Jerez de los Caballeros, Spain), explorer, who died while searching for gold on the banks of the Mississippi R.

1840 Signing of the Treaty of Waitangi by Maori chiefs of New Zealand and representatives of Queen Victoria, granting sovereignty over New Zealand to the queen.

1851 Discovery of gold in Australia.

1881 Formation of the US Lawn Tennis Association, in New York.

1884 Completion of the Statue of Liberty; designed by French sculptor Auguste Bartholdi (1834–1904), and shipped to New York to be assembled and dedicated in 1886.

1894 Formal opening of the Manchester Ship Canal, length 57 km/ 35 miles, by Queen Victoria.

1916 Introduction of Daylight Saving Time in Britain.

1921 Birth of Andrey Sakharov in Moscow (d.1989), physicist, who was awarded the 1975 Nobel Peace Prize.

1927 Aviator Charles Lindbergh (1902–74) landed at Le Bourget Field near Paris in the aircraft 'The Spirit of St Louis', the first solo non-stop transatlantic flight.

1929 Death of Archibald Philip Primrose, 5th Earl of Rosebery (b.1847 in London), British prime minister (1894–5).

1932 US aviator Amelia Earhart (1897–1937) became the first woman to fly solo across the Atlantic.

1945 Marriage of Humphrey Bogart (1899–1957) to Lauren Bacall (b.1924).

1956 Testing of the first known airborne US hydrogen bomb over Bikini Atoll in the Pacific.

1965 Death of Sir Geoffrey de Havilland (b.1882 in Haslemere, Surrey), aircraft designer, who built his first plane in 1908.

1966 US boxer Muhammad Ali (b.1942) beat Britain's Henry Cooper (b.1934), retaining the world heavyweight championship.

1991 Death of Rajiv Gandhi (b.1944 in Mumbai (Bombay), India), former prime minister of India, assassinated by a bomb in a basket of flowers.

MAY

22

Feast of St Rita of Cascia, patron saint of hopeless cases and unhappily married women.

1455 The first battle of the Wars of the Roses was fought, the Battle of St Albans.

1783 Birth of William Sturgeon, in Whittington, Lancashire (d.1850), scientist, who built the first practical electromagnet (1825).

1813 Birth of Richard Wagner in Leipzig, Germany (d.1883), composer, whose 'Ring' cycle was first performed as a whole at the Bayreuth theatre in 1876.

1859 Birth of Sir Arthur Conan Doyle in Edinburgh (d.1930), writer, whose first book, *A Study in Scarlet* (1887), introduced the character of Sherlock Holmes.

1868 $98,000 was stolen by the Reno Gang in the Great Train Robbery at Marshfield, Indiana.

1895 Beginning of the retrial of writer Oscar Wilde, for offences arising from his friendship with Lord Alfred Douglas.

1897 Official opening of the Blackwall Tunnel under the R Thames, London.

1900 Patenting of the pianola by Edwin Votey of Detroit, Michigan.

1965 The Beatles' song, 'Ticket To Ride', became their eighth consecutive No.1 hit when it reached the top spot of the US singles list.

1969 In a rehearsal for the first Moon landing, Apollo 10's lunar module separated from the command module and flew to within nine miles of the Moon's surface.

1972 Ceylon adopted a new constitution and became the republic of Sri Lanka.

1972 Death of C(ecil) Day-Lewis (b.1904 in Ballintubber, Co Kildare, Ireland), poet and novelist, who became poet laureate in 1968.

1972 Richard Nixon visited the USSR, the first US president to do so.

1981 'Yorkshire Ripper' Peter Sutcliffe (b.1946) was jailed for life at the Old Bailey, London.

1986 United Artists film studio signed Sylvester Stallone (b.1946) to a 10-film deal over six years, making him the wealthiest Hollywood actor at the time.

1990 US computer company Microsoft released Windows 3.0.

1993 'Hairgate': President Bill Clinton kept Los Angeles airport closed for 40 minutes while he had his hair cut on board Air Force One.

2004 Marriage of Prince Felipe (b.1968), crown prince of Spain, to Letizia Ortiz (b.1972), former Spanish television anchorwoman, the first commoner in Spanish history to enter the line of succession.

MAY
23

1430 Capture and sale of Joan of Arc to the British at Compiègne by John of Luxembourg.

1533 The marriage of Henry VIII (1491–1547), king of England, to Catherine of Aragon (1485–1536) was declared null and void.

1701 Death of William Kidd (b.c.1645 probably in Greenock, Inverclyde), sea captain, hanged for piracy and murder.

1785 US scientist Benjamin Franklin (1706–90) described his latest invention, the first bi-focal spectacles, in a letter to a friend.

1788 South Carolina became the 8th state of the Union.

1868 Death of Kit Carson (b.1809 in Madison Co, Kentucky), frontiersman, soldier, and Indian agent.

1873 Formation of the North West Mounted Police in Canada; they were later renamed the Royal Canadian Mounted Police.

1910 Birth of Artie Shaw in New York (d.2004), clarinet player and bandleader, who became internationally known after recording 'Begin the Beguine' (1938).

1931 Opening of Whipsnade Zoo, in the Chiltern Hills, Bedfordshire.

1933 Birth of Joan Collins in London, actress, who made her film debut in 1951.

1934 Death of US outlaws Bonnie Parker (b.1911 in Rowena, Texas) and Clyde Barrow (b.1909 in Telico, Texas), notorious robbery partners, killed by police in Louisiana.

1937 Death of John D(avison) Rockefeller (b.1839 in Richford, New York), industrialist and philanthropist, who established the Rockefeller Foundation (1913).

1941 Death of Herbert Austin, Baron Austin of Longbridge (b.1866 in Little Missenden, Buckinghamshire), manufacturer of the Austin car.

1945 Death of Heinrich Himmler (b.1900 in Munich, Germany), Nazi leader and chief of police, who committed suicide a day after being captured.

1945 Resignation of Sir Winston Churchill (1874–1965) as British prime minister.

1951 Birth of Anatoly Yevgenyevich Karpov in Zlatoust, Russia, chess player and world champion (1975–85).

1960 Capture of Adolf Eichmann (1906–62), Nazi leader wanted for war atrocities, by Israeli agents in Argentina.

1969 Release of the rock opera *Tommy* by British rock group The Who.

1971 British racing driver Jackie Stewart (b.1939) won the Monaco Grand Prix, driving for Tyrrell.

MAY

24

1543 Death of Nicolaus Copernicus (b.1473 in Toruń, Poland), founder of modern astronomy.

1738 [Old Style calendar, New Style 4 June] Birth of George III in London (d.1820), king of Great Britain and Ireland (1760–1820).

1809 Opening of Dartmoor Prison at Princetown, Devon, to house French prisoners of war; from 1850 the prison was used for convicts.

1819 Birth of Queen Victoria in London (d.1901), queen of Great Britain (1837–1901) and (from 1876) empress of India.

1830 The children's nursery rhyme 'Mary Had a Little Lamb' was written by Sarah Josepha Hale, and later published in a collection called *Poems for Our Children*.

1830 Opening of the first US passenger railroad, the Baltimore & Ohio.

1844 Inventor Samuel Morse (1791–1872) sent the first Morse message over the first telegraph line from Washington to Baltimore: 'What hath God wrought?'.

1883 Opening of the Brooklyn Bridge linking Manhattan and Brooklyn, New York.

1930 British aviator Amy Johnson (1903–41), first woman to fly solo from England to Australia, landed her De Havilland Gypsy Moth biplane in Darwin.

1941 Birth of Bob Dylan in Duluth, Minnesota, folk singer and songwriter, whose songs include 'Blowin' in the Wind' (1963).

1956 The first Eurovision Song Contest was held in Lugano, Switzerland.

1959 Celebration of the first Commonwealth Day, previously called Empire Day.

1969 British pop group The Beatles reached the top of the US charts with their song 'Get Back'.

1970 Fire severely damaged the Menai tubular railway bridge linking Anglesey to mainland Wales.

1972 Opening of Britain's most complicated road interchange, Spaghetti Junction, in Birmingham.

1976 First commercial flights for the British and French Concordes from London and Paris respectively to Washington Dulles international airport, in just under four hours.

1983 Centenary celebrations were held for New York's Brooklyn Bridge.

1988 Opening of the restored Albert Dock, Liverpool, as a business and leisure centre by HRH the Prince of Wales.

1995 Death of Harold Wilson (b.1916 in Huddersfield, West Yorkshire), British prime minister (1964–70, 1974–6).

2000 Israeli troops pulled out from south Lebanon, ending 18 years of occupation.

MAY

25

Feast of St Bede (c.673–735), patron saint of scholars.

1085 Alfonso VI (1130–1109), king of León and Castile, took Toledo from the Muslims.

1661 Marriage of Charles II (1630–85), king of England, to Catherina of Braganza (1638–1705).

1768 Captain James Cook (1728–79) set sail to Tahiti on his first voyage in the *Endeavour*.

1833 The first flower show in Britain was held by the Royal Horticultural Society.

1871 Britain's House of Commons passed the Bank Holiday Act.

1879 Birth of Max Aitken, Lord Beaverbrook, in Maple, Ontario (d.1964), British statesman and newspaper owner.

1889 Birth of Igor Sikorsky in Kiev, Ukraine (d.1972), aeronautical engineer and helicopter pioneer.

1913 Birth of Richard (Frederick) Dimbleby in Richmond-on-Thames, London (d.1965), broadcaster, who became the BBC's first foreign correspondent and first war correspondent.

1935 US track and field athlete Jesse Owens (1913–80) broke three world records and equalled a fourth in just 45 minutes.

1951 Escape of British traitors Guy Burgess (1910–63) and Donald Maclean (1913–83) from England to Moscow.

1962 Consecration of the new Coventry Cathedral, designed by Sir Basil Spence (1907–76).

1969 Release of *Midnight Cowboy*, the only X-rated film to win an Oscar for best picture.

1975 Launch of the first Skylab space laboratory.

1981 Amateur stuntman Daniel Goodwin (b.1956) scaled Sears Tower, Chicago, in $7\frac{1}{2}$ hours, wearing a Spiderman costume.

1983 Opening of the film *Return of the Jedi* in 1002 cinemas in the USA; it broke previous box-office records with takings of $6,219,629.

1986 Thirty million people ran in Bob Geldof's 'Race Against Time', to raise money for the starving in Africa.

1988 Louise Kinkel, Eric P. Hoffman, and co-workers announced that the protein dystrophin is absent in cases of Duchenne muscular dystrophy, making early diagnosis of the disease possible.

1994 The Camelot consortium won the contract to run Britain's first national lottery.

2005 Death of Ismail Merchant (b.1936 in Mumbai (Bombay), India), film director, who formed Merchant-Ivory Productions with James Ivory.

MAY

26

1521 The Edict of Worms declared religious reformer Martin Luther (1483–1546) an outlaw, and banned his writings, because of his religious beliefs.

1703 Death of Samuel Pepys in London (b.1633), naval administrator, best known for the diary he kept from 1 January 1660 to 31 May 1669.

1799 [Old Style calendar, New Style 6 June] Birth of Alexander Sergeyevich Pushkin in Moscow, Russia (d.1837), poet and writer, whose works include *Eugene Onegin* (1828).

1805 Coronation of Napoleon Bonaparte (1769–1821) as king of Italy in Milan Cathedral.

1865 Surrender of Confederate general Edmund Kirby Smith (1824–93) in Texas, ending the American Civil War.

1886 Birth of Al Jolson in Srednike, Russia (d.1950), actor and singer, brought to the USA in 1893, who became known in the 1920s for such sentimental songs as 'Mammy'.

1906 Official opening of Vauxhall Bridge over the R Thames, London.

1907 Birth of John Wayne (Marion Michael Morrison) in Winterset, Iowa (d.1979), actor, who made over 80 films, including *True Grit* (1969, Oscar).

1910 Birth of Laurance Rockefeller in New York, business executive and conservationist, who oversaw the donation of 33,000 acres of Rockefeller land to the Grand Teton National Park.

1913 Founding of the Actors' Equity Association in New York.

1938 Completion of the first Volkswagen car at the factory in Wolfsburg, Germany.

1950 End of petrol rationing in Britain.

1956 Opening of the first mobile bank, in Long Island, New York, a 14-m/46-ft trailer, which received $100,000 of deposits on its first day of trading.

1966 Birth of Helena Bonham-Carter in London, actress, whose film credits include *Hamlet* (1990).

1969 John Lennon and Yoko Ono, on honeymoon, began their 'Bed-In' for world peace.

1972 Sale of state-owned British travel firm Thomas Cook & Son to a consortium of private businesses headed by the Midland Bank.

1978 Opening of the first legal casino in the USA outside Nevada, in Atlantic City.

1986 The film *Cobra*, starring Sylvester Stallone (b.1946), took $12·4 million in ticket sales on its opening day, setting a new sales record for a non-sequel film.

1994 Marriage of Michael Jackson (b.1958), US pop star, and Lisa Marie Presley (b.1968).

MAY
27

1647 Death of Alse Young in Hartford, Connecticut, the first person in America to be executed as a witch.

1679 Passing of the 'habeas corpus' act in Britain, a common-law right that requires a person who detains another to appear in court and justify that detention.

1703 Founding of St Petersburg by Peter the Great (1672–1725), tsar of Russia.

1794 Birth of Cornelius Vanderbilt on Staten Island, New York (d.1877), steamship owner, who later became a railroad financier.

1837 Birth of James Butler 'Wild Bill' Hickok in Troy Grove, Illinois (d.1876), frontiersman, sharpshooter, and scout.

1910 Death of Robert Koch (b.1843 in Clausthal-Zellerfeld, Germany), bacteriologist, who discovered the bacillus of both tuberculosis and cholera.

1911 Birth of Vincent Price in St Louis, Missouri (d.1993), actor and writer, who starred in Gothic horror movies such as *The Abominable Dr Phibes* (1971).

1915 Ending of the second stage of the Battle of Ypres, one of the major battles in World War 1.

1922 Birth of Christopher Lee in London, actor, whose films include *Dracula* (1958) and its sequels.

1933 Release in the USA of Walt Disney's Academy Award-winning animation *The Three Little Pigs*.

1936 Opening of Britain's first open prison, at New Hall near Wakefield, West Yorkshire.

1937 Opening of the Golden Gate Bridge at San Francisco, California; length of main span, 1280 m/ 4200 ft.

1941 Sinking of the German battleship *Bismarck*.

1943 Birth of Cilla Black in Liverpool, singer and television game-show hostess, especially known for *Blind Date*.

1963 Election of Jomo Kenyatta (c.1889–1978) as first prime minister of Kenya.

1964 Death of Jawaharlal Nehru (b.1899 in Allahabad, India), first prime minister of independent India.

1988 Death of Ernst Ruska (b.1906 in Heidelberg, Germany), scientist, who developed the electron microscope.

1994 Return to Russia of Nobel Prize-winning author Alexander Solzhenitsyn (b.1918), after 20 years in exile.

1996 Opening of Shakespeare's Globe , a replica of the original, in London.

1999 Indictment of Slobodan Milošević (1941–2006), former president of Serbia, by the Hague International War Crimes Tribunal for crimes against humanity.

MAY
28

Feast of St Bernard of Menthon (923–1008), known as the Apostle of the Alps, patron saint of mountaineers.

1533 The marriage of King Henry VIII and Anne Boleyn was declared valid.

1660 Birth of George I in Osnabrück, Germany (d.1727), king of Great Britain and Ireland (1714–27).

1742 Opening of England's first indoor swimming pool, in London, entry fee one guinea.

1759 Birth of William Pitt 'the Younger' in Hayes, London (d.1806), British prime minister (1783–1801, 1804–6).

1843 Death of Noah Webster (b.1758 in Hartford, Connecticut), lexicographer, who compiled the first major US dictionary (1828).

1878 Death of Lord John Russell (b.1792 in London), British prime minister (1846–52, 1865–6).

1908 Birth of Ian Fleming in London (d.1964), writer and journalist, who achieved worldwide fame as the creator of James Bond.

1934 Birth of the Dionne quintuplets – Emilie (d.1954), Yvonne (d.2001), Cécile, Marie (d.1970), and Annette – in Callender, Ontario, the first documented set of quintuplets to survive.

1940 The evacuation began of the Allied armies from Dunkirk.

1951 Broadcast of the first *Goon Show* by the BBC.

1957 Foundation of the National Academy of Recording Arts and Sciences in the USA, which each year presents the Grammys, annual popular music awards.

1959 Launch into space of monkeys Able and Baker, the first living creatures to survive a space flight.

1967 Arrival of Sir Francis Chichester in Plymouth, after his successful solo circumnavigation of the world in *Gipsy Moth IV*.

1972 Death of Edward VIII (b.1894 in Richmond, London), king of the United Kingdom (Jan–Dec 1936).

1982 Arrival in Britain of Pope John Paul II, the first papal visit to the country since 1531.

1984 Death of Eric Morecambe, originally Eric Bartholomew (b.1926 in Morecambe, Lancashire), comedian, who teamed up with Ernie Wise to become Morecambe and Wise.

1987 Mathias Rust (b.1968), 19-year-old West German pilot, evaded Soviet air defences and landed a private plane in Moscow's Red Square.

MAY
29

526 Destruction of Antioch in a massive earthquake which killed most of the population, c.250,000, including Euphrasius, patriarch of Antioch.

1453 Ending of the Byzantine Empire, when Constantinople fell to Muhammad II; Emperor Constantine XI Dragases was killed, and the city renamed Istanbul.

1660 Restoration of Charles II (1630–85) to the English throne after nine years' exile in France.

1781 Birth of John Walker in Stockton-on-Tees (d.1859), chemist, who invented the first friction matches.

1790 Rhode Island became the 13th state of the Union.

1829 Death of Humphry Davy (b.1778 in Penzance, Cornwall), chemist, the inventor of the miner's safety lamp.

1848 Wisconsin became the 30th state of the Union.

1871 The first Bank Holiday in Britain was celebrated on Whit Monday.

1874 Birth of G(ilbert) K(eith) Chesterton in London (d.1936), critic and writer, who gained popularity with the amiable detective-priest introduced in *The Innocence of Father Brown* (1911).

1898 Birth of Beatrice Lillie in Toronto, Ontario (d.1989), revue singer, who became renowned from 1914 in music hall and the new vogue of 'intimate revue'.

1903 Birth of Bob Hope (Leslie Towne Hope) in London (d.2003), comedian, who appeared in the highly successful *Road to …* comedies (1940–52).

1917 Birth of John F. Kennedy in Brookline, Massachusetts (d.1963), 35th president of the USA (1961–3).

1942 Singer and film star Bing Crosby (1904–77) recorded Irving Berlin's 'White Christmas' for Decca Records, the biggest-selling record ever.

1953 Mountaineer and explorer Sir Edmund Hillary (b.1919) and Tenzing Norgay (1914–86), known as Sherpa Tenzing, became the first people to reach the summit of Mt Everest.

1968 Manchester United became the first English football club to win the European Cup, beating Portuguese side Benfica 4–1.

1985 Thirty-five people died when rioting Liverpool fans caused a wall to collapse at the European Cup soccer final at Heysel Stadium, Brussels, Belgium.

1992 The diary of Albert Pierrepoint, Britain's last hangman, fetched £18,000 at auction.

1995 Christopher Reeve (1952–2004), US actor and star of the *Superman* films, was paralysed after falling from his horse.

1999 Space shuttle Discovery completed the first-ever docking procedure with the international space station.

MAY
30

Feast of St Ferdinand (III), patron saint of engineers.

Feast of St Joan of Arc, patron saint of France and soldiers.

Feast of St Walstan of Bawburgh, patron saint of agricultural workers.

1431 Joan of Arc was burnt at the stake in Rouen, France, for heresy.

1536 Marriage of Henry VIII (1491–1547), king of England, to Jane Seymour (1509–37), eleven days after the execution of Anne Boleyn, his second wife.

1593 Death of Christopher Marlowe (b.1564 in Canterbury, Kent), poet and playwright, killed in a tavern brawl in Deptford.

1757 Birth of Henry Addington, 1st Viscount of Sidmouth, in London (d.1844), British prime minister (1801–4).

1846 Birth of Peter Carl Fabergé in St Petersburg, Russia (d.1920), goldsmith and jeweller, known for the creation of elaborate and fantastic objects.

1848 Ratification of the Treaty of Guadalupe Hidalgo by Mexico, giving the USA New Mexico, California, and parts of Nevada, Utah, Arizona, and Colorado in return for $15 million.

1909 Birth of Benny Goodman in Chicago, Illinois (d.1986), clarinettist and bandleader, who formed his own orchestra in New York (1934).

1911 The first Indianapolis 500 motor race was won by Ray Harroun with an average speed of 74.59 mph.

1942 Over a thousand bombers attacked Cologne, Germany, in the RAF's first 1000-bomber raid of World War 2.

1959 Launch of the first full-sized experimental hovercraft at Cowes, Isle of Wight, built by Saunders-Roe.

1961 Birth of Harry Enfield in Sussex, comedian, actor, and writer, known for his character-based comedy shows.

1977 Launch of the US space probe Mariner 9 towards Mars.

1981 Death of Ziaur Rahman (b.1935), president of Bangladesh, assassinated in a failed military coup.

1982 Spain became the sixteenth member of NATO, the first to enter the alliance since West Germany in 1955.

1989 British pop singer Cliff Richard (b.1940) released his 100th single.

1996 The marriage of Prince Andrew (b.1960) and Sarah Ferguson (b.1959) was ended by decree.

2002 A ceremony was held at Ground Zero, New York, to mark the end of the clean-up operation following the terrorist attacks $8\frac{1}{2}$ months previously.

MAY

31

1809 Death of Franz Josef Haydn (b.1732, in Rohrau, Austria), composer, whose works include *The Creation* (1798).

1837 Death of Joseph Grimaldi (b.1779 in London), dancer and actor, whose white-faced act marked the birth of the English circus clown.

1859 First day of operation for Big Ben, in the clock tower of the Houses of Parliament, London.

1872 Birth of Heath Robinson in London (d.1944), artist, cartoonist, and book illustrator, whose fame rests mainly on his humorous drawings satirizing the machine age.

1902 Signing of the Treaty of Vereeniging in Pretoria, ending the Boer War.

1907 First day of operation for taxis in New York.

1911 Launch of the British liner *Titanic* from the Harland and Wolff shipyard in Belfast.

1916 The Battle of Skagerrak was fought at Jutland between British and German fleets during World War 1.

1922 Birth of Denholm Elliott in London (d.1992), actor, who received an Oscar nomination for *A Room with a View* (1986).

1928 Australian World War 1 ace Sir Charles Kingsford-Smith (1897–1935) took off from Oakland, California, for Australia, on the first flight across the Pacific.

1930 Birth of Clint Eastwood in San Francisco, California, actor and director, who rose to international stardom with the spaghetti Western *A Fistful of Dollars* (1964).

1939 Birth of Terry Waite in Bollington, Cheshire, consultant and negotiator, who was kidnapped in Beirut (1987–91).

1961 South Africa left the Commonwealth and became an independent republic.

1962 Death of Adolf Eichmann (b.1906 in Solingen, Germany), Gestapo official, hanged in Israel for his role in the Holocaust.

1969 Ex-Beatle John Lennon (1940–80) and Yoko Ono (b.1933) recorded 'Give Peace a Chance'.

1974 Signing of the Israel–Syria Disengagement Agreement on the Golan Heights.

1977 Completion of the trans-Alaska oil pipeline after three years of work.

1988 The World Health Organization voted to eradicate polio from the world by the year 2000.

1996 Benjamin Netanyahu (b.1949) beat Shimon Peres (b.1923) in the Israeli prime ministerial election.

2002 The World Cup soccer tournament opened in Asia for the first time, with a match held in South Korea.

JUNE

1

Feast of St Justin the Martyr (c.100–c.165), patron saint of philosophers.

1792 Kentucky became the 15th state of the Union.

1794 The Battle of the Glorious First of June, a naval battle fought off the Isle d'Ouessant (near Brest) between the British and the French.

1796 Tennessee became the 16th state of the Union.

1869 Patenting of an electric voting machine by US inventor and physicist Thomas Edison (1847–1931).

1880 The first public telephone box went into service, in New Haven, Connecticut.

1907 Birth of Sir Frank Whittle in Coventry, West Midlands, inventor and pioneer of jet propulsion.

1926 Birth of Marilyn Monroe in Los Angeles, California (d.1962), actress, whose films include *Gentlemen Prefer Blondes* (1953).

1935 Implementation of compulsory driving tests in Britain.

1938 First appearance of Superman, in DC Comics' *Action Comics* series, issue no. 1.

1946 Issue of the first British television licences, price £2.

1949 Subscribers to the weekly US *Newsweek* magazine were offered the periodical in microfilm form for the first time, at an annual subscription of $15.

1957 Computer ERNIE (Electronic Random Number Indicator Equipment) picked the first Premium Bond winners, top prize £1000.

1967 The Beatles released their album *Sergeant Pepper's Lonely Hearts Club Band*, which became No. 1 throughout the world.

1968 Death of Helen Keller (b.1880 in Tuscumbia, Alabama), writer and lecturer, who lost her sight and hearing after an illness at 19 months, but was taught to speak, read, and write.

1973 British Honduras changed its name to Belize.

1976 Signing of a deal between Iceland and the UK, ending the third 'Cod War'.

1980 Debut of Cable News Network (CNN) as television's first all-news service, with 24-hour news broadcasts.

1983 Jockey Lester Piggott (b.1935) rode the Derby winner for a record ninth time, on 'Teenoso'.

2001 Crown Prince Dipendra of Nepal (1971–2001) killed at least eight members of the royal family before shooting himself.

JUNE

2

Feast of St Erasmus, patron saint of navigators, and sufferers from colic and intestinal disease.

1537 Pope Paul III banned enslavement of Indians in the New World.

1780 Beginning of the 'No Popery' or 'Gordon Riots'.

1840 Birth of Thomas Hardy in Upper Bockhampton, Dorset (d.1928), novelist and poet, whose works include *The Return of the Native* (1878).

1850 Birth of Sir Jesse Boot, Baron Trent, in Nottingham, Nottinghamshire (d.1931), drug manufacturer, who by 1900 had built up the largest pharmaceutical retail trade in the world.

1857 Birth of Sir Edward Elgar in Broad Heath, Hereford and Worcester (d.1934), composer, whose works include the *Enigma Variations* (1899).

1868 Beginning of the first Trades Union Congress, held in Manchester.

1886 Marriage of Grover Cleveland (1837–1908) to Frances Folsom (1864–1947), the first US president to wed in the White House.

1896 Issue of the first patent for a system of communication by electromagnetic waves, to physicist Guglielmo Marconi (1874–1937).

1910 British co-founder of Rolls-Royce, Charles Stewart Rolls (1877–1910), became the first man to fly an aeroplane non-stop across the English Channel and back.

1924 US citizenship was granted to all American Indians.

1938 Robert and Edward Kennedy opened Regent's Park Children's Zoo in London.

1941 Beginning of clothes rationing in Britain.

1941 Death of Lou Gehrig (b.1903 in New York), baseball player, of amyotrophic lateral sclerosis, a rare paralysis now termed Lou Gehrig's disease.

1953 Coronation of Queen Elizabeth II of the United Kingdom in Westminster Abbey.

1962 Opening of the Metropole in Brighton, Britain's first legal casino.

1966 Landing of the US Surveyor spacecraft on the Moon.

1979 Arrival of Pope John Paul II (1920–2005) in his native Poland, the first papal visit to a Communist country.

1985 English football clubs were banned from playing in European competitions, after continued hooliganism by their fans when travelling abroad.

JUNE

3

Feast of St Genesius of Rome, patron saint of actors, clowns, and comedians.

1098 Capture of Antioch after a five-month siege during the First Crusade.

1657 Death of William Harvey (b.1578 in Folkestone, Kent), physician, who first described the circulation of the blood.

1865 Birth of George V, born in London (d.1936), king of the United Kingdom (1910–36).

1867 Introduction of lacrosse into Britain, from Montreal.

1871 Wild West outlaw Jesse James (1847–82) and his gang stole $15,000 from the Obocock Bank, Corydon, Iowa.

1898 Death of Samuel Plimsoll (b.1824 in Bristol, Avon), social reformer, and originator of the Plimsoll line (enforced 1894) for the safe loading of ships.

1906 Birth of Josephine Baker in St Louis, Missouri (d.1975), dancer and entertainer, who became an instant success when she appeared at the Folies Bergères.

1922 Birth of Alain Resnais in Vannes, France, director, whose films include *L'Année dernière à Marienbad* (1961, Last Year at Marienbad).

1925 Birth of Tony Curtis in New York, actor, whose films include *Some Like It Hot* (1959).

1937 Marriage of the Duke of Windsor to Mrs Wallis Warfield Simpson, following his abdication as king.

1956 Abolition of third-class rail travel in Britain, in line with continental travel.

1965 Ed White spent 21 minutes outside Gemini 4, the first US astronaut to walk in space.

1969 Broadcasting of the final episode of the television series *Star Trek* on NBC in the USA.

1973 Crash of a Soviet supersonic airliner at the Paris air show, killing 15 people.

1979 Exploratory oil well Ixtoc 1 spilled over 140 million gallons of oil into the Bay of Campeche, off the coast of Mexico.

1981 Racehorse Shergar won the Derby.

1989 Death of the Ayatollah Khomeini (b.1900 in Khomeyn, Iran), political and religious leader of Iran.

2001 US actor and comedian Mel Brooks' musical comedy *The Producers* won a record 12 Tony Awards.

JUNE

4

1391 A mob led by Ferrand Martinez, archdeacon of Ecija, surrounded and set fire to the Jewish quarter of Seville, Spain.

1738 [24 May, Old Style calendar] Birth of George III in London (d.1820), king of Great Britain and Ireland (1760–1820).

1798 Death of Giacomo Casanova (b.1725 in Venice, Italy), adventurer and spy, known as one of the world's great lovers.

1805 The first 'Trooping of the Colour' was held at Horse Guards Parade, London.

1878 Cyprus came under British administration in exchange for assistance against Russian encroachment in eastern Turkey.

1893 Production of the first petrol-driven motor car by manufacturer Henry Ford (1863–1947).

1910 Birth of Sir Christopher Cockerell in Cambridge (d.1999), engineer, who invented the amphibious hovercraft.

1911 Discovery of gold in Indian Creek, Alaska.

1913 Death of Emily Davison (b.1872 in London), suffragette, who died after being trampled by the king's horse in the 1913 Derby when she tried to catch its reins.

1924 Dedication of the eternal light at Madison Square, New York, to the memory of soldiers from New York State who died in World War 1.

1935 Patenting of invisible glass by Londoners Gerald Brown and Edward Pollard.

1937 Introduction of the first super-market trolleys, in Oklahoma.

1940 British prime minister Winston Churchill delivered his famous 'We shall fight on the beaches … we shall never surrender' speech to the House of Commons.

1942 Start of the Battle of Midway in the Pacific; the Allied air victory in the battle was a turning point in World War 2.

1946 Installation of Juan Perón (1895–1974) as president of Argentina.

1948 Birth of Bob Champion in Yorkshire, jump jockey, known for his Grand National win on Aldaniti in 1981.

1958 Presentation of the first Duke of Edinburgh Awards at Buckingham Palace, London.

1970 Tonga became completely independent and a member of the Commonwealth.

1989 Tiananmen Square, Beijing, was the scene of mass protests by students against the Chinese government.

JUNE

5

Feast of St Boniface (c.680–c.754), patron saint of Germany.

468 BC Suggested date for the birth of Socrates in Athens, Greece (d.399 BC), Greek philosopher.

1661 Admission of Isaac Newton (1642–1727) as a student to Trinity College, Cambridge.

1783 Aeronautical inventors Joseph Michel Montgolfier (1740–1810) and Jacques Etienne Montgolfier (1745–99) made the world's first manned balloon flight.

1819 Birth of John Couch Adams in Laneast, Cornwall (d.1892), mathematician and astrologer, who (independently of Leverrier) predicted the existence of the planet Neptune.

1826 Death of Carl von Weber (b.1786 in Eutin, Germany), composer and pianist, who died in London, where he was staying for the premiere of his opera, *Oberon*.

1882 [Old Style calendar, New Style 17 June] Birth of Igor Stravinsky near St Petersburg, Russia (d.1971), composer, whose works include *The Firebird* (1910).

1898 Birth of Federico García Lorca in Fuente Vaqueros, Spain (d.1936), poet, whose works include *The Gypsy Ballads* (1928, 1935).

1916 HMS *Hampshire* struck a mine off Orkney, and was lost at sea.

1928 Birth of Tony Richardson in Shipley, West Yorkshire (d.1991), director, whose films include *Tom Jones* (1963, Oscar).

1939 Birth of Margaret Drabble in Sheffield, South Yorkshire, novelist and biographer.

1945 Premiere of Benjamin Britten's *Peter Grimes*, the first opera to be performed at Sadler's Wells Theatre, London.

1947 US secretary of state George C. Marshall (1880–1959) outlined an aid programme for Europe that came to be known as the Marshall Plan.

1967 Start of the 'Six Day War' between the Arab states and Israel.

1968 Shooting of Robert Kennedy in Los Angeles during his presidential campaign; he died in hospital the following day.

1975 Reopening of the Suez Canal to international shipping, eight years after its closure during the war with Israel (1967).

1981 The US Centers for Disease Control and Prevention reported the first cases of the disease later known as AIDS.

1988 Australian yachtswoman Kay Cottee (b.1954) sailed into Sydney Harbour, the first woman to sail round the globe single-handedly.

2004 Death of Ronald Wilson Reagan (b.1911 in Tampico, Illinois), 40th president of the USA, as a result of Alzheimer's disease.

JUNE
6

Feast of St Claude, patron saint of sculptors, turners, and toymakers.

Feast (Eastern Church) of St Martha, patron saint of cooks, hoteliers, housewives, laundry-workers, lay-sisters, servants, and waiters.

1654 Queen Christina of Sweden abdicated and converted to Catholicism.

1683 Opening of the first museum in Britain to the public, the Ashmolean Museum in Oxford.

1844 Founding of the YMCA (Young Men's Christian Association) in London.

1882 Patenting of the electric flat-iron by H. W. Seely of New York.

1912 Eruption of Mt Katmai volcano in Alaska, the largest volcanic eruption during the 20th c.

1925 Founding of Chrysler, the car manufacturing company, by Walter Percy Chrysler (1875–1940).

1932 A federal tax of 1 penny per gallon on gasoline (petrol) was imposed in the USA.

1933 Opening of the first drive-in cinema, in Camden, New Jersey.

1934 Establishment of the US Securities and Exchange Commission, to protect the interests of investors.

1944 D-Day: the Allies launched the greatest amphibious operation in history (code-named 'Overlord'), invading German-occupied Europe.

1949 Publication of George Orwell's novel *Nineteen Eighty-Four*.

1954 Inauguration of the Eurovision television link; the participating countries were Britain, Belgium, Denmark, France, West Germany, Italy, The Netherlands, and Switzerland; the opening broadcast was a message from Pope Pius XII in Rome.

1962 EMI producer George Martin auditioned a new pop group, The Beatles.

1966 US civil-rights activist James Meredith (b.1933), the first African-American to enrol in the University of Mississippi, was shot and wounded during a civil-rights march.

1968 Death of Robert Kennedy (b.1925 in Boston, Massachusetts), after being shot in Los Angeles on 5 June during his presidential campaign.

1976 Death of J. Paul Getty (b.1892 in Minneapolis, Minnesota), oil billionaire and art collector.

1985 Exhumation in Brazil of a body later identified as the remains of Dr Josef Mengele (1911–79), the 'Angel of Death' of the Nazi Holocaust.

JUNE

7

1329 Death of Robert Bruce (b.1274), king of Scots.

1614 Dissolution of the Addled Parliament (James I's second parliament), which passed no bills after its first meeting on 5 April 1614.

1778 Birth of George Bryan (Beau) Brummell in London (d.1840), dandy, and a leader of early 19th-c fashion.

1909 US actress Mary Pickford (1893–1979) made her screen debut at age 16 in *The Violin Maker of Cremona*.

1912 The US army tested the first aeroplane-mounted machine-gun.

1917 Birth of Dean Martin in Steubenville, Ohio (d.1995), actor and singer, whose films include *Rio Bravo* (1959).

1928 Birth of James Ivory in Berkeley, California, film director, who formed Merchant-Ivory Productions with Ismail Merchant.

1929 The Lateran Treaty reintroduced the Papal State, extinct since 1870, as the State of Vatican City.

1931 Birth of Virginia McKenna in London, actress, whose roles include Joy Adamson in *Born Free* (1966).

1939 Arrival of George VI and Queen Elizabeth in New York, on the first visit to the USA by a reigning British monarch.

1940 Birth of Sir Tom Jones in Pontypridd, Wales, singer, whose 'Green Green Grass of Home' (1966) was his biggest-selling single.

1946 Television resumed after the war, and announcer Leslie Mitchell said: 'As I was saying before I was so rudely interrupted … '

1948 Resignation of President Edvard Beneš, after the Communist take-over of Czechoslovakia.

1950 Broadcast of the first episode of the BBC radio serial *The Archers*, created by Godfrey Basely.

1952 Birth of Liam Neeson in Ballymena, Northern Ireland, actor, whose screen credits include the title role in *Rob Roy* (1995).

1965 The first domestic videotape recorder, manufactured by Sony, went on sale for $995.

1967 Israel captured the Western Wall in East Jerusalem, on the third day of the Six-Day War.

1977 Across the UK, celebrations began, and beacons were lit, to mark the Silver Jubilee of Queen Elizabeth II.

1994 Death of Dennis Potter (b.1935 in the Forest of Dean, Gloucestershire), playwright, whose works include *The Singing Detective* (1986).

JUNE
8

Feast of St Médard, patron saint of toothache sufferers.

632 Death of the Prophet Muhammad (b.570), the founder of Islam, in Mecca.

1695 Death of Christiaan Huygens (b.1629 in The Hague), physicist and astronomer, who discovered the rings and fourth satellite of Saturn (1655).

1786 Ice-cream was manufactured commercially for the first time, in New York.

1810 Birth of Robert Schumann in Zwickau, Germany (d.1856), composer, whose works include four symphonies.

1829 Birth of Sir John Everett Millais in Southampton (d.1896), painter, a founder member of the Pre-Raphaelite Brotherhood.

1861 Tennessee became the 11th and last state to secede from the Union.

1869 Birth of Frank Lloyd Wright in Richmond Center, Wisconsin (d.1959), architect, who became known for his controversial designs.

1869 Patenting of the suction vacuum cleaner by Ives McGaffey of Chicago, Illinois.

1876 Death of Gerard Manley Hopkins (b.1844 in Stratford, London), poet, whose works include 'The Wreck of the *Deutschland*' (1875).

1916 Birth of Francis Crick in Northampton, Northamptonshire, biophysicist, joint Nobel Prize winner (1962) for the discovery of the structure of DNA.

1933 Birth of Joan Rivers in Larchmont, New York, comedienne and writer, who hosted *Hollywood Squares* (from 1987).

1953 Ruling by the US Supreme Court that restaurants in Washington, DC, could not refuse to serve African-Americans.

1965 US troops were authorized to engage in offensive operations in South Vietnam.

1968 Arrest of James Earl Ray, killer of Martin Luther King Jr, in London.

1978 Yachtswoman Dame Naomi James arrived home, having circumnavigated the world two days faster than Sir Francis Chichester.

1982 Ronald Reagan predicted that Marxism-Leninism would end up 'on the ash heap of history', in the first speech by a US president to a joint session of British parliament.

2003 US photographer Spencer Tunick (b.1967) photographed more than 7000 nude people in Barcelona, Spain, as part of a temporary artwork installation.

2003 Work began on one of the world's longest bridges, the 22-mile, $1.4 billion bridge across Hangzhou Bay, linking Shanghai to the port of Ningbo.

2004 The planet Venus made a rare transit across the face of the Sun.

JUNE
9

Feast of St Columba (Colmcille) (521–97), patron saint of poets.

68 Death of Nero Claudius Caesar (b.37), emperor of Rome (54–68), who was blamed for the Great Fire of Rome (64) and forced to commit suicide.

1549 Adoption of the Book of Common Prayer by the Church of England.

1781 Birth of George Stephenson in Wylam, Northumberland (d.1848), railway engineer, whose engine, the *Rocket*, running at 58 km/36 miles an hour, was built in 1829.

1790 *The Philadelphia Spelling Book* was the first book to be copyrighted.

1853 Birth of Walter Weeden Grossmith in London (d.1919), writer, who with his brother, George Grossmith (1847–1912) wrote 'Diary of a Nobody' in *Punch* magazine (1892).

1870 Death of Charles Dickens (b.1812 in Landport, Hampshire), novelist.

1874 Death of Cochise (b.1812 in present-day Arizona or New Mexico), Chiricahua Apache chief.

1898 Britain leased Hong Kong from China for 99 years; it reverted to Chinese sovereignty at midnight on 30 June 1997.

1904 Inaugural concert for the London Symphony Orchestra, the first independent, self-governing orchestra in the UK; the conductor was Hans Richter.

1934 Launch of Donald Duck in his first film, Disney's *The Wise Little Hen*.

1957 Birth of Patricia Cornwell in Miami, Florida, novelist, known especially for the character of medical examiner Dr Kay Scarpetta, introduced in her first novel *Postmortem* (1990).

1958 Opening of Gatwick airport, London, by Queen Elizabeth II, thought to be the first airport in the world to combine airport, trunk road, and rail facilities in one unit.

1961 Birth of Michael J. Fox in Edmonton, Alberta, actor, whose films include the *Back to the Future* series.

1963 Birth of Johnny Depp in Owensboro, Kentucky, actor, whose films include *Edward Scissorhands* (1990).

1976 Death of Dame Sybil Thorndike (b.1882 in Gainsborough, Lincolnshire), actress, whose Shakespearian roles include Lady Macbeth and Portia (both 1922).

1993 Marriage of Naruhito (b.1960), crown prince of Japan, to commoner Masako Owada (b.1963).

JUNE

10

1190 Death of Frederick I (b.c.1123), Holy Roman emperor, who drowned crossing the Saleph R during the Third Crusade.

1692 Hanging of the first of the Salem 'witches' in Massachusetts.

1801 Tripoli declared war on the USA in a dispute over the safe passage of merchant vessels through the Mediterranean.

1829 Oxford won Britain's first Boat Race, competing with Cambridge.

1854 Official opening of the Crystal Palace, at Sydenham, South London.

1854 Graduation of the first students at the US Naval Academy, Annapolis, Maryland.

1865 Premiere of Wagner's opera *Tristan und Isolde* in Munich, Germany.

1901 Birth of Frederick Loewe in Vienna, Austria (d.1988), composer, whose musicals include *My Fair Lady* (1956).

1909 First use of the SOS distress signal, by Cunard liner SS *Slavonia*, wrecked off the Azores.

1911 Birth of Sir Terence Rattigan in London (d.1977), playwright, whose plays include *The Winslow Boy* (1946).

1922 Birth of Judy Garland in Grand Rapids, Minnesota (d.1969), actress and singer, best known for her lead role in *The Wizard of Oz* (1939).

1923 Birth of Robert Maxwell in Slatinske Doly, Czech Republic (d.1991), British publisher and politician, and chairman of the Mirror group of newspapers.

1943 US patent given on ball-point pens, devised by Hungarian Lazlo Biró (1899–1985).

1967 Death of Spencer Tracy (b.1900 in Milwaukee, Wisconsin), actor, who co-starred with Katharine Hepburn in nine films.

1967 Ending of the Six-Day War between Israel and the Arab states.

1976 A record-breaking crowd of 67,100 fans came to hear the group Wings, with ex-Beatle Paul McCartney, at an indoor concert in Seattle, Washington.

1991 Eruption of Mt Pinatubo volcano in the Philippines.

1993 Opening of director Steven Spielberg's film *Jurassic Park* in the USA.

2000 Opening of the Millennium Bridge, a pedestrian suspension bridge over the R Thames, London; it was closed after three days to correct excessive swaying, and reopened in 2002.

JUNE

11

Feast (Eastern Church) of St Bartholomew, patron saint of butchers, bookbinders, leather-workers, and tanners.

1509 Marriage of King Henry VIII of England (1491–1547) to his first wife, Catherine of Aragon (1485–1536).

1572 Birth of Ben Jonson in London (d.1637), playwright, whose works include *The Alchemist* (1610).

1770 Captain James Cook, commander of the British ship *Endeavour*, discovered the Great Barrier Reef by running on to it.

1776 Birth of John Constable in East Bergholt, Suffolk (d.1837), landscape painter, whose works include *Haywain* (1821).

1798 Napoleon Bonaparte (1769–1821) occupied Malta.

1864 Birth of Richard Strauss in Munich, Germany (d.1949), composer, whose works include *Der Rosenkavalier* (1911).

1910 Birth of Jacques Cousteau in Saint-André, France (d.1997), naval officer and underwater explorer, whose films include *The Golden Fish* (1960, Oscar).

1935 Birth of Gene Wilder in Milwaukee, Wisconsin, actor, writer, and director, whose films include *Blazing Saddles* (1974).

1955 Crash of a Mercedes-Benz racing car during the Le Mans race, France, killing driver Pierre Levegh and more than 80 spectators.

1959 Launch of the hovercraft, invented by Christopher Cockerell

(1910–99), in Southampton, Hampshire.

1963 Buddhist monk Quang Duc (b.1897) burned himself to death in Saigon in a protest against the government of South Vietnamese president Ngo Dinh Diem.

1964 Martin Luther King was jailed by officials for his involvement in the organizing of protest demonstrations and marches in St Augustine, Florida.

1975 Britain's North Sea oilfields pumped ashore their first oil.

1979 Death of John Wayne, originally Marion Michael Morrison (b.1907 in Winterset, Iowa), actor, who achieved stardom as the Ringo Kid in *Stagecoach* (1939).

1982 Opening of director Steven Spielberg's *E.T. The Extra-Terrestrial* in the USA.

1987 Margaret Thatcher (b.1925) became the first British prime minister in 160 years to win a third consecutive term of office.

1990 Refusal of the US Supreme Court to pass a federal law prohibiting desecration of the American flag.

2001 Execution of Timothy McVeigh, who admitted planting a bomb killing 168 people in the Oklahoma City federal building.

2002 Marriage of Sir Paul McCartney (b.1942), musician, songwriter, composer, and ex-Beatle, to former model Heather Mills (b.1968).

JUNE

12

1819 Birth of Charles Kingsley in Holne, Devon (d.1875), clergyman, best known for his story *The Water Babies* (1863).

1839 A new game, baseball, was played for the first time, in Cooperstown, New York.

1842 Death of Thomas Arnold (b.1795 in East Cowes, Isle of Wight), educationist, scholar, and headmaster of Rugby School.

1897 Patenting of a penknife, later known as the Swiss army knife, by Swiss cutlery maker Carl Elsener.

1901 Birth of Sir Norman Hartnell in London (d.1978), fashion designer and court dressmaker, whose work included Princess Elizabeth's wedding and coronation gowns.

1915 Birth of David Rockefeller in New York, banker and philanthropist.

1921 Final Sunday postal delivery in Britain.

1924 Birth of George H. W. Bush in Milton, Massachusetts, 41st president of the USA (1989–93).

1929 Birth of Anne Frank in Frankfurt, Germany (d.1945), Jewish diarist, whose family fled to The Netherlands in 1933.

1935 Signing of the truce ending the Chaco War, a conflict fought between Bolivia and Paraguay over disputed territory (1932–5).

1939 Dedication of the National Baseball Hall of Fame and Museum in Cooperstown, New York, on the 100th anniversary of the day it is thought the sport was invented.

1962 Using spoons, prisoners finally dug their way out of the high-security prison of Alcatraz, San Francisco Bay, California.

1963 Premiere of *Cleopatra* starring Elizabeth Taylor (b.1932), at that time the most expensive film ever made, with production costs of $40 million.

1967 Refusal of the US Supreme Court to pass state laws prohibiting interracial marriages.

1978 Serial killer David Berkowitz, 'Son of Sam', was sentenced to life imprisonment six times over.

1980 Death of Sir Billy Butlin (b.1899 in Cape Town, South Africa), holiday-camp promoter, who opened his first camp at Skegness, Lincolnshire, in 1936.

1987 The title Princess Royal was conferred upon Princess Anne.

2003 Final flight of Air France's Concorde; it is now on display at the Smithsonian Air and Space Museum, Washington Dulles airport.

JUNE
13

Feast of St Antony of Padua (1195–1231), patron saint of donkeys, horses, lost articles, the poor, Portugal, the starving, and travellers.

323 BC Suggested date for the death of Alexander the Great.

1381 A peasant army led by Wat Tyler marched into London.

1795 Birth of Thomas Arnold in East Cowes, Isle of Wight (d.1842), educationist, scholar, and headmaster of Rugby School.

1854 Birth of Sir Charles Parsons in London (d.1931), engineer, and developer of the high-speed steam turbine.

1865 Birth of William Butler Yeats near Dublin, Ireland (d.1939), poet and playwright, whose works include the narrative poem 'The Wanderings of Oisin' (1888).

1886 Death of Ludwig II of Bavaria (b.1864 in Munich, Germany), drowned in Lake Starnberg, Germany.

1893 The first ladies' golf tournament was held at Royal Lytham & St Annes, UK.

1931 Death of Sir Jesse Boot, Baron Trent (b.1850 in Nottingham, Nottinghamshire), drug manufacturer, who opened his first chemist's shop in Nottingham (1877).

1943 Birth of Malcolm McDowell in Leeds, West Yorkshire, actor, who played the lead in *If …* (1968).

1944 Landing of Hitler's 'secret weapon', the V-1 flying bomb, on England for the first time.

1944 Patenting of the wire recorder, the precursor of the magnetic tape recorder, by Marvin Camras.

1966 US police required to give all suspects a right-to-silence warning – the 'Miranda warning'.

1971 Birth of nine children to Geraldine Broderick of Sydney, Australia; one of the few recorded instances of nonuplets.

1981 Six blank shots were fired by a teenage boy at Queen Elizabeth II, during the Trooping the Colour ceremony in London.

1983 Pioneer 10, the world's first outer-planetary probe, left the solar system.

1986 Death of Benny Goodman (b.1909 in Chicago, Illinois), clarinettist and bandleader, one of the best-known leaders of the big-band era.

1991 Lightning killed a spectator during the first round of the US Open golf tournament at Hazeltine, Minnesota.

2000 The first meeting was held between Kim Jong Il, president of North Korea, and Kim Dae Jung, president of South Korea.

2004 Former US president George Bush celebrated his 80th birthday with a 13,000 ft parachute jump in College Station, Texas.

JUNE

14

1645 Defeat of the Cavaliers by the Roundheads at the Battle of Naseby, Northamptonshire, during the English Civil War.

1775 Founding of the US Army, when Continental Congress authorized the muster of troops under its sponsorship.

1777 Adoption of the 'Stars and Stripes' as the USA's official flag.

1789 Arrival of Captain William Bligh (1754–1817) in Timor, in the small boat in which he and 18 of his men were cast adrift when the crew of HMS *Bounty* mutinied.

1811 Birth of Harriet Beecher Stowe in Litchfield, Connecticut (d.1896), novelist, who became famous with her first novel, *Uncle Tom's Cabin* (1852).

1864 Birth of Alois Alzheimer in Marktbreit, Germany (d.1915), psychiatrist and neuropathologist, known for his work on pre-senile dementia (Alzheimer's disease).

1881 Patenting of a self-operating 'player' piano by John McTammany, of Cambridge, Massachusetts.

1919 Birth of Sam Wanamaker in Chicago, Illinois (d.1993), actor, director, and founder (1970) of The Globe Trust, a project to build a replica of Shakespeare's Globe Theatre, London (completed 1996).

1927 Death of Jerome K. Jerome (b.1859 in Walsall, Staffordshire), novelist and playwright, whose works include *Three Men in a Boat* (1889).

1928 Birth of Che Guevara in Rosario, Argentina (d.1967), revolutionary leader, who played an important part in the Cuban revolution (1956–9).

1941 Birth of Mike Yarwood in Stockport, Cheshire, impressionist.

1946 Birth of Donald Trump in New York, real-estate developer, who built the Trump Tower, New York (1982).

1961 Birth of Boy George in Eltham, Kent, pop singer and songwriter.

1964 Nelson Mandela (b.1918) was sentenced to life imprisonment for treason.

1967 Launch of space probe Mariner 5 from Cape Kennedy on its flight past Venus.

1970 Footballer Bobby Charlton played his last game for England at the World Cup in Mexico City.

1982 Surrender of Argentine forces to British troops, ending the Falklands War.

1991 Death of Peggy Ashcroft (b.1907 in London), actress, whose notable stage roles included Juliet (1935) and Hedda Gabler (1954).

2005 Jamaican athlete Asafa Powell (b.1983) broke the world 100 m sprint record with a time of 9.77 seconds during the Athens Olympics.

JUNE
15

Feast of St Vitus (4th c), patron saint of actors, comedians, dancers, dogs, epileptics, and sufferers from nervous diseases.

1215 The Magna Carta was stamped with the Royal Seal by King John at Runnymede, Surrey.

1330 Birth of Edward the Black Prince in Woodstock, Oxfordshire (d.1376), eldest son of Edward III.

1381 Death of Wat Tyler, leader of the Peasants' Revolt, beheaded in London.

1667 Jean-Baptiste Denys (1640–1704), personal physician to Louis XIV of France, transferred c.350 ml (12 fluid oz) of lamb's blood into a sick boy; the first successful human transfusion.

1752 Benjamin Franklin (1706–90) conducted his famous kite experiment, demonstrating that lightning is an electrical discharge.

1775 George Washington was unanimously voted head of the Continental Army by the Second Continental Congress.

1836 Arkansas became the 25th state of the Union.

1843 Birth of Edvard Grieg in Bergen, Norway (d.1907), composer, whose works include *Peer Gynt* (1876).

1846 Establishment of the border between Canada and the USA.

1864 Establishment of Washington's Arlington Cemetery as a military cemetary.

1869 Patenting of celluloid by US inventor John Wesley Hyatt (1837–1920).

1919 Completion of the first non-stop transatlantic plane flight, by aviators Sir John William Alcock (1892–1919) and Sir Arthur Whitten Brown (1886–1948), in 16 hours 27 minutes.

1937 Birth of Waylon Jennings in Littlefield, Texas (d.2002), country music singer, whose albums include *Honky Tonk Heroes* (1973).

1945 Introduction of family allowance payments in Britain for second and subsequent children (5 shillings per week per child).

1964 Birth of Courtney Cox-Arquette in Birmingham, Alabama, actress, best known for her role as Monica in the sitcom *Friends* (1994–2004).

1971 British MP Margaret Thatcher caused protests with her plans to end free school milk.

1978 Marriage of King Hussein of Jordan (1935–99) to Lisa Halaby (b.1951), who then became Queen Noor.

1996 Death of Ella Fitzgerald (b.1917 in Newport News, Virginia), jazz singer, often referred to as 'the first lady of song'.

1996 Explosion of an IRA bomb in Manchester, injuring more than 200 and badly damaging the city's main shopping centre.

JUNE
16

1487 Henry VII of England won the Battle of Stoke, the final battle in the Wars of the Roses.

1567 Imprisonment of Mary, Queen of Scots (1542–87), in Lochleven Castle, Scotland.

1829 Birth of Geronimo along the Gila R in present-day Arizona (d.1909), Chiricahua Apache war chief.

1890 Birth of Stan Laurel (Arthur Stanley Jefferson) in Ulverston, Lancashire (d.1965), film comedian, who teamed up with Oliver Hardy (1892–1957) in 1926.

1896 Birth of Jean Peugeot in Valentigney, France (d.1966), car manufacturer.

1904 James Joyce's novel, *Ulysses*, takes place on this day in Dublin, Ireland.

1922 The first helicopter flight was made by Henry Berliner, in Maryland.

1930 Death of Elmer Ambrose Sperry (b.1860 in Cortland, New York), electrical engineer, who invented the gyroscopic compass (1911) and stabilizers for ships and aeroplanes.

1935 Passing of the 'New Deal' programme by the US Congress, to help America recover from the Great Depression.

1958 Introduction of yellow lines on British roads, to indicate 'no waiting'.

1959 Death of George Reeves (b.1914 in Woodstock, Iowa), actor, best known for his role as Superman during the 1950s; Reeves shot himself.

1961 Defection of Soviet ballet dancer Rudolf Nureyev (1938–93) at Le Bourget airport, Paris, while travelling with the Leningrad Kirov Ballet.

1963 Cosmonaut Valentina Tereshkova (b.1937) became the first woman in space on the launch of the three-day Vostok 6 flight.

1972 Arrest of terrorist Ulrike Meinhof (1934–76), the last of the German Baader-Meinhof gang to be caught.

1972 Opening of the New York Jazz Museum, the only museum devoted exclusively to jazz.

1978 First demonstration of the electronic game 'Space Invaders'.

1978 Premiere of the film *Grease* in New York, starring John Travolta and Olivia Newton-John.

1980 Opening of the film *The Blues Brothers* in Chicago, Illinois, starring John Belushi and Dan Aykroyd.

1981 In British politics, an alliance was formed between the Liberal Party and the SDP (Social Democratic Party).

1996 First independent presidential election in Russia, eventually won by Boris Yeltsin (b.1931).

JUNE
17

1239 Birth of Edward I in London (d.1307), king of England (1272–1307), who won renown as a crusader to the Holy Land in the Eighth Crusade (1270–72).

1579 Sir Francis Drake anchored in San Francisco Bay, and claimed it for England.

1703 Birth of John Wesley in Epworth, Lincolnshire (d.1791), evangelist and founder of Methodism.

1719 Death of Joseph Addison (b.1672 in Milston, Wiltshire), essayist and politician, who co-founded *The Spectator* with Sir Richard Steele in 1711.

1775 Beginning of the American War of Independence with the Battle of Bunker Hill, near Boston.

1823 Patenting of waterproof material by chemist Charles Macintosh (1766–1843).

1837 Patenting of rubber by US inventor Charles Goodyear (1800–1860).

1885 Arrival in New York of the French naval ship *Isère*, carrying the wooden crates with the component pieces of the Statue of Liberty.

1898 Death of Sir Edward Coley Burne-Jones (b.1833 in Birmingham, West Midlands), painter and designer, much influenced by William Morris and Rossetti.

1920 Birth of Beryl Reid in Hereford, Hereford and Worcester (d.1996), character actress, whose films include *The Killing of Sister George* (1968).

1928 US aviator Amelia Earhart (1897–1937) participated in a transatlantic flight with Wilmer Stultz and Louis Gordon, becoming the first woman to fly the Atlantic.

1929 First showing of Hitchcock's film *Blackmail*, in London.

1941 WNBT-TV in New York gained the right to run a commercial television station, the first in the USA.

1944 Iceland became an independent republic.

1946 Birth of Barry Manilow (Barry Alan Pincus) in Brooklyn, New York, singer, whose songs include 'I Write The Songs' (1975).

1950 The first kidney transplant was carried out in Chicago.

1970 First sale in Britain of decimal postage stamps, values 10p, 20p, and 50p.

1972 Five burglars were caught breaking into the Watergate offices of the Democratic National Committee in Washington, DC, triggering a political scandal.

1974 Explosion of an IRA bomb at the Houses of Parliament, London, injuring 11 people, and causing extensive damage.

2003 British football star David Beckham (b.1975) signed a four-year contract worth c.£25 m with Real Madrid, Spain.

JUNE
18

1815 Defeat of Napoleon Bonaparte (1769–1821) at the Battle of Waterloo.

1817 Opening of the Waterloo Bridge over the R Thames, London, designed by civil engineer John Rennie (1761–1821).

1873 US women's rights leader Susan B. Anthony was fined $100 for casting a ballot in the 1872 presidential election.

1887 Opening of Hammersmith Bridge over the R Thames, London.

1898 Opening of Steel Pier in Atlantic City, New Jersey; the 9½-mile-long pier offered facilities including amusements, concerts, food, and beverages.

1901 Birth of Jeanette MacDonald in Philadelphia, Pennsylvania (d.1965), soprano, best known for roles opposite Nelson Eddy in film operettas such as *Rose Marie* (1936).

1927 First day of sale for the first US postage stamp to feature the name of a living American, aviator Charles A. Lindbergh (1902–74).

1928 Death of Roald Amundsen (b.1872 in Borge, Norway), explorer, best known for having reached the South Pole in December 1911, one month ahead of Captain Scott.

1942 Birth of Beatle Paul McCartney in Liverpool.

1948 Adoption of the Universal Declaration of Human Rights by the UN.

1952 Birth of Isabella Rossellini in Rome, actress, and daughter of Roberto Rossellini (1906–77) and Ingrid Bergman (1915–82).

1953 Egypt became a republic, with Mohammed Neguib (1901–84) as first president.

1959 Broadcast by American NBC-TV of the first television programme received from England.

1975 Death of Faisal Ibn Musaid Abdul Aziz, Saudi prince, beheaded for killing his uncle King Faisal ibn Abd al-Aziz.

1978 Birth of 'Garfield', comic-strip cat created by Jim Davis (b.1945).

1979 Signing of the SALT (Strategic Arms Limitation Treaty) treaty by Supreme Soviet President Leonid Brezhnev (1906–82) and US President Jimmy Carter (b.1924).

1983 Dr Sally Ride (b.1951) was the first American woman in space.

1999 Disappeareance of the uninhabited islands of Tebua Tarawa and Abanuea in Kiribati under the rising ocean.

JUNE

19

1269 Decree by Louis IX of France that all Jews must wear a *rouelle*, a badge of shame; those Jews appearing in public without the badge were fined ten *livres*.

1566 Birth of James I in Edinburgh (d.1625), the first Stuart king of England (1603–25).

1623 Birth of Blaise Pascal in Clermont-Ferrand, France (d.1662), mathematician, physicist, and theologian, who invented a calculating machine, barometer, and hydraulic press.

1829 Founding of the London Metropolitan Police by British prime minister Sir Robert Peel (1788–1850).

1846 The first baseball match was played at Hoboken, New York – New York Nine beat Knickerbocker Club 23–1.

1867 Death of Ferdinand Joseph Maximilian (b.1832, in Vienna, Austria), emperor of Mexico.

1895 Opening of the Kiel Canal, a 98-km/61-mile link between the North Sea and the Baltic, by Emperor Wilhelm II.

1896 Birth of Wallis Simpson in Blue Ridge Summit, Pennsylvania (d.1986), Duchess of Windsor, and wife of abdicated King Edward VIII.

1910 Founding of Father's Day in the USA by Mrs John Bruce Dodd.

1917 Adoption of the name of Windsor by the British Royal family, renouncing all German titles and names.

1924 Disappearance of climber George Mallory, 1000 ft from the summit of Everest; his body was discovered on 1 May 1999 by the Mallory and Irvine Research Expedition.

1937 Death of Sir J. M. Barrie (b.1860 in Kirriemuir, Scotland), novelist and playwright, whose plays include *Peter Pan* (1904).

1961 Independence of Kuwait.

1978 England cricketer Ian Botham (b.1955) became the first in the history of the game to score a century and take eight wickets in one innings of a Test match.

1981 Opening day of film *Superman II*, which broke the one-day record for box office takings when $5.5 million was paid in cinema tickets.

1993 Death of William Golding (b.1911 near Newquay, Cornwall), novelist, whose works include *Lord of the Flies* (1954).

1997 British politician William Hague (b.1961) became the youngest leader of the Conservative Party in nearly 200 years.

1999 Marriage of Prince Edward (b.1964) and Sophie Rhys-Jones (b.1965) at St George's Chapel, Windsor.

JUNE
20

1597 Death of William Barents (b.1550), Dutch navigator and cartographer, who discovered and charted the Spitsbergen group of islands.

1756 Imprisonment of surviving British defenders overnight in a small, badly ventilated room – the Black Hole of Calcutta – causing many to perish.

1782 US Congress approved the Great Seal of the USA, and the eagle as its symbol.

1789 Meeting of the Third Estate on an indoor tennis court; they swore not to disband until a New French constitution had been adopted.

1819 The *Savannah* became the first steamship to cross the Atlantic, arriving in Liverpool nearly a month after leaving Savannah, Georgia, on 24 May.

1837 Death of William IV (b.1765 in London), king of Great Britain and Ireland, and king of Hanover (1830–7).

1837 Accession of Queen Victoria to the British throne.

1863 West Virginia became the 35th state of the Union.

1887 Opening of the second Tay Bridge, Scotland, at the time the longest bridge in Britain.

1900 Beginning of the Boxer Rebellion in China.

1906 Birth of Dame Catherine Cookson in East Jarrow, Tyne and Wear (d.1998), novelist, whose books include *Branded Man* (1997).

1909 Birth of Errol Flynn in Hobart, Tasmania, Australia (d.1959), actor, who became a hero of historical adventure films such as *The Adventures of Robin Hood* (1938).

1911 Opening of Britain's first trolleybus service, in Leeds, West Yorkshire.

1963 The White House, USA, and the Kremlin, USSR, agreed a method of emergency communication; although tested, the system was never used.

1967 Birth of Nicole Kidman in Honolulu, Hawaii, actress, whose films include *Moulin Rouge* (2000).

1969 A rock star was paid the largest amount to date for a single appearance, when US rock guitarist Jimi Hendrix (1942–70) earned $125,000 at the Newport Jazz Festival, Los Angeles.

1975 Release of the film *Jaws*, directed by Steven Spielberg.

1977 Opening of the trans-Alaskan pipeline, allowing oil to flow in Alaska.

1985 Treasure hunters found the Spanish galleon *Nuestra Señora de Atocha*, which sank off the coast of Florida in 1622; the ship contained over $400 million in coins and silver ingots.

JUNE
21

Summer Solstice (non-leap years).
Feast of St Luigi Gonzaga, known as St
Aloysius (1568–91), patron saint of youth.

1527 Death of Niccolò Machiavelli
(b.1469 in Florence, Italy), statesman, writer, and political theorist,
whose masterpiece was *Il Principe*
(1532, The Prince).

1652 Death of Inigo Jones (b.1573 in
London), architect, who introduced the Italian Palladian style
into England.

1675 Start of the reconstruction of St
Paul's Cathedral, London, designed
by Sir Christopher Wren (1632–1723)
to replace the building destroyed
by the Great Fire of London (1666).

1788 New Hampshire became the 9th
state of the Union.

1854 During the Russian War, sailor
Charles Lucas (1834–1914) saved his
ship by picking up a live shell from
the deck and throwing it overboard, for which he was awarded
the first Victoria Cross in 1857.

1868 The first performance of
Wagner's opera *Die Meistersinger*
took place in Munich, Germany.

1891 Birth of Pier Luigi Nervi in Son-
drio, Italy (d.1979), architect, whose
building designs include the Pirelli
building (1955, the first skyscraper
in Italy).

1905 Birth of Jean-Paul Sartre in Paris
(d.1980), existentialist philosopher
and writer, who was awarded, but
declined, the 1964 Nobel Prize for
Literature.

1919 Despite the surrender of Germany, German sailors scuttled 72
German warships at Scapa Flow in
the Orkneys, in the greatest act of
self-destruction in modern military
history.

1921 Birth of Jane Russell in Bemidji,
Minnesota, actress, who became
one of the leading Hollywood sex
symbols of the 1950s, with films
including *Gentlemen Prefer Blondes*
(1953).

1935 Birth of Françoise Sagan in Paris,
novelist, who wrote the best-selling
Bonjour tristesse (1954, Hello Sadness) at the age of 18.

1937 First television broadcast of lawn
tennis from Wimbledon, London.

1948 Tom Kilburn with Freddie Williams ran the first program on the
world's first computer, at Manchester University.

1953 Birth of Benazir Bhutto in Karachi, Pakistan, prime minister of
Pakistan (1988–91, 1993–6).

1970 Tony Jacklin (b.1944) became the
first British golfer in 50 years to win
the US Open.

1978 The musical *Evita* was first produced in London.

1981 Fire broke out at Goodge Street
tube station, London, killing one
and injuring 16.

2001 The first total solar eclipse of the
21st c took place.

JUNE

22

Summer Solstice (leap years only).
Feast of St Thomas More (1478–1535) and St John Fisher (1469–1535), patron saints of lawyers.

1611 English navigator Henry Hudson (1580–1611) and eight others were cast adrift in present-day Hudson Bay when his crew mutinied.

1814 Lord's Cricket Ground, London, hosted its first match.

1824 Birth of Lord Kelvin in Belfast (d.1907), mathematician and physicist, known for his research into thermodynamics.

1870 Creation of the Department of Justice by US Congress.

1906 Birth of Billy Wilder in Sucha, Poland, formerly Austria (d.2002), US director, whose films include *Some Like It Hot* (1959).

1911 First day of action for Great George, the Liver Clock in Liverpool.

1932 Birth of Prunella Scales in Abinger, Surrey, actress, whose roles include Sybil in British television's *Fawlty Towers* (1975–9).

1936 US stuntman Harry Froboess, whose films include *The Alamo* (1960), made a successful 110-m dive from an airship into the Bodensee.

1937 US boxer Joe Louis (1914–81) won the world heavyweight title.

1941 Invasion of Russia by German troops, in violation of the 1939 Russo-German non-aggression pact.

1945 End of the World War 2 Battle of Okinawa; 12,520 US troops and 110,000 Japanese died during the 81-day campaign.

1949 Birth of Meryl Streep in Summit, New Jersey, actress, whose films include Oscar-winning roles in *Kramer vs. Kramer* (1979) and *Sophie's Choice* (1982).

1969 Death of Judy Garland (b.1922 in Grand Rapids, Minnesota), actress and singer, who starred in *The Wizard of Oz* (1939).

1978 Discovery of Charon, Pluto's only known satellite, discovered photographically by James W. Christy and Robert S. Harrington at the US Naval Observatory in Washington, DC.

1981 Mark Chapman pleaded guilty to the murder of ex-Beatle John Lennon in New York.

1984 First flight of a new low-price airline, Virgin Atlantic.

1995 Resignation of British prime minister John Major (b.1943) as leader of the Conservative Party.

JUNE

23

Midsummer's Eve.

1757 Defeat of the Nawab of Bengal, India, by the British at the Battle of Plassey.

1848 Patenting of the saxophone by musician and inventor Adolphe Sax (1814–94).

1868 Patenting of the typewriter by US inventor Christopher Latham Sholes (1819–90).

1894 Birth of Alfred Kinsey in Hoboken, New Jersey (d.1956), sexologist and zoologist, known for his controversial studies of human sexual behaviour.

1902 Founding of the Order of Merit by King Edward VII of the United Kingdom; it is awarded for exceptional service to the Crown or for the advancement of the arts, learning, law, and literature.

1912 Birth of Alan Turing in London (d.1954), mathematician, logician, and computer pioneer, who carried out code-breaking during World War 2.

1914 The naval wing of Britain's Royal Flying Corps became the Royal Naval Air Service.

1927 Birth of Bob Fosse in Chicago, Illinois (d.1987), actor, dancer, and choreographer, who choreographed and directed *Cabaret* (1972).

1929 Birth of Valerie June Carter in Maces Springs, Virginia (d.2003), country music singer, wife of Johnny Cash, and a founder member of the Carter Family trio.

1940 Birth of Adam Faith in London (d.2003), pop singer and actor, whose TV credits include the title role in *Budgie* (1971).

1951 Defection to the USSR of British traitors Guy Burgess (1910–63) and Donald Maclean (1913–83).

1959 Release of Communist spy and naturalized Briton Klaus Fuchs (1912–88) from prison in England, following a jail term for disclosing nuclear secrets to Russia.

1973 Degree ceremony for the first graduates of Britain's Open University.

1976 Opening of the CN Tower in Toronto, Canada, the world's tallest self-supporting tower at 555·3 m/1822 ft.

1980 Death of Sanjay Gandhi (b.1946 in New Delhi, India), eldest son of prime minister Indira Gandhi, killed in a plane crash.

1995 Death of Jonas Salk (b.1914 in New York), immunologist, who developed the first vaccination against poliomyelitis.

JUNE

24

Midsummer's Day.
Feast of St John the Baptist (1st c), patron saint of bird-dealers, lambs, monks, and tailors.

1314 Defeat of King Edward II of England by Robert the Bruce at the Battle of Bannockburn, near Stirling, Scotland.

1340 The French fleet at Sluys was destroyed by the British fleet during the Hundred Years' War.

1509 Coronation of King Henry VIII of England (1509–47).

1519 Death of Lucrezia Borgia (b.1480 in Rome), noblewoman, a patron of art and education.

1717 Inauguration of the first Freemason Lodge, London.

1777 Birth of Sir John Ross at Balsaroch, Dumfries and Galloway (d.1856), British naval officer and Arctic explorer.

1825 Birth of W. H. Smith in London (d.1891), who secured the privilege of selling books and newspapers at railway stations (1849).

1850 Birth of Lord Kitchener in Ballylongford, Co Kerry, Ireland (d.1916), British field marshal and secretary for war.

1859 Defeat of Austria at the Battle of Solferino in Lombardy by Emperor Napoleon III.

1895 Birth of Jack Dempsey in Manassa, Colorado (d.1983), boxing champion, who won the world heavyweight championship in 1919 by knocking out Jess Willard.

1901 Pablo Picasso had his first Paris exhibition.

1912 Birth of Brian Johnston in Little Berkhamsted, Hertfordshire (d.1994), British broadcaster and commentator, who specialized in cricket commentary on radio and television.

1947 A report by US pilot Kenneth Arnold of objects like 'saucers skipping across the water' in the sky near Mt Rainier, Washington, led to the term 'flying saucers'.

1953 Announcement of the engagement between John F. Kennedy and Jacqueline Bouvier.

1971 Opening of the first part of the second Mersey road tunnel, Liverpool.

1973 Resignation of Eamon de Valera as president of Ireland – at 90 years of age, the world's oldest statesman.

1978 Discovery of a black hole in the constellation of Scorpio.

2003 Arrival in London of Russian president Vladimir Putin – the first state visit to Britain by a Russian leader since Tsar Alexander II in 1874.

JUNE
25

1788 Virginia became the 10th state of the Union.

1796 Birth of Nicholas I in Tsarskoye Selo, near St Petersburg, Russia (d.1855), tsar of Russia, despot, who attempted to Russianize all the inhabitants of the empire.

1857 Trial of French author Gustave Flaubert for public immorality in relation to his novel *Madame Bovary*.

1867 Patenting of barbed wire by Lucien Smith of Ohio.

1876 General Custer and the 7th cavalry were destroyed by Sioux Indians at the Battle of Little Big Horn.

1891 *Strand Magazine* published its first Sherlock Holmes story by Arthur Conan Doyle (1859–1930).

1898 Physicists Pierre and Marie Curie announced the discovery of radium.

1903 Birth of George Orwell in Motihari, Bengal (d.1950), British novelist, whose works include *Nineteen Eighty-Four* (1949).

1924 Birth of Sidney Lumet in Philadelphia, Pennsylvania, director, whose films include *Murder on the Orient Express* (1974).

1945 Birth of Carly Simon in New York, singer and songwriter, whose songs include 'You're So Vain' (1972).

1950 Invasion of South Korea by North Korea.

1951 First commercial colour broadcast, with the CBS transmission of a one-hour special from New York to Baltimore, Philadelphia, Boston, and Washington, DC.

1963 Birth of George Michael in Finchley, London, singer and songwriter, who partnered Andrew Ridgeley in the band Wham!

1968 Death of Tony Hancock (b.1924 in Birmingham, West Midlands), comedian, who achieved national popularity with the radio and TV series *Hancock's Half Hour* (1954–61).

1975 Independence of Mozambique from Portugal, with Samora Machel (1933–86) as president.

1976 Death of Johnny Mercer (b.1909 in Savannah, Georgia), composer, lyricist, and singer, whose musicals include *Seven Brides for Seven Brothers* (1954).

1991 Independence of Croatia and Slovenia from Yugoslavia.

1993 Kim Campbell (b.1947) became the first female prime minister of Canada.

1997 Auction of dresses owned by Diana, Princess of Wales, raising $3.5 million for charity.

1997 Crash of an unmanned cargo vessel into Mir space station during a docking practice, causing a partial power failure and damaging a pressurized laboratory.

JUNE
26

1243 Defeat of the Seljuk Turks by the Baiju Mongol army in the Battle of Kösedag.

1541 Death of Francisco Pizarro (b.1478 in Trujillo, Spain), conquistador who founded Lima (1535), assassinated in Lima.

1827 Death of Samuel Crompton (b.1753 in Firwood, Greater Manchester), inventor of the spinning-mule in 1779.

1830 Death of George IV (b.1762 in London), king of Great Britain and Hanover (1820–30).

1836 Death of Claude Joseph Rouget de Lisle (b.1760 in Lons-le-Saunier, France), French army officer, who wrote and composed the 'Marseillaise'.

1846 Repeal of the Corn Laws, which imposed high duties on the import of foreign corn into Britain.

1857 Queen Victoria awarded the first Victoria Crosses in Hyde Park, London; there were 62 recipients, representing the Army, the Navy, and the Royal Marines.

1870 The first performance of Richard Wagner's *Die Walküre* (The Valkyries) took place in Munich.

1892 Birth of Pearl S. Buck in Hillsboro, West Virginia (d.1973), writer, who was was awarded the 1938 Nobel Prize for Literature.

1904 Birth of Peter Lorre in Rosenberg, Hungary (d.1964), actor, whose films include *The Maltese Falcon* (1941).

1905 Founding of Britain's Automobile Association, in a meeting at the Trocadero restaurant in London; an initial 100 members had grown to 83,000 by 1914.

1906 The first Grand Prix was raced at Le Mans in France.

1909 Opening of the Victoria and Albert Museum in London.

1914 Birth of Laurie Lee in Stroud, Gloucestershire (d.1997), poet and author, whose works include the autobiographical *Cider With Rosie* (1959).

1945 Signing of the United Nations Charter in San Francisco, California.

1963 Visit of US president John F. Kennedy to the Berlin Wall, where he said, 'Ich bin ein Berliner' (I am a Berliner).

1973 First performance of the musical *Grease* in London.

1979 Boxer Muhammad Ali (b.1942) announced his retirement.

1997 Leader of Fianna Fáil Bertie Ahern (b.1951) became tenth taoiseach of the Republic of Ireland.

JUNE

27

1746 Escape of Bonnie Prince Charlie to the Isle of Skye, disguised as a maid, with the help of Flora Macdonald.

1778 Relocation of the Liberty Bell, rung at the proclamation of the Declaration of Independence (1776), to Philadelphia, Pennsylvania.

1844 Death of Joseph Smith (b.1805 in Sharon, Vermont), founder of the Church of Jesus Christ of Latter-day Saints (the Mormons).

1865 Birth of Sir John Monash in Melbourne, Victoria, Australia (d.1931), Australian soldier, who commanded the 4th Australian Brigade at Gallipoli (1914–15).

1880 Birth of Helen Keller in Tuscumbia, Alabama (d.1968), author and lecturer, deaf and blind from the age of nineteen months.

1905 Seizure of battleship *Potemkin* in the Black Sea by Russian soldiers, who threw the commander and several officers overboard.

1939 Flight of the first transatlantic airline, Pan American Airways, from Newfoundland to Southampton, with 19 passengers.

1944 Capture of Cherbourg from the Germans by the Allies, three weeks after D-Day.

1950 Responding to a request to member nations by the UN Security Council, US president Truman ordered the US Air Force and Navy to aid South Korea repel an invasion from the North.

1954 The first atomic power station began production, at Obinsk, near Moscow.

1961 Enthronement of Michael Ramsey (1904–88) as the 100th Archbishop of Canterbury.

1962 Birth of Michael Ball in Leicester, Leicestershire, actor and singer, known for his work in such shows as *Les Misérables* (1985).

1963 Decca Records signed US singer Brenda Lee on a new recording contract, guaranteeing her $1 million over the following 20 years.

1967 Installation of Britain's first hole-in-the-wall cash machine, by Barclays Bank at Enfield, London.

1969 Clash between police and patrons at the Stonewall Inn, a gay bar in Greenwich Village, New York, in what is considered to be the birth of the US gay rights movement.

1977 Death of Lady Olave Baden-Powell (b.1889 in Chesterfield, Derbyshire), who became English Chief Guide in 1918.

2001 Death of Jack Lemmon (b.1925 in Boston, Massachusetts), actor, whose films include *Some Like It Hot* (1959).

JUNE
28

1461 Coronation of King Edward IV of England (r.1461–70, 1471–83).

1577 Birth of Peter Paul Rubens in Siegen, Germany (d.1640), Flemish artist, whose works include the triptych *The Descent from the Cross* (1611–14).

1712 Birth of Jean Jacques Rousseau in Geneva, Switzerland (d.1778), political philosopher, whose works include *The Social Contract* (1762).

1778 Defeat of the British at the Battle of Monmouth in New Jersey by George Washington (1732–99), during the American War of Independence.

1836 Death of James Madison (b.1751 in Port Conway, Virginia), 4th president of the USA (1809–17).

1838 Coronation of Queen Victoria of Great Britain (1837–1901) in Westminster Abbey, London.

1861 Death of Robert Burke (b.1820 in St Clerans, Co Galway, Ireland), explorer, who crossed the Australian continent from S to N; he died on the return journey.

1902 Birth of Richard Rodgers in New York (d.1979), composer, who collaborated with lyricist Lorenz Hart (1895–1943), and later Oscar Hammerstein II (1895–1960).

1909 Birth of Eric Ambler in London (d.1998), novelist and playwright, who specialized in the writing of thrillers, such as *Epitaph for a Spy* (1938).

1910 Consecration of Westminster Cathedral, London.

1914 Death of Franz Ferdinand (b.1863), heir to the Austrian throne, and his wife in Sarajevo, assassinated by Serbian nationalists in an incident which precipitated World War 1.

1919 Signing of the Treaty of Versailles by Germany and the Allies, ending World War 1.

1926 Birth of Mel Brooks (Melvin Kaminsky) in New York, actor and director, whose films include *Blazing Saddles* (1974).

1935 Fort Knox, Kentucky, was proposed as the site for a building to hold the federal gold reserves.

1950 Capture of Seoul by North Korea, enforcing a move to Taejon by the government of the Republic of Korea.

1976 The Seychelles in the Indian Ocean became an independent republic.

1997 Disqualification of US boxer Mike Tyson during a WBA heavyweight title fight in Las Vegas for biting the ear of opponent Evander Holyfield.

2001 Serbia handed over former Yugoslav leader Slobodan Miloševic to the UN war crimes tribunal.

2004 Diplomatic links between the USA and Libya were resumed after a 24-year break.

JUNE

29

48 BC Defeat of Pompey (106–48 BC) by Julius Caesar (c.101–44 BC), who became absolute ruler of Rome.

1534 Discovery of Prince Edward Islands, Canada, by French explorer Jacques Cartier (1491–1557).

1613 Destruction by fire of the original Globe Theatre in London.

1767 The British parliament approved the Townshend Revenue Acts, imposing import duties on glass, lead, paint, paper, and tea shipped to America; the acts were repealed in 1770.

1801 Publication of Britain's first census results.

1855 First publication in London of the *Daily Telegraph*.

1861 Death of Elizabeth Barrett Browning (b.1806 in Durham, UK), poet, and wife of Robert Browning.

1868 Founding of the Press Association News Agency in London.

1871 An Act of Parliament granted legal recognition to Labour Unions in Britain.

1901 Birth of Nelson Eddy in Providence, Rhode Island (d.1967), singer and actor, whose films include *Naughty Marietta* (1935).

1910 Birth of Frank Loesser in New York (d.1969), composer and lyricist, whose works include the music and lyrics of *Guys and Dolls* (1950).

1941 Birth of Stokely Carmichael in Port of Spain, Trinidad (d.1998), African-American civil rights leader, who popularized the phrase 'black power'.

1953 Passing of the US Federal Highway Act, which allowed the building of the interstate highway system.

1956 Marriage of playwright Arthur Miller (1915–2005) to actress Marilyn Monroe (1926–62).

1967 Death of Jayne Mansfield (b.1933 in Bryn Mawr, Pennsylvania), actress, whose films include *The Female Jungle* (1955).

1974 Isabel Perón (b.1931) became the first female president of Argentina.

1980 Election of Vigdís Finnbogadóttir (b.1930) as president of Iceland, Europe's first democratically elected female head of state.

1995 Collapse of a department store in Seoul, South Korea, killing over 500 and injuring more than 900.

2002 Death of Rosemary Clooney (b.1928 in Maysville, Kentucky), actress and singer.

2003 Death of Katharine Hepburn (b.1907 in Old Saybrook, Connecticut), Academy Award-winning actress, whose films include *The African Queen* (1952).

JUNE

30

1470 Birth of Charles VIII in Amboise, France (d.1498), king of France (1483–98).

1520 Death of Montezuma II (b.1466), the last Aztec emperor.

1837 The British parliament abolished use of the pillory as a form of punishment.

1859 French acrobat and tightrope walker Charles Blondin (1824–97) walked across a tightrope over the Niagara Falls.

1884 Birth of Georges Duhamel in Paris (d.1966), poet and novelist, whose works include *Chronique des Pasquier* (1933–44, The Pasquier Chronicles).

1891 Birth of Sir Stanley Spencer in Cookham, Windsor and Maidenhead (d.1959), painter, whose main works interpret the Bible in terms of everyday life.

1894 Opening of Tower Bridge, London, designed by Sir Horace Jones and Sir J. Wolfe Barry; it is a 'bascule' (French 'see-saw') bridge, on a level with the adjoining streets, with two arms that can be raised or lowered.

1934 Night of the Long Knives, when Adolf Hitler eliminated all his political critics and opponents.

1936 Publication of the book *Gone With the Wind* by US novelist Margaret Mitchell (1900–49), which won a Pulitzer Prize.

1939 Final day of service for the Mersey Ferry between Liverpool and Rock Ferry, Merseyside.

1953 Full production began of the hand-built Corvette car at General Motors, Flint, Michigan; 300 Corvettes were produced that year.

1957 First day of service for the lion stamped on British eggs.

1960 Opening of Alfred Hitchcock's film *Psycho* in New York.

1963 Enthronement of Giovanni Battista Montini (1897–1978) as Pope Paul VI, 262nd head of the Roman Catholic Church.

1966 Birth of Mike Tyson in New York, boxer and world heavyweight champion.

1971 The three-man crew of Russian cosmonauts were found dead in Soyuz 11, after a normal landing; the cause was decompression of their capsule during the descent.

1974 Defection of Soviet ballet dancer Mikhail Baryshnikov (b.1948) to the West, while on tour in Canada with the Bolshoi Ballet.

1980 Last day of legal tender for the British sixpence.

JULY

1

Feast (Eastern Church) of St Cosmas and St Damian (3rd c), twin brothers, and patron saints of chemists, doctors, hairdressers (men's), midwives, and surgeons.

1690 The Battle of the Boyne was fought near Drogheda, Co Louth, Ireland, between William of Orange and the exiled James II.

1837 First registration of births, marriages, and deaths in Britain.

1847 First sales of adhesive stamps in the USA.

1858 Naturalist Charles Darwin (1809–82) announced his theory of evolution to the Linnean Society.

1899 Birth of Charles Laughton in Scarborough, North Yorkshire (d.1962), actor, whose films include *Mutiny on the Bounty* (1935).

1904 [Old Style calendar, New Style 14 July] Death of Anton Chekhov (b.1860 in Taganrog, Russia), playwright and short-story writer, whose plays include *Uncle Vanya* (1900).

1910 Birth of Estée Lauder in New York, businesswoman, who co-founded a perfume firm with her husband Joseph Lauder in 1946.

1916 Launch of the distinctive Coca-Cola bottle.

1916 Beginning of the Battle of the Somme; on this day Britain suffered 54,470 casualties, including 19,240 dead, an unprecedented total in the history of the British army.

1934 Birth of Sydney Pollack in South Bend, Indiana, director and producer, whose films include *Out of Africa* (1985, 2 Oscars).

1937 First operation of the 999 telephone service in Britain.

1940 Beginning of the Battle of Britain during World War 2, as German air forces attacked Britain.

1941 Transmission of the first television advertisement, in the USA, by the Bulova Clock and Watch Company.

1967 BBC2 broadcast its first colour television programmes.

1969 Investiture of Prince Charles as the Prince of Wales at Caernarfon Castle, North Wales.

1974 Opening of the first Laura Ashley shop in the USA, in San Francisco.

1980 Death of C(harles) P(ercy) Snow (b.1905 in Leicester, Leicestershire), novelist and physicist, whose works include an 11-volume novel series, *Strangers and Brothers* (1940–70).

1990 The Deutschmark became official currency for East and West Germany.

1997 Hong Kong was handed back to China by Britain.

185

JULY
2

1566 Death of Nostradamus (b.1503 in St Rémy, France), physician and astrologer, best known for his *Centuries* of predictions (two collections, 1555–8).

1644 During the English Civil War, the Royalist Cavaliers were beaten by the Roundheads at the Battle of Marston Moor, near York.

1778 Death of Jean Jacques Rousseau (b.1712 in Geneva, Switzerland), French philosopher, best known for his *Social Contract* (1762).

1850 Patenting of the gas mask by B. J. Lane of Cambridge, Massachusetts.

1865 Foundation of the Salvation Army by religious leader William Booth (1829–1912) in the East End of London.

1900 First airship flight by German army officer Count Ferdinand Zeppelin (1838–1917).

1900 Opening of the 2nd Olympic Games, in Paris.

1903 Birth of Sir Alec Douglas-Home in London (d.1995), British prime minister (1963–4).

1913 Birth of Marcus Joseph Sieff in Manchester (d.2001), chairman (1972–84), then president, of Marks and Spencer.

1940 Sinking of British prison ship *Andora Star* by a German submarine, while carrying German and Italian internees to Canada.

1961 Death of Ernest Hemingway (b.1899 in Oak Park, Illinois), writer, whose works include *For Whom the Bell Tolls* (1940).

1964 Signing of the US Civil Rights Bill by President Lyndon B. Johnson.

1973 Death of Betty Grable (b.1916 in Louis, Minnesota), film actress and World War 2 pin-up girl.

1980 The musical *Sweeny Todd* was performed for the first time in London.

1982 Los Angeles truck driver Larry Walters flew 16,000 ft into the air with 42 helium balloons attached to a garden chair.

1988 German tennis player Steffi Graf (b.1969) defeated Martina Navratilova (b.1956), winning her first Wimbledon title.

1997 Death of James Stewart (b.1908 in Indiana, Pennsylvania), film star, whose films include *The Philadelphia Story* (1940, Oscar).

1999 Death of Mario Puzo (b.1920 in New York), novelist, whose works include *The Godfather* (1969).

2001 Mr Robert Tools of Kentucky became the first person to receive a self-contained artificial heart.

2002 US adventurer Steve Fossett became the first to fly a balloon solo around the globe, travelling 19,428 miles in 13 days, 12 hours, 16 minutes, 13 seconds.

JULY
3

Feast of St Thomas the Apostle (1st c), patron saint of architects, the blind, builders, and Portugal (also 21 December).

1608 Founding of Quebec as a trading post by Samuel de Champlain (1567–1635).

1841 Discovery of the planet Neptune, almost simultaneously, by astronomers John Couch Adams (1819–92) and Urbain Leverrier (1811–77).

1863 Ending of the Battle of Gettysburg, with victory for the North, during the American Civil War.

1883 Birth of Franz Kafka in Prague, Czech Republic (d.1924), novelist, whose posthumous works include *Der Prozess* (1925, The Trial).

1890 Idaho became the 43rd state of the Union.

1901 Butch Cassidy's Wild Bunch committed its last US robbery, stealing $65,000 from a Great Northern train.

1927 Birth of Ken Russell in Southampton, Hampshire, director, whose films include *Women in Love* (1969).

1928 Electrical engineer John Logie Baird (1888–1946) made the first television broadcast in colour from the Baird Studios, London.

1937 Birth of Sir Tom Stoppard in Zlín, Czech Republic, playwright, who made his name in 1967 with *Rosencrantz and Guildenstern are Dead*.

1945 The Ford Motor Company completed the first civilian passenger car constructed since February 1942, when manufacture was diverted to vehicle production for World War 2.

1954 Ending of food rationing in Britain.

1962 Birth of Tom Cruise in Syracuse, New York, actor, whose films include *Eyes Wide Shut* (1999).

1964 Birth of Joanne Harris in Barnsley, South Yorkshire, novelist, whose works include *Chocolat* (1999, filmed 2000).

1971 Death of Jim Morrison (b.1943 in Melbourne, Florida), rock singer with The Doors (1965).

1986 Relighting of the renovated Statue of Liberty, in a gala ceremony presided over by US president Ronald Reagan.

1987 The Octopus publishing group was bought by Reed International for £540 million.

1996 Sir Cliff Richard began a sing-along to keep the crowd entertained when rain stopped play at Wimbledon's centre court.

JULY

4

USA Independence Day.

1631 Opening of the first employment agency, in Paris.

1776 Adoption of the Declaration of Independence by the Continental Congress.

1826 Death of John Adams (b.1735 in Braintree (now Quincy), Massachusetts), 2nd president of the USA (1797–1801).

1829 Introduction of Britain's first scheduled bus service, in London.

1845 Birth of Thomas John Barnardo in Dublin, Ireland (d.1905), doctor and philanthropist, who founded homes for children which came to be known as the 'Dr Barnardo's Homes'.

1872 Birth of John Calvin Coolidge in Plymouth, Vermont (d.1933), 30th president of the USA (1923–9).

1885 Birth of Louis B. Mayer in Minsk, Belarus (d.1957), US film mogul, who helped form the Metro–Goldwyn–Mayer film company (1924).

1901 Birth of Louis Armstrong in New Orleans, Louisiana (d.1971), jazz singer and trumpeter, who established the central role of the improvising soloist in jazz.

1904 Construction began on the Panama Canal, linking the Atlantic and Pacific Oceans, opened to traffic on 15 August 1914.

1918 Birth of Ann Landers, pseudonym of Esther Pauline Friedman, in Sioux City, Iowa (d.2002), journalist, who became an institution as an advice columnist.

1927 Birth of Neil Simon in New York, playwright, whose shows include *Lost in Yonkers* (1991, Pulitzer, Tony).

1934 Death of Marie Curie (b.1867 in Warsaw, Poland), physicist, who worked in Paris with her French husband Pierre Curie (1859–1906) on magnetism and radioactivity.

1946 Independence of the Philippines from US sovereignty.

1974 Death of Georgette Heyer (b.1902 in London), writer, whose work includes historical novels, fictional studies of real figures, and comedy detective novels.

1976 Rescue of most of the passengers and crew from an Air France aeroplane hijacked by pro-Palestinians when Israeli commandos stormed Entebbe airport, Uganda.

1976 The USA celebrated its bicentennial.

1985 Ruth Lawrence (b.1971) became the youngest British person to gain a first-class degree, and the youngest-known graduate of Oxford University.

1999 Lindsey Davenport (USA) beat Steffi Graf (Germany) to become Wimbledon's women's singles champion.

2004 The cornerstone, a 20-ton inscribed granite slab, was laid for the Freedom Tower skyscraper, New York, to replace the twin towers of the World Trade Center, destroyed 11 September 2001.

JULY

5

1201 An earthquake in Syria and upper Egypt killed c.1.1 million people.

1810 Birth of P. T. Barnum in Bethel, Connecticut, showman, who joined with his rival James Anthony Bailey (1847–1906) to found the Barnum and Bailey circus (1881).

1811 Independence of Venezuela, the first South American country to declare independence from Spain.

1817 Sovereigns became legal tender in Britain.

1826 Death of Sir Stamford Raffles (b.1781 at sea, off Port Morant, Jamaica), colonial administrator and naturalist, who established a settlement at Singapore (1819).

1841 Arrangement of England's first railway excursion, from Leicester to Loughborough, by tourist pioneer Thomas Cook (1808–92).

1853 Birth of Cecil Rhodes in Bishop's Stortford, Hertfordshire (d.1902), statesman and financier, who founded scholarships at Oxford for Americans, Germans, and colonials.

1865 Britain imposed the world's first road speed-limit, 4 mph, under the 'Red Flag Act': mechanical vehicles had to follow a man carrying a red flag.

1889 Birth of Jean Cocteau in Maisons-Lafitte, France (d.1963), poet, novelist, artist, and director, whose works include the film *Beauty and the Beast* (1945).

1911 Birth of Georges Pompidou in Montboudif, France (d.1974), prime minister (1962, 1962–6, 1966–7, 1967–8) and president (1969–74) of France.

1924 Opening of the 8th Olympic Games, in Paris.

1946 Modelling of the first bikini at a Paris fashion show, made by French designer Louis Réard (1897–1984).

1948 Britain's National Health Service came into being.

1965 US opera singer Maria Callas (1923–77) gave her last stage performance, in *Tosca*, at Covent Garden, London.

1969 Death of Walter Gropius (b.1883 in Berlin, Germany), architect, who formed the Bauhaus, an influential school of arts and crafts (1919).

1975 Arthur Ashe (1943–93) became the first black man to win the Wimbledon singles title, defeating Jimmy Connors (b.1952).

1977 Overthrow in Pakistan of the government of Zulfikar Ali Bhutto, in a military coup by General Mohammad Zia-ul-Haq.

1981 Riots began in the Toxteth district of Liverpool.

1997 Swiss tennis player Martina Hingis (b.1980) became the youngest Wimbledon singles champion of the 20th c when she beat Jana Novotna (b.1968) in the women's finals.

JULY
6

1483 Coronation of King Richard III of England (1483–5).

1553 Death of King Edward VI of England (b.1537 in London, r.1547–53) from tuberculosis.

1886 Introduction of box numbers in the classified advertisements of newspapers, pioneered by Britain's *Daily Telegraph*.

1912 Opening of the 5th Olympic Games in Stockholm, Sweden.

1919 Beginning of the first airship crossing of the Atlantic, by British airship R34, taking 108 hours.

1923 Formal constitution of the Union of Soviet Socialist Republics.

1928 Strand Theatre, New York, screened the first all-talking feature film, *Lights of New York*.

1932 Death of Kenneth Grahame (b.1859 in Edinburgh), novelist, best known for his children's story *The Wind in the Willows* (1908).

1935 Birth of Tenzin Gyatso in Taktser, China, 14th Dalai Lama.

1936 Birth of Dave Allen in Firhouse, Co Dublin, Ireland (d.2005), comedian and actor, known for his TV comedy series *Dave Allen at Large* (1971, 1975).

1946 Birth of Sylvester Stallone in New York, actor, best known as an action-film hero in such films as *Rocky* (1976, 2 Oscars).

1946 Birth of George W. Bush in New Haven, Connecticut, who became 43rd president of the USA (2001) following five weeks of legal argument over the voting procedure.

1952 Final journey of trams in London.

1957 Althea Gibson (1927–2003) became the first female African-American tennis player to win a Wimbledon singles title, defeating fellow American Darlene Hard (b.1936).

1958 Birth of Jennifer Saunders in Sleaford, Lincolnshire, comedy writer and actress, co-star of *Absolutely Fabulous*.

1971 Announcement by the British government that the wearing of crash helmets by motorcyclists was to be compulsory.

1971 Death of Louis Armstrong (b.1901 in New Orleans, Louisiana), jazz singer and trumpeter, who established the central role of the improvising soloist in jazz.

1988 Explosion of the Piper Alpha oil platform in the North Sea, killing 167 people.

2005 Awarding of the 2012 Olympics to London, which brings the games back to the British capital for the first time since 1948.

JULY

7

1307 Death of King Edward I of England (b.1239 in London, r.1272–1307).

1456 Annulment of the heresy charges against Joan of Arc (c.1412–31), 25 years after her execution.

1816 Death of Richard Brinsley Sheridan (b.1751 in Dublin, Ireland), playwright, whose comedies include *The School for Scandal* (1777).

1846 The annexation of California by the USA was announced at Monterey, following the surrender of a Mexican garrison.

1860 Birth of Gustave Mahler in Kalist, Czech Republic, formerly Bohemia (d.1911), composer, whose works include nine symphonies.

1887 Birth of Marc Chagall in Vitebsk, Belarus (d.1985), painter, first to be described as a Surrealist.

1899 Birth of George Cukor in New York (d.1988), director, whose films include *My Fair Lady* (1964, Oscar).

1919 Birth of John Pertwee in Chelsea, London (d.1996), actor, whose television roles include the third Dr Who and Worzel Gummidge.

1927 Christopher Stone (1882–1965) presented the first BBC programme of recorded music on radio, becoming the first disc jockey.

1930 Death of Sir Arthur Conan Doyle (b.1859 in Edinburgh), writer, whose first book, *A Study in Scarlet* (1887), introduced the character of Sherlock Holmes.

1940 Birth of Ringo Starr in Liverpool, drummer, singer, songwriter, and actor, who replaced Pete Best as drummer in The Beatles pop group.

1946 Canonization of Italian-born Mother Frances Xavier Cabrini (1850–1917), the first US saint.

1950 Britain's first air display took place at Farnborough.

1956 Explosion of seven army trucks carrying dynamite in Cali, Columbia, killing 1100–1200 people, and destroying 2000 buildings.

1970 Death of Sir Allen Lane (b.1902 in Bristol, Avon), publisher, who formed Penguin Books in 1935.

1979 Martina Navratilova (b.1956) won the women's tennis singles final at Wimbledon.

1979 Björn Borg (b.1956) won the men's tennis singles final at Wimbledon.

1981 Flight of the first solar-powered aircraft, the Solar Challenger, across the English Channel.

2001 Banning of a National Front rally led to race riots in Bradford, West Yorkshire, in which 80 police officers were injured.

2005 A terrorist attack on London transport during rush hour left 52 people dead and over 700 injured.

JULY
8

1497 Portuguese navigator Vasco da Gama (c.1469–1525) sailed from Lisbon to Calicut, India, a journey which opened the Far East to European trade and colonial expansion.

1663 Charles II of England granted a charter to Rhode Island, New England, guaranteeing freedom of worship.

1709 Defeat of Charles XII of Sweden at the Battle of Poltava, Ukraine, by Peter the Great of Russia, effectively ending the Swedish Empire.

1776 First public reading of the Declaration of Independence, given by Colonel John Nixon (1828–98) at Independence Square, Philadelphia, Pennsylvania.

1822 Death of Percy Bysshe Shelley (b.1792 near Horsham, West Sussex), poet, drowned while sailing off the coast of Italy.

1838 Birth of Count Zeppelin in Konstanz, Germany (d.1917), army officer, who in 1897–1900 constructed his first airship, setting up a factory at Friedrichshafen.

1839 Birth of John D. Rockefeller in Richford, New York (d.1937), industrialist and philanthropist, who in 1913 established the Rockefeller Foundation.

1884 Foundation of the National Society for the Prevention of Cruelty to Children (NSPCC), in London.

1889 First day of publication for the *Wall Street Journal*, when the Dow Jones business newsletter became a fully fledged newspaper.

1892 The first conviction took place using fingerprints as evidence, in Buenos Aires Province, Argentina.

1907 Presentation of the first *Follies* production, by US theatre manager Florenz Ziegfeld (1869–1932).

1918 First sales of National Saving stamps in Britain.

1948 Celebration in Moscow of the 500th anniversary of the Russian Orthodox church.

1949 The first enlisted woman, Vietta M. Bates, was sworn into the US Army, when legislation made the Women's Auxiliary Army Corps part of the regular army.

1951 Birth of Angelica Huston in Los Angeles, California, actress, whose films include *The Addams Family* (1991).

1958 Presentation of the first gold disc, to the soundtrack record of *Oklahoma!*, by the Recording Industry Association of America (RIAA).

1965 First use of starting gates in British horse racing, at Newmarket, for the Chesterfield Stakes.

1985 Death of Frank Hampson (b.1918 in Manchester), strip cartoonist, who in 1950 designed the *Eagle* comic for boys.

JULY

9

1386 Defeat of Leopold III of Austria and his 6000-strong army by 1600 Swiss pikemen at the Battle of Sempach during the Swiss–Swabian wars.

1441 Death of Jan van Eyck (b.1389 near Maastricht, The Netherlands), painter, whose works include *Arnolfini Wedding Portrait* (1434).

1816 Independence of Argentina from Spain.

1819 Birth of Elias Howe in Spencer, Massachusetts (d.1867), inventor, who constructed and patented the first sewing machine in 1846.

1872 Patenting of the doughnut cutter, by John Blondel of Thomaston, Maine.

1877 The All England Croquet and Lawn Tennis Club began its first lawn tennis tournament at Wimbledon, London.

1888 Birth of Simon Marks in Leeds, West Yorkshire (d.1964), businessman, who collaborated with Israel Sieff to develop Marks and Spencer into a major retail chain.

1901 Birth of Barbara Cartland in Edgbaston, West Midlands (d.2000), popular romantic novelist, who, after her first novel, *Jigsaw* (1923), wrote over 600 books.

1916 Birth of Edward Heath in Broadstairs, Kent, British prime minister (1970–74).

1922 Swimmer and film star Johnny Weissmuller (1904–84) became the first person to swim 100 m in under a minute.

1932 Death of King C. Gillette (b.1855 in Fond du Lac, Wisconsin), inventor of the safety razor.

1938 British civilians were issued with gas masks in anticipation of World War 2.

1947 Birth of O. J. Simpson in San Francisco, California, player of American football, who joined the Buffalo Bills in 1968, leading the League as top rusher four times (1972–6).

1956 Birth of Tom Hanks in Oakland, California, actor, whose films include *Forrest Gump* (1994).

1972 Ex-Beatle Paul McCartney (b.1942) made his first stage appearance after a six-year break when his group, Wings, played in the south of France.

1979 US Voyager 2 space probe passed close to Jupiter.

1982 A man broke into Buckingham Palace, London, and spent ten minutes talking to Queen Elizabeth II in her bedroom.

1984 Fire destroyed the roof of York Minster, North Yorkshire.

2000 Pete Sampras (b.1971) became the most successful player in men's tennis when he won his seventh Wimbledon singles title.

JULY

10

1460 Defeat of Henry VI by Richard, Duke of York, at the Battle of Northampton during the Wars of the Roses.

1802 Birth of Robert Chambers in Peebles, Borders (d.1871), publisher and writer, who began as a bookseller in Edinburgh (1818).

1806 Death of George Stubbs (b.1724 in Liverpool), painter, best known for his paintings of horses.

1834 Birth of James McNeill Whistler in Lowell, Massachusetts (d.1903), artist, whose works include a famous portrait of his mother (1871–2).

1890 Wyoming became the 44th state of the Union.

1913 Recording of the highest temperature in Death Valley, California, when it reached 134°F.

1925 Establishment of TASS, official news agency of the Soviet Union.

1929 US paper currency was first issued in the size that is still in use.

1943 Invasion of Sicily by Britain, the USA, and Canada as part of Operation Husky in World War 2.

1958 Introduction of parking meters into Britain, in Mayfair, London; a total of 625 were installed.

1962 Launch of Telstar 1 in the USA, the world's first television telecommunications satellite; it weighed 171 lbs and had a diameter of 34 in.

1965 British rock group The Rolling Stones reached No. 1 in the US pop charts, with their record '(I Can't Get No) Satisfaction'.

1973 Independence of the Bahamas within the Commonwealth, a British colony since 1783.

1985 Sinking of Greenpeace ship *Rainbow Warrior* by French security forces near New Zealand.

1989 Rangers football club, Scotland, signed Catholic footballer Maurice ('Mo') Johnston, a significant move away from the club's Protestant-only policy.

1992 Panama soldier and politician Manuel Noriega (b.1939) received a 40-year jail sentence in the USA for drug-trafficking.

1999 The US ladies soccer team beat China 5–4 in a penalty shoot-out, winning the World Cup at the Rose Bowl in Pasadena, California.

2003 Opening in Granada of the first mosque in Spain since the Moors were expelled in 1492.

JULY

11

Feast (Western Church) of St Benedict of Nursia (c.480–c.547), patron saint of Europe, monks, and speleologists.

1274 Birth of Robert Bruce (d.1329), king of Scots, and hero of the Scottish War of Independence.

1754 Birth of Thomas Bowdler in Ashley, Somerset (d.1825), doctor and man of letters, immortalized as the editor of *The Family Shakespeare* (1818).

1776 Captain James Cook (1728–79) set off on his third and final voyage of discovery, hoping to find a passage round the north coast of America from the Pacific.

1848 Official opening of Waterloo Station, one of London's main railway terminuses.

1914 Debut of Babe Ruth (1895–1948) in major-league baseball as a pitcher for the Boston Red Sox.

1915 Birth of Yul Brynner in Vladivostock, Russia (d.1985), US actor, whose films include *The King and I* (1956).

1921 Independence of Mongolia from China.

1934 Franklin D. Roosevelt became the first US president to sail through the Panama Canal.

1937 Death of George Gershwin (b.1898 in New York), composer and songwriter, whose works include the jazz-opera *Porgy and Bess* (1935).

1950 First transmission of the BBC children's television programme *Andy Pandy*.

1959 Birth of Richie (Richard Stephen) Sambora in Perth Amboy, New Jersey, rock guitarist with Bon Jovi.

1974 China's Great Terracotta Army was uncovered at Mount Li, the burial place of Qin Shihuangdi, first emperor of China (259–210 BC).

1979 Return to earth of the US Skylab 1 (launched 14 May 1973), after 34,981 orbits of the earth.

1980 Opening of the Britannia Road Bridge, built on top of the railway line over the Menai Straits between mainland Wales and Anglesey.

1989 Death of Sir Laurence Olivier (b.1907 in Dorking, Surrey), actor, producer, and director, who played all the great male Shakespearean roles.

1995 The Bosnian Serb army seized the UN 'safe area' of Srebrenica, after the forced withdrawal of Dutch peacekeepers.

2000 Death of Robert Runcie (b.1921 in Crosby, Lancashire), former archbishop of Canterbury.

JULY

12

1543 Marriage of King Henry VIII of England (1491–1547) to his sixth and last wife, Catherine Parr (1512–48).

1730 Birth of Josiah Wedgwood in Burslem, Staffordshire (d.1795), potter, who invented unglazed black basalt and blue jasper ware with raised designs in white.

1794 British admiral Lord Nelson lost his right eye during the siege of Calvi, Corsica.

1817 Birth of Henry David Thoreau in Concord, Massachusetts (d.1862), writer and naturalist.

1851 Death of Louis Daguerre (b.1789 in Cormeilles, France), photographic pioneer, who perfected the photographic process named after him.

1854 Birth of George Eastman in Waterville, New York (d.1932), inventor and philanthropist, who produced the transparent celluloid film which made possible the moving-picture industry (1889).

1895 Birth of Oscar Hammerstein II in New York (d.1960), librettist, who with Richard Rodgers (1902–79) wrote such musicals as *Oklahoma!* (1943).

1910 Death of C. S. Rolls (b.1877 in London), motorist and aeronaut, who formed a partnership with Henry Royce in 1906 for car production.

1930 Australian cricketer Don Bradman (1908–2001) scored 309 in one day during the third Test against England at Headingley, the highest score ever for one day of a Test match.

1935 Death of Alfred Dreyfus (b.1859 in Mulhouse, France), army officer, sent to Devil's Island having been falsely accused of selling military secrets.

1937 Birth of Bill Cosby in Philadelphia, Pennsylvania, comedian and actor, best known for *The Cosby Show* (from 1984).

1951 Boxer Randolph Turpin beat Ray Robinson at Earls Court, London, becoming European middleweight champion.

1958 'Yakety Yak', by the Coasters, reached No. 1 in the US charts, the first stereo record to make that spot.

1960 First sales of the popular children's toy Etch-A-Sketch.

1969 British golfer Tony Jacklin (b.1944) became the first home winner of the British Open golf championship since Max Faulkner in 1951.

1979 Independence of Kiribati, formerly the Gilbert Islands, from the UK.

1982 *E.T. The Extra-Terrestrial* broke box-office records when over $100 million in ticket sales were taken in the first month following its release.

2003 Commissioning of USS *Ronald Reagan*, the first aircraft-carrier named after a living president.

JULY

13

Feast (Eastern Church) of St Margaret of Antioch, patron saint of the dying and of women in childbirth.

1643 Defeat of the Parliamentarians by the Royalists at the Battle of Roundway Down, Devizes, Wiltshire, during the English Civil War.

1779 Birth of William Hedley in Newburn, Tyne and Wear (d.1843), inventor, whose locomotive, 'Puffing Billy', was the first commercial steam locomotive.

1793 Murder of Jean Paul Marat (b.1743), French revolutionary, in his bath by Charlotte Corday (1768–93).

1837 Queen Victoria took up residence at Buckingham Palace in London.

1863 Around 1000 people died in riots in New York against the Civil War military draft.

1875 Patenting of the first money-carrying system – a basket, wire, and pulley construction – by David Brown of Lebanon, New Jersey.

1908 Opening of the 4th Olympic Games, in London.

1919 Completion of the first Atlantic round trip, by British airship R34.

1923 A bill was passed by the British parliament making the sale of alcohol to people under 18 illegal.

1930 The first World Cup football match was played between France and Mexico in Montevideo; France won 4–1.

1940 Birth of Patrick Stewart in Mirfield, Yorkshire, actor, who played Captain Jean-Luc Picard in the follow-up series of *Star Trek* (from 1987).

1943 Defeat of German forces in the Battle of Kursk, the largest tank battle in history, with over 6000 tanks, 2 million troops, and 4000 aircraft.

1955 Hanging of murderer Ruth Ellis (b.1926), the last woman to receive the death penalty in Britain.

1960 Birth of Ian Hislop in Mumbles, Swansea, writer, broadcaster, and editor of *Private Eye* (from 1986).

1977 Arrest of around 3000 people when looters rampaged through the New York area during a 25-hour power blackout.

1985 Over £42 million was raised for famine victims in Africa by British and American 'Live Aid' pop concerts, organized by rock musician and philanthropist Bob Geldof (b.1954).

2002 Celebration of the marriage of Mohammed VI (b.1963), king of Morocco, to Lalla Salma (b.1978), a computer engineer, with two days of festivities.

JULY

14

Bastille Day (France).
Feast of St Camillus of Lellis, patron saint of hospitals, nurses, and sick people.
Feast of St Phocas of Sinope (also 22 September), patron saint of agricultural workers, gardeners, and sailors.

1798 US Congress passed the Sedition Act, making it a crime to publish false, scandalous, or malicious writing about the US government.

1833 Launch of the Oxford Movement within the Church of England, seeking the revival of high doctrine and ceremonial.

1857 Birth of Emmeline Pankhurst in Manchester (d.1928), suffragette, who was arrested and went on hunger strike in support of her cause.

1865 British Alpine climber Edward Whymper (1840–1911) led the first climbers to the summit of the Matterhorn.

1867 First demonstration of dynamite, by chemist and industrialist Alfred Bernhard Nobel (1833–96), in a quarry in Redhill, Surrey.

1881 Death of Billy the Kid, originally William H. Bonney (b.1859 in New York), outlaw, shot by Sheriff Pat Garrett in Fort Sumner, New Mexico.

1911 Birth of Terry-Thomas in Finchley, London (d.1990), actor who played the gap-toothed villain in dozens of post-World War 2 comedies.

1913 Birth of Gerald Ford in Omaha, Nebraska, 38th president of the USA (1974–7).

1918 Birth of Ingmar Bergman in Uppsala, Sweden, director and writer, whose films include *Through a Glass Darkly* (1961, Oscar).

1930 Transmission of the first BBC TV play, *The Man with a Flower in His Mouth*.

1933 The Nazi Party under Adolf Hitler banned all opposition parties in Germany.

1950 Birth of Bruce Oldfield in London, fashion designer.

1958 Death of Faisal II (b.1935 in Baghdad), king of Iraq, assassinated with his entire household during a military coup, after which Iraq became a republic.

1959 Launch of the first nuclear warship, USS *Long Beach*.

1967 Legalization of abortion in the UK.

1987 End of 37 years of martial law in Taiwan.

2002 Failure of an assassination attempt on French president Jacques Chirac (b.1932) during a Bastille Day parade.

JULY

15

Feast of St Swithin (?–862); the planned removal of his body on this day in 971 to Winchester Cathedral was apparently delayed by violent rains – leading to the belief that if it rains on this day, it will rain for 40 days more.

1573 Birth of Inigo Jones in London (d.1652), first of the great English architects, whose designs include the Queen's House at Greenwich (1616–35).

1606 Birth of Rembrandt in Leyden, The Netherlands (d.1669), painter, whose works include *The Night Watch* (1642).

1741 Danish navigator Vitus Bering (1681–1741) landed on the Alaskan coast, during his last voyage.

1795 Adoption of the 'Marseillaise' as the French National Anthem.

1865 Birth of Alfred Harmsworth, 1st Viscount Northcliffe, near Dublin, Ireland (d.1922), journalist and newspaper magnate, who introduced mass circulation journalism to the UK.

1869 Patenting of margarine by French chemist Hippolyte Mège-Mouriès (1817–80).

1912 Introduction of national insurance payments in Britain.

1916 Founding of the Boeing Co, originally Pacific Aero Products, by William Boeing (1881–1956) in Seattle, Washington.

1919 Birth of Dame Iris Murdoch in Dublin, Ireland (d.1999), novelist and philosopher, whose works include *The Sea, The Sea* (1978, Booker).

1936 Lifting of economic sanctions against Italy by the League of Nations, imposed following Italy's invasion of Ethiopia.

1945 In Britain, wartime blackouts ended and 'the lights came on again'.

1948 Foundation of Alcoholics Anonymous in London.

1958 Landing of 5000 US marines in Lebanon at the request of President Chamoun, to help end a short-lived civil war.

1959 Death of Ernest Bloch (b.1880 in Geneva, Switzerland), composer, whose works include *America* (1926).

1965 The first close-up pictures of Mars were sent back by US spacecraft Mariner 4.

1968 First direct air services began between the USA and the Soviet Union, flying between New York and Moscow, operated by Aeroflot and Pan American.

1997 Death of Gianni Versace (b.1946 in Reggio di Calabria, Italy), fashion designer, whose trademark designs were the siren dresses made using innovative materials and techniques.

2005 Marriage of world heavyweight boxing champion Lennox Lewis (b.1965) to Miss Jamaica runner-up Violet Chang (b.1975).

JULY
16

622 Muhammad fled from Mecca to Medina, so beginning the Islamic Era, the Hejira.

1377 Coronation of King Richard II of England (r.1377–99).

1557 Death of Anne of Cleves (b.1515), German princess, and queen consort of England, the fourth wife of Henry VIII.

1790 Washington, DC, became the seat of federal government in the USA.

1821 Birth of Mary Baker Eddy in Bow, New Hampshire (d.1910), founder of the Church of Christ: Scientist.

1827 Death of Josiah Spode (b.1755 in Stoke-on-Trent, Staffordshire), potter, who made transfer-printed earthenware, stoneware, and highly decorated bone-china.

1867 Patenting of reinforced concrete by Joseph Monier of Paris.

1872 Birth of Roald Amundsen in Borge, Norway (d.1928), explorer, and locator of the Magnetic North Pole.

1907 Birth of Barbara Stanwyck in New York (d.1990), actress, whose films include *Double Indemnity* (1944).

1911 Birth of Ginger Rogers in Independence, Missouri, actress, who danced with Fred Astaire in several films, and won an Oscar for her role in *Kitty Foyle* (1940).

1918 Murder of Tsar Nicholas II of Russia and his family by Bolsheviks at Ekaterinburg.

1926 Publication of the first underwater colour photographs, by the US journal *National Geographic*.

1935 First installation and use of parking meters, in Oklahoma City.

1945 Detonation of the first atomic bomb, at Alamogordo Air Base in New Mexico.

1951 Publication of *The Catcher in the Rye*, by US author J. D. Salinger (b.1919).

1965 Opening of the Mont Blanc road tunnel, a 12-km/7-mile link between Italy and France.

1969 Launch of the first crewed mission to the Moon, Apollo 11, undertaken by NASA at the direction of President Kennedy.

1979 Saddam Hussein (b.1937) became president of Iraq and chairman of the Revolutionary Command Council.

1989 Death of Herbert von Karajan (b.1908 in Salzburg, Austria), principal conductor with the Berlin Philharmonic.

1999 Death of John F. Kennedy Jr, together with his wife and sister-in-law, when the aeroplane he was flying crashed into the sea near Martha's Vineyard, Massachusetts.

JULY

17

Feast of St Alexis of Rome, patron saint of beggars.

1603 Arrest of Sir Walter Raleigh (1552–1618) on false charges of conspiracy; his death sentence was suspended, but he remained in the Tower of London for 13 years.

1717 Handel's *Water Music* was played for George I of Great Britain during a royal barge trip on the R Thames, London.

1761 Opening of Britain's Bridgewater Canal, linking Worsley to Manchester, and continuing to Liverpool, length 64 km/40 miles.

1763 Birth of John Jacob Astor in Waldorf, Germany (d.1912), fur trader and financier, who went to the USA in 1784, and founded the America Fur Co.

1790 Death of Adam Smith (b.1723 in Kirkcaldy, Fife), economist and philosopher, who published the first major work of political economy (1776).

1821 Spain ceded Florida to the USA.

1841 Publication of the first issue of *Punch* magazine, in London.

1898 Surrender of Spain to the USA at Santiago, Cuba, ending the Spanish–American War.

1899 Birth of James Cagney in New York (d.1986), actor, who won an Oscar for his role in *Yankee Doodle Dandy* (1942).

1903 Death of James McNeill Whistler (b.1834 in Lowell, Massachusetts), artist, known for his evening scenes, such as 'Old Battersea Bridge' (c.1872–5).

1935 Birth of Donald Sutherland in St John, New Brunswick, Canada, actor, whose films include *M*A*S*H* (1970).

1955 Opening of Disneyland theme park in Anaheim, California.

1968 London premiere of *Yellow Submarine*, the full-length cartoon featuring The Beatles.

1975 The US Apollo and Russian Soyuz spacecraft docked in orbit.

1979 Athlete Sebastian Coe (b.1956) ran the mile in a new record time of 3 minutes 48·95 seconds.

1981 Formal opening by Queen Elizabeth II of the Humber Estuary Bridge, length of main span 1410 m/4626 ft.

1998 Burial of Nicholas II (1868–1918), last tsar of Russia, 80 years after he and his family were executed by the Bolsheviks.

JULY
18

1536 An Act of Parliament declared the pope's authority void in England.

1811 Birth of William Makepeace Thackeray in Calcutta, India (d.1863), novelist, whose works include *Vanity Fair* (1847–8).

1817 Death of Jane Austen (b.1775 in Steventon, Hampshire), novelist, whose works include *Pride and Prejudice* (1813).

1848 Birth of W(illiam) G(ilbert) Grace in Downend, Gloucestershire (d.1915), cricketer, whose career in first-class cricket as batsman and bowler won him the title 'The Great Cricketer'.

1872 Introduction of the Ballot Act in Britain, allowing people to vote by secret ballot.

1892 Death of Thomas Cook (b.1808 in Melbourne, Derbyshire), tourist pioneer, who organized his first railway excursion in 1841, from Leicester to Loughborough.

1919 Unveiling of the Cenotaph in Whitehall, London, designed by Sir Edwin Lutyens, a memorial to those who gave their lives during World War 1.

1925 Publication of the first volume of Adolf Hitler's *Mein Kampf.*

1934 Opening by King George V of the Mersey (Queensway) tunnel under the R Mersey, the longest road tunnel in Britain.

1936 Beginning of the Spanish Civil War, when General Franco led an uprising of army troops based in Spanish North Africa.

1947 Signing of the Presidential Succession Act, giving a line of succession of vice president, followed by the Speaker of the House, the Senate president, and the president's cabinet by rank.

1950 Birth of Richard Branson in Sharnley Green, Surrey, businessman, and founder of the Virgin empire of companies.

1966 Launch of the US spacecraft Gemini 10, with astronauts John Young and Michael Collins on board.

1976 Opening of the 21st Olympic Games, at Montreal, Quebec.

1976 The first perfect score of 10 at the Olympics was awarded to 14-year-old Romanian gymnast Nadia Comaneci (b.1961), who then scored six more tens and won three gold medals.

1998 A 23-foot tsunami along the coast of Papua New Guinea killed nearly 3000 people.

2001 Death of Roy Gilchrist (b.1934 in Seaforth, Jamaica), cricketer, who played Test cricket for the West Indies.

JULY

19

1333 Defeat of the Scots army by Edward III at the Battle of Halidon Hill during the war of Scottish Independence.

1545 The *Mary Rose*, a warship built in 1511 for King Henry VIII, keeled over and sank in the Solent.

1814 Death of Matthew Flinders (b.1774 in Donington, Lincolnshire), explorer, who circumnavigated Australia (1800–1803); Flinders River and the Flinders Range are named after him.

1821 Coronation of George IV, king of Great Britain and Hanover (1820–30), in Westminster Abbey, London.

1834 Birth of Edgar Degas in Paris (d.1917), Impressionist artist, whose works include *Dancer Lacing Her Shoe* (1880).

1837 Launch of the *Great Western* steamship, designed by Isambard Kingdom Brunel (1806–59), at Bristol, Avon.

1843 Launch of the first ocean screwsteamer, the *Great Britain*, designed by Isambard Kingdom Brunel (1806–59), from Wapping Dock, London.

1865 Birth of Charles Horace Mayo in Rochester, Minnesota (d.1939), surgeon, who with his older brother, William James Mayo, established the Mayo Foundation (1915).

1870 Beginning of the Franco–Prussian war.

1896 Birth of A(rchibald) J(oseph) Cronin in Cardross, Argyll and Bute (d.1981), novelist, whose books include *The Citadel* (1937).

1900 Opening of the Paris underground rail system, the Métro.

1903 French cyclist Maurice Garin (1871–1957) won the first Tour de France cycle race.

1911 Opening of the Royal Liver Building at Pier Head, Liverpool.

1941 British prime minister Winston Churchill (1874–1965) launched his 'V for Victory' campaign in Europe.

1952 Opening of the 15th Olympic Games, in Helsinki, Finland.

1966 Marriage of US actor and singer Frank Sinatra (1915–98) to actress Mia Farrow (b.1945).

1973 Death of Bruce Lee (b.1940 in San Francisco, California), martial arts film star who made Kung fu popular, best known for *Enter the Dragon* (1973).

1980 Opening of the 22nd Olympic Games, in Moscow.

2003 Death of Bill Bright (b.1921 in Coweta, Oklahoma), businessman and evangelist, winner of the Templeton Prize in 1996.

JULY
20

Feast (Western Church) of St Margaret of Antioch, patron saint of the dying and of women in childbirth.
Feast of St Wilgefortis (Uncumber), patron saint of women unhappily married.

1304 Birth of Petrarch in Arezzo, Italy (d.1374), poet and scholar, best known for a series of love poems, the *Canzoniere*.

1837 Opening of Euston, London's first railway station.

1871 Charles Alcock, secretary of the Football Association, put forward the idea of an FA Cup competition.

1881 Surrender of Sioux Indian leader Sitting Bull (1831–90), a fugitive since the Battle of the Little Big Horn, to federal troops.

1885 Professionalism was legalized by the Football Association.

1890 Death of Sir Richard Wallace (b.1818 in London), art collector and philanthropist, who bequeathed the *Wallace Collection* to the nation in 1897.

1919 Birth of Sir Edmund Hillary in Auckland, New Zealand, mountaineer and explorer, who with Tenzing Norgay reached the summit of Mt Everest in 1953.

1923 Death of Pancho Villa (b.1878 in Hacienda de Río Grande, Mexico), Mexican revolutionary, who led a successful revolt against the regime of Victoriano Huerta (1914).

1937 Death of Guglielmo Marconi (b.1874 in Bologna, Italy), physicist and inventor, who established a worldwide radio telegraph network for the British government.

1938 Birth of Diana Rigg in Doncaster, South Yorkshire, actress, whose roles include Emma Peel in the television series *The Avengers* (1961–9).

1940 First publication of singles record charts, in the USA.

1944 Unsuccessful assassination attempt on Adolf Hitler (1889–1945) by Claus von Stauffenberg (1907–44), who placed a bomb at Hitler's headquarters in Rastenburg.

1947 Birth of Carlos Santana in Autlan, Jalisco, Mexico, rock guitarist, whose songs include 'The Game of Love' (2001, Grammy).

1962 Introduction of the first regular Hovercraft passenger service, between Rhyl in North Wales and Wallasey on the Dee Estuary.

1969 US astronaut Neil Armstrong (b.1930) became the first person to walk on the Moon.

1972 Llyn Brianne Dam, Ceredigion, Wales, became operational, the highest dam in the UK.

1976 US space probe Viking sent back pictures of Mars.

1999 Raising of the Liberty Bell Seven Mercury capsule from the Atlantic, 38 years after its splashdown.

JULY

21

1542 Launch of the Inquisition against Protestants by Pope Paul III.

1693 Birth of Thomas Pelham, 1st Duke of Newcastle (d.1768), British prime minister (1754–6, 1757–62).

1796 Death of Robert Burns (b.1759 in Alloway, South Ayrshire), Scotland's national poet, and author of 'Auld Lang Syne'.

1797 British admiral Horatio Nelson (1758–1805) lost his right arm during an attempt to seize a Spanish ship at Santa Cruz.

1816 Birth of Paul Julius Reuter in Kassel, Germany (d.1899), founder of the first news agency.

1861 Victory for the Confederates at the first Battle of Bull Run, during the American Civil War.

1873 Wild West outlaw Jesse James (1847–82) and his gang stole $3000 from the Rock Island Express in Iowa.

1890 Opening of Battersea Bridge over the R Thames, London.

1897 Official opening of the Tate Gallery, London, as the National Gallery of British Art.

1899 Birth of Ernest Hemingway in Oak Park, Illinois (d.1961), writer, whose works include *A Farewell to Arms* (1929).

1920 Birth of Isaac Stern in Kremenets, Belarus (d. 2001), violinist, who achieved outstanding success at his Carnegie Hall debut in 1943.

1952 Birth of Robin Williams in Chicago, Illinois, actor and comedian, whose films include *Good Morning, Vietnam* (1987).

1959 Launch of US *Savannah* in Camden, New Jersey, the first nuclear merchant ship.

1961 Opening of Runcorn Bridge over the R Mersey, then the longest steel arch bridge in the UK.

1967 Death of Basil Rathbone (b.1892 in Johannesburg, South Africa), actor, best known for his portrayal of the fictional character Sherlock Holmes.

1987 US television personality Mary Hart (b.1950) insured her legs for $1 million with Lloyds of London.

1998 Death of Alan Shepard (b.1923 in East Derry, New Hampshire), astronaut and NASA administrator, the first American to travel in space.

2002 Ernie Els (b.1969) of South Africa won the British Open in the first sudden-death finish in the history of the golf tournament.

JULY

22

Feast of St Mary Magdalene (1st c), patron saint of glovemakers, hairdressers (ladies'), perfumers, repentant prostitutes, and penitents.

1298 Defeat of the Scots, led by William Wallace, by the English at the Battle of Falkirk.

1796 Founding of the city of Cleveland, Ohio, by Moses Cleaveland (1754–1806).

1812 Defeat of the French by the Duke of Wellington at the Battle of Salamanca in Spain.

1822 Birth of Gregor Mendel in Heinzendorf, Austria (d.1884), botanist and biologist, whose laws governing the nature of inheritance formed the basis of modern genetics.

1844 Birth of William Archibald Spooner in London (d.1930), Anglican clergyman, whose name is associated with the *spoonerism*, e.g. 'a half-warmed fish' for 'a half-formed wish'.

1894 The first motor race took place between Paris and Rouen, France.

1923 Birth of Bob Dole in Russell, Kansas, US representative and senator, defeated by Bill Clinton in the presidential election (1996).

1928 Birth of Jimmy Hill in Balham, London, television sports presenter, and ex-professional footballer.

1933 Completion of the first solo flight round the world, taking 7 days, 18 hours, 49 minutes, by pioneer US aviator Wiley Post (1900–1935).

1934 Death of John Dillinger (b.1903 in Indianapolis, Indiana), gangster, who specialized in armed bank robberies, shot dead by FBI agents.

1939 Birth of Terence Stamp in London, actor, whose films include *Far From the Madding Crowd* (1967).

1943 Capture of Palermo, Sicily, by US forces during Operation Husky.

1946 Introduction of bread rationing in Britain.

1964 Birth of Bonnie Langford in Hampton Court, Surrey, actress, whose TV credits include *Doctor Who* (1986–7).

1976 First performance of the stage show *A Chorus Line* in London.

1981 Turkish extremist Mehmet Ali Agca (b.1958) received a life sentence for his failed assassination attempt on Pope John Paul II.

2003 Evacuation of over 3000 people from the Eiffel Tower, Paris, following an electrical fire on the top floor.

2004 Death of Sacha Distel (b.1933 in Paris), guitarist, singer, and composer, well known for his version of the song 'Raindrops Keep Falling on My Head' (1970).

JULY

23

Feast of St Birgitta (c.1302–73), patron saint of scholars.

1403 Death of Sir Henry Percy, 'Harry Hotspur' (b.1364), killed at the battle of Shrewsbury fought by the Percys against King Henry IV.

1757 Death of Domenico Scarlatti (b.1685 in Palermo, Sicily, Italy), composer, mainly remembered for his 555 sonatas written for the harpsichord.

1759 Defeat of Prussia by Russia at the battle of Kay (or Paltzig), during the Seven Years' War.

1875 Death of Isaac Singer (b.1811 in Pittstown, New York), inventor, who manufactured sewing machines.

1888 Birth of Raymond Chandler in Chicago, Illinois (d.1959), writer, creator of the detective antihero Philip Marlowe.

1891 Birth of Ras Tafari Makonnen, Haile Selassie, near Harer, Ethiopia (d.1975), emperor of Ethiopia, who led the revolution in 1916.

1914 Issue of an ultimatum by Austria and Hungary to Serbia, following the assassination of Archduke Ferdinand (1863–1914); the dispute led to World War 1.

1916 Death of Sir William Ramsay (b.1852 in Glasgow), chemist, who identified helium, neon, krypton, and xenon, and was awarded the 1904 Nobel Prize for Chemistry.

1940 Britain's Local Defence Volunteers were renamed the Home Guard.

1940 Beginning of the blitz in London, with an all-night German air raid.

1945 Trial of Henri Pétain (1856–1951), French marshal, and head of the Vichy government during World War 2, on charges of treason; his death sentence was commuted.

1947 Birth of David Essex in London, singer and actor, who made his stage debut as Jesus in the hit musical *Godspell* (1971).

1952 Overthrow of Farouk I, Egypt's last reigning monarch, in a military coup led by Gamal Abdel Nasser (1918–70).

1962 US communications satellite Telstar sent the first live television programmes to Europe.

1986 Marriage of Prince Andrew to Sarah Ferguson in Westminster Abbey, London.

1994 Return of space shuttle Columbia to Earth after a 15-day mission which included experiments on the effects of weightlessness on aquatic animals.

1995 Discovery of the Hale-Bopp comet by US astronomers Alan Hale (b.1958) and Thomas Bopp (b.1949).

2002 Election of Rowan Williams, archbishop of Wales (b.1950), as 104th archbishop of Canterbury.

JULY

24

1567 Mary, Queen of Scots (1542–87), was forced to abdicate in favour of her year-old son, James VI.

1799 Defeat of the Ottoman Turks by Napoleon Bonaparte at the Battle of Aboukir Bay, NE of Alexandria.

1802 Birth of Alexander Dumas in Villers-Cotterêts, France (d.1870), novelist and playwright, whose works include *The Count of Monte Cristo* (1844–5).

1824 Publication of the results of the first public opinion poll, held in Wilmington, Pennsylvania, to determine voters' allegiances before the 1824 US presidential election.

1847 Arrival of Brigham Young (1801–77) and his followers in present-day Utah, the first members of the Church of Jesus Christ of Latter Day Saints (Mormons).

1847 Patenting of the rotary type printing press by Richard Hoe of New York.

1880 Birth of Ernest Bloch in Geneva, Switzerland (d.1959), composer, whose works include *America* (1926).

1897 Birth of Amelia Earhart in Atchison, Kansas (d.1937), aviator, the first woman to fly the Atlantic as a passenger, followed by a solo flight (1932).

1911 Discovery of Machu Picchu, a lost Inca city in Peru, by archaeologist Hiram Bingham (1875–1956).

1929 Birth of Peter Yates in Aldershot, Hampshire, director, whose films include *Summer Holiday* (1963).

1936 Introduction of the speaking clock by Britain's General Post Office, with the voice of Jean Cain, accessed by dialling TIM on the telephone.

1965 Former British champion boxer Freddie Mills (b.1919) was found shot dead in his car in Soho, London.

1970 Birth of Jennifer Lopez in the Bronx, New York, singer and actress, whose films include *Monster-in-Law* (2005).

1974 Death of Sir James Chadwick (b.1891 in Manchester), physicist, who discovered the neutron (1932), and led the UK's work on the atomic bomb in World War 2.

1980 Death of Peter Sellers (b.1925 in Southsea, Hampshire), actor and comedian, who starred as Inspector Clouseau in the *Pink Panther* films.

1985 Opening of *The Black Cauldron*, the 25th full-length cartoon film by Walt Disney Studios, and its most expensive to date at $25 million.

1987 US mountaineer Hulda Crooks (c.1896–1997) became the oldest woman (age 91) to climb Mt Fuji, Japan's highest peak.

JULY

25

1603 Coronation of King James I of England (1566–1625).

1834 Death of Samuel Taylor Coleridge (b.1772 in Ottery St Mary, Devon), poet, whose works include 'Kubla Khan' (1797).

1843 Death of Charles Macintosh (b.1766 in Glasgow), manufacturing chemist, who developed a method of waterproofing cloth (1823).

1848 Birth of Arthur James Balfour, 1st Earl Balfour, in Whittinghame, East Lothian (d.1930), British statesman and philosopher.

1887 Death of Henry Mayhew (b.1812 in London), writer, who founded *Punch* magazine with Mark Lemon in 1841.

1909 French airman Louis Blériot (1872–1936) made the first flight across the English Channel from Baraques to Dover in a small 24-hp monoplane.

1917 The Dutch spy known as Mata Hari was sentenced to death for passing secrets to the Germans during World War 1.

1946 The USA tested the first underwater atomic bomb, at Bikini Atoll.

1948 Ending of bread rationing in Britain.

1959 First crossing of the English Channel by Hovercraft, the *SRN I*, making the journey between Dover and Calais in just over two hours.

1966 Death of Billy Smart (b.1893 in London), circus manager.

1971 The world's first heart and lung transplant was carried out by Christiaan Barnard (1922–2001) in South Africa.

1978 Birth of Louise Joy Brown in Oldham, Lancashire, the first test-tube baby.

1984 Soviet cosmonaut Svetlana Savitskaya (b.1948) became the first woman to walk in space, performing over 3 hours of experiments outside space station Salyut 7.

1987 The *London Daily News* ceased publication after only five months.

1994 Signing of a declaration by Yitzhak Rabin, prime minister of Israel, and King Hussein of Jordan, ending their countries' 46-year formal state of war.

2000 Crash of supersonic airliner Concorde in Gonesse, France, killing all 109 people on board, and four on the ground.

2004 US cyclist Lance Armstrong (b.1971) won the Tour de France for a record-breaking sixth time.

JULY

26

Feast (Western Church) of St Anne (fl.1st c BC–1st c AD) with St Joachim, patron saint of broom-makers, cabinet makers, Canada, carpenters, housewives, lacemakers, miners, old-clothes dealers, seamstresses, stable-men, and turners.

1775 Foundation of the US postal system by the 2nd Continental Congress.

1788 New York became the 11th state of the Union.

1847 Liberia became the first independent republic in Africa.

1856 Birth of George Bernard Shaw in Dublin, Ireland (d.1950), playwright, essayist, and pamphleteer, whose plays include *Pygmalion* (1913).

1875 Birth of Carl Jung in Kesswil, Switzerland (d.1961), psychiatrist, who developed his own brand of analytical psychology.

1881 First publication of the London *Evening News*.

1882 Premiere of *Parsifal*, Richard Wagner's final opera, in Bayreuth, Germany.

1894 Birth of Aldous Huxley in Godalming, Surrey (d.1963), novelist and essayist, whose works include *Brave New World* (1932).

1908 Inauguration of the FBI (Federal Bureau of Investigation) in Washington, DC.

1922 Birth of Blake Edwards in Tulsa, Oklahoma, director, producer, and actor, whose films include the *Pink Panther* series (1964–93).

1928 Birth of Stanley Kubrick in New York (d.1999), screenwriter, producer and director, whose films include *2001: A Space Odyssey* (1968).

1943 Birth of Mick Jagger in Dartford, Kent, rock singer, whose group, The Rolling Stones, made its debut in 1962.

1952 Death of Eva Perón (b.1919 in Los Toldos, Argentina), second wife of Argentinian president Juan Perón; the musical *Evita* (1979) was based on her life.

1956 Nationalization of the Suez Canal by President Nasser on his take-over of Egypt.

1958 Final presentation of debutantes at the royal court in Britain.

1963 An earthquake destroyed Skopje, Macedonia (former Yugoslavia), and killed over 1000 people.

1971 Launch of Apollo 15 from Kennedy Space Center, Florida, the fourth mission to land men on the Moon.

1987 Stephen Roche (b.1959) won the Tour de France, the first Irish winner.

JULY

27

Feast of St Pantaleon, patron saint of midwives.

1245 A council at Lyons deposed Holy Roman Emperor Frederick II, finding him guilty of sacrilege.

1667 Birth of Johann Bernoulli in Basel, Switzerland (d.1748), mathematician, who found the length and area of curves, isochronous curves, and curves of quickest descent.

1694 Foundation of the Bank of England, the central bank of Britain, in state ownership only since 1946.

1768 Birth of Charlotte Corday in St Saturnin, France (d.1793), noblewoman, who stabbed and killed revolutionary leader Jean Paul Marat in his bath (1793).

1784 Publication of the first French newspaper in the USA, the *Courier de l'Amerique*.

1866 Installation of the transatlantic telegraph cable was completed when the *Great Eastern* arrived in Newfoundland.

1882 Birth of Sir Geoffrey de Havilland in Haslemere, Surrey (d.1965), aircraft designer, who built his first plane in 1908.

1904 Birth of Anton Dolin in Slinfold, West Sussex (d.1983), dancer and choreographer, who co-founded the Markova–Dolin Ballet.

1930 Birth of Baroness Shirley Williams in London, daughter of Vera Brittain, and co-founder of the Social Democratic Party (1981).

1940 Debut of cartoon character Bugs Bunny, in the Warner Bros film *A Wild Hare*.

1949 First flight for the world's first jet-propelled airliner, the UK-built De Havilland DH 106 Comet, at Hatfield, Hertfordshire.

1953 The Korean War ended.

1974 In America the House Judiciary Committee voted to impeach President Nixon, so bringing Watergate to a head.

1982 Opening of *Little Shop of Horrors* by Alan Menken (b.1949) and Howard Ashman (1950–91), at the Orpheum Theatre, Memphis, Tennessee.

1995 Dedication in Washington, DC, of the Korean War Veterans Memorial, by US president Bill Clinton and South Korean president Kim Young-sam.

1996 Explosion of a bomb in an entertainment park during the Olympic Games in Atlanta, Georgia, killing one person and wounding 110.

2003 Death of Bob Hope, originally Leslie Towne Hope (b.1903 in Eltham, London), comedian, whose work includes the classic 'Road' films with Bing Crosby and Dorothy Lamour.

JULY

28

1540 Execution of Thomas Cromwell (b.c.1485 in London), chief minister to Henry VIII.

1576 Discovery of Frobisher Bay, Canada, by English navigator Martin Frobisher (c.1535–94).

1586 Mathematician and scientist Thomas Harriot (1560–1621) brought the first potatoes to Britain, from Colombia.

1741 Death of Antonio Vivaldi (b.1678 in Venice, Italy), violinist and composer, whose works include *The Four Seasons* (1725).

1750 Death of Johann Sebastian Bach (b.1685 at Eisenach, Germany), composer and musician.

1794 Death by guillotine of Maximilien Robespierre (b.1758 in Arras, France), French revolutionary leader.

1851 The first image of a total solar eclipse was captured on a daguerreotype photograph.

1858 First use of fingerprints as a means of identity.

1866 Birth of Beatrix Potter in London (d.1943), writer of children's books such as *Peter Rabbit* (1900) and *Benjamin Bunny* (1904).

1866 Introduction of the metric system, standardizing weights and measures in the USA.

1883 A water tricycle was pedalled by a Mr Ferry across the English Channel from Dover to Calais, 32.19 km/20 miles in under eight hours.

1925 Birth of John Stonehouse in Southampton, Hampshire (d.1988), Labour politician, who in 1974 tried to fake his own death by supposed drowning.

1928 Opening of the 9th Olympic Games in Amsterdam.

1929 Birth of Jacqueline Kennedy Onassis in Southampton, New York (d.1994), US first lady (1961–3).

1959 Introduction of postcodes in Britain by the postmaster-general.

1967 Renationalization of Britain's steel industry.

1976 An earthquake in Tangshan, China, killed at least 242,000 people, the highest known earthquake casualty toll in modern times.

1984 Death of George Gallup (b.1901 in Jefferson, Iowa), public opinion expert, who evolved the Gallup polls for testing the state of public opinion.

1984 Opening of the 23rd Olympic Games in Los Angeles.

2001 Death of Eric Bedford (b.1909), architect, who designed London's Post Office Tower.

JULY

29

Feast (Western Church) of St Martha, patron saint of cooks, hoteliers, housewives, laundry-workers, lay-sisters, servants, and waiters.
Feast of St Olaf I Haraldsson, patron saint of Norway.

1588 Defeat of the Spanish Armada by the English fleet.

1801 Birth of George Bradshaw in Salford, Greater Manchester (d.1853), mapmaker, best known for the series of railway guides (*Bradshaws*) which he began in 1839.

1833 Death of William Wilberforce (b.1759 in Kingston-upon-Hull), politician, evangelist, and philanthropist, who in 1788 began the movement which led to the abolition of the slave trade in the British West Indies in 1807.

1883 Birth of Benito Mussolini in Predappio, Romagna, Italy (d.1945), dictator of Italy.

1890 Death of Vincent Van Gogh (b.1853 in Groot-Zundert, The Netherlands), painter, a pioneer of Expressionism, whose works include *Sunflowers* (1888).

1900 Death of Umberto I (b.1844 in Turin, Italy), king of Italy, assassinated at Monza by anarchist Gaetano Bresci (1869–1901).

1905 Birth of Clara Bow in New York (d.1965), film actress, known as the 'It Girl' of silent films.

1921 Adolf Hitler (1889–1945) became president of the Nationalist Social-ist German Workers' Party, the Nazis.

1948 Opening of the 14th Olympic games in London.

1957 Establishment of the IAEA (International Atomic Energy Agency) as an autonomous organization under the UN.

1958 Foundation of NASA, the National Aeronautics and Space Administration agency, in the USA.

1965 Premiere of The Beatles' film *Help!* at the London Pavillion, Piccadilly Circus.

1966 Bob Dylan crashed his motor cycle and suffered serious injuries.

1968 Issue of the encyclical *Humanae Vitae* by Pope Paul VI.

1974 Death of Cass Elliot (b.1943 in Baltimore, Maryland), singer, and member of the pop group The Mamas and the Papas.

1975 Gerald R. Ford became the first US president to visit the Auschwitz Nazi concentration camp site in Poland, paying tribute to its victims.

1981 Marriage of Prince Charles and Lady Diana Spencer at St Paul's Cathedral, London.

1996 England player Alan Shearer (b.1970) became the world's most expensive footballer, when Newcastle United paid his £15 million transfer fee.

JULY

30

1718 Death of William Penn (b.1644 in London), Quaker reformer and colonialist, who founded Pennsylvania.

1729 Founding of Baltimore, Maryland.

1818 Birth of Emily Brontë in Thornton, West Yorkshire (d.1848), author of the novel *Wuthering Heights* (1847).

1824 Italian composer Gioacchino Rossini (1792–1868) became director of the Théâtre-Italien, Paris.

1844 Founding of the New York Yacht Club, oldest yacht club in the USA.

1863 Birth of Henry Ford in Dearborn, Michigan (d.1947), automobile engineer and manufacturer, who produced his first petrol-driven motor car in 1893.

1898 Birth of Henry Moore in Castleford, West Yorkshire (d.1986), sculptor, whose style was based on the organic forms and undulations found in the landscape.

1909 Birth of C(yril) Northcote Parkinson in Barnard Castle, Durham, political scientist, originator of the law that 'work expands to fill the time available for its completion'.

1932 Opening of the 10th Olympic Games in Los Angeles.

1935 Publication of the first Penguin paperback book.

1938 The first edition of the *Beano* children's comic went on sale.

1945 Sinking of USS *Indianapolis* with the deaths of nearly 900 men, torpedoed by a Japanese submarine in one of the greatest naval losses of World War 2.

1947 Birth of Marc Bolan in London (d.1977), rock star, and lead vocalist with T Rex.

1948 Opening of the world's first radar station, at Liverpool port.

1956 Adoption of the national motto, 'In God We Trust', by the USA.

1958 Birth of Daley Thompson in London, athlete, who was world decathlete champion (1983) and Olympic champion (1980, 1984).

1966 England beat Germany 4–2 at Wembley Stadium, London, winning the football World Cup for the first time since the tournament began in 1930.

1975 Disappearence of former Teamsters labour union president Jimmy Hoffa (b.1913) from a restaurant car park in Detroit, Michigan; presumed dead, his remains have never been found.

1980 Independence of Vanuatu.

2004 First sales of a new Austrian postage stamp, featuring Austrian-born US actor Arnold Schwarzenegger, on sale for his 57th birthday.

JULY

31

Feast of St Ignatius Loyola (1491 or 1495–1556), patron saint of retreatants. Feast (Eastern Church) of St Joseph, patron saint of Belgium, bursars, cabinetmakers, Canada, carpenters, fathers, and manual workers. Feast (Eastern Church) of St Joseph of Arimathea (1st c), patron saint of grave-diggers and funeral directors.

1485 Publication of Sir Thomas Mallory's *Le Morte Darthur* by William Caxton.

1886 Death of Franz Liszt (b.1811 in Raiding, Hungary), composer, and virtuoso pianist.

1908 Inauguration of the Boy Scout movement by Lord Robert Stephenson Smyth Baden-Powell (1857–1941).

1910 Murderer Hawley Harvey Crippen (1862–1910) was the first criminal apprehended by the use of a radio telegraph message, sent ship-to-shore by the captain of the SS *Montrose*.

1917 Beginning of the third stage of the Battle of Ypres, Canadian infantrymen eventually taking Passchendaele after months of trench warfare.

1928 Leo, the MGM lion, roared for the first time at the beginning of MGM's first sound film, *White Shadows on the South Seas*.

1950 Opening of Sainsbury in London, Britain's first self-service store.

1954 A team of Italian mountaineers became the first to climb K2, Pakistan, the world's second-highest mountain.

1962 Birth of Wesley Snipes in Orlando, Florida, actor, whose films include *Passenger 57* (1992).

1964 Death of Jim Reeves (b.1924 in Galloway, Texas), country-and-western singer, whose hits include 'Welcome to My World'.

1964 The first close-up pictures of the surface of the Moon were sent back by Ranger 7.

1965 Birth of J(oanne) K(athleen) Rowling in Gloucestershire, writer, famous for the enormously popular *Harry Potter* series of books.

1968 Inauguration of the cross-Channel hovercraft service.

1969 Pope Paul VI became the first reigning pope to visit sub-saharan Africa, arriving in Uganda.

1971 Apollo 15 astronauts James Irwin and David Scott went for a drive on the Moon.

1990 During the Test match between England and India at Lords cricket ground, London, after 1603 minutes of play, the combined scores of both teams reached 1603 runs.

1991 Signing of the Strategic Arms Reduction Treaty in Moscow by US president George H. W. Bush and Soviet president Mikhail Gorbachev.

AUGUST

1

Lammas Day in the UK, a former church festival.
Feast of St Alfonso Maria de' Liguori, also known as St Alphonsus Liguori (1696–1787), patron saint of theologians.

1715 The first rowing of the Doggetts Coat and Badge race (after Thomas Doggett, joint manager of the Drury Lane Theatre) took place on the R Thames; it is the oldest annually contested event in the British sporting calendar.

1774 Discovery of oxygen by British chemist and clergyman Joseph Priestley (1733–1804); he called it 'dephlogisticated air'.

1793 Introduction of the first metric weight, the kilogram, in France.

1798 Horatio Nelson destroyed the French fleet off Aboukir in the Battle of the Nile.

1819 Birth of Herman Melville in New York (d.1891), writer, whose works include *Moby Dick* (1851).

1831 Opening of the New London Bridge, designed by John Rennie.

1834 Abolition of slavery in the British Empire.

1873 First successful test run of the first cable-car, overseen by its inventor, British-born engineer Andrew Smith Hallidie (1836–1900), in San Francisco.

1876 Colorado became the 38th state of the Union.

1883 Introduction of parcel post in Britain.

1936 Opening of the 11th Olympic Games in Berlin, Germany.

1944 Final entry in the diary of Anne Frank (1929–45), which documented the two years she spent hiding from the Nazis with her family in a sealed-off office flat in Amsterdam.

1944 Introduction of the first postcodes, in Germany.

1965 Birth of Sam Mendes in Reading, Berkshire, director, whose films include *American Beauty* (1999, Oscar).

1965 Cigarette advertising was banned from the television in the UK.

1969 The old British halfpenny ceased to be legal tender.

1971 Madison Square Gardens in New York hosted a Concert for Bangladesh, which raised over $11 million.

1976 Austrian motor-racing champion Niki Lauda (b.1949) suffered severe burns and injuries in the German Grand Prix at the Nürburgring.

AUGUST
2

1100 Death of William II (b.c.1056), king of England, shot with an arrow while hunting in the New Forest.

1704 Beginning of the Battle of Blenheim during the War of the Spanish Succession, in which Louis XIV's armies were defeated.

1784 The first purpose-built Royal Mail coach ran, between Bristol and London.

1824 Opening of New York's Fifth Avenue.

1835 Birth of Elisha Gray in Barnesville, Ohio (d.1901), inventor, and manufacturer of telegraphic apparatus.

1858 The government of India was taken over from the East India Company by the British government.

1865 First publication of *Alice's Adventures in Wonderland* by Lewis Carroll, soon withdrawn due to poor printing quality; of 2000 copies, only 23 copies are known to have survived.

1870 Opening of Tower Subway, the world's first underground tube railway, under the R Thames, London; it had steam-operated lifts, and a 12-seat carriage that shuttled by means of a wire rope.

1875 Opening of Britain's first rollerskating rink to the public, in Portsdown Road (later Randolph Avenue), Paddington, London.

1876 Death of Wild Bill Hickok (b.1837 in Troy Grove, Illinois), frontier figure, killed while playing poker in Deadwood, South Dakota; his hand, with two black aces and two black eights, became known as 'the dead man's hand'.

1880 The British parliament officially adopted GMT (Greenwich Mean Time).

1894 Introduction of death duties in Britain.

1922 Death of Alexander Graham Bell (b.1847 in Edinburgh), educationist, the inventor of the articulating telephone (1875).

1932 Birth of Peter O'Toole in Connemara, Co Galway, Ireland, actor, whose films include *Lawrence of Arabia* (1962).

1934 Adolf Hitler became sole leader of Germany on the death of President Paul von Hindenburg (1847–1934).

1980 Explosion of a huge bomb at Bologna railway station, Italy, killing 85 people and injuring nearly 300.

1987 Re-release of the Disney cartoon classic *Snow White and the Seven Dwarfs*, with box-office receipts of nearly $20 million taken in the following fortnight.

1990 Invasion of Kuwait by Iraqi tanks and infantry.

AUGUST

3

1610 Discovery of Hudson Bay, Northwest Territories, Canada, by Henry Hudson (?–1611).

1778 Opening of La Scala Opera House in Milan, Italy.

1792 Death of Sir Richard Arkwright (b.1732 in Preston, Lancashire), inventor of mechanical cotton-spinning, who set up his celebrated spinning-frame in Preston in 1768.

1801 Birth of Sir Joseph Paxton near Woburn, Bedfordshire (d.1865), gardener and architect, who designed the Crystal Palace for the Great Exhibition of 1851.

1805 The first recorded cricket match, between Eton and Harrow, played at Lord's Old Ground at Dorset Fields; Eton won by an innings and two runs.

1811 Birth of Elisha Otis in Halifax, Vermont (d.1861), inventor, who designed and installed the first elevator to incorporate an automatic brake (1852).

1858 Discovery of Lake Victoria, the source of the Nile, by English explorer John Speke (1827–64).

1887 Birth of Rupert Brooke in Rugby, Warwickshire (d.1915), poet, who wrote *1914 and Other Poems*.

1914 Germany declared war on France.

1920 Birth of P. D. James in Oxford, Oxfordshire, detective-story writer, whose novels include *Original Sin* (1994).

1933 First production of the Mickey Mouse watch, which sold for $2.75.

1938 Birth of Terry Wogan in Limerick, Ireland, broadcaster and writer, who joined the BBC in 1965.

1955 English-language premiere of *Waiting for Godot* (1954) by Samuel Beckett (1906–89), at the Arts Theatre, London, directed by Peter Hall (b.1930).

1957 John Charles (1931–2004) became the first British footballer to be transferred to a foreign club, when he joined Juventus from Leeds United for £65,000.

1958 The nuclear-powered submarine *Nautilus* became the first vessel to cross the North Pole underwater.

1971 Formation of Wings, the new band fronted by ex-Beatle Paul McCartney (b.1942).

1997 Soufriere Hills volcano, Montserrat, began a period of violent eruption, virtually destroying Plymouth, the capital city.

2003 Hottest recorded day to date in Britain, as the temperature rose to 38·1° C (100·6° F) in Gravesend, Kent.

2003 First use of the taser, or stun gun, by British police officers, when they dealt with an armed man in Hounslow, London.

AUGUST

4

Feast of St Jean-Baptiste-Marie Vianney
(1786–1859), patron saint of parish priests.
Feast of St Sithney, patron saint of mad dogs.

1265 Death of Simon de Montfort, Earl
of Leicester (b.c.1208 in Montfort,
France), killed at the Battle of Evesham.

1492 Christopher Columbus
(1451–1506) set sail on the voyage
that was to find America.

1792 Birth of Percy Bysshe Shelley at
Field Place, near Horsham, West
Sussex (d.1822), poet, who lived in
Italy from 1818.

1870 Lord Wantage established the
Red Cross Society in Britain, a
branch of the international agency
founded by the Geneva Convention (1864).

1875 Death of Hans Christian Andersen (b.1805 in Odense, Denmark),
writer, remembered for his fairy-
tales for children.

1900 Birth of Elizabeth Bowes-Lyon,
HM Queen Elizabeth, the Queen
Mother, in St Paul's Waldenbury,
Hertfordshire (d.2002).

1914 Britain declared war on Germany.

1929 Birth of Yasser Arafat in Egypt
(d.2004), Palestinian leader, and
co-founder of the Fatah resistance
group, which in 1969 took control
of the Palestine Liberation Organization.

1939 First British transatlantic mail
service, Southampton to Montreal
and Southampton to New York, a
weekly service by two BOAC flying
boats.

1944 Anne Frank and her family were
discovered in hiding in Amsterdam
by the Gestapo.

1954 Maiden flight of Britain's first
supersonic fighter plane, the English Electric Lightning P-1, at RAF
Boscombe Down, Salisbury, Wiltshire.

1972 Ugandan dictator Idi Amin
(c.1925–2003) gave Uganda's
50,000 Asians 90 days to leave the
country.

1975 Michael Angelow became the
first streaker to run on to the field
during a Test cricket match in
England, on the fourth day of the
England v. Australia match at
Lord's, London.

1983 Thomas Sankara (1949–87), head
of state of Upper Volta, renamed his
country Burkina Faso (Land of
Upright Men).

1997 Australian athlete Cathy Freeman (b.1973) won the women's
400 m final at the World Championships in Athens, Greece, the
first Aboriginal to win a world title.

1999 Appointment by NATO of British
defence secretary George Robert-
son (b.1946) as its secretary general,
a post he held until 2003.

1999 Death of Victor Mature (b.1915 in
Louisville, Kentucky), actor, whose
films include *My Darling Clementine*
(1946).

AUGUST

5

Opening of the oyster season.

1305 Death of William Wallace (b.1270 probably in Elderslie, Renfrewshire), Scottish knight, and champion of the independence of Scotland.

1583 English navigator Sir Humphrey Gilbert (c.1539–83) claimed St John's, Newfoundland, as the first English colony in North America.

1729 Death of Thomas Newcomen (b.1663 in Dartmouth, Devon), inventor, who by 1698 had invented the atmospheric steam engine.

1844 The Statue of Liberty's cornerstone was laid on what is now Liberty Island, New York.

1858 Greetings passed between Queen Victoria and President Buchanan at the opening of the first transatlantic cable, laid by HMS *Agamemnon* and USS *Niagara*.

1862 Birth of Joseph Merrick in Leicester, Leicestershire (d.1890), known as 'The Elephant Man' because of his disfigurement; he was believed to have had Proteus Syndrome.

1891 Cashing of the first American Express traveller's cheque.

1901 Opening of the first full-time cinema in Britain, at the Mowhawk Hall, Islington, London.

1914 Erection of the first electric traffic lights, in Cleveland, Ohio.

1930 Birth of Neil Armstrong in Wapakoneta, Ohio, astronaut, the first man to set foot on the Moon (1969).

1962 Death of Marilyn Monroe (b.1926 in Los Angeles, California), actress, from an overdose of sleeping pills.

1963 Signing of the Nuclear Test-Ban Treaty by Britain, the USA, and the Soviet Union.

1970 Penalty kicks were used for the first time as a tie-breaker in a Watneys Cup match between Hull City and Manchester United (Man Utd won 4-3).

1976 Metal fatigue caused the first and only major breakdown of Big Ben, part of the Great Clock of Westminster, London.

1983 Twenty-two members of the IRA were jailed for a total of more than 4000 years, following one of Northern Ireland's biggest mass trials.

1984 Death of Richard Burton (b.1925 in Pontrhydfen, Wales), actor, who received six Oscar nominations.

2000 Death of Sir Alec Guinness (b.1914 in London), actor, whose films include *The Bridge on the River Kwai* (1957).

AUGUST
6

Feast of the Transfiguration – described in the Gospels, when Jesus was temporarily changed in appearance on a mountain in front of his disciples Peter, James, and John.

1504 Birth of Matthew Parker, nickname 'Nosey', in Norwich, Norfolk (d.1575), second Protestant archbishop of Canterbury.

1809 Birth of Alfred, Lord Tennyson, in Somersby, Lincolnshire (d.1892), poet, who became poet laureate in 1850.

1889 Opening of the Savoy Hotel, London.

1890 US murderer William Kemmler (b.1860) was the first to be executed in the electric chair, in Auburn Prison, New York.

1893 Opening of the Corinth Canal, bisecting the Isthmus of Corinth in Greece, built 1881–93, length 6.5 km/4 miles.

1917 Birth of Robert Mitchum in Bridgeport, Connecticut (d.1997), actor, whose films include *The Sundowners* (1960).

1926 US Olympic swimmer Gertrude Ederle (1905–2003) became the first woman to swim the English Channel, in 14 hours 31 minutes, nearly two hours faster than the existing men's record.

1928 Birth of Andy Warhol in Pittsburgh, Pennsylvania (d.1987), pop artist and film-maker, a pioneer in 1961 of Pop Art.

1932 Inauguration of the first film festival, held in Venice.

1934 Birth of Sir Chris Bonington in London, mountaineer and photojournalist, a member of the first British team that conquered the north face of the Eiger (1962) and Everest (1972).

1937 Birth of Barbara Windsor in Shoreditch, London, actress, best known for her roles in the *Carry On* series of comedies.

1945 Dropping of the first atomic bomb, on Hiroshima, Japan.

1962 Independence of Jamaica, a British colony for more than 300 years.

1964 Release of The Beatles' first film *A Hard Day's Night*.

1971 British yachtsman Chay Blyth (b.1940) became the first to sail the world non-stop in the 'wrong' direction (east to west), aboard his yacht *British Steel*.

1991 British network designer Tim Berners-Lee (b.1955) put the first website (http://info.cern.ch/) online.

1994 Opening of Buckingham Palace to the public, to raise money for the restoration of Windsor Castle after the 1992 fire.

2001 Death of Dame Dorothy Tutin (b.1931 in London), actress, whose films include *Savage Messiah* (1972).

2005 Death of Robin Cook (b.1946 in Bellshill, North Lanarkshire), British statesman, secretary of state for foreign and commonwealth affairs (1997) and leader of the House of Commons (2001).

AUGUST

7

1782 George Washington (1732–99), 1st US president, ordered the creation of the Badge of Military Merit to honour soldiers wounded in battle, later renamed the Purple Heart.

1834 Death of Joseph Marie Jacquard (b.1952 in Lyon, France), silk weaver, and inventor of the *Jacquard loom*.

1840 The British parliament passed an act prohibiting the employment of boys as chimney sweeps.

1858 Ottawa became the capital city of Canada.

1876 Birth of Mata Hari in Leeuwarden, The Netherlands (d.1917), dancer, shot in Paris after being found guilty of espionage for the Germans.

1888 Patenting of the revolving door by Theophilus Van Kannel of Philadelphia, Pennsylvania.

1888 Martha Turner, first victim of Jack the Ripper, was found in the Spitalfields district of Whitechapel, London.

1903 Birth of Louis S. B. Leakey in Kabete, Kenya (d.1972), physical anthropologist, who found remains of several early species in East Africa.

1925 The British Summer Time Act was made permanent.

1926 The first British Grand Prix was run at Brooklands in Surrey.

1931 Death of Bix Beiderbecke (b.1903 in Davenport, Iowa), cornettist and composer, a celebrated jazz performer of the 1920s.

1942 Marines landed on Guadalcanal, Solomon Islands, the first major Allied landing during World War 2.

1947 Anthropologist Thor Heyerdahl (1914–2002) reached the Tuamotu Archipelago 101 days after setting off from Peru on the *Kon-Tiki*, a balsa-wood raft.

1957 Death of Oliver Hardy (b.1892 near Atlanta, Georgia), comedian, who with Stan Laurel formed Hollywood's first film comedy team.

1959 Launch of Explorer 6 into Earth orbit from Cape Canaveral, Florida; it returned the first pictures of Earth seen from space.

1960 Independence of the Ivory Coast, official name Côte d'Ivoire.

1974 French high-wire artist Philippe Petit (b.1949) made eight crossings between the unfinished twin towers of the World Trade Center, New York, a quarter of a mile above the ground.

1987 US open-water swimmer Lynne Cox (b.1957) swam the 4·3-km/ 2·7-mile Bering Strait in 2 hours, 6 minutes, becoming the first person to swim from the USA to the Soviet Union.

2000 Death of Sir Robin Day (b.1923 in London), journalist and broadcaster, who presented BBC television's *Question Time* (1979–89).

AUGUST
8

Feast of St Dominic (c.1170–1221), patron saint of astronomers.

1588 Review of the troops at Tilbury by Queen Elizabeth I.

1786 First ascent of Mont Blanc, by Jacques Balmat and Michel-Gabriel Paccard.

1829 Testing of *The Stourbridge Lion* at Honesdale, Pennsylvania, the first steam locomotive to run on a commercial line in the USA.

1834 Passing of the Poor Law Amendment Act in Britain.

1844 Creation of the leading body of the Mormon Church, by Brigham Young (1801–77) and the Quorum of Twelve, at a meeting in Nauvoo, Illinois.

1899 Patenting of the refrigerator by A. T. Marshall of Brockton, Massachusetts.

1900 Beginning of the first Davis Cup tennis competition, named after Dwight Filley Davis (1879–1945), at Longwood Cricket Club, Massachusetts; USA beat Britain 3–0.

1919 Death of Frank W. Woolworth (b.1852 in Rodman, New York), businessman, who built a chain of similar stores from 1905.

1925 First national congress of the Ku Klux Klan; 40,000 members marched down Pennsylvania Avenue, Washington, DC.

1929 Graf Zeppelin LZ-127 left Lakehurst, New Jersey, on the first round-the-world flight by an airship; piloted by Hugo Eckener, it completed the circumnavigation in 21 days, 7 hours.

1937 Birth of Dustin Hoffman in Los Angeles, California, actor, who received Oscars for his roles in *Kramer vs Kramer* (1979) and *Rain Man* (1988).

1954 Birth of Nigel Mansell in Birmingham, West Midlands, motor-racing driver, champion in both Formula 1 and Indy car-racing.

1963 Theft of £2½ million pounds from the Glasgow-to-London mail train at Sears Crossing, Buckinghamshire, in the Great Train Robbery.

1979 Death of Nicholas Monsarrat (b.1910 in Liverpool), novelist, who wrote the best-selling novel *The Cruel Sea* (1951).

1988 Eighty-eight, Kentucky, named for the number of cents in its founder's pocket, was inundated by visitors wanting to buy postcards to be franked at 8.08 a.m. with the 88 postmark.

1991 Journalist John McCarthy was freed after being held hostage for more than five years by the Islamic Jihad in the Lebanon.

1996 Death of Sir Frank Whittle (b.1907 in Coventry, West Midlands), aviator, and inventor of the British jet engine.

AUGUST
9

1593 Birth of Sir Izaak Walton in Stafford, Staffordshire (d.1683), writer, best known for his treatise on fishing and country life, *The Compleat Angler* (1653).

1721 Six prisoners at Newgate Prison, London, were offered a full pardon if they submitted to the 'Royal Experiment' of smallpox variolation; all were inoculated, survived, and released.

1757 Birth of Thomas Telford in Langholm, Dumfries and Galloway (d.1834), engineer, whose projects include the road from London to Holyhead.

1842 Signing of the Webster-Ashburton Treaty between the USA and Britain, agreeing the frontier between the USA and Canada from Maine to the Great Lakes.

1870 Britain passed the Elementary Education Act, giving compulsory free education to every child in England and Wales aged five to 13.

1902 Coronation of Edward VII, king of the United Kingdom (1901–10).

1910 Patenting of the electric washing machine by A. J. Fisher of Chicago, Illinois.

1914 Sinking of the U-15 German submarine by HMS *Birmingham* during World War 1, the first to be sunk by the Royal Navy.

1922 Birth of Philip Larkin in Coventry, West Midlands (d.1985), poet, librarian, and jazz critic.

1938 Birth of Rod Laver in Rockhampton, Queensland, Australia, tennis player, who won two grand slams and was the first player to make more than $1 million.

1941 Capture of RAF fighter pilot Douglas Bader (1910–82) by German troops, after a collision with an enemy aircraft over Béthune, France, during World War 2.

1945 The US exploded a nuclear bomb over Nagasaki, Japan.

1957 Birth of Melanie Griffith in New York, actress, whose films include *Bonfire of the Vanities* (1990).

1967 Death of Joe Orton (b.1933 in Leicester, Leicestershire), playwright and actor, whose plays include *Loot* (1964–5).

1968 Birth of Gillian Anderson in Chicago, Illinois, actress, whose television roles include Dana Scully in *The X-Files* (1993–2002).

1972 First performance of the London production of *Jesus Christ Superstar*.

1974 Resignation of President Richard Nixon (1913–94) over the Watergate scandal.

1979 The first nudist beach in Britain was established in Brighton, West Sussex.

AUGUST

10

Feast of St Laurence (d.258), patron saint of cooks, deacons, fire-fighters, and restaurateurs.

1675 The foundation stone of the Royal Greenwich Observatory was laid.

1782 Birth of Sir Charles James Napier in London (d.1853), British soldier, the conqueror of Sind (now part of Pakistan).

1792 Abolition of the French monarchy, and the beginning of the French Revolution.

1821 Missouri became the 24th state of the Union.

1829 Death of Thomas Young (b.1773 in Milverton, Somerset), physicist, physician, and Egyptologist, who played an important role in deciphering the Rosetta Stone.

1842 The passing of the Mines Act in Britain prohibited women and young children from working underground.

1846 An Act of Congress established the Smithsonian Institution, a foundation for the promotion of knowledge, opened in Washington, DC, in 1855.

1885 Opening of the first electric street railway in the USA, in Baltimore, Maryland.

1889 Patenting of the screwcap bottle, by Dan Rylands of Hope Glass Works, Yorkshire.

1895 The first Promenade Concert was held at the old Queen's Hall, London, conducted by Sir Henry Wood.

1897 Foundation of the RAC (Royal Automobile Club), first known as the Automobile Club of Great Britain and Ireland; its royal patron was King Edward VII.

1911 British MPs voted to be salaried for the first time, receiving £400 a year.

1928 Birth of Eddie Fisher in Philadelphia, Pennsylvania, singer and actor, who became Elizabeth Taylor's fourth husband.

1932 Death of Rin Tin Tin, US canine film-star.

1960 Birth of Antonio Banderas in Málaga, Spain, actor, whose films include *The Legend of Zorro* (2005).

1966 Launch of Orbiter I by the USA, its first Moon satellite.

1990 Arrival of the Magellan spacecraft at the planet Venus, after a 15-month journey from Earth.

1995 Outbreak of Ebola fever in Zaire (now the Democratic Republic of Congo).

1998 British soccer club Manchester United became the first club in the world to have its own television channel – MUTV.

AUGUST

11

Feast of St Clare of Assisi (1194–1253), patron saint of embroiderers, television, and washerwomen.

1711 Queen Anne of Great Britain and Ireland attended the first Royal Ascot racing meeting.

1797 The English Home Office suspected poets William Wordsworth (1770–1850) and Samuel Taylor Coleridge (1772–1834) of being spies, because of their habit of wandering the countryside making detailed observations of the landscape.

1873 Birth of Bertram Mills in London (d.1938), circus manager.

1877 Discovery of Phobos and Deimos, the two moons of Mars, by US astronomer Asaph Hall (1829–1907).

1897 Birth of Enid Blyton in London (d.1968), children's writer, who published over 600 books.

1919 Meeting of the National Constituent Assembly at Weimar, Germany, to draw up a constitution for the Weimar Republic, the name by which the German Federal Republic was known until 1933.

1919 Death of Andrew Carnegie (b.1835 in Dunfermline, Fife), industrialist and philanthropist, who gave generously to public institutions.

1921 Birth of Alex Haley in Ithaca, New York (d.1992), journalist and writer, best known for the novel *Roots* (1976).

1934 Arrival of the first group of prisoners at Alcatraz Federal Penitentiary, a high-security prison in San Francisco Bay, California.

1942 Traffic was allowed across the new Waterloo Bridge over the R Thames, London.

1950 Birth of Steve Wozniak in San Jose, California, electrical engineer and computer inventor, who formed Apple Computers with Steve Jobs in 1976.

1956 Death of Jackson Pollock (b.1912 in Cody, Wyoming), abstract expressionist painter.

1965 Premiere of The Beatles' film *A Hard Day's Night*.

1971 British prime minister Edward Heath steered his yacht *Morning Cloud* to victory in the British Admiral's Cup race.

1984 Unaware that he was on air during a microphone check, US president Ronald Reagan said, 'My fellow Americans, I'm pleased to tell you that I just signed legislation that would outlaw Russia forever. We begin bombing in five minutes.'

1994 Death of Peter Cushing (b.1913 in Kenley, Greater London), actor, whose films include *Star Wars* (1977).

2003 NATO took over command of the peace-keeping force in Afghanistan, its first major operation outside the Euro-Atlantic area in its 54-year history.

AUGUST
12

British grouse shooting season begins.

1762 Birth of George IV in London (d.1830), king of Great Britain and Hanover (1820–30).

1774 Birth of Robert Southey in Bristol, Avon (d.1843), writer and poet laureate.

1827 Death of William Blake (b.1757 in London), poet, painter, and engraver, best known for *Songs of Innocence* (1789) and *Songs of Experience* (1794).

1851 Patenting of the double-treadle sewing machine by US inventor Isaac Singer (1811–75).

1865 British surgeon Joseph Lister (1827–1912) introduced antiseptic conditions during surgery, which greatly reduced surgical mortality.

1881 Birth of Cecil B. de Mille in Ashfield, Massachusetts (d.1959), director, whose films include *The Greatest Show on Earth* (1952).

1883 Death of the Quagga mare in Amsterdam Zoo; it was not realized until many years later that she was the last of the species.

1918 Commencement of a regular airmail service between Washington and New York.

1925 Birth of Ross (d.1975) and Norris (d.2004) McWhirter in Winchmore Hill, London, publishers and writers, who compiled the first edition of *The Guinness Book of Records* in 1954.

1944 The first PLUTO (Pipe Line Under the Ocean) went into operation, supplying petrol from the Isle of Wight to Allied forces in France during World War 2.

1953 First Soviet test of a thermo-nuclear weapon (hydrogen bomb).

1955 Death of Thomas Mann (b.1875 in Lübeck, Germany), novelist, whose works include *Death in Venice* (1913).

1960 Launch of US Echo I, the first communications satellite.

1961 Preparations began for the construction of the Berlin Wall, dividing East Germany from the West.

1977 The US space shuttle made its maiden flight on the back of a Boeing 747.

1981 Announcement of the IBM PC 5150, the company's first popular personal computer, at a press conference in New York.

1994 British 400 m hurdler Sally Gunnell (b.1966) became the first woman to hold Olympic, World, European, and Commonwealth titles and the world record at the same time.

1997 Decision by the British Tourist Authority to drop the Union flag as its logo.

AUGUST

13

Feast of St Concordia, patron saint of nannies, children's nurses, and nursing mothers.
Feast (Western Church) of St Hippolytus (170–235), patron saint of horses.

1422 Birth of William Caxton, possibly in Tenterden, Kent (d.c.1491), the first English printer, who printed the first book in English in 1475.

1814 The Cape of Good Hope Province was ceded to Britain, after 150 years of Dutch rule.

1826 Death of René Laënnec (b.1781 in Quimper, France), physician, and inventor of the stethoscope (1819).

1889 Patenting of a coin-operated telephone by William Gray of Hartford, Connecticut.

1899 Birth of Sir Alfred Hitchcock in London (d.1980), film director.

1910 Death of Florence Nightingale (b.1820 in Florence, Italy), hospital reformer, who formed an institution for the training of nurses in London.

1913 Invention of rustless steel, later stainless steel, by Harry Brearley (1871–1948) using an electric furnace.

1918 Birth of Dr Frederick Sanger in Rendcombe, Gloucestershire, biochemist, who was awarded Nobel Prizes for Chemistry in 1958 and 1980.

1927 Birth of Dr Fidel Castro near Birán, Cuba, Cuban revolutionary, prime minister (1959), and president (from 1976).

1934 First appearance of the comic strip 'Li'l Abner', by US strip cartoonist Al Capp.

1946 Death of H(erbert) G(eorge) Wells (b.1866 in Bromley, Kent), writer, whose books include *War of the Worlds* (1898).

1959 Building commenced on the Verrazano-Narrows Bridge across the entrance to New York harbour, completed 1964, length 1298 m/4260 ft.

1961 Closure of the Brandenburg Gate by East Germany, completing the divide between East and West Berlin.

1966 Announcement by China of plans for a New Leap Forward, after the first meeting in four years of the Communist Party's Central Committee.

1970 Birth of Alan Shearer in Newcastle-upon-Tyne, England footballer, who scored his 250th Premiership goal in 2005.

1977 Death of Henry Williamson (b.1895 in Brockley, London), author, whose classic nature stories include *Tarka the Otter* (1927).

2004 Opening of the 28th Olympic Games in Athens, Greece; the first time the city had hosted the modern Summer Games since 1896.

AUGUST

14

1820 Founding of the New York Eye Infirmary, the first US eye hospital, by Edward Delafield (1812–75) and John Kearney Rodgers (1793–1851), in two rented rooms in an old building opposite City Hall.

1867 Birth of John Galsworthy in Kingston Hill, Surrey (d.1933), novelist and playwright, who was awarded the 1932 Nobel Prize for Literature.

1880 Completion of Cologne Cathedral, Germany, after 632 years; rebuilding started in 1248 following a fire.

1893 Introduction of motor-vehicle registration plates, in France.

1901 *Islander*, a steamer, sank off Alaska after hitting an iceberg, with the loss of 70 lives, and £3 million in gold.

1908 Britain hosted the first international beauty competition, in Folkestone, Kent.

1920 Opening of the 7th Olympic games in Antwerp, Belgium.

1922 Death of Lord Alfred Harmsworth (b.1865 near Dublin, Ireland), journalist and newspaper magnate, who revolutionized Fleet Street with his *Daily Mail* (1896).

1941 Issue of the Atlantic Charter in a secret meeting off Newfoundland by US president Roosevelt and British prime minister Winston Churchill.

1945 Unconditional surrender of Japan, ending World War 2.

1948 Australian cricketer Don Bradman (1908–2001) played his final innings.

1951 Death of William Randolph Hearst (b.1863 in San Francisco, California), newspaper publisher and owner.

1966 Birth of Halle Berry in Cleveland, Ohio, actress, whose films include *Die Another Day* (2002).

1969 British troops were moved into Northern Ireland to restore order.

1979 Several people died and many yachts were lost in the Fastnet Yacht race, when freak storms hit the Irish Sea.

1980 Strike of 16,000 shipyard workers at the Lenin shipyard, Gdańsk, Poland.

1984 Death of J(ohn) B(oynton) Priestley (b.1894 in Bradford, West Yorkshire), writer, whose works include *The Good Companions* (1929).

1988 Death of Enzo Ferrari (b.1898 in Modena, Italy), racing-car designer, who became a racing driver in 1920, and founded the Ferrari company in 1929.

2000 Start of an unsuccessful operation to rescue more than 100 sailors on board Russian submarine *Kursk*, grounded at the bottom of the Barents Sea following an explosion.

2003 NE USA and S Canada suffered the worst power blackout in history, affecting more than 50 million customers.

AUGUST
15

Feast of Our Lady of the Assumption, patron saint of France, India, and South Africa. Feast of St Tarsicius, patron saint of altar servers.

1769 Birth of Napoleon I in Ajaccio, Corsica (d.1821), French general, consul, and emperor (1804–15).

1771 Birth of Sir Walter Scott in Edinburgh (d.1832), novelist and poet, the most popular author of the day, whose books include *Ivanhoe* (1819).

1843 Opening of the Tivoli Gardens in Copenhagen, an amusement park founded by Georg Carstensen (1812–57).

1848 US patenting of the rising/falling/reclining dental chair.

1872 Britain's first parliamentary election by secret ballot was held in Pontefract, West Yorkshire.

1888 Birth of T(homas) E(dward) Lawrence in Tremadoc, Gwynedd (d.1935), soldier, writer, and adviser on Arab affairs to the Colonial Office (1921–2), known as 'Lawrence of Arabia'.

1914 Opening of the Panama Canal linking the Atlantic and Pacific Oceans, a project that had begun in 1881.

1935 Death of Wiley Post (b.1900 in Grand Saline, Texas), pioneer aviator, who completed the first solo flight round the world in 1933.

1945 Celebration of VJ Day, following Japan's surrender to the Allies in World War 2.

1947 Independence of India.

1951 Birth of Princess Anne, the Princess Royal, in London.

1960 Opening of Britain's first motorway restaurant, on the M1 at Newport Pagnell, Buckinghamshire.

1967 The UK Marine Broadcasting Offences Act came into force, making it illegal to participate in offshore pirate radio.

1969 Opening of Woodstock, the three-day rock festival held as part of the Woodstock Music and Art Fair, in upstate New York.

1971 Disqualification of British showjumper Harvey Smith (b.1938) from the Hickstead Derby for making his famous two-fingered gesture; he was later reinstated.

1980 First public sales of *I Me Mine*, autobiography of ex-Beatle George Harrison (1943–2001).

1987 Caning was officially banned in Britain.

1998 Explosion of a terrorist bomb in Omagh, Northern Ireland, killing 29 people and injuring 220.

AUGUST
16

Feast of St Roch, patron saint of invalids, prisoners, and tilemakers.

Feast of St Stephen I of Hungary (c.975–1038), patron saint of Hungary.

1513 Defeat of the French at Guinegate, France, by Henry VIII of England in the Battle of the Spurs, so called because of the haste with which the French left the battlefield.

1780 The Battle of Camden was fought in South Carolina, during the American War of Independence.

1819 The Peterloo Massacre took place in St Peter's Field, Manchester, when a mass meeting about parliamentary reform was forcibly broken up by the Manchester Yeomanry.

1867 The Grand National Croquet Club's first open championship was played at Evesham, Worcestershire.

1897 Public opening of the Tate Gallery, London.

1899 Death of Robert Wilhelm Bunsen (b.1811 in Göttingen, Germany), chemist and physicist, whose inventions include the Bunsen burner and the grease-spot actinometer.

1930 Opening of the first British Empire Games, now The Commonwealth Games, in Hamilton, Canada, with 400 competitors representing 11 countries.

1948 Death of Babe Ruth (b.1895 in Baltimore, Maryland), baseball player, who achieved fame with the New York Yankees.

1952 Flash floods hit Lynmouth, Devon, after nine inches of rain had fallen in 24 hours on Exmoor; 34 people died.

1956 Death of Bela Lugosi (b.1884 in Lugos, Hungary), actor, whose greatest success was *Dracula* (1931).

1958 Birth of Madonna (Madonna Louise Veronica Ciccone) in Rochester, Michigan, pop singer, actress, and star of the film *Evita* (1996).

1960 Cyprus became an independent republic.

1961 Britain applied to join the European Economic Community.

1977 Death of Elvis Presley (b.1935 in Tupelo, Mississippi), rock singer and actor, who made 45 records that sold in millions.

1996 At Brookfield Zoo, Chicago, gorilla Binti Jua picked up a three-year-old boy who had fallen 18 feet into her enclosure, and placed him carefully by a door where he was retrieved for treatment.

2004 Flash floods hit Boscastle, Cornwall, destroying buildings and carrying 50 cars into the sea, after the area's average rainfall for August fell in two hours.

AUGUST
17

1601 Birth of Pierre de Fermat (d.1665) in Beaumont-de-Lomagne, France, mathematician, known for his 'last theorem' (solved in 1994).

1648 Oliver Cromwell's army won the Battle of Preston, during the English Civil War.

1786 Birth of Davy Crockett in Limestone, Tennessee (d.1836), backwoodsman, who distinguished himself against the Creek Indians in Jackson's campaign of 1814.

1892 Birth of Mae West in New York (d.1980), actress, whose name was given to a pneumatic life jacket.

1896 Death of Bridget Driscoll of Croydon, Surrey, the first person to die in a car accident; the car was travelling at a 'reckless pace' of around 6·4 kph/4 mph.

1896 First gold claims staked in Bonanza Creek, Yukon.

1915 Patenting of the electric self-starter for cars by Charles Kettering of Detroit, Michigan.

1926 Birth of George Melly in Liverpool, jazz singer, who sang with Mick Mulligan and John Chilton.

1939 Premiere of the film *The Wizard of Oz*, starring Judy Garland.

1943 Birth of Robert de Niro in New York, actor and director, whose films include *The Godfather, Part II* (1974, Oscar).

1945 Independence of Indonesia.

1962 Death of Peter Fechter (b.1944), bricklayer, one of the first victims of the Berlin Wall, shot by East German border guards while attempting to cross into West Berlin.

1977 Birth of Thierry Henry in Les Ulis, Paris, footballer, who was signed for English side Arsenal in 1999 for an estimated £10·5 million, and became the club's leading goal-scorer in 2005.

1983 Death of Ira Gershwin (b.1896 in New York), songwriter, who with his brother produced such hits as 'They Can't Take That Away From Me' (1938).

1987 Death of Rudolf Hess (b.1894 in Alexandria, Egypt), German politician and Hitler's former deputy, who committed suicide in Spandau Prison, Berlin.

1989 Richard Hart, accused of theft, became the first suspect to be supervised by electronic tagging in Britain.

1998 US president Bill Clinton (b.1946) admitted having an inappropriate relationship with former White House intern Monica Lewinsky.

1999 An earthquake in Izmit, Turkey, killed more than 17,000 people and caused damage totalling $6·5 billion.

AUGUST
18

1227 Death of Genghis Khan (b.1162 in Temujin, Mongolia), ruler of Mongolia, whose empire stretched from the Black Sea to the Pacific.

1587 Birth of Virginia Dare, born in Roanoke, Virginia, the first child to English New World settlers, seven days after the landing of Walter Raleigh's second expedition.

1750 Birth of Antonio Salieri in Verona, Italy (d.1825), composer, a famous rival of Mozart.

1826 Scottish explorer Alexander Gordon Laing (1793–1826) became the first European to reach Timbuktu.

1868 Discovery of helium in the solar spectrum by French astronomer Pierre Janssen (1824–1907), while observing an eclipse of the sun.

1891 A rainmaking experiment in Midland, Texas, proved inconclusive; it consisted of 12 hours of balloon and ground explosions, and cost $9000.

1894 US Congress established the Bureau of Immigration, precursor of the Immigration and Naturalization Service.

1919 Formation of the Anti-Cigarette League of America in Chicago, Illinois.

1920 Ratification of the 19th Amendment to the US Constitution, giving women the right to vote.

1933 Birth of Roman Polanski in Paris, Polish film-maker and actor, whose films include *Rosemary's Baby* (1968).

1937 Birth of Robert Redford in Santa Barbara, California, actor and director, whose films include *Ordinary People* (1980, Oscar).

1937 Birth of William Rushton in Chelsea, London (d.1996), comic actor, writer, novelist, and cartoonist, one of the founders of *Private Eye*.

1941 Establishment of the National Fire Service by the British government.

1948 Twelve-year-old British jockey Lester Piggott (b.1935) rode his first winner, *The Chase*, at Haydock Park, in only his 7th professional ride.

1957 Argentinian racing driver Juan Manuel Fangio (1911–95) won his 5th and last world championship, finishing second behind Stirling Moss in the Pescara Grand Prix, Italy.

1960 Launch of the birth control pill in the USA.

1964 Banning of South Africa from the Olympic Games because of its racial policies.

1982 A new record was set on the stock market when 132,690,000 shares were traded at the New York Stock Exchange in a single day.

1989 Anouncement of the sale of Manchester United Football Club to property tycoon Michael Knighton for £20 million, in the biggest takeover deal of British football. The deal subsequently fell through.

AUGUST
19

1274 Coronation of King Edward I of England (r.1272–1307).

1561 Arrival of Mary Queen of Scots in Scotland to assume the throne, after 13 years in France.

1646 Birth of John Flamsteed in Denby, Derbyshire (d.1719), Britain's first Astronomer Royal.

1743 Birth of Comtesse du Barry in Vaucouleurs, France (d.1793), favourite mistress of Louis XV of France.

1808 Birth of James Nasmyth in Edinburgh (d.1890), engineer, who devised and patented a steam hammer (1842).

1839 Release of the details of Louis Daguerre's first practical photographic process in Paris, called the 'Daguerreotype'.

1848 The *New York Herald* published the first news stories about the discovery of gold in California, USA.

1879 Construction began on the new Eddystone Lighthouse, when the foundation stone was laid by the Duke of Edinburgh and the Prince of Wales, the future Edward VII.

1883 Birth of Coco Chanel, popular name of Gabrielle Chanel, in Saumur, France (d.1971), couturier, who revolutionized women's fashions during the 1920s.

1897 Britain's first taxi began operation, in the City and London's West End.

1930 During its construction, the two halves of Sydney Harbour Bridge, Australia, were successfully joined.

1942 Launch by British and Canadian troops of the raid on Dieppe, France, during World War 2, with heavy Allied casualties and total loss of equipment.

1953 England's cricket team won the Ashes for the first time in 19 years, when they beat Australia by two wickets in the 5th Test Match at The Oval, London.

1960 US pilot Francis Gary Powers (b.1929) was sentenced to 10 years in prison by a Soviet military court after pleading guilty to spying for the CIA.

1960 Launch of the Soviet Union's Sputnik 5, with two dogs, 40 mice, 2 rats, and a variety of plants on board; the spacecraft returned safely to earth next day.

1988 Death of Sir Frederick Ashton (b.1906 in Guayaquil, Ecuador), British choreographer, whose works include *Façade* (1931).

1991 Overthrow of Soviet president Mikhail Gorbachev after a coup by Communist hardliners; the coup was declared a failure two days later, and Gorbachev returned to power.

AUGUST
20

Feast of St Bernard of Clairvaux (1090–1153), patron saint of bee-keepers.

1882 First performance of Tchaikovsky's *1812 Overture* at the consecration of the Cathedral of Christ the Saviour, Moscow.

1897 Discovery of malarial parasites in mosquitoes, by British physician Sir Ronald Ross (1857–1932), laying the foundation for the treatment of malaria.

1905 Birth of Jack Teagarden in Vernon, Texas (d.1964), jazz trombonist and band leader.

1912 Death of William Booth (b.1829 in Nottingham, Nottinghamshire), founder and general of the Salvation Army.

1924 Scottish sprinter Eric Liddell won the gold medal in the 400 m in a world record time of 47·6 seconds at the Olympic Games in Paris.

1924 Birth of Jim Reeves in Galloway, Texas (d.1964), country-and-western singer.

1940 Death of Leon Trotsky (b.1879 in Yanovka, Ukraine), Russian revolutionary, assassinated by one of Stalin's agents.

1940 British prime minister Winston Churchill (1874–1965) made his famous tribute to the RAF Battle of Britain pilots: 'Never in the field of human conflict was so much owed by so many to so few.'

1956 First day of operation for the world's first large-scale atomic power station, at Calder Hall, Cumbria.

1967 The *New York Times* reported a noise-reduction system for album and tape recording, developed by Dr Ray Dolby (b.1933).

1968 The Soviet Union invaded Czechoslovakia to crush the 'Prague Spring' liberalization drive of Alexander Dubček's regime.

1975 NASA launch of Viking 1 to Mars.

1977 Launch of US Voyager 2 space probe towards Jupiter, Saturn, and Uranus.

1980 Italian climber Reinhold Messner (b.1944) became the first man to make a solo ascent of Mt Everest.

1981 The US Voyager 2 space probe passed close to Saturn.

1989 The *Marchioness* pleasure-boat sank on London's R Thames, killing 51 people, after colliding with a dredger.

2001 Death of Sir Fred Hoyle (b.1915 in Bingley, West Yorkshire), astronomer, mathematician, and science-fiction writer, who coined the term 'Big Bang'.

AUGUST
21

1754 Birth of William Murdock in Old Cumnock, Strathclyde (d.1839), engineer, and pioneer of coal gas for lighting.

1808 Defeat of the French by British troops at the Battle of Vimiero during the Peninsular War.

1831 Nat Turner (1800–1831) led an unsuccessful slave rebellion in Southampton Co, Virginia, killing 60 people before being stopped by a 3000-man militia.

1872 Birth of Aubrey Beardsley in Brighton (d.1898), artist and illustrator, a major figure in the Aesthetic movement.

1888 Patenting of the adding machine by US inventor William Seward Burroughs (1855–98) of St Louis, Missouri.

1904 Birth of Count Basie in Red Bank, New Jersey (d.1984), jazz pianist, who formed his own band in 1935.

1911 Theft of Leonardo da Vinci's *Mona Lisa* from the Louvre in Paris (recovered in 1913).

1930 Birth of Princess Margaret at Glamis Castle, Angus (d.2002), British princess, the second daughter of George VI.

1933 Birth of Barry Norman in London, writer and television film critic, best known for hosting his long-running BBC series (1973–81, 1983–97).

1938 Birth of Kenny Rogers in Houston, Texas, popular singer and guitarist, whose songs include *Lucille* (1977).

1944 Representatives from the USA, the UK, the Soviet Union, and China began a series of meetings at Dumbarton Oaks, Washington, DC, to plan the formation of the United Nations.

1959 Hawaii became the 50th state of the Union.

1960 Release of Kenyan nationalist leader Jomo Kenyatta (c.1889–1978), after nine years in prison and exile.

1962 Maiden voyage of *Savannah*, the world's first nuclear-powered merchant ship.

1965 Launch of spacecraft Gemini 5, used to demonstrate the new capabilities of extravehicular activity.

1976 Mary Joy Langdon joined the East Sussex Fire and Rescue Service, becoming the first female firefighter in Britain.

1991 Independence of Latvia from the Soviet Union.

1996 First performance at the new Shakespeare's Globe theatre, London a short, unofficial 'Prologue Season' presentation of *The Two Gentlemen of Verona*.

1999 The town council of St Pierre-de-Trivisye, near Albi, France, home of Roquefort cheese, imposed a symbolic 100 per cent tax on Coca-Cola, in retaliation for US tariffs on European goods.

AUGUST

22

1485 The Battle of Bosworth Field was fought in Leicestershire, the last battle of the Wars of the Roses.

1642 Beginning of the English Civil War.

1654 Jacob Barsimson from Holland became the first Jewish settler in America when he arrived in New Amsterdam, later to be called New York.

1788 Founding of the British settlement in Sierra Leone, to secure a home in Africa for freed slaves and homeless Africans from England.

1806 Death of Jean Honoré Fragonard (b.1732 in Grasse, France), painter and engraver, best known for his light-hearted paintings of court life.

1851 First race around the Isle of Wight for a trophy originally named the 100 Guineas Cup – later renamed the America's Cup.

1862 Birth of Claude Debussy in St Germain-en-Laye, France (d.1918), composer, whose works include *La Mer* (1905).

1864 Foundation of the International Red Cross organization.

1901 Founding of the Cadillac Motor Company, in Detroit, Michigan.

1902 President Theodore Roosevelt (1858–1919) became the first US chief executive to ride in an automobile.

1906 Production began on the Victrola, a hand-cranked record-player produced by the Victor Talking Machine Company of Camden, New Jersey.

1922 Death of Michael Collins (b.1890 near Clonakilty, Co Cork, Ireland), Irish politician and Sinn Féin leader, killed in an ambush.

1932 The BBC made its first experimental television broadcast in Britain.

1940 Death of Sir Oliver Joseph Lodge (b.1851 in Penkhull, Staffordshire), physicist, and pioneer of radio-telegraphy.

1957 Birth of Steve Davis in London, snooker player, who won the world championship six times: 1981, 1983–4, and 1987–9.

1968 Arrival of Pope Paul VI in Bogota, Colombia, the first papal visit to Latin America.

1974 Death of Jacob Bronowski (b.1908 in Poland), mathematician and biologist, who wrote and presented the BBC television series *The Ascent of Man* (1973).

1988 Passing of a new law allowing all-day (11 a.m.–11 p.m.) drinking in English pubs, clubs, and wine bars, every day except Sunday.

2004 Theft by armed robbers of two Edvard Munch paintings, *The Scream* and *Madonna*, from the Munch Museum, Oslo.

AUGUST
23

Feast of St Rose of Lima, patron saint of florists, the Philippines, and South America.

410 The Visigoths sacked Rome.

1305 Death of Sir William Wallace (b.c.1270, probably in Elderslie, Renfrewshire), champion of the independence of Scotland, executed in London following his capture by English troops near Glasgow.

1617 An Act of Common Council established the first one-way streets in London, to regulate the 'disorder and rude behaviour of Carmen, Draymen and others using Cartes'.

1793 Introduction in France of the first national conscription for all unmarried men between 18 and 25.

1821 Independence of Mexico.

1852 Birth of Arnold Toynbee in London (d.1883), economic historian and social reformer, whose books include *The Industrial Revolution in England* (1884).

1913 The statue of the 'Little Mermaid' was placed on Langelinie Pier, Copenhagen.

1914 British expeditionary forces fought the first battle of World War 1 at Mons.

1926 Death of Rudolph Valentino, originally Rodolpho Guglielmi (b.1895 in Castellaneta, Italy), actor, the leading 'screen lover' of the 1920s.

1938 England Test cricketer Len Hutton (1916–90) scored a then world record Test score of 364 in the Fifth Test against Australia at The Oval, London.

1947 Birth of Willy Russell in Whiston, Lancashire, playwright, whose works include *Educating Rita* (1979).

1947 Birth of Keith Moon in London (d.1978), drummer with rock band The Who.

1948 Founding of the World Council of Churches as 147 different churches from many countries met in Amsterdam to commit themselves to the ecumenical movement.

1970 Birth of River Phoenix in Madras, Oregon (d.1993), actor, whose films include *Indiana Jones and the Last Crusade* (1989).

1979 Defection of Russian ballet dancer Alexander Godunov (1949–95) to the West, while on tour with the Bolshoi Ballet in New York.

1984 Sale of South Fork Ranch, near Dallas, Texas, home of the fictitious Ewing family of the CBS-TV show *Dallas*, to transform it from a tourist attraction into a hotel.

1989 More than one million people from Estonia, Latvia, and Lithuania, occupied by the Soviet Union, joined hands in the 'Baltic Way', an uninterrupted 600-km/373-mile human chain, to demand freedom and independence.

AUGUST
24

Feast (Western Church) of St Bartholomew, patron saint of butchers, bookbinders, leather-workers and tanners.

79 Eruption of Vesuvius smothered the cities of Pompeii, Stabiae, and Herculaneum.

79 Death of Pliny the Elder (b.23 in Novum Comum (now Como), Gaul), Roman scholar, killed while observing the eruption of Vesuvius.

1349 An outbreak of bubonic plague was blamed on Jews in Mainz, Germany: 6000 were killed in one day.

1456 Completion of the printing of the Gutenberg Bible.

1572 Slaughter of French Huguenots in the St Bartholomew's Day Massacre, Paris, ordered by King Charles IX.

1662 Parliament passed the Act of Uniformity, requiring England's college fellows and clergymen to accept the newly published Book of Common Prayer or be expelled.

1680 Death of Captain Thomas Blood, Irish adventurer, known for his activities during the English Civil War and Restoration.

1724 Birth of George Stubbs in Liverpool, Merseyside (d.1806), anatomist, painter, and engraver, who published *Anatomy of the Horse* (1766), illustrated by his own engravings.

1770 Death of Thomas Chatterton (b.1752 in Bristol, Avon), poet, who took his own life at 17.

1814 British troops captured Washington, DC, and burnt down the White House.

1954 Signing of the Communist Control Act by US president Dwight D. Eisenhower, taking away privileges and immunities from the Communist Party in America.

1957 Birth of Stephen Fry in London, writer, actor, and comedian, whose films include *Wilde* (1997).

1967 Three of The Beatles pop group, John Lennon, Paul McCartney, and George Harrison, met Maharishi Mahesh Yogi for the first time, at the Park Lane Hilton, London.

1968 Explosion of a hydrogen bomb near Fugataufa Atoll in the Pacific Ocean, making France the world's fifth nuclear power.

1981 Mark Chapman was given a life sentence for killing ex-Beatle John Lennon.

1990 Release of Irish hostage Brian Keenan (b.1950) in Beirut by his Islamic kidnappers, after more than four years in captivity in Lebanon.

1991 Resignation of Mikhail Gorbachev (b.1931) as first secretary of the Communist Party in the Soviet Union.

1992 Hurricane Andrew hit S Florida, killing over 50 people and causing millions of dollars of damage.

AUGUST
25

Feast of St Genesius of Arles, patron saint of secretaries. Feast of St Louis IX (1215–70), patron saint of builders, distillers, France, haberdashers, hairdressers, kings, and sculptors.

1688 Death of Sir Henry Morgan (b.1635 in Llanrumney, Wales), buccaneer, whose most famous exploit was the sacking of Porto Bello and Panama (1671).

1718 New Orleans was founded by French colonists as La Nouvelle-Orléans, under the direction of Jean-Baptiste Le Moyne de Bienville, who named it after the Duc d'Orléans.

1819 Birth of Allan Pinkerton in Glasgow (d.1884), detective, who founded the Pinkerton National Detective Agency (1850) in the USA.

1822 Death of Sir William Herschel (b.1738 in Hanover, Germany), English astronomer, who built the largest reflecting telescopes of the day.

1867 Death of Michael Faraday (b.1791 in Newington Butts, Surrey), chemist, experimental physicist, and natural philosopher.

1875 English swimmer Matthew Webb (1848–83) became the first person to swim the English Channel, swimming from Dover to Calais in 21 hours 45 minutes.

1918 Birth of Leonard Bernstein in Lawrence, Massachusetts (d.1990), conductor, pianist, and composer, best known for *West Side Story* (1957).

1919 Commencement of the daily air service between London and Paris.

1928 Opening of the stand and covered terracing at the Kop End of Englands's Liverpool Football Club, Anfield.

1930 Birth of Sean Connery in Edinburgh, actor, whose role as James Bond in the film *Dr No* (1963) established him as an international star.

1938 Birth of Frederick Forsyth in Ashford, Kent, writer of suspense thrillers, whose novels include *The Day of the Jackal* (1971).

1944 Liberation of Paris by the Allies.

1960 The 17th Olympic Games opened in Rome, Italy.

1964 British pop group The Beatles won a gold disc for their record 'A Hard Day's Night'.

1967 Death of George Lincoln Rockwell (b.1918 in Bloomington, Illinois), founder of the American Nazi Party, shot by party member John Patler.

1989 US spacecraft Voyager sent back pictures of Triton and two previously unknown moons of Neptune.

2001 Marriage of Crown Prince Haakon of Norway to Mette-Marit Tjessern Hoiby.

AUGUST
26

55 BC First invasion of Britain by Rome, under Emperor Julius Caesar.

1364 The Battle of Crécy took place between France and England during the Hundred Years' War.

1676 Birth of Sir Robert Walpole, 1st Earl of Orford, in Houghton, Norfolk (d.1745), leading minister (1721–42) of George I and George II.

1743 Birth of Antoine Laurent Lavoisier in Paris (d.1794), chemist, the founder of modern chemistry.

1819 Birth of Prince Albert at Schloss Rosenau, near Coburg, Germany (d.1861), Prince Consort to Queen Victoria.

1833 Birth of Henry Fawcett in Salisbury, Wiltshire (d.1884), postmaster-general, who introduced postal orders and parcel post.

1846 First performance of Mendelssohn's oratorio *Elijah*, at the Birmingham Festival, UK.

1873 Birth of Lee De Forest in Council Bluffs, Iowa (d.1961), inventor, widely honoured as 'the father of radio' and 'the grandfather of television'.

1875 Birth of John Buchan in Perth, Perth and Kinross (d.1940), writer and statesman, whose books include *The Thirty-nine Steps* (1915).

1895 Electricity was first transmitted commercially from the first large-scale usage of Niagara Falls' power.

1930 Death of Lon Chaney (b.1883 in Colorado Springs, Colorado), actor, whose films include *The Hunchback of Notre Dame* (1924).

1936 The Anglo-Egyptian Treaty established Egypt as a sovereign state after 50 years of British occupation.

1940 The RAF bombed Berlin, Germany, for the first time.

1942 Beginning of the Battle of Stalingrad, fought between Nazi German and Soviet troops during World War 2.

1959 British car manufacturers Austin and Morris launched their small family car, the Mini, designed by Sir Alec Issigonis (1906–88).

1972 Opening of the 20th Olympic Games in Munich, Germany.

1972 Death of Sir Francis Chichester (b.1901 in Barnstaple, Devon), pioneer air navigator and yachtsman, who made a solo circumnavigation of the world (1966–7) in *Gipsy Moth IV*.

1994 Arthur Cornhill, aged 62, was given the first battery-operated heart in a pioneering operation at Papworth Hospital, Cambridgeshire.

AUGUST
27

Feast of St Monica, patron saint of married women, mothers, and widows.

1660 Burning of books by the English poet John Milton (1608–74) in London, as a result of Milton's attacks on King Charles II.

1859 Beginning of the first commercial oil-well drilling near Titusville, Pennsylvania.

1869 Oxford University defeated Harvard in coxed-fours on the R Thames in the first transatlantic boat race.

1877 Birth of C. S. Rolls in London (d.1910), motorist and aeronaut, who formed a partnership with Henry Royce in 1906 for motor-car production.

1882 Birth of Samuel Goldwyn in Warsaw, Poland (d.1974), film producer, who emigrated to the USA, and in 1917 founded the Goldwyn Pictures Corporation.

1883 Destruction of the volcanic island of Krakatoa, in the Sunda Strait between Java and Sumatra, when the volcano erupted.

1896 The Anglo–Zanzibar War was fought between Britain and Zanzibar (the British were the victors); lasting about 45 minutes, it holds the record for being the shortest war in recorded history.

1908 Birth of Don Bradman in Cootamundra, New South Wales, Australia (d.2001), cricketer, whose batting records include the highest score (452 not out).

1910 Birth of Mother Teresa of Calcutta, in Skopje, Macedonia, former Yugoslavia (d.1997), Christian missionary in India, who was awarded the 1979 Nobel Peace Prize.

1939 First flight of the world's first jet-propelled aeroplane, the Heinkel 178.

1950 The BBC made the first television transmission from the Continent.

1962 Launch of US spacecraft Mariner 2 in the first planetary flyby.

1979 Death of Louis Mountbatten (b.1900 in Windsor, UK), British admiral and statesman, assassinated by Irish terrorists while fishing near his summer home, Classiebawn Castle, Co Sligo, Ireland.

1990 Launch of the BBC's first new radio network for 23 years, when Radio 5 opened with a mixture of sports, news, and children's programmes.

2003 Closest approach by Mars to Earth in 59,619 years, passing approximately 55.76 million km/34.65 million miles from Earth.

2003 The world's most powerful storage battery system became fully operational, providing Fairbanks, Alaska, with emergency power.

AUGUST
28

Feast of St Augustine (354–430), patron saint of printers and theologians.

1207 Liverpool was made a borough by King John of England (1199–1216).

1749 Birth of Johann Wolfgang von Goethe in Frankfurt, Germany (d.1832), poet, dramatist, and scientist, whose works include *Faust* (1808, 1832).

1828 [Old Style calendar, New Style 9 September] Birth of Count Leo Tolstoy at Yasnaya Polyana, Russia (d.1910), writer and moralist, whose novels include *War and Peace* (1865–9).

1837 Pharmacists John Lea and William Perrins of Worcester, Hereford and Worcester, first made Worcestershire sauce, from a recipe given to them by Lord Sandys, governor of Bengal.

1840 Birth of Ira David Sankey in Edinburgh, Pennsylvania (d.1908), evangelist, hymn-writer, and collaborator with Dwight L. Moody (1837–1899).

1850 The first English Channel telegraph cable was laid between Dover, UK, and Cap Gris Nez, France, and was broken by a French fisherman within hours; a second cable was laid in 1851.

1850 Premiere of Richard Wagner's opera *Lohengrin*, conducted by Franz Liszt, in Weimar, Germany.

1922 Broadcast of the first radio commercial in New York, advertising property.

1930 Birth of Windsor Davies in London, actor, best known for his comic role as the sergeant-major in the British television series *It Ain't Half Hot, Mum* (1973–7).

1933 The BBC broadcast the first appeal over the air on behalf of the police, for wanted murderer Stanley Hobday.

1958 Launch of Sputnik 3 by the Soviet Union, with two dogs on board.

1963 Civil rights leader Martin Luther King (1929–68) made his famous 'I Have a Dream' speech at a civil rights rally in Washington, DC.

1987 Death of John Huston (b.1906 in Nevada, Missouri), director, screenwriter, and actor, whose films include *The Treasure of the Sierra Madre* (1948, Oscar).

1992 The Russian kopek, worth three millionths of a UK penny, was withdrawn from circulation.

1994 Thousands of shops in England and Wales opened legally on a Sunday for the first time, following a change in trading laws.

1996 Divorce of the Prince and Princess of Wales, Charles and Diana, after fifteen years of marriage.

2004 British athlete Kelly Holmes (b.1970) won the 800 m and 1500 m gold medals in Athens, Greece, becoming the first Briton in 84 years to achieve the Olympic middle-distance double.

AUGUST
29

1533 Atahualpa, the last ruler of the Incas, was killed by Francisco Pizarro (c.1476–1541).

1831 Demonstration by physicist Michael Faraday (1791–1867) of the first electrical transformer at the Royal Institute, London.

1833 Passing of the Factory Act in Britain, regulating the employment of children.

1842 The Treaty of Nanking leased the Hong Kong territories to Britain.

1862 Capture of Garibaldi (1807–82), on his way to take Rome, by Italian forces at the Battle of Aspromonte.

1885 Patenting of the first motorcycle, built by Daimler in Germany.

1897 Creation of chop suey, a dish devised by a US chef to cater for both Chinese and US tastes.

1904 Opening of the 3rd Olympic games in St Louis, Missouri.

1915 Birth of Ingrid Bergman in Stockholm, Sweden (d.1982), actress, whose films include *Gaslight* (1944, Oscar).

1920 Birth of Charlie Parker in Kansas City, Kansas (d.1955), jazz saxophonist, a leading proponent of bebop music.

1923 Birth of Sir Richard Attenborough in Cambridge, Cambridgeshire, actor and director, whose films include *Gandhi* (1982).

1957 Testing of the first breathalyser in the USA, formerly known as a 'drunkometer'.

1958 Birth of Michael Jackson in Gary, Indiana, pop singer, whose first major solo album was *Off The Wall* (1979).

1958 Birth of Lenny Henry in Dudley, West Midlands, comedian, whose shows include the *Lenny Henry Show* (1984–95).

1979 Hurricane David devastated the tiny Caribbean island of Dominica as it travelled through the Caribbean.

1987 Death of Lee Marvin (b.1924 in New York), actor, whose films include *The Dirty Dozen* (1967).

1988 A 14-year-old boy, Matthew Sadler (b.c.1974), became Britain's youngest ever international chess master at a tournament in London, England.

1991 Suspension of all activities of the Communist Party by the Supreme Soviet, the parliament of the USSR, bringing an end to the institution.

1992 Death of Mary Pearson Norton (b.1903 in Leighton Buzzard, Bedfordshire), children's author, best known for *The Borrowers* series (1952–82).

2005 Hurricane Katrina made landfall along the American southern seaboard; over 1400 people were killed and $75 billion worth of damage caused.

AUGUST

30

Feast of St Fiacre (Fiachrach) (?–670), patron saint of gardeners, sufferers from venereal diseases, and taxi-drivers (also 1 September).

30 BC Death of Cleopatra (b.69 BC), queen of Egypt, the daughter of Ptolemy Auletes.

1483 Death of Louis XI, king of France (b.1423), who united most of France under one crown.

1797 Birth of Mary Shelley in London (d.1851), writer, whose works include the novel *Frankenstein, or the Modern Prometheus* (1818).

1860 Opening of the first British tramway, in Birkenhead, Merseyside.

1862 US soldier Thomas 'Stonewall' Jackson (1824–63) led the Confederates to victory at the second Battle of Bull Run, during the American Civil War.

1871 Birth of Ernest Rutherford near Nelson, New Zealand (d.1937), physicist, a pioneer of subatomic physics.

1884 Birth of Dr Collis Browne, medical doctor, who while practising in India invented Chlorodyne, a patent medicine for stomach upsets.

1901 Patenting of the electrically powered vacuum cleaner by British engineer Hubert Cecil Booth (1871–1955).

1905 Ty Cobb (1886–1961), a member of baseball's Hall of Fame, made his major league debut with the Detroit Tigers.

1926 British cricketer Jack Hobbs (1882–1963) scored 316 runs at Lords, the highest individual score recorded at the ground.

1932 Nazi leader Hermann Goering (1893–1946) was elected president of the Reichstag.

1939 Birth of John Peel in Heswall, Merseyside (d.2004), disc jockey and radio presenter, whose programmes include *Home Truths* (1998–2004).

1939 Beginning of the evacuation of women and children from British cities, in anticipation of World War 2 bombing.

1941 The Germans cut the railway line to Leningrad, in preparation for the siege which began a week later.

1945 Britain reclaimed Hong Kong, which had been occupied for four years by Japan.

1963 Opening of the 'hot line' telephone communications link between the Kremlin and the White House.

1972 Birth of Cameron Diaz in San Diego, California, actress, whose films include *Charlie's Angels* (2000).

1991 Azerbaijan declared independence from the Soviet Union.

2003 Death of Charles Bronson (b.1921 in Ehrenfield, Pennsylvania), actor, known for his 'tough-guy' roles in such films as *Death Wish* (1974).

AUGUST
31

Feast of St Raymond Nonnatus, patron saint of midwives, and women in childbirth.

1385 England's King Richard II (1367–1400) invaded Scotland with an army of 14,000 men.

1829 Italian composer Gioacchino Rossini's (1792–1868) final opera, *William Tell*, was produced in Paris for the Grand Opera.

1852 Authorization of pre-stamped envelopes by the US Congress.

1870 Birth of Maria Montessori in Rome (d.1952), doctor, who developed a new system of education.

1887 Inventor Thomas A. Edison (1847–1931) received a patent for his *Kinetoscope*, a device which produced moving pictures.

1913 Birth of Sir Bernard Lovell in Oldland Common, Gloucestershire, astronomer, director of Jodrell Bank, and pioneer of radio astronomy.

1918 Birth of Alan Jay Lerner in New York (d.1986), librettist, best known for such hit musicals as *My Fair Lady* (1956).

1936 Britain's first female television announcer, Elizabeth Cowell, made her first broadcast from Alexandra Palace.

1942 The British 8th Army, under General Montgomery, defeated Field Marshal Rommel's Afrika Korps in the Battle of Alam Halfa in Egypt.

1946 Death of Harley Granville-Barker (b.1877 in London), actor, playwright, and critic, whose writing included a series of prefaces to Shakespeare's plays (1927–45).

1949 Birth of Richard Gere in Philadelphia, Pennsylvania, actor, whose films include *American Gigolo* (1980).

1951 Issue of the first 33 rpm record, by the West German company Deutsche Grammophon Gesellschaft.

1962 Chris Bonnington and Ian Clough became the first Britons to conquer the north face of the Eiger.

1972 US swimmer Mark Spitz (b.1950) won the first of his seven gold medals at the Munich Olympic Games.

1979 The comet Howard-Koomur-Michels became the first recorded comet to collide with the Sun.

1986 Death of Henry Moore (b.1898 in Castleford, West Yorkshire), sculptor.

1994 Troops of the former Soviet Union ended half a century of military presence on German soil with a farewell ceremony.

1997 Death of Diana, Princess of Wales (b.1961 at Sandringham, Norfolk), in a car crash in Paris.

SEPTEMBER

1

Opening of the partridge-shooting season in Britain.

Feast of St Giles (?–c.700), patron saint of beggars, cancer sufferers, childless women, cripples, hermits, horses, and lepers.

1853 Issue of the world's first triangular postage stamps by the Cape of Good Hope.

1859 First observation of a solar flare, by British astronomer Richard C(hristopher) Carrington (1826–75).

1866 Birth of 'Gentleman Jim' James John Corbett in San Francisco, California (d.1933), boxer, who knocked out John L(awrence) Sullivan in 1892.

1875 Birth of Edgar Rice Burroughs in Chicago, Illinois (d.1950), writer, who made his name with the Tarzan stories, beginning with *Tarzan of the Apes* (1914).

1878 The first female telephone operator, Emma Nutt, started work at an exchange in Boston, Massachusetts.

1886 Opening of the Severn Tunnel, UK, for goods traffic.

1923 Tokyo and Yokohama in Japan were destroyed by earthquake, causing c.100,000 deaths.

1923 Birth of Rocky Marciano in Brockton, Massachusetts (d.1969), heavyweight boxer, who made his name by defeating the former world champion, Joe Louis, in 1951.

1939 Broadcasting began on the BBC's Home Service; it was renamed as BBC Radio 4 on 30 September 1967.

1939 Invasion of Poland by Hitler, precipitating World War 2.

1946 Birth of Barry Gibb in Douglas, Isle of Man, rock musician, who with his two younger brothers formed The Bee Gees.

1957 Birth of Gloria Estefan in Cuba, pop singer, and member of the group the Miami Sound Machine.

1971 Britain's old penny and three-penny coins were no longer legal tender.

1972 Extension of fishing limits around Iceland from 12 to 50 miles (c.20 to 80 km).

1983 A Korean Air Lines Boeing 747 was shot down by a Soviet fighter plane near Sakhalin Island, killing all 269 on board.

1985 Location of the remains of RMS *Titanic* by a joint US-French expedition, 563 km/350 miles SE of Newfoundland in 3962 m/13,000 ft of water.

SEPTEMBER

2

31 BC Defeat of Antony and Cleopatra at the Battle of Actium by Augustus Octavian.

1666 Start of the Great Fire of London, which engulfed four-fifths of the city.

1834 Death of Thomas Telford (b.1757 in Langholm, Dumfries and Galloway), engineer, whose projects include the Ellesmere (1793–1805) and Caledonian (1803–23) canals.

1843 Publication of the first edition of *The Economist* by James Wilson.

1898 Defeat of the Mahdists by Lord Kitchener (1850–1916) at the Battle of Omdurman.

1910 Death of Henri Rousseau (b.1844 in Laval, France), primitive painter, who produced painstaking portraits, imaginary landscapes, and dreams.

1930 Completion of the first non-stop flight from Paris to New York, by French aviators Dieudonné Costes and Maurice Bellonte.

1939 Conscription of men between the ages of 19 and 41, under Britain's National Service Bill.

1945 Formal surrender of Japan to the Allies at the end of World War 2 aboard the US aircraft carrier *Missouri* in Tokyo Bay.

1952 Birth of Jimmy Connors in Belleville, Illinois, tennis player, who became Wimbledon champion in 1974 and 1982.

1964 Birth of Keanu Reeves in Beirut, Lebanon, US actor, whose films include *The Matrix* (1999) and its sequels.

1965 The Beatles were awarded a gold disc for their record 'Help'.

1973 Death of J(ohn) R(onald) R(euel) Tolkien (b.1892) in Bloemfontein, South Africa, philologist and writer, whose interest in language and saga led to the book *The Lord of the Rings* (1954–5).

1978 Marriage of George Harrison (1943–2001), former member of The Beatles, to Olivia Trinidad Arias (b.1948).

1987 Launch of the CD-video, combining digital sound with high-definition video, by Philips.

1993 A robot was used by police in Washington, DC, to control a murder suspect.

1994 Death of Roy Castle (b.1932 in Scholes, West Yorkshire), musician, dancer, and actor, known for such programmes as BBC television's *Record Breakers*.

1995 British boxer Frank Bruno (b.1961) beat US boxer Oliver McCall (b.1965) over 12 rounds at Wembley Stadium, London, to win the WBC world heavyweight championship.

2001 Death of Professor Christiaan Barnard (b.1922 in Beaufort West, South Africa), surgeon, who performed the first successful human heart transplant (1967).

SEPTEMBER

3

Feast of St Gregory I the Great (c.540–604), patron saint of musicians, popes, singers, and teachers (also 12 March).

1189 Coronation of King Richard I of England (r.1189–99), known as Richard the Lionheart.

1658 Death of Oliver Cromwell (b.1599 in Huntingdon, Cambridgeshire), English soldier and statesman.

1777 The American stars and stripes flag was carried into battle for the first time at the Battle of Cooch's Bridge, Delaware, during the Revolutionary War.

1783 Signing of peace in Paris, ending the War of American Independence.

1833 Publication of the first penny newspaper, the *New York Sun*, in the USA.

1856 Failure of the Royal British Bank, with debts of over £500,000.

1875 Birth of Ferdinand Porsche in Hafersdorf, Germany (d.1951), automobile designer, who produced the Volkswagen and (1950) sports car.

1916 The first Zeppelin airship over Britain during World War 1 was shot down in Cuffley, Hertfordshire.

1935 Briton Sir Malcolm Campbell (1885–1948) set a new world land speed record with two runs over a 1·61-km/1-mile course, averaging 484·62 kph/301·13 mph in *Bluebird* at Bonneville Salt Flats, Utah.

1939 Beginning of World War 2, when Britain and France declared war on Germany.

1942 US singer Frank Sinatra left the Tommy Dorsey Band to begin his solo singing career.

1954 Transmission of the last episode of the radio series *The Lone Ranger*, after 2596 episodes.

1962 Opening of the 4800-mile Trans-Canada highway, linking St John's, Newfoundland to Victoria, British Columbia.

1967 Sweden's traffic system switched from left- to right-lane driving.

1969 Death of Ho Chi Minh (b.1892 in Kim-Lien, North Vietnam), North Vietnamese president (1954–69).

1976 Landing of Viking 2 on Mars, on Utopia Planitia, after nearly a year's journey.

1991 Death of Frank Capra (b.1897 in Palermo, Italy), director, whose films include *You Can't Take It with You* (1938, Oscar).

2004 Ending of the siege at Beslan, North Ossetia-Alania, Russia, when over a thousand hostages were held by 32 Islamic terrorists for 52 hours; over 340 died, more than half of them children.

SEPTEMBER

4

1781 Founding of 'El Pueblo de Nuestra Señora la Reina de Los Angeles' (The Village of Our Lady, the Queen of the Angels), modern-day Los Angeles.

1833 Ten-year-old Barney Flaherty became the first US newspaper delivery boy, when he answered an advertisement in the *New York Sun*.

1870 Forces of the Third Republic deposed Emperor Napoleon III of France, following his capture at the Battle of Sedan two days previously.

1885 Opening of the Exchange Buffet in New York, the first self-service cafeteria in the USA.

1896 Birth of Anton Bruckner in Ansfelden, Austria (d.1896), composer, organist, and professor of composition at the Vienna Conservatory (1868–91).

1907 Death of Edvard Grieg (b.1843 in Bergen, Norway), composer, whose works include the *Piano Concerto in A Minor*.

1909 Britain's Crystal Palace hosted the world's first Boy Scout rally.

1937 Birth of Dawn Fraser in Balmain, New South Wales, Australia, swimmer, who won the Olympic 100 m Freestyle gold medal in 1956, 1960, and 1964.

1940 Demonstration of colour television by the Columbia Broadcasting System in the USA.

1949 Birth of Tom Watson in Kansas City, Missouri, professional golfer, whose tournament wins include the Open championship (1975, 1977, 1980, 1982–3) and the US Masters (1977, 1981).

1955 Broadcasters Richard Baker (b.1925) and Kenneth Kendall (b.1924) became the first BBC newsreaders to be seen on British television.

1957 An Arkansas governor called out the National Guard to prevent nine African-American students from entering the Central High School in Little Rock, Arkansas.

1961 Introduction of the ITA (Initial Teaching Alphabet), devised by British educationist James Pitman (1901–85), in 19 British schools.

1964 Opening of the Forth Road Bridge (1876 m/6156 ft) at Queensferry, Lothian.

1970 Defection of Russian ballerina Natalia Makarova (b.1940) of the Kirov Ballet to the West.

1972 At the Munich Olympics, US swimmer Mark Spitz (b.1950) became the first to win seven gold medals in a single Olympiad; all seven wins set world records.

1985 Remote-control cameras photographed the wreck of the *Titanic* on the bed of the Atlantic.

1989 Death of Georges Simenon (b.1903 in Liège, Belgium), crime novelist, whose works include the Inspector Maigret novels (from 1933).

2001 Computer firms Hewlett-Packard and Compaq announced a $55 billion merger.

SEPTEMBER
5

1638 Birth of Louis XIV in St Germain-en-Laye, France (d.1715), king of France (1643–1715), whose long reign marked the cultural ascendancy of France within Europe.

1698 Introduction of a tax on beards by Peter I the Great, tsar of Russia (1682–1721) and emperor (1721–5).

1800 Surrender of Malta by French troops to the British Navy, following a lengthy naval blockade.

1826 Birth of John Wisden in Brighton (d.1884), cricketer for Sussex, who compiled the Wisden record books.

1897 Birth of A(rthur) C(harles) Nielsen in Chicago, Illinois (d.1980), businessman and market-researcher, who established a national television rating service (1950).

1902 Birth of Darryl F. Zanuck in Wahoo, Nebraska (d.1979), film producer, who co-founded Twentieth-Century Pictures (later Twentieth-Century Fox) in 1933.

1914 Beginning of the Battle of the Marne, early in World War 1, halting German forces that were approaching Paris.

1930 Charles Creighton and James Hagris completed a drive from New York to Los Angeles and back in a 1929 Ford Model A – all in reverse gear; the trip took 42 days.

1940 Birth of Raquel Welch in Chicago, Illinois, actress, launched as a sex symbol after her appearance in *One Million Years BC* (1966).

1959 Inauguration of Britain's first trunk dialling system, when the deputy Lord Mayor of Bristol dialled the Lord Mayor of London.

1960 US boxer Cassius Clay (b.1942, later Muhammad Ali) won the gold medal in light heavyweight boxing at the Olympic Games in Rome.

1975 Explosion of an IRA bomb in the lobby of the Hilton Hotel, London, killing two people and injuring 63.

1977 Launch of Voyager 1, the first spacecraft to leave the solar system.

1982 Death of Sir Douglas Bader (b.1910 in London), wartime aviator, who overcame the loss of both legs in a flying accident to become an RAF hero during World War 2.

1997 Death of Mother Teresa of Calcutta (b.1910 in Skopje, Macedonia, former Yugoslavia), Christian missionary in India, who was awarded the 1979 Nobel Peace Prize.

2001 UK kayaker Peter Bray became the first person to cross the North Atlantic Ocean in a kayak, in 74 days.

SEPTEMBER
6

1191 Richard I, king of England, defeated the Saracens at the Battle of Arsouf.

1620 The *Mayflower*, a three-masted carrack, set sail from Plymouth to North America, a journey lasting 66 days.

1666 End of the Great Fire of London, which began on 2 September, and engulfed c.160 hectares/400 acres.

1766 Birth of John Dalton in Eaglesfield, Cumbria (d.1844), chemist, the first to describe colour blindness (1794).

1852 Opening of Britain's first free lending library, in Campfield, Manchester.

1879 Opening of Britain's first telephone exchange, in Lombard Street, London.

1882 The USA held its first Labour Day parade in New York.

1927 Opening in the USA of the film *The Jazz Singer*, starring Al Jolson, the first 'talkie'.

1939 Death of Arthur Rackham (b.1867 in London), water-colourist and book illustrator, known for his Romantic and grotesque pictures in books of fairy tales.

1942 Birth of Brit Ekland in Stockholm, Sweden, actress, whose films include *The Man with the Golden Gun* (1973).

1948 First breaking of the sound barrier in Britain, by John Derry in a De Havilland DH 108 aeroplane, during a dive.

1952 Death of Gertrude Lawrence (b.1898 in London), actress, a leading lady in many of Noel Coward's productions.

1952 A jet fighter aeroplane broke up and fell into the crowd at Farnborough Air Show, Hampshire, killing at least 27 people and injuring more than 60.

1959 Mattel Toy Corporation sold the first Barbie doll.

1987 For the first time since 1315, the Venice Regatta took place without the city's 230 gondoliers, on strike in protest at the damage caused by powerboats.

1989 Following a computer error, over 40,000 Parisians received letters charging them with murder, extortion, and organized prostitution, instead of traffic offence notifications.

1990 Death of Sir Leonard Hutton (b.1916 in Fulneck, West Yorkshire), Yorkshire cricketer, and captain of the England team that regained the Ashes in 1953.

1997 The funeral of Diana, Princess of Wales, took place at Westminster Abbey, London; more than a million people lined the route of the funeral cortège.

1998 Death of Akira Kurosawa (b.1910 in Tokyo), director, whose films include *The Seven Samurai* (1954).

SEPTEMBER

7

1533 Birth of Elizabeth I in Greenwich, London (d.1603), queen of England and Ireland (1558–1603).

1813 First use of the nickname 'Uncle Sam' as a symbolic reference to the USA, when it appeared in the New York newspaper *Troy Post*.

1836 Birth of Sir Henry Campbell-Bannerman in Glasgow (d.1908), British prime minister (1905–8).

1838 Grace Darling (1815–42) and her father William (1795–1860), a lighthouse-keeper on the Farne Islands, UK, rescued the crew of the *Forfarshire*, a steamer wrecked off the Northumberland coast.

1867 Birth of J. P. Morgan in Hartford, Connecticut (d.1913), banker, financier, and art collector, who built his father's firm into the most powerful private banking house in the USA.

1887 Birth of Dame Edith Sitwell in Scarborough, North Yorkshire (d.1964), poet, whose experimental poetry, *Façade* (1922), was controversially received.

1892 US boxer James J. Corbett (1866–1933) knocked out John L. Sullivan (1858–1918) in the 21st round in New Orleans, Louisiana, winning the first championship boxing match using padded gloves under the Queensberry Rules.

1896 A. H. Whiting won the first motor-race held on a closed circuit, in Cranston, Rhode Island.

1901 Signing of the Peace of Peking, ending the Boxer Rebellion which attempted to drive all foreigners out of China.

1914 Birth of James Van Allen in Mount Pleasant, Iowa, physicist, who gave his name to radiation belts surrounding the earth.

1921 America held its first Miss America beauty contest, in Atlantic City, won by Margaret Gorman of Washington, DC.

1936 Birth of Buddy Holly in Lubbock, Texas (d.1959), rock singer, songwriter, and guitarist, whose hits include 'Peggy Sue' (1957).

1940 Beginning of nightly blitz bombing by the Germans over London, continuing until 2 November.

1981 Death of Christy Brown (b.1932 in Dublin, Ireland), novelist and painter, handicapped from birth with cerebral palsy.

1986 Desmond Tutu (b.1931) became archbishop of Cape Town, South Africa.

2001 Children in over 3000 schools across Britain jumped off chairs or up and down at precisely 11 a.m., in an experiment at the beginning of Science Year to see if humans can create earthquakes.

SEPTEMBER
8

1157 Birth of King Richard I of England in Oxford, Oxfordshire (d.1199), son of Eleanor of Aquitaine and Henry II of England.

1504 Unveiling of Michelangelo's *David* in front of the Palazzo Vecchio, Florence, the first large statue of a nude to be exhibited in a public place in Italy since antiquity.

1664 The Dutch colony of New Amsterdam surrendered to the British and was renamed New York.

1831 Coronation of William IV, king of Great Britain and Ireland, and king of Hanover (1830–37).

1841 Birth of Antonín Dvořák near Prague, Czech Republic (d.1904), composer, whose works are known for their colourful Slavonic motifs.

1886 Founding of Johannesburg, South Africa.

1888 The first season of the English Football League began with 12 member clubs.

1921 Birth of Sir Harry Secombe in Swansea, Wales (d.2001), comedian, singer, actor, and media personality.

1925 Birth of Peter Sellers in Southsea, Hampshire (d.1980), actor and comedian, who starred as Inspector Clouseau in the *Pink Panther* series of films.

1930 The first roll of Scotch Cellophane Tape, invented by Richard Drew, was sent to a prospective customer.

1931 Birth of Jack Rosenthal in Manchester (d.2004), playwright, whose television plays include *The Knowledge* (1979).

1932 Birth of Patsy Cline in Winchester, Virginia, country music singer, whose hits include 'Crazy' (1961).

1941 Beginning of the siege of Leningrad by Germany, lasting until January 1944; around 650,000 residents of Leningrad died.

1944 Landing of the first German V-2 rocket during World War 2, on Chiswick, London, killing three people.

1966 Transmission of the first episode of *Star Trek*, called 'The Man Trap', on NBC-TV.

1968 UK tennis player Virginia Wade (b.1945) beat the top-seeded American Billie Jean King (b.1943) to win the US Open women's singles title.

1974 President Gerald Ford pardoned ex-President Richard Nixon for all federal crimes he might have committed while in office.

2000 Report by NASA that the hole in the ozone layer over Antarctica had grown to its largest to date, measuring 28·3 million sq km/10·9 million sq miles.

2001 Michael Jackson (b.1958) performed live at Madison Square Garden, New York, to celebrate his 30th year as a performer.

SEPTEMBER

9

Feast of St Peter Claver, patron saint of race relations.

1087 Death of William the Conqueror, the first Norman king of England (r.1066–87).

1513 The English won the Battle of Flodden Field, near Branxton, Northumberland, where James IV of Scotland was killed.

1737 Birth of Luigi Galvani in Bologna, Italy (d.1798), physiologist, known for his studies of the role of electrical impulses in animal tissue.

1754 Birth of Captain William Bligh in Plymouth, Devon (d.1817), British naval officer, who lost his ship HMS *Bounty* to mutineers in 1789.

1835 The British Municipal Corporations Act came into force, creating modern local government.

1850 California became the 31st state of the Union.

1901 Death of Henri de Toulouse Lautrec (b.1864 in Albi, France), painter and lithographer, known for his paintings of Montmartre society.

1941 Birth of Otis Redding in Dawson, Georgia (d.1967), soul singer, whose songs include 'Mr Pitiful' (1965).

1948 Proclamation of the Democratic People's Republic of Korea, after the withdrawal of Soviet forces from North Korea.

1950 Ending of soap rationing in Britain.

1958 First race riots in Britain at the annual Notting Hill carnival.

1960 Birth of Hugh Grant in London, actor, whose films include *Notting Hill* (1999).

1970 The first hijacking of a British aircraft took place, near Beirut, Lebanon.

1975 Defection of Czech tennis player Martina Navratilova (b.1956) to the West, requesting political asylum in the USA; she became a US citizen in 1981.

1976 Death of Mao Zedong (b.1893 in Shaoshan, Hunan Province, China), Chinese revolutionary leader, who launched the 'Great Leap Forward' and the 'Cultural Revolution'.

1979 Tracy Austin, aged 16 years, eight months, 28 days, became the youngest US Open women's singles champion, beating Chris Evert Lloyd.

1988 England cricket captain Graham Gooch, and seven other squad members, were refused visas to India for their involvement in South African cricket, leading to the cancellation of the tour.

1998 Announcement of the closure of the Royal Opera House, London, due to serious financial problems, cancelling nearly all its 1999 performances in an emergency rescue bid.

SEPTEMBER

10

1753 Birth of Sir John Soane in Goring, Oxfordshire (d.1837), architect, whose designs include the Bank of England (1792–1833, now rebuilt).

1771 Birth of Mungo Park in Foulshiels, Scottish Borders (d.1806), surgeon and explorer, who found the true course of the Niger in Africa.

1823 Simon Bolivar (1783–1830) became dictator of Peru.

1846 Patenting of the lock-stitch sewing machine by US inventor Elias Howe (1819–67).

1897 George Smith, a London taxi-driver, was the first motorist to be convicted of driving while under the influence of alcohol.

1921 Completion of Germany's first motorway.

1929 Birth of Arnold Palmer in Latrobe, Pennsylvania, champion golfer, credited with turning golf from an exclusive sport into a popular pastime.

1935 NBC Radio broadcast the first *Popeye* show, based on the popular comic strip by US cartoonist Elzie Segar (1894–1938).

1960 Transmission of the first live television football match in the UK, when the BBC covered the last 50 minutes of the league match between Blackpool (0) and Bolton Wanderers (1).

1963 Launch of the American Express sterling credit card in Britain.

1973 Independence of Guinea-Bissau.

1977 Death of Hamida Djandoubi (b.1949), Tunisian immigrant, the last person to be guillotined in France, convicted of the murder of Elisabeth Bousquet in Marseille.

1981 Return of Picasso's *Guernica* to Spain from New York.

1984 Accidental discovery of DNA fingerprinting by Professor Alec Jeffreys (b.1950) of Leicester University while tracing genetic markers through families to understand inheritance patterns of illness.

1985 Death of Jock Stein (b.1922 in Burnbank, South Lanarkshire), footballer and manager, who collapsed during the Wales v. Scotland World Cup match, and died shortly afterwards.

1988 German tennis player Steffi Graf became the third woman to complete the Grand Slam, defeating Gabriela Sabatini in the final of the US Open.

1998 Meeting at Stormont, Belfast, between Ulster Unionist leader David Trimble and Sinn Féin leader Gerry Adams, the first meeting between a Republican and Loyalist leader since 1922.

SEPTEMBER

11

1297 Defeat of Edward I by Scottish patriot William Wallace at the Battle of Stirling Bridge.

1649 Oliver Cromwell's troops besieged Drogheda, Ireland, killing nearly 3500 people and fuelling Catholic–Protestant strife for over three centuries.

1777 The Battle of the Brandywine was fought at Brandywine Creek, near Philadelphia, Pennsylvania, during the American War of Independence.

1816 Birth of Carl Zeiss in Weimar, Germany (d.1888), optician and industrialist, whose factory at Jena produced lenses, microscopes, and other optical instruments.

1855 During the Crimean War, the Russians surrendered, and Sebastopol was taken by the Allies.

1883 Patenting of the mail chute by US inventor James Cutler.

1895 Theft of the original FA Cup from a football outfitter's window in Birmingham, West Midlands; in 1958, 83-year-old Harry Burge claimed that he had stolen it to make counterfeit half-crown coins.

1915 Foundation of Britain's first Women's Institute, in Llan-fairpwllgwyngyllgogerychwyrn-drobwllllantysiliogogogoch, Anglesey.

1945 Birth of Franz Beckenbauer in Munich, Germany, footballer, who became the first person to win the World Cup as both a captain (1974) and a manager (1990).

1951 US swimmer Florence Chadwick (1918–95) became the first woman to swim the English Channel in both directions, swimming from England to France in 16 hours and 22 minutes.

1962 Recording of The Beatles' first single, 'Love Me Do'.

1971 Death of Nikita Khrushchev (b.1894 in Kalinovka, Ukraine), Soviet prime minister (1958–64).

1972 First transmission of the BBC TV quiz programme *Mastermind*, hosted by Magnus Magnusson (b.1929).

1973 Death of Salvador Allende, president of Chile, when his government was overthrown by a military junta led by General Augusto Pinochet.

1978 Death of Georgi Markov (b.1929 in Sofia, Bulgaria), fatally stabbed with a poisoned umbrella while walking down a London street.

1994 Death of Jessica Tandy (b.1909 in London), actress, whose films include *Driving Miss Daisy* (1989).

1997 In a national referendum on devolution, Scotland voted to create its own parliament for the first time in more than 300 years.

2001 Two planes were crashed by terrorists into the twin towers of The World Trade Center in New York.

SEPTEMBER
12

Defenders' Day, an optional bank holiday in Maryland, commemorating the defence of Fort McHenry against the British in 1814.

1440 Founding of Eton College near Windsor, Berkshire, by Henry VI to provide free education for 70 poor scholars.

1609 English explorer Henry Hudson sailed into New York harbour, and further inland along what is now called the Hudson R.

1818 Birth of Richard Jordan Gatling in Maney's Neck, North Carolina (d.1903), inventor, best remembered for his rapid-fire Gatling gun (1861–2).

1878 Erection of Cleopatra's Needle on the Thames Embankment, London.

1888 Birth of Maurice Chevalier in Paris (d.1972), film and vaudeville actor, whose films include *Gigi* (1958).

1910 Alice Wells became the first policewoman on her appointment to Los Angeles Police Department.

1913 Birth of Jesse Owens in Danville, Alabama (d.1980), athlete, who won four gold medals at the 1936 Berlin Olympic Games.

1940 Discovery of prehistoric cave paintings at Lascaux, near Montignac, France, by four teenagers.

1944 Birth of Barry White in Galveston, Texas, pop and soul singer.

1951 Birth of Bertie Ahern in Dublin, Ireland, taoiseach of Ireland, a key participant in the Northern Ireland peace process after the signing of the 1998 Good Friday Agreement.

1953 Marriage of John F. Kennedy to Jacqueline Lee Bouvier in St Mary's Church, Newport, Rhode Island.

1954 Debut of *Lassie* on CBS, the long-running US television series about a collie dog and her various owners; the last show was transmitted on 12 September 1971.

1959 Launch of Luna 2, one of a series of unmanned Soviet lunar probes, the first spacecraft to strike the Moon.

1960 Introduction of Ministry of Transport tests on motor vehicles in Britain.

1970 Supersonic aircraft Concorde made its first landing at Heathrow airport, London, triggering complaints about the noise.

1972 Sinking of two British trawlers by an Icelandic gunboat, beginning the second 'Cod War'.

1977 Death of Steve Biko (b.1946 in King William's Town, Cape Province, South Africa), political activist, who died in detention.

2003 Death of Johnny Cash (b.1932 in Kingsland, Arkansas), singer, guitarist, and songwriter, one of the greatest stars of country music.

SEPTEMBER

13

Feast of St John Chrysostom (c.347–407), patron saint of preachers.

490 BC Defeat of the Persians by the Greeks at the Battle of Marathon.

1515 Defeat of the Swiss by Francis I of France at the Battle of Marignano, near Milan.

1672 Release of John Bunyan from Bedford jail after 12 years, following his arrest for preaching without a licence.

1788 New York became the federal capital of the USA.

1894 Birth of J(ohn) B(oynton) Priestley in Bradford, West Yorkshire (d.1984), novelist and playwright, whose works include *The Good Companions* (1929).

1902 The Metropolitan Police made Britain's first conviction on the evidence of fingerprints, in a case at the Old Bailey against Harry Jackson.

1903 Birth of Claudette Colbert in Paris (d.1996), actress, whose films include *It Happened One Night* (1934, Oscar).

1916 Birth of Roald Dahl in Llandaff, Cardiff (d.1990), writer, whose children's books include *Charlie and the Chocolate Factory* (1964).

1922 The highest temperature recorded on Earth to date, 136°F, was registered in Azizia, Libya.

1943 Re-election of General Chiang Kai-shek as president of China.

1969 Birth of Shane Warne in Melbourne, Victoria, Australia, cricketer, whose leg-spinners made him the first bowler to take both 500 and 600 Test Match wickets.

1970 The first New York Marathon was run, with 127 athletes each paying $1 in a race that circled several times inside Central Park; 55 runners crossed the finishing line.

1971 Birth of Goran Ivanisevic in Split, Croatia, tennis player, who won the 2001 Wimbledon men's singles title in a dramatic five-set final against Pat Rafter of Australia.

1987 Death of Bob Fosse (b.1927 in Chicago, Illinois), actor, dancer, and choreographer, whose work includes *Cabaret* (1972).

1993 Signing of the first peace accord between Israel and Palestine at the White House in Washington, DC, giving Palestine limited self-government on the Gaza Strip and in Jericho.

SEPTEMBER

14

1742 George Frideric Handel completed his oratorio, *Messiah*.

1752 Replacement of the Julian calendar by the Gregorian calendar in Britain – the last day of the Julian calendar was 2 September, and the intervening eleven days 'disappeared'.

1759 The earliest dated board game in England, 'A Journey Through Europe; or, The Play of Geography', was sold at 8s (40p) by its inventor John Jeffreys from his house in London.

1812 Napoleon Bonaparte's French army entered the city of Moscow, the turning point in the invasion of Russia.

1814 Publication of the poem 'The Defence of Fort McHenry' by lawyer and poet Francis Scott Key (1799–1843), adopted in 1931 as the US national anthem, 'The Star-Spangled Banner'.

1849 [Old Style calendar, New Style 26 September] Birth of Ivan Pavlov in Ryazan, Russia (d.1936), physiologist, known for his studies of animal behaviour.

1852 Death of Arthur Wellesley, 1st Duke of Wellington (b.1769 in Dublin, Ireland), British general and prime minister (1828–30), best known for his victory at Waterloo (1815).

1866 First patenting of the typewriter ribbon by George Kerr Anderson of Memphis, Tennessee.

1891 Joseph Heath of Wolverhampton Wanderers took the first penalty kick in English league football, in a game against Accrington Stanley at Molineux; he scored to set Wolves up for a 5–0 win.

1909 Birth of Sir Peter Scott in London (d.1989), artist, ornithologist, and broadcaster, a leading popularizer of natural history.

1927 Death of Isadora Duncan (b.1877 in San Francisco, California), dancer and choreographer, a pioneer of modern dance.

1938 Birth of Walter Koenig in Chicago, Illinois, actor, best known as Chekov in the original *Star Trek* television series and films.

1960 Founding of OPEC (Organization of the Petroleum Exporting Countries) in Baghdad, with founder members Iran, Iraq, Kuwait, Saudi Arabia, and Venezuela.

1975 Canonization of Elizabeth Ann Seton (1774–1821), founder of the Sisters of Charity (1813), the first American-born saint.

1982 Death in a car accident of Grace Kelly, Princess Grace of Monaco (b.1929 in Philadelphia, Pennsylvania), actress, who married Prince Rainier III of Monaco.

1987 Skateboarder Tony Magnuson set a record when he cleared the top of a U-ramp by 2·9 m/9·5 ft.

260

SEPTEMBER
15

1784 The first hydrogen balloon ascent in England was made by Vincenzo Lunardi of Lucca, Italy.

1830 First fatal rail accident, when British statesman William Huskisson (1790–1830) was injured by Stephenson's Rocket at the opening of the Liverpool and Manchester Railway.

1857 Patenting of the typesetting machine by Timothy Alder of New York.

1877 Death of Crazy Horse (b.1842 in South Dakota), Sioux chief, one of the leaders in the victory at Little Big Horn (1876).

1891 Birth of Dame Agatha Christie, née Miller, in Torquay, Devon (d.1976), writer of over 70 detective stories and plays, including the long-running *The Mousetrap* (1952).

1901 Birth of Sir Donald Bailey in Rotherham, South Yorkshire (d.1985), engineer, who designed the Bailey bridge, widely used in World War 2.

1904 First launch of a meteorological (weather) balloon in the USA, in St Louis, Missouri.

1907 Birth of Fay Wray in Cardston, Alberta (d.2004), actress, whose roles include the screaming victim in *King Kong* (1933).

1916 The first use of tanks, at the Battle of the Somme, during World War 1.

1928 Bacteriologist Sir Alexander Fleming (1881–1955) discovered penicillin, for which he shared the 1945 Nobel Prize for Physiology or Medicine.

1938 Meeting between British prime minister Neville Chamberlain and Adolf Hitler to negotiate a compromise over German expansionism in Europe.

1940 The Battle of Britain ended with a British victory.

1949 First episode of *The Lone Ranger* on ABC television, in a three-part story telling the history of the masked man of the West.

1960 London's first traffic wardens began work.

1971 The fishing boat *Greenpeace* set off in an attempt to prevent a US nuclear weapons test in the Aleutian Islands.

1972 Watergate charges were brought against President Richard Nixon's aides.

1978 US boxer Muhammad Ali (b.1942) became the first to win the world heavyweight championship three times, when he defeated 1976 Olympic champion Leon Spinks (b.1953).

1984 Birth of Harry (Henry Charles Albert David), son of Charles and Diana, Prince and Princess of Wales.

1985 The US golf team lost the Ryder Cup for the first time since 1957, when they were beaten by Europe.

SEPTEMBER
16

1400 Owen Glendower (Owain Glyndwr) rebelled against Henry IV and proclaimed himself Prince of Wales.

1620 Departure of the *Mayflower* from Plymouth, England, with 102 passengers; the voyage to Massachusetts took 66 days.

1685 Birth of John Gay in Barnstaple, Devon (d.1732), poet and playwright, who wrote *The Beggar's Opera* (1728).

1736 Death of Gabriel Daniel Fahrenheit (b.1686 in Gdańsk, Poland), physicist, who invented the alcohol thermometer (1709) and the mercury thermometer (1714).

1782 First use of the Great Seal of the United States, by Charles Thomson, US Congress secretary, to verify a document authorizing the negotiation of a prisoner-of-war agreement with the British.

1847 Purchase of Shakespeare's birthplace, in Stratford-upon-Avon, Warwickshire, by the United Shakespeare Company for £3000, the first building in Britain to be bought for preservation.

1861 Introduction of the Post Office Savings Bank in Britain.

1893 Birth of Sir Alexander Korda in Puszta, Hungary (d.1956), producer, whose films include *The Third Man* (1949).

1908 Founding of the General Motors Company by William Crapo Durant, with the merger of the Buick and Olds car companies.

1925 Birth of B. B. King in Itta Bena, Mississippi, blues singer and guitarist, who became known as the 'Beale Street Blues Boy'.

1955 A military coup ousted Argentine president Juan Perón during his second term in office, and began an exile lasting 18 years.

1963 Premiere of *The Outer Limits* on ABC-TV, with the first episode, *The Galaxy Being*.

1966 Launch of *Resolution*, Britain's first Polaris submarine.

1968 Introduction of the two-tier postal system in Britain.

1969 Opening of Biba in Kensington High Street, London, the shop that epitomized the 'swinging sixties'.

1975 Full independence of Papua New Guinea from Australia, self-governing since December 1973.

1977 Death in a car crash of Marc Bolan (b.1947 in London), rock star and lead vocalist with T Rex.

1992 Withdrawal of Britain from the European Exchange Rate Mechanism.

1998 Sale of the Union Jack dress worn by former Spice Girl Geri Halliwell for £41,320 at Sotheby's, London; it was bought by Peter Morton, of the Hard Rock Hotel, Las Vegas, Nevada.

SEPTEMBER

17

Constitution Day, USA.
Feast of St Lambert, patron saint of children.

1701 Death of James II (b.1633 in London), king of England and Ireland (1685–8).

1862 Withdrawal of the Confederates at the Battle of Antietam, Maryland, during the American Civil War.

1894 Opening of *A Gaiety Girl*, the first British musical staged on Broadway, at Daly's Theater; it ran for 81 performances.

1904 Birth of Sir Frederick Ashton in Guayaquil, Ecuador (d.1988), British choreographer, who became co-director of Sadler's Wells (1952–63), then director (1963–70).

1928 Birth of Roddy McDowall in Herne Hill, London (d.1998), actor, whose films include *Planet of the Apes* (1968).

1930 Construction of the Boulder (now Hoover) Dam began at Black Canyon on the Nevada–Arizona border.

1931 Launch of 33 rpm long-playing records at a demonstration in the Savoy Plaza Hotel, New York.

1939 Invasion of E Poland by the Soviet Union and Germany.

1940 London Underground first employed female workers, as porters and ticket collectors.

1942 Birth of Desmond Lynam in Ennis, Co Clare, Ireland, sports and media broadcaster, whose television appearances include *Grandstand*.

1944 Easing of blackout regulations in Britain to allow lights on buses, trains, and at railway stations, for the first time since 1939.

1961 A CND Ban-the-Bomb rally in London ended in violent clashes, with the arrest of more than 1000 people.

1972 Premiere of *M*A*S*H* on CBS-TV, which ran for 251 episodes until February 1983.

1981 A team of 12 divers began recovering £40 million worth of gold ingots from HMS *Edinburgh*, which sank off Norway in 1942.

1983 Vanessa Williams (b.1963) became the first African-American to be crowned Miss America, but was forced to resign her title in 1984 after revelations that she had appeared in *Penthouse* magazine.

1986 Death of Pat Phoenix (b.1923 in Portnum, Co Galway, Ireland), actress, best known as Elsie Tanner in the television soap *Coronation Street*.

1988 Opening of the 24th Olympic Games in Seoul, South Korea.

SEPTEMBER
18

Feast of St Joseph (Cupertino), patron saint of aviators, air passengers, and astronauts.

1709 Birth of Samuel Johnson, known as Dr Johnson, in Lichfield, Staffordshire (d.1784), lexicographer, critic, and poet.

1819 Birth of Léon Foucault in Paris (d.1868), physicist, who hung a 67 m/220 ft pendulum in the dome of the Panthéon, Paris, to demonstrate the rotation of the Earth.

1838 Economist and politician Richard Cobden (1804–65) established the Anti-Corn-Law League.

1850 US Congress declared the Fugitive Slave Act, allowing slave owners to claim slaves who had escaped into other states.

1851 First day of publication for the *New York Times*.

1879 First year of the annual illuminations in Blackpool, Lancashire.

1905 Birth of Greta Garbo in Stockholm, Sweden (d.1990), actress, based in the USA from 1925, whose films include *Anna Karenina* (1935).

1912 Birth of Peter Finch in London (d.1977), actor, whose films include *Network* (1976), for which he received the first-ever posthumous Oscar.

1939 William Joyce, Fascist politician and Nazi sympathizer known as 'Lord Haw-Haw', began his propaganda broadcasts to the UK during World War 2.

1949 Birth of Peter Shilton in Leicester, Leicestershire, international footballer, the first England goalkeeper to gain 100 caps.

1955 First showing of *The Ed Sullivan Show* on CBS-TV.

1967 Death of Sir John Douglas Cockcroft (b.1897 in Todmorden, West Yorkshire), nuclear physicist, who with Ernest Walton split the atom in 1932.

1970 Death of Jimi Hendrix, popular name of James Marshall Hendrix (b.1942 in Seattle, Washington), rock guitarist, singer, and songwriter.

1971 Birth of Lance Armstrong in Plano, Texas, racing cyclist, who overcame cancer to become a record-breaking seven-times winner of the Tour de France (1999–2005).

1976 800 million Chinese people, a fifth of the world's population, stood in a three-minute silent tribute at the start of a memorial service for their dead leader, Mao Zedong.

1981 Abolition of capital punishment in France.

1997 The Welsh electorate voted in favour of devolution and the creation of the National Assembly for Wales.

SEPTEMBER
19

1777 General Burgoyne suffered heavy casualties at the Battle of Bemis Heights, New York, during the American War of Independence.

1839 Birth of George Cadbury in Birmingham, West Midlands (d.1922), businessman, who expanded his father's chocolate-making business.

1840 Founding of Auckland, New Zealand.

1851 Birth of William Hesketh Lever, 1st Viscount Leverhulme, in Bolton, Greater Manchester (d.1925), soap-maker and philanthropist.

1876 Patenting of the carpet sweeper by US inventor Melville Bissell (1843–89).

1888 Spa, Belgium, held the first-ever beauty contest.

1893 New Zealand granted women citizens the right to vote.

1905 Death of Thomas John Barnardo (b.1845 in Dublin, Ireland), doctor and philanthropist, who founded homes for destitute children.

1922 Birth of Emil Zatopek in Kopřivnice, Czech Republic (d.2000), athlete, who won gold medals in the 10,000 m, the 5000 m, and the marathon in the 1952 Helsinki Olympics.

1934 Birth of Brian Epstein in Liverpool (d.1967), manager of rock groups, including The Beatles.

1943 Birth of Cass Elliot in Baltimore, Maryland (d.1974), singer, and member of the pop group The Mamas and the Papas.

1948 Birth of Jeremy Irons in Cowes, Isle of Wight, actor, whose TV credits include *Brideshead Revisited* (1981).

1949 Birth of Twiggy, professional name of Lesley Lawson, *née* Hornby, in London, fashion model, actress, and singer, a symbol of London's 'swinging sixties'.

1957 The USA conducted its first underground nuclear test, the Rainier event, in the Nevada desert test site.

1959 Soviet premier Nikita Khrushchev did not visit Disneyland 'for reasons of security' during a goodwill tour of the USA; it later emerged that Walt Disney had refused him entry.

1968 First publication of the *TV Times* weekly magazine for Britain's independent television station.

1970 The first Glastonbury Festival took place over two days; the 1500 people who attended paid £1 each.

1975 The BBC broadcast the first episode of *Fawlty Towers*, starring John Cleese and Prunella Scales.

1991 Discovery of Ötzi the Iceman, the mummified body of a man from about 3300 BC in a glacier in the Ötztaler Alps on the Austria–Italy border.

SEPTEMBER
20

Feast (Western Church) of St Eustace, patron saint of hunters.

356 BC Birth of Alexander the Great at Pella (d.323 BC), king of Macedonia, whose conquests spread Greek language and culture across the continent to the East.

1519 Portuguese navigator Ferdinand Magellan (c.1480–1521) began his circumnavigation of the world from Seville.

1643 The first battle of Newbury was fought in Berkshire in the English Civil War; more than 3500 men were killed.

1803 Death of Robert Emmet (b.1778 in Dublin, Ireland), Irish patriot, hanged for his part as a leader in the uprisings.

1842 Birth of Sir James Dewar in Kincardine, Fife (d.1923), chemist and physicist, who invented the Dewar flask (or thermos flask) in the 1870s.

1854 The Battle of Alma, the first engagement of the Crimean War (1854–6), was fought near the R Alma in the Crimea.

1885 Birth of Jelly Roll Morton in Gulfport, Louisiana (d.1941), jazz pianist, composer, bandleader, and pioneer of jazz.

1914 Birth of Kenneth More in Gerards Cross, Buckinghamshire (d.1982), actor, whose film roles include *Reach For the Sky* (1956).

1917 Opening of the first Royal Society for the Prevention of Cruelty to Animals clinic, in Liverpool.

1931 Removal of British sterling currency from the gold standard.

1934 Birth of Sophia Loren in Rome, film star, whose films include *The Millionairess* (1961).

1946 Opening of the first annual Cannes Film Festival; 18 nations were represented at one of the first great post-war cultural events.

1967 Launch of the British liner *Queen Elizabeth II* at Clydebank, Scotland.

1988 Death of Roy Kinnear (b.1934 in Wigan, Greater Manchester), comedy actor, known for his roles as the blustering, perspiring sidekick.

1995 The Bosman Ruling decreed that football federation rules restricting the number of foreign players in football teams, or involved in transfers, were contrary to European Community law.

SEPTEMBER
21

Feast of St Matthew (1st c), patron saint of accountants, bankers, book-keepers, and tax-collectors.

19 BC Death of Virgil (b.70 BC in Andes, near Mantua), Latin poet, whose works include the *Aeneid*.

1745 Defeat of the English at the Battle of Prestonpans, Scotland, by Charles Edward Stuart (Bonnie Prince Charlie) and his Jacobite army.

1756 Birth of John Loudon McAdam in Ayr, Strathclyde (d.1836), inventor of macadamized roads.

1784 First publication of the *Pennsylvania Packet and General Advertiser*, America's first successful daily newspaper.

1792 France was declared a republic.

1860 Death of Arthur Schopenhauer (b.1788 in Gdańsk, Poland), philosopher, and a major influence on existentialism.

1866 Birth of H(erbert) G(eorge) Wells in Bromley, Kent (d.1946), writer, who rose to fame with scientific fantasies such as *The Time Machine* (1895).

1874 Birth of Gustav Holst in Cheltenham, Gloucestershire (d.1934), Swedish composer, whose works include the suite *The Planets* (1914–16).

1895 Birth of Juan de la Cierva in Murcia, Spain (d.1936), aeronautical engineer, who developed the autogiro, which flew successfully in 1923.

1902 Birth of Sir Allen Lane in Bristol (d.1970), publisher, who founded Penguin Books in 1935.

1915 Purchase of Stonehenge at auction for £6600 by Cecil Chubb at the New Theatre, Salisbury, Wiltshire; he donated it to the nation in 1918.

1937 Publication of the first UK edition of *The Hobbit*, written by J(ohn) R(onald) R(euel) Tolkien (1892–1973), limited to just 1500 copies.

1947 Birth of Stephen King in Portland, Maine, novelist, known for his vivid treatment of horrific and supernatural themes.

1949 Opening of Britain's first comprehensive school, in Holyhead, Anglesey.

1955 Announcement by the Admiralty that Britain had formally claimed Rockall, an uninhabited rocky islet west of Scotland, to prevent the Soviet Union from spying on UK missile tests.

1961 Argentine swimmer Antonio Abertondo became the first to swim the English Channel both ways non-stop, making the return swim in 43 hours and 5 minutes, with only a four-minute break.

1962 First transmission of the BBC television quiz *University Challenge*, hosted by Bamber Gascoigne.

1965 North Sea oil was first struck in the Ekofisk Field, in Norwegian waters, by BP (British Petroleum).

SEPTEMBER
22

Feast of St Maurice, patron saint of dyers, infantry, Piedmont, Savoy, Sardinia, and weavers.
Feast of St Phocas of Sinope (also 14 July), patron saint of agricultural workers, gardeners, and sailors.

1515 Birth of Anne of Cleves (d.1557), German princess and queen consort of England, the fourth wife of Henry VIII.

1735 Number 10 Downing Street became the official home of Britain's prime ministers, when Sir Robert Walpole (1676–1745) took up residence.

1761 Coronation of George III, king of Great Britain and Ireland (1760–1820).

1791 Birth of Michael Faraday in Newington Butts, Surrey (d.1867), chemist, physicist, and natural philosopher.

1827 Joseph Smith (1805–44), founder of the Mormons, announced the discovery of the Book of Mormon.

1862 Issue of the Emancipation Proclamation by President Abraham Lincoln, ordering the freeing of slaves.

1880 Birth of Dame Christabel Pankhurst in Manchester (d.1958), suffragette, the daughter of Emmeline Pankhurst.

1888 The units ohm, volt, and ampere were made official at the Electrical Conference in Paris.

1902 Maiden flight for Britain's first airship, built by Stanley Spencer, head of the British balloon-manufacturers Spencer Brothers.

1927 Gene Tunney (1898–1978) successfully defended his world heavyweight boxing title against Jack Dempsey (1895–1983) in the famous 'long-count' fight.

1934 Death of 265 miners in a pit disaster at the Gresford Mine, Wrexham.

1943 Proposal to introduce PAYE (Pay As You Earn) in Britain, in which tax is deducted at source.

1955 An advertisement for Gibbs SR toothpaste was the first shown when British Independent Television began broadcasting.

1958 Birth of Andrea Bocelli in Lajatico, Tuscany, Italy, tenor, whose albums include *Romanza* (1997).

1960 Independence of Mali.

1980 Founding of Solidarity in Poland as an organization to coordinate the activities of the emerging independent trade union following protracted industrial unrest.

1982 Birth of Billie Piper in Swindon, Wiltshire, pop singer and actress, whose roles include Rose Tyler in the cult BBC television series *Doctor Who*.

1989 Death of Irving Berlin (b.1888 in Temun, Russia), composer, whose musicals include *Annie Get Your Gun* (1946).

2001 The first images of Comet Borrelly were received from the Deep Space 1 probe.

SEPTEMBER

23

Autumn Equinox (northern hemisphere).

480 BC Defeat of the Persians by the Greeks at the Battle of Salamis.

1846 Discovery of Neptune by German astronomer Johann Galle (1812–1910), although the planet's existence had been postulated by French astronomer Urbain Leverrier (1811–77).

1848 First commercial production of chewing gum, by John Curtis on his stove in Bangor, Maine.

1879 Invention of the *Audiophone* by Richard S. Rhodes (1843–1902) of Chicago, Illinois, a fan-shaped device that enabled the deaf to hear through the medium of the teeth.

1889 Birth of Walter Lippmann in New York (d.1974), journalist, and special writer for the New York *Herald Tribune*.

1912 Release of Mack Sennett's first Keystone Kops film, *Cohen Collects a Debt*.

1920 Birth of Mickey Rooney in New York, actor, whose films include *Boys Town* (1938).

1930 Birth of Ray Charles in Albany, Georgia (d.2004), singer and pianist, blind from childhood, who developed an original blend of music identified as 'soul'.

1939 Death of Sigmund Freud (b.1856 in Freiberg, Moravia – now Pribor, Czech Republic), psychiatrist, the founder of psychoanalysis.

1940 During his Empire broadcast message, George VI announced the institution of the George Cross, to recognize civilian heroism by men and women of the Commonwealth.

1949 Birth of Bruce Springsteen in Freehold, New Jersey, rock musician, whose albums include *Born in the USA* (1984).

1952 US boxer Rocky Marciano (1923–69) became world heavyweight champion when he knocked out Jersey Joe Walcott in round 13.

1957 Buddy Holly and the Crickets' song 'That'll Be the Day' reached No. 1 in the US music charts.

1964 The first performance of the musical *Fiddler on the Roof* took place in New York.

1974 Inauguration of CEEFAX, the BBC TV teletext service.

1992 $5 million damages were awarded to a Florida teenager who had been given to the wrong parents at birth.

2000 British rower Steve Redgrave (b.1962) won a fifth consecutive Olympic gold medal, a feat accomplished by no other athlete, in the coxless fours during the Olympic Games in Sydney, Australia.

SEPTEMBER
24

1776 The St Leger horse race was run for the first time at Doncaster, South Yorkshire.

1853 Publication in Liverpool of England's first provincial daily newspaper, the *Northern Daily Times*.

1869 Black Friday: an attempted fraud caused a severe fall in the price of gold and a US financial crisis.

1890 Birth of A(lan) P(atrick) Herbert in Elstead, Surrey (d.1971), politician and writer, who wrote the libretti for many comic operas.

1896 Birth of F. Scott Fitzgerald in St Paul, Minnesota (d.1940), novelist, who captured the spirit of the 1920s jazz era in *The Great Gatsby* (1925).

1898 Birth of Sir Howard Walter Florey in Adelaide, South Australia (d.1968), pathologist, who worked with Sir Ernest Boris Chain (1906–79) to isolate penicillin.

1930 First performance of Noel Coward's *Private Lives*, at the Phoenix Theatre, London, with himself, Gertrude Lawrence, and Laurence Olivier in the cast.

1936 Birth of Jim Henson in Greenville, Mississippi (d.1990), puppeteer, and creator of the Muppets.

1941 Birth of Linda McCartney in New York (d.1998), photographer, musician, animal rights activist, businesswoman, and wife of ex-Beatle Paul McCartney.

1948 Founding of the Honda Motor Company by Japanese industrialist Soichiro Honda (1906–91), who responded to the need in Japan for cheap basic transport by fitting engines to bicycles.

1960 Launch of the first nuclear-powered aircraft carrier, USS *Enterprise*, from Newport, Virginia.

1962 Birth of Jack Dee in Petts Wood, near Orpington, Kent, comedian and actor, known for his deadpan humour.

1975 Dougal Haston (1940–77) and Doug Scott (b.1941) became the first Britons to reach the summit of Mt Everest via the previously unclimbed south-west face.

1980 Escalation of the Iran–Iraq conflict into full-scale war when Iraqis blew up the Abadan oil refinery.

1991 Death of Theodor Seuss Geisel (b.1904 in Springfield, Massachusetts), better known as Dr Seuss, writer and illustrator of children's books such as *The Cat in the Hat* (1957).

2004 Death of Françoise Sagan (b.1935 in Cajarc, France), novelist, whose works include *Bonjour tristesse* (1954, Hello Sadness).

SEPTEMBER
25

1066 Defeat of the Norwegians at Stamford Bridge by Harold II, king of England.

1513 Spanish explorer Vasco Núñez de Balboa (1475–1519) crossed the Isthmus of Panama and became the first European to sight the Pacific Ocean.

1660 English diarist Samuel Pepys (1633–1703) recorded in his diary that he had tasted tea for the first time.

1818 First blood transfusion using human blood, in London.

1897 Birth of William Faulkner in New Albany, Mississippi (d.1962), author, whose works include *The Sound and the Fury* (1929); he was awarded the 1949 Nobel Prize for Literature.

1897 First motorized bus service in Britain, operated by the Yorkshire Motor Car Company, with omnibuses daily from Bradford Town Hall to Four Lane Ends; the 2-mile journey cost sixpence.

1929 Birth of Ronnie Barker in Bedford, Bedfordshire (d.2005), comic actor, whose television appearances include *Porridge* (1974–7).

1933 Exhibition of the Shroud of Turin for the first time in 400 years, in Turin Cathedral, Italy.

1944 Birth of Michael Douglas in New Brunswick, New Jersey, actor and producer, whose films include *Fatal Attraction* (1987).

1952 Birth of Christopher Reeve in New York (d.2004), actor, who became universally known as the star of *Superman* (1978) and its sequels.

1956 Opening of transatlantic telephone cables between Britain and North America.

1957 Enforcement of desegregation in Little Rock, Arkansas, when National Guardsmen escorted nine African-American children into school.

1962 US boxer Sonny Liston (1932–70) knocked out Floyd Patterson (b.1935) in round 1 to become heavyweight champion of the world.

1968 Birth of Will Smith in Philadelphia, Pennsylvania, actor and rapper, whose film appearances include *Men in Black* (1997).

1969 Birth of Catherine Zeta-Jones in Swansea, Wales, actress, whose films include *Entrapment* (1999).

1977 Beginning of the Skytrain service set up by entrepreneur Sir Freddie Laker (b.1922), with flights from Gatwick, London, to New York.

1983 Escape of 38 prisoners from the high-security Maze Prison near Lisburn, Northern Ireland.

1987 Death of Emlyn Williams (b.1905 in Pen-y-ffordd, Flintshire), actor, playwright, and director, whose works include the play *Night Must Fall* (1935).

SEPTEMBER
26

Dominion Day, New Zealand.
World Language Day.
Feast (Western Church) of Sts Cosmas and Damian (3rd c), twin brothers, and patron saints of chemists, doctors, hairdressers (men's), midwives, and surgeons.
Feast (Eastern Church) of St John the Apostle, patron saint of publishers, writers, and theologians.

1087 Coronation of William II of England (r.1087–1100).

1580 English seaman Francis Drake (c.1540–96) returned to Plymouth in the *Golden Hind*, becoming the first English explorer to circumnavigate the earth.

1687 The Venetians bombarded Athens, severely damaging the Parthenon and Propyleiea.

1820 Death of Daniel Boone (b.1734 in Berks Co, Pennsylvania), legendary pioneer, who made a trail through the Cumberland Gap and became one of the first to explore Kentucky.

1871 Patenting of cement in the USA by David Saylor, first US producer of Portland cement.

1887 Patenting of the gramophone by German inventor Emile Berliner (1851–1929).

1898 Birth of George Gershwin in New York (d.1937), composer, whose works include the jazz-opera *Porgy and Bess* (1935).

1934 Launch of the British liner *Queen Mary*, at Clydebank, Scotland.

1944 Birth of Anne Robinson in Liverpool, Merseyside, journalist and television presenter, whose programmes include *The Weakest Link* (from 2000).

1945 Birth of Bryan Ferry in Washington, Co Durham, singer, pianist, and composer, one of the leading members of the rock band Roxy Music.

1948 Birth of Olivia Newton-John in Cambridge, Cambridgeshire, singer, whose films include *Grease*.

1953 Ending of sugar rationing in Britain, after almost 14 years.

1955 First sales of fish fingers in the UK, priced 1s 8d (8½p); invented by US businessman Clarence Birdseye (1886–1956); in their first year, 600 tons of fish fingers were eaten.

1960 First televised debate between two White House candidates, Republican vice-president Richard M. Nixon and Democrat senator John F. Kennedy, watched by more than 60 million in the USA.

1972 Norway voted against joining the EEC (European Economic Community).

1983 Australia won the America's Cup yacht race.

1992 Swiss firm Swatch made its 100-millionth watch.

SEPTEMBER

27

Feast of St Vincent de Paul (c.1580–1660), patron saint of charitable societies.

1540 Pope Paul III officially recognized and approved the Jesuits.

1822 Announcement by Jean-François Champollion (1790–1832), founder of Egyptology, that he had deciphered Egyptian hieroglyphics using the Rosetta Stone.

1825 Railway engineer George Stephenson (1781–1848) drove the first public train in Britain, pulled by the steam engine Active, on the Stockton and Darlington Railway.

1840 Birth of Thomas Nast in Landau, Germany (d.1902), US cartoonist, who created the Republican elephant, the Democratic donkey, and helped form the American notion of Santa Claus.

1888 London's Central News Agency received a letter signed 'Jack the Ripper', the first time this name had been used.

1892 Patenting of book matches by Joshua Pusey (1842–1906) of Lima, Ohio.

1907 Birth of Sir Bernard Miles in Uxbridge, London (d.1991), actor, stage director, and founder of the Mermaid Theatre (1959).

1917 Death of Edgar Degas (b.1834 in Paris), Impressionist artist, whose works include *Dancer Lacing Her Shoe* (1880).

1937 Opening of a school for Santa Clauses in Albion, New York, where students trained in Santa Claus techniques, including Santa's history, and perfecting his 'Ho! Ho! Ho!'

1938 Launch of the British liner *Queen Elizabeth*, largest passenger ship built, at Clydebank, Scotland.

1948 Birth of Michele Dotrice in Cleethorpes, Lancashire, actress, whose roles include the long-suffering wife in the television series *Some Mothers Do 'Ave 'Em*.

1960 Opening of Europe's first moving pavement, the 'travelator', at Bank Underground station, London, linking the Waterloo & City line station at Bank with the main tube station concourse.

1963 British singer Cilla Black (b.1943) released her first single, 'Love of the Loved'.

1964 Release of the report concluding that Lee Harvey Oswald, acting alone, assassinated John F. Kennedy.

1967 The passenger liner *Queen Mary* completed her final transatlantic crossing.

1979 Death of Gracie Fields (b.1898 in Rochdale, Greater Manchester), singer, actress, and comedienne, best known for 'Sally', which became her theme song.

1987 America suffered its first home defeat in the Ryder Cup when Europe won 15–13 at Muirfield Village Golf Club, Ohio.

SEPTEMBER
28

Feast of St Bernardino (Feltre), patron saint of bankers and pawnbrokers.
Feast of St Thiemo, patron saint of engravers.
Feast of St Wenceslaus (c.903–35), known as Good King Wenceslas, patron saint of brewers.

1066 William of Normandy landed in Pevensey, Sussex, heralding the start of the Norman Conquest of England.

1542 Arrival of Spanish explorer Juan Rodríguez Cabrillon at San Diego Bay, California, with the first European expedition.

1745 First performance of the British national anthem, 'God Save the King', in London's Drury Lane Theatre.

1864 Founding of the International Workingmen's Association, later the First International, St Martin's Hall, London; among the attendees was Karl Marx.

1865 Britain's first female doctor, Elizabeth Garrett Anderson (1836–1917), graduated from medical school.

1894 Opening of a Penny Bazaar, the first Marks and Spencers, in Manchester.

1895 Death of Louis Pasteur (b.1822 in Dôle, France), chemist and microbiologist, who established the pasteurization process for milk.

1902 Birth of Ed Sullivan (d.1974) in New York, newspaper columnist and broadcaster, host of *The Ed Sullivan Show* (1948–71).

1909 Birth of Al Capp in New Haven, Connecticut, strip cartoonist, who created the hillbilly character L'il Abner (1934).

1923 First publication of Britain's *Radio Times*.

1934 Birth of Brigitte Bardot in Paris, actress, who retired from the screen in 1973 and devoted herself to campaigning for animal rights.

1953 Death of Edwin Hubble (b.1889 in Marshfield, Missouri), astronomer.

1973 First performance in Sydney Opera House, Australia, when the Australian Opera staged a production of Prokofiev's *War and Peace*.

1978 Death of John Paul I (b.1912 in Forno di Canale, Italy), pope (Aug–Sep 1978), who died after just 33 days in office.

1994 5000th Broadway performance of the musical *Cats* at the Wintergarden Theater, New York.

1994 Sinking of the Estline car and passenger ferry *Estonia* in the Baltic Sea off Finland, with the loss of c.900 lives, after a loading bay door was left open.

2000 A referendum in Denmark rejected a proposal to join the single currency and adopt the euro by 53 to 47 percent.

SEPTEMBER
29

Feast (Western Church) of St Gabriel (also 24 March), patron saint of broadcasters, diplomats, messengers, postal, radio, and television workers.
Feast of St Michael, patron saint of Germany, grocers, hatters, paratroopers, police officers, radiologists, and sick people.

1399 Richard II became the first English monarch to abdicate.

1758 Birth of Horatio Nelson in Burnham Thorpe, Norfolk (d.1805), British admiral, who led the victory at the Battle of Trafalgar.

1810 Birth of Mrs Elizabeth Gaskell in London (d.1865), novelist, whose works include *Wives and Daughters* (1865).

1829 The first policemen, known as 'bobbies' or 'peelers', patrolled London's streets.

1885 Opening of the first electric street tramway in Britain, in Blackpool, Lancashire.

1899 Birth of Billy Butlin in Cape Town, South Africa (d.1980), holiday camp promoter, who opened his first camp in Skegness, Lincolnshire (1936).

1916 US industrialist John D. Rockefeller (1839–1937) became the world's first billionaire when his net worth officially surpassed $1 billion.

1943 Birth of Lech Wałęsa in Popowo, Poland, president of Poland (1990–95), who was awarded the 1983 Nobel Peace Prize.

1946 First day of broadcasting for BBC Radio 3, the 'Third Programme'.

1950 Testing of the first automatic telephone answering machine by the Bell Telephone Company, USA.

1952 Death of John Rhodes Cobb (b.1899 in Esher, Surrey), holder of the world land speed record, when his boat *Crusader* crashed on Loch Ness, Scotland, in an attempt on the world water speed record.

1963 Beginning of The Rolling Stones' first tour, as a support act for the Everly Brothers and Bo Diddley at the Gaumont in Southampton, Hampshire.

1973 Death of W(ystan) H(ugh) Auden (b.1907 in York, North Yorkshire), poet and essayist, a leading figure in the left-wing literary movement of the 1930s.

1977 US boxing judge Eva Shain (1918–99) became the first woman to officiate at a world heavyweight boxing championship, at the fight between US boxers Muhammad Ali and Earnie Shavers.

1979 Pope John Paul II made the first papal visit to Ireland, where he made an impassioned plea for an end to the violence between Catholics and Protestants in Northern Ireland.

SEPTEMBER

30

Feast of St Jerome (c.342–420), patron saint of archaeologists, librarians, and students.

1772 Death of James Brindley (b.1716 in Thornsett, Derbyshire), engineer, who built the canal between Worsley and Manchester, completed in 1772.

1791 First performance of Mozart's *The Magic Flute* in Vienna.

1840 The foundation stone for Nelson's Column was laid in Trafalgar Square, London.

1846 First use of ether as an anaesthetic, by US dental surgeon Dr William Morton (1819–68).

1863 First performance of Bizet's *The Pearl Fishers* in Paris.

1882 The world's first hydroelectric power plant, later known as the Appleton Edison Light Company, began operation on Fox River in Appleton, Wisconsin.

1902 First patenting of artificial silk (rayon), a textile fibre formed from cellulose.

1921 Birth of Deborah Kerr in Helensburgh, Argyll and Bute, actress, whose films include *From Here to Eternity* (1953).

1924 Birth of Truman Capote in New Orleans, Louisiana (d.1984), writer, whose books include *Breakfast at Tiffany's* (1958).

1936 Opening of Pinewood Studios at Iver Heath, Buckinghamshire; the first complete film made there was *Talk of the Devil* (1937) directed by Carol Reed (1906–76).

1938 Prime Minister Neville Chamberlain returned to Britain with a signed agreement from Hitler, saying there would be 'peace in our time'.

1949 Ending of the Berlin Airlift, after 277,264 flights carried 2·3 million tons of supplies, and the loss of 17 American and 7 British planes due to crashes.

1951 Final day of the Festival of Britain; around 8·5 million people visited the exhibition, which included the Royal Festival Hall, the Skylon, and the Dome of Discovery.

1955 Death of James Dean in a car crash (b.1931 in Marion, Indiana), actor, who starred in the film *East of Eden* (1955).

1967 Launch of BBC Radio 1, with Tony Blackburn's Breakfast Show.

1980 Birth of Martina Hingis in Kosice, Slovak Republic, Swiss tennis player, who in 1997 became the youngest singles Grand Slam tournament winner of the 20th c.

1985 Death of Charles Richter (b.1900 near Hamilton, Ohio), seismologist, who devised, with Beno Gutenberg (1889–1960), the Richter scale of earthquake strength.

OCTOBER

1

Opening of the pheasant-shooting season in Britain.

1800 Louisiana was ceded by Spain to France; its later purchase by the USA effectively doubled its size.

1843 First day of publication for the British Sunday newspaper *News of the World*.

1867 Publication of *Das Kapital* by Karl Marx (1818–83), social philosopher and founder of international Communism.

1870 Introduction of postcards and the halfpenny postage stamp by the British Post Office.

1873 Death of Sir Edwin Landseer (b.1802 in London), artist, whose most famous sculptures are the bronze lions in Trafalgar Square (1867).

1880 Manufacture of the first electric light bulbs, by the Edison Lamp Works in New Jersey.

1908 Completion of the first model T Ford car, in Detroit, Michigan.

1930 Birth of Richard Harris in Co Limerick, Ireland (d.2002), actor, whose last role was as Albus Dumbledore in the first two Harry Potter films.

1931 Opening of the world's then largest commercial hotel, the Waldorf Astoria on Park Avenue, New York.

1949 Founding of the People's Republic of China, under chairman Mao Zedong.

1955 Opening of O'Hare international airport, Chicago, at the time the world's busiest airport.

1958 Transfer of the administration of Christmas Island, south of Java, from Britain to Australia.

1963 Nigeria became a republic.

1969 Supersonic airliner Concorde broke the sound barrier for the first time.

1971 Opening of Disney World at Lake Buena Vista, Orlando, Florida, the world's largest theme park, 122 sq km/47 sq miles; the Magic Kingdom was later supplemented by Epcot, Disney MGM Studios, and Disney's Animal Kingdom.

1974 Commencement of the US Watergate trial, resulting in the first resignation of a president in US history (Richard Nixon, in office 1968–74).

1989 The first legal gay marriage took place, held in Copenhagen, between Axel and Eigil Axgil.

2003 Abolition in China of the requirement for couples to gain permission from their employers before marriage.

OCTOBER
2

322 BC Death of Aristotle (b.384 BC in Stagira, Macedonia), Greek philosopher, scientist, and physician.

1608 Demonstration of the first telescope by Dutch optician Hans (or Jan) Lippershey (c.1570–1619).

1836 Return of naturalist Charles Darwin (1809–82) to Britain on the HMS *Beagle* after a five-year voyage to explore the southern oceans.

1852 Birth of Sir William Ramsay in Glasgow, Strathclyde (d.1916), chemist, who discovered the inert gases.

1866 Patenting of the tin can with key opener by J. Osterhoudt of New York.

1869 Birth of M. K. Gandhi in Poorbandar, Kathiawar, India (d.1948), political and religious leader.

1870 Rome replaced Florence as the capital city of Italy, following a vote by papal states in favour of union with Italy.

1895 Publication of 'The Yellow Kid', first cartoon comic in a newspaper, created by US illustrator Richard F. Outcault (1863–1928) for *New York World*.

1902 Launch of the British navy's first submarine, *Holland 1*, named after Irish engineer John Philip Holland (1841–1914), at Barrow-in-Furness, Cumbria.

1909 A flight altitude record of 1600 ft was set by US aviator Orville Wright (1871–1948), beating French aviator Hubert Latham's previous record of 508 ft.

1925 London's famous red double-decker buses began operating.

1945 Introduction of fluorescent lighting in Britain, on Piccadilly Circus Underground station.

1950 First appearance of 'Peanuts', the comic strip created by Charles M. Schulz (1922–2000), published in seven newspapers as 'Li'l Folks'.

1951 Birth of Sting, originally Gordon Sumner, in Newcastle-upon-Tyne, singer and actor, former vocalist and lyricist of rock group The Police.

1954 Publication of a paper by doctors at the UK's Medical Research Council, demonstrating that cancer can be caused by smoking.

1968 Birth of Britain's first recorded live sextuplets, to Sheila Thorns of Birmingham, West Midlands.

1977 Motor-racing driver Niki Lauda (b.1949) won the Formula 1 world championship in Austria.

1983 Neil Kinnock (b.1942) became the new leader of the UK Labour Party.

1991 Fiftieth anniversary of international charity Oxfam (Oxford Committee for Famine Relief).

OCTOBER

3

Feast of St Theresa of Lisieux, also known as the Little Flower (1873–97), patron saint of florists, France, and missionaries.

1863 President Abraham Lincoln announced that Thanksgiving Day would be recognized each year in the USA on the last Thursday in November.

1867 Death of Elias Howe (b.1819 in Spencer, Massachusetts), inventor of the sewing machine (patented 1846).

1896 Death of William Morris (b.1834 in London), craftsman, poet, and political activist, who revolutionized the art of house decoration and furniture in England.

1906 The Berlin Radio Conference accepted SOS as the international distress signal.

1911 Birth of Michael Hordern in Berkhamsted, Hertfordshire (d.1995), actor, whose performances include Tom Stoppard's *Jumpers* (1972).

1922 The first faxed photograph was sent through telephone lines in Washington, DC.

1932 Full independence of Iraq, when it was admitted into the League of Nations.

1942 First successful test flight of a V-2 missile, from the German rocket research station at Peenemunde; it flew 190 km/118 miles and to an altitude of 85 km/53 miles.

1952 Test-detonation of Britain's first atomic bomb, on the Monte Bello Islands off the coast of Australia; in 1998, levels of radiation limited a visit to the islands to one hour.

1956 First appearance of the Bolshoi Ballet at Covent Garden, London.

1959 Introduction of British postal codes began in Norwich, Norfolk, to assist in the automatic sorting of mail.

1962 Release of The Beatles' first single, 'Love Me Do'.

1964 57 people tunnelled under the Berlin Wall from the east to the west, the largest mass escape.

1967 Death of Woody Guthrie (b.1912 in Okemah, Oklahoma), folk musician, whose songs lauded migrant workers, pacifists, and underdogs of all kinds.

1981 Irish Nationalists in the Maze Prison, Belfast, Northern Ireland, called off their seven-month hunger strike after ten people had died.

1988 Death of Sir Alec Issigonis (b.1906 in Smyrna, Turkey), car designer, best known for the Morris Minor (1948–71) and the Mini (launched in 1959).

1993 Russian president Boris Yeltsin (b.1931) declared a state of emergency in Moscow when armed opponents of his economic reforms stormed the streets and seized control of key buildings.

OCTOBER

4

National Day, Lesotho.
Feast of St Francis of Assisi (?1181–1226),
patron saint of animals, birds, and
ecologists.

1669 Death of Rembrandt (b.1606 in
Leyden, The Netherlands), painter,
whose work includes *The Night
Watch* (1642).

1814 Birth of Jean François Millet in
Gruchy, France (d.1875), painter,
known for his paintings of rustic
life, such as *The Gleaners* (1857).

1824 Mexico became a federal republic.

1853 Beginning of the Crimean War,
fought by Britain, France, Turkey,
Piedmont, and Austria against
Russia.

1883 The Orient Express made its first
run linking Istanbul and Paris by
rail.

1895 First US Open golf tournament
was won by 19-year-old English
professional golfer Horace Rawlins,
in Newport, Rhode Island.

1911 Opening of Britain's first public
escalator, at Earl's Court Underground station, London.

1927 Carving began on the gigantic
sculptures of four past US
presidents (Washington, Jefferson,
Roosevelt, and Lincoln) on Mt
Rushmore, South Dakota.

1931 Birth of Sir Terence Conran in
Esher, Surrey, designer and busi-
nessman, who founded and ran the
Habitat Company (1971).

1946 Birth of Susan Sarandon in New
York, actress, whose films include
Thelma and Louise (1991).

1947 Death of Max Planck (b.1858 in
Kiel, Germany), physicist, who was
awarded the 1918 Nobel Prize for
Physics.

1952 The first external pacemaker was
fitted, developed by US cardiologist
Dr Paul Zoll (1911–99).

1957 Launch of Sputnik 1 by Russia,
the first space satellite.

1958 Beginning of the first scheduled
transatlantic passenger jetliner service, by BOAC, with flights between
London and New York.

1966 Independence of Lesotho.

1970 Death of Janis Joplin (b.1943 in
Port Arthur, Texas), blues rock
singer, whose life was told in the
film *The Rose* (1979).

1976 Introduction of the Inter-City 125
(mph) High Speed Train, to provide
a regular fast service between Cardiff, Bristol, and London.

2004 SpaceShip-One was the first private manned spacecraft to fly to the
edge of space and back, winning
the Ansari X Prize for the Mojave
Aerospace Ventures LLC team led
by aviation pioneer Burt Rutan.

OCTOBER

5

1713 Birth of Denis Diderot in Langres, France (d.1784), writer and philosopher, chief editor of the *Encyclopédie* (1751–65).

1830 The world's first bathing costume went on sale in Baker Street, London.

1880 Patenting of the earliest ball pen, with its own ink supply and retractable tip, by Alonzo T. Cross (b.1846).

1914 The first air battle was fought between French and German aircraft during World War 1.

1916 Adolf Hitler (1889–1945) was wounded in the leg by shrapnel while stationed at Bapaume, near Arras, France, during World War 1.

1917 Donation of Chequers by Sir Arthur Lee to Britain, as a country retreat for the prime minister.

1919 Birth of Donald Pleasence in Worksop, Nottinghamshire (d.1995), actor, known for his villainous or eccentric characters.

1923 Birth of Glynis Johns in Pretoria, South Africa, British actress, who successfully made the transition from child star to adult performer.

1927 The British Labour Party voted to nationalize the coal industry.

1930 Crash of the British airship R101 near Beauvais, France, killing all but six of the passengers and crew.

1936 Start of the Jarrow March to London by unemployed shipbuilding and mining workers in the Tyne and Wear town, to put the case for the unemployed.

1952 Ending of tea rationing in Britain.

1954 Birth of Bob Geldof in Dublin, Ireland, rock musician and philanthropist, who founded the pop charity 'Band Aid' trust in 1984.

1967 Brighton Quarter sessions accepted Britain's first majority verdict by a jury in a trial, of 10 to 2.

1969 *Monty Python's Flying Circus* made its debut on BBC Television; it ran on British television until 1974.

1975 Birth of Kate Winslet in Reading, Berkshire, actress, whose films include *Titanic* (1997).

1984 Death of Leonard Rossiter (b.1926 in Liverpool), actor, whose television series include *The Fall and Rise of Reginald Perrin* (1976–80).

1989 The Dalai Lama (b.1935), exiled leader of Tibet, was awarded the Nobel Peace Prize in recognition of his commitment to the nonviolent liberation of his homeland.

OCTOBER
6

Feast of St Thomas the Apostle (Greek),
patron saint of architects, the blind, builders,
and Portugal.

1683 Arrival of the first Mennonites in America aboard the *Concord*, creating Germantown in present-day Philadelphia, one of America's oldest settlements.

1732 Birth of Nevil Maskelyne in London (d.1811), Astronomer Royal, known for his work on methods and instruments of observation.

1829 The steam train *Rocket*, constructed by railway engineer George Stephenson (1781–1848), won trials to find a locomotive to run on the Liverpool and Manchester Railway.

1846 Birth of George Westinghouse in Central Bridge, New York State (d.1914), engineer, a pioneer in the use of alternating current for distributing electric power.

1889 Opening of the Moulin Rouge in Paris to the public for the first time.

1895 Conductor Sir Henry Wood (1869–1944) helped to found Britain's Promenade Concerts.

1914 Birth of Thor Heyerdahl in Larvik, Norway (d.2002), anthropologist and explorer, who developed and tested theories about the migration patterns of ancient peoples.

1928 Chiang Kai-shek (1887–1975) became president of China.

1951 Death of W. K. Kellogg (b.1860 in Battle Creek, Michigan), cereal manufacturer and philanthropist.

1954 Edward T. Lyon, nurse anaesthetist, joined 3500 women in the US Army Nurse Corps, the first man to be commissioned to the corps by an amendment to the 1947 Army–Navy Nurses Act.

1966 Lysergic acid diethylamide (LSD) was declared illegal by the US government.

1968 British drivers Jackie Stewart, Graham Hill, and John Surtees took the first three places in the US Grand Prix.

1978 London Underground's first female train-driver took up employment.

1980 Death of Hattie Jacques (b.1924 in Sandgate, Kent), comic actress, who appeared in 14 *Carry On* films.

1981 Death of Anwar el-Sadat (b.1918 in the Tala district, Egypt), president of Egypt, assassinated in Cairo by extremists.

1987 US computer company Microsoft introduced Excel, its first Windows application.

1989 Death of Bette Davis (b.1908 in Lowell, Massachusetts), actress, whose roles included *Jezebel* (1938, Oscar).

1992 Death of Denholm Elliott (b.1922 in London), actor, who received an Oscar nomination for *A Room with a View* (1986).

1995 Marriage of film star Elizabeth Taylor to Larry Fortensky, her eighth husband.

OCTOBER

7

1571 Defeat of the Turkish fleet by Don John of Austria at the Battle of Lepanto, Greece.

1799 HMS *Lutine*, with its cargo of gold bullion, sank off the coast of Holland.

1806 Patenting of carbon paper, which he called 'stylographic writer', by Ralph Wedgwood of London.

1849 Death of Edgar Allan Poe (b.1809 in Boston, Massachusetts), novelist and poet, whose works include *The Pit and the Pendulum* (1843).

1908 Crete revolted against Turkish domination and united with Greece.

1919 Foundation of the oldest existing airline, the Dutch company KLM, which began regular service in 1920.

1922 The Prince of Wales (later Edward VIII) made the first royal broadcast on 2LO, eleven days before the company's name changed to the British Broadcasting Company (BBC).

1922 Death of Marie Lloyd (b.1870 in London), music-hall singer and entertainer, whose songs include 'Oh, Mr Porter'.

1939 Birth of Clive James in Sydney, New South Wales, Australia, writer, satirist, broadcaster, and critic.

1949 Formation of the German Democratic Republic.

1956 Death of Clarence Birdseye (b.1886 in New York), businessman and inventor, best known for developing a process for freezing food in small packages suitable for retailing.

1957 Birth of Jayne Torvill in Nottingham, Nottinghamshire, figure-skater, world ice dance champion (1981–4) and Olympic champion (1984) with Christopher Dean (b.1958).

1959 Russian spacecraft Lunik III took the first pictures of the far side of the Moon.

1959 Death of Mario Lanza (b.1921 in Philadelphia, Pennsylvania), tenor and actor, who appeared in *The Great Caruso* (1951).

1985 Palestinian militants seized the Italian cruise liner *Achille Lauro*, with 400 passengers on board.

1986 First day of publication for the *Independent*, a British national daily newspaper with no political allegiance.

1992 Installation of the first braille cash dispenser, by Northern Rock Building Society in Gateshead, Tyne and Wear.

1996 Demolition of 25 Cromwell St, Gloucester, where the murders committed by Frederick and Rosemary West took place.

2000 Davo Karnicar of Slovenia became the first person to ski non-stop down Mt Everest.

OCTOBER
8

1085 Consecration of St Mark's Cathedral in Venice.

1754 Death of Henry Fielding (b.1707 at Sharpham Park, Glastonbury, Somerset), founder of the English novel, best known for *The History of Tom Jones, A Foundling* (1749).

1871 Beginning of the Great Fire of Chicago, which burned for four days, killed over 250 people, made 98,000 homeless, and destroyed 17,450 buildings.

1891 The first street collection for charity was made, in Manchester and Salford; the day was designated 'Lifeboat Day'.

1895 Foundation of the Berliner Gramophone Company in Philadelphia, Pennsylvania.

1906 Demonstration of a machine to put permanent waves in hair, by Karl Nessler, in London; the six-hour process involved a dozen brass curlers, each weighing 2 lb, and cost 10 guineas.

1925 Jockey Eileen Joel was the first woman to win an open race in Britain, at Newmarket, Suffolk.

1932 Birth of Ray Reardon in Tredegar, Wales, snooker player, who was world professional champion six times (1970, 1973–6, 1978).

1940 Birth of Paul Hogan in Lightning Ridge, New South Wales, Australia, comedian and actor, best known for *Crocodile Dundee* (1986) and its sequels.

1941 Birth of Jesse Jackson in Greenville, South Carolina, civil rights activist.

1943 Birth of Chevy Chase in Woodstock, New York, actor, whose films include *National Lampoon's Vacation* (1983).

1949 Birth of Sigourney Weaver in New York, actress, best known for her role as astronaut Ripley in the film *Alien* (1979) and its sequels.

1965 Opening of the Post Office Tower (177 m/580 ft) in Maple Street, London.

1967 The first motorist was breathalysed in Britain, at Flax Bourton, Somerset.

1967 Death of Clement Richard Attlee, 1st Earl Attlee (b.1883 in London), British prime minister (1945–51).

1970 Birth of Matt Damon in Cambridge, Massachusetts, actor, whose films include *Saving Private Ryan* (1998).

1973 First day of broadcasting for Britain's first legal commercial radio station, LBC (London Broadcasting).

1999 Professional boxing debut of Laila Ali (b.1977), daughter of Muhammad Ali (b.1942), in Verona, New York; she knocked out April Fowler 31 seconds into the contest.

OCTOBER

9

National Day, Uganda.
Leif Eriksson Day, Norway.
Feast of St Denis or Denys (3rd c), patron saint of France.

1855 Patenting of the sewing machine motor, by US inventor Isaac Singer (1811–75).

1875 Foundation of the Universal Postal Union in Berne, Switzerland.

1900 Birth of Alistair Sim in Edinburgh (d.1976), actor, whose films include *Scrooge* (1951).

1908 Birth of Jacques Tati in Le Pecq, France (d.1982), actor and director, whose films include *Mon Oncle* (1958).

1923 Birth of Donald Sinden in Plymouth, Devon, actor, whose films include *The Cruel Sea* (1952).

1934 Death of Alexander I, king of Yugoslavia (b.1888 in Cetinje, Montenegro), and Louis Barthou (b.1862), French foreign minister, assassinated by Croatian separatists in Marseille, France.

1937 Birth of Brian Blessed in Mexborough, West Yorkshire, actor, whose credits include *I Claudius* (1976) for British television.

1940 Birth of John Lennon in Liverpool (d.1980), pop star, composer, songwriter, and Beatle.

1946 First manufactured electric blanket was on sale in Petersburg, Virginia, price $39.50.

1955 Birth of Steve Ovett in Brighton, athlete, who won the gold medal in the 800 m and bronze in the 1500 m at the 1980 Olympics.

1962 Independence of Uganda after nearly 70 years of British rule.

1963 A landslide behind Vaiont Dam, north of Venice, caused a 200 m-high wave which destroyed several communities along the Piave valley, and killed 3000 people.

1967 Assassination in Bolivia of Che Guevara (b.1928 in Rosario, Argentina), Latin-American revolutionary.

1973 Divorce of rock singer Elvis Presley from Priscilla.

1974 Death of Oskar Schindler (b.1908 in Zwittau, Czech Republic), industrialist, who saved 1200 Jews from the Holocaust.

1988 Death of Jackie Millburn (b.1924 in Ashington, Northumberland), footballer, and uncle of Jackie and Bobby Charlton.

1991 Beginning of a sumo wrestling tournament at the Royal Albert Hall, London, the first held outside Japan in the sport's 1500-year history.

OCTOBER
10

Feast of St Francis Borgia, patron saint of Portugal.
Feast of St Gereon, patron saint of headache sufferers.

1865 Patenting of the billiard ball by US inventor John Wesley Hyatt (1837–1920).

1877 Birth of William Richard Morris, 1st Viscount Nuffield, in Worcester, UK (d.1963), motor magnate and philanthropist, first to develop the mass production of cheap cars (Morris).

1886 Birth of the dinner jacket, first worn at a ball in the Tuxedo Park Country Club, New York, from which its alternative name was derived.

1903 Formation of the *Women's Social and Political Union* by suffragettes Emmeline Pankhurst (1858–1928) and her daughter Christabel (1880–1958).

1913 US president Woodrow Wilson triggered the charge to demolish the Gamboa Dike, completing the Panama Canal, the link between the Atlantic and Pacific Oceans.

1930 Birth of Harold Pinter in London, playwright, whose works include *The Birthday Party* (1958).

1946 Birth of Charles Dance in Redditch, Hereford and Worcester, actor, whose films include *Michael Collins* (1996).

1957 Detection of a major radiation leak at Windscale Nuclear Plant, Cumbria, following an accident three days earlier.

1961 Evacuation of the entire population of the South Atlantic island of Tristan da Cunha to Britain, following a volcanic eruption.

1964 Opening of the 18th Olympic Games, in Tokyo, Japan.

1972 Appointment of Sir John Betjeman (1906–84) to the post of Britain's poet laureate, an office he held until his death.

1975 Remarriage of film stars Richard Burton and Elizabeth Taylor.

1983 Death of Sir Ralph Richardson (b.1902 in Cheltenham, Gloucestershire), actor, whose films include *The Fallen Idol* (1948).

1985 Death of Orson Welles (b.1915 in Kenosha, Wisconsin), director, producer, writer, and actor, whose film *Citizen Kane* (1941) is a landmark in cinema.

1985 Death of Yul Brynner (b.1915 in Vladivostok, Russia), US actor, whose films include *Westworld* (1972).

2004 Death of Christopher Reeve (b.1952 in New York), actor, whose credits include the *Superman* films (1978–87).

OCTOBER
11

1216 King John's luggage was lost in The Wash, the shallow inlet of the North Sea on the east coast of England.

1521 The title 'Defender of the Faith' was conferred on Henry VIII.

1727 Coronation of George II, king of Great Britain and Ireland (r.1727–60).

1821 Birth of Sir George Williams in Dulverton, Somerset (d.1905), social reformer, who founded the YMCA (Young Men's Christian Association) in 1844.

1844 Birth of H. J. Heinz in Pittsburgh, Pennsylvania (d.1919), food manufacturer, and co-founder of F. & J. Heinz.

1899 Beginning of the Boer War in South Africa.

1919 Serving of the first airline meals by Handley Page Transport on a London-to-Paris service; passengers were offered a pre-packed lunch box, costing 3 shillings (15p).

1930 Birth of Sir Michael Edwardes in South Africa, British business executive, who saved British Leyland from commercial collapse.

1937 Birth of Sir Bobby Charlton in Ashington, Northumberland, Manchester United and England footballer.

1956 The record was set for the slowest scoring in a cricket Test match: Australia scored 80 and Pakistan 15 during a full day's play in Karachi.

1957 The radio telescope at Jodrell Bank in Macclesfield, Cheshire, went into operation.

1957 Birth of Dawn French in Holyhead, Anglesey, comedy writer and actress, known for her work with Jennifer Saunders, and for her comedy series *The Vicar of Dibley* (1994).

1958 First broadcast of *Grandstand*, the BBC television sports programme.

1963 Birth of Beatlemania, as the UK pop group The Beatles appeared at the London Palladium.

1968 Launch of Apollo 7 by NASA.

1975 Marriage of Bill Clinton (b.1946) to Hillary Rodham (b.1947) in Fayetteville, Arkansas.

1976 The 'Gang of Four', the Shanghai-based radical leaders of China's Cultural Revolution (1966–76), were arrested in Beijing.

1982 Lifting of the wreck of the *Mary Rose*, flagship of King Henry VIII of England, from the Solent 437 years after she sank while still in harbour.

1984 Kathryn D. Sullivan, astronaut with space shuttle *Challenger*, became the first American woman to walk in space.

OCTOBER

12

1492 First sighting of what was to be San Salvador by Christopher Columbus (1451–1506).

1823 Scottish manufacturing chemist Charles Macintosh (1766–1843) began selling raincoats.

1845 Death of Elizabeth Fry (b.1780 in Norwich, Norfolk), Quaker prison reformer, who also founded hostels for the homeless and charitable societies.

1849 Patenting of the safety pin by British inventor Charles Rowley, unaware of the patent granted to Walter Hunt of New York six months previously.

1858 Birth of Isaac Newton Lewis in New Salem, Pennsylvania (d.1931), US army officer, who invented the Lewis machine-gun.

1859 Death of Robert Stephenson (b.1803 in Willington Quay, Tyne and Wear), engineer, who devised the tubular design of the Menai Straits Britannia Bridge (1850).

1872 Birth of Ralph Vaughan Williams in Down Ampney, Gloucestershire (d.1958), composer, known for his national style of music.

1901 The Executive Mansion in Washington, DC, was renamed The White House.

1915 Death of Edith Cavell (b.1865 in Swardeston, Norfolk), nurse, shot as a spy by a German firing squad in Brussels, Belgium.

1948 Completion of the first Morris Minor car at Cowley, Oxfordshire.

1964 Launch of Soviet spacecraft Voskhod 1, the first multi-manned spacecraft; in the haste to launch before the US Gemini flights, the Soviet crew had no spacesuits, ejection seats, or escape tower.

1968 Opening of the 19th Olympic Games, in Mexico City.

1969 Death of Sonja Henie (b.1912 in Oslo, Norway), figure-skater and actress, who won three Olympic gold medals.

1971 Opening of the musical *Jesus Christ Superstar* on Broadway.

1984 Explosion of an IRA bomb at the Grand Hotel, Brighton, during the Tory Party Conference.

1986 Queen Elizabeth II was the first British monarch to visit China.

1989 The Museum of London announced the discovery of the original Globe Theatre foundations on the South Bank of the Thames in London.

1997 Death of John Denver (b.1943 in Rockwell, New Mexico), singer and songwriter, whose songs include 'Take Me Home, Country Roads'.

2000 A terrorist bomb killed seventeen US sailors aboard the USS *Cole*, in the port of Aden, Yemen.

OCTOBER
13

Feast of St Edward the Confessor
(c.1003–66), patron saint of kings.

54 Death of Claudius I, Roman emperor (r.41–54).

1399 Coronation of Henry Bolingbroke as King Henry IV of England (r.1399–1413).

1792 President George Washington laid the foundation stone of the White House, Washington, DC.

1853 Birth of Lillie Langtry in Jersey, Channel Isles (d.1929), actress, known as the 'Jersey Lily'.

1884 Adoption of Greenwich as the universal time meridian of longitude, used to calculate standard times worldwide.

1894 The first Merseyside derby football match was played between Liverpool and Everton at Goodison Park, Liverpool; Everton won 3–0.

1910 Birth of Art Tatum in Toledo, Ohio (d.1956), jazz pianist, the first keyboard jazz virtuoso.

1921 Birth of Yves Montand in Monsummano Alto, Italy (d.1991), French actor and singer, whose films include *Let's Make Love* (1960).

1925 Birth of Baroness Margaret Thatcher in Grantham, Lincolnshire, British prime minister (1979–90).

1927 First British veteran car rally took place in London.

1941 Birth of Paul Simon in Newark, New Jersey, singer and songwriter, who teamed up with Art Garfunkel in the duo Simon and Garfunkel.

1944 Liberation of Athens by the Allies during World War 2.

1972 Abolition of bank rates in Britain, replaced by a minimum lending rate.

1972 A plane crashed in the Andes, stranding survivors without food, the subject of the book and film *Alive* (1992).

1974 Death of Ed Sullivan (b.1902 in New York), newspaper columnist and broadcaster, host of *The Ed Sullivan Show* (1948–71).

1984 Broadcasting of the first televised nine-dart perfect 501 game in the history of the sport, achieved by British player John Lowe in the quarter-finals of the MFI world matchplay championships.

1996 British racing driver Damon Hill (b.1960) won the Japanese Grand Prix, clinching his first, and only, Formula 1 world championship.

2004 Launch of the Russian Soyuz spacecraft, carrying two Russians and an American to replace the crew of the international space station.

OCTOBER
14

National Day, Madagascar.

1066 The Battle of Hastings was fought between the Normans and the Anglo-Saxons, in which King Harold II was killed.

1633 Birth of James II in London (d.1701), king of England and Ireland (1685–8).

1712 Birth of George Grenville in London (d.1770), British prime minister (1763–5).

1884 Patenting of photographic film by US inventor and philanthropist George Eastman (1854–1932).

1888 Birth of Katherine Mansfield in Wellington, New Zealand (d.1923), writer, whose works include *Bliss* (1920).

1894 Birth of E(dward) E(stlin) Cummings in Cambridge, Massachusetts (d.1962), writer and painter, known for his use of lower-case letters.

1896 Birth of Bud Flanagan in London (d.1968), comedian and singer, who teamed up with Chesney Allen, and was a member of the Crazy Gang.

1912 Theodore Roosevelt (1858–1919), US presidential candidate, was shot in the chest in Milwaukee, Wisconsin, but his thick coat and the documents he was carrying saved his life.

1913 Death of 439 people at Universal Colliery, Glamorgan, Britain's worst pit disaster.

1939 Sinking of Royal Navy battleship HMS *Royal Oak* by a German submarine torpedo in Scapa Flow, Orkney, with the loss of 810 lives.

1940 Birth of Cliff Richard in Lucknow, India, British pop singer and actor, who formed his own band, The Shadows, in 1958.

1944 Death of Erwin Rommel (b.1891 in Heidenheim, Germany), field marshal, who committed suicide rather than face execution for charges of conspiracy against Adolf Hitler.

1947 Aviator and test pilot Chuck Yeager (b.1923) was the first to break the sound barrier, when he flew the Bell X-1 rocket at 670 mph in level flight.

1958 Independence of Malagasy republic.

1968 Opening of the new Euston Station in London.

1969 Introduction of the 50p coin in Britain.

1977 Death of Bing Crosby (b.1904 in Tacoma, Washington), singer and film star, whose recordings include 'White Christmas'.

1982 At a ceremony in Seoul, South Korea, 5837 couples were married, or had their marriages blessed, by Korean evangelist Sun Myung Moon.

1994 A record £12,650 was paid by a French engineer for a 1938 Dinky Toy van.

OCTOBER

15

Feast of St Teresa of Avila (1515–82), patron saint of France and Spain.

70 BC Birth of Virgil in Andes, near Mantua (d.19 BC), Latin poet, whose works include the *Aeneid*.

1581 Performance in Paris of the *Ballet Comique de la Reine*, commissioned by Catherine de' Medici, often considered to be the first major ballet.

1582 First day of the Gregorian Calendar after it was adopted by Pope Gregory XIII. Ten days were eliminated: thus 5 October 1582 became 15 October.

1608 Birth of Evangelista Torricelli in Faenza, Italy (d.1647), physicist and mathematician, who gave the first description of a barometer, or Torricellian tube (1643).

1815 Napoleon Bonaparte (1769–1821) began his exile on the island of St Helena, where he was sent by the British after his defeat at the Battle of Waterloo.

1851 Ending of the Great Exhibition at Hyde Park, London.

1880 Birth of Marie Stopes in Edinburgh (d.1958), pioneer advocate of birth control, suffragette, and palaeontologist.

1895 Britain's first motor show was held at Tunbridge Wells, Kent.

1905 Birth of C(harles) P(ercy) Snow in Leicester, Leicestershire (d.1980), novelist and physicist, known for his controversial lecture, *The Two Cultures and the Scientific Revolution* (1959).

1917 Death of Mata Hari (b.1876 in Leeuwarden, The Netherlands), dancer and spy, executed by a French firing squad in Paris, guilty of espionage for the Germans during World War 1.

1920 Birth of Mario Puzo in New York (d.1999), novelist, best known for his epic best-selling mafia story *The Godfather* (1969).

1928 German airship *Graf Zeppelin* made its first transatlantic flight, from Friedrichshafen to Lakehurst, New Jersey.

1956 The last RAF Lancaster bomber was retired from active service.

1961 Formation of Amnesty International to investigate the abuse of human rights.

1964 Death of Cole Porter (b.1892 in Peru, Indiana), composer, who wrote lyrics and music for many stage successes, including *Kiss Me Kate* (1948).

1997 Andy Green (b.1962), in the British jet-powered car *Thrust SSC*, set a new land speed record with an average run of 1227·98 kph/763.035 mph, and broke the sound barrier, at Black Rock Desert, Nevada.

OCTOBER
16

Feast of St Gerard Majella, patron saint of lay-brothers.

1758 Birth of Noah Webster in Hartford, Connecticut (d.1843), lexicographer, whose works include the *American Dictionary of the English Language* (1828).

1793 Execution by guillotine of Queen Marie Antoinette in Paris (b.1755 in Vienna), during the French Revolution.

1813 Beginning of the Battle of Leipzig, which ended with Emperor Napoleon's defeat and retreat.

1846 First use of ether as an anaesthetic in a major operation, in Massachusetts.

1847 Publication of *Jane Eyre*, by Charlotte Brontë.

1854 Birth of Oscar Wilde in Dublin, Ireland (d.1900), writer and wit, whose works include *Lady Windermere's Fan* (1892).

1881 First publication of British newspaper the *People*.

1888 Birth of Eugene O'Neill in New York (d.1953), playwright, whose works include *The Iceman Cometh* (1946); awarded the Nobel Prize for Literature (1936).

1902 Opening of Britain's first detention centre, in Borstal, Kent.

1908 First aeroplane flight in England, at Farnborough, Hampshire, by US aviator Samuel Franklin Cody (1862–1913).

1916 Opening of the first birth-control clinic in the USA, by Margaret Sanger in Brooklyn, New York.

1922 Birth of Max Bygraves in Rotherhithe, London, singer and entertainer, known for his catchphrase, 'I wanna tell you a story.'

1925 Birth of Angela Lansbury in London, actress, whose films include *Bedknobs and Broomsticks* (1971).

1945 Institution of the Food and Agricultural Organization to improve nutrition and standards of living.

1958 Birth of Tim Robbins in West Govina, California, actor and director, whose films include *The Shawshank Redemption* (1994).

1958 First broadcast by the BBC of Britain's most popular children's television programme, *Blue Peter*, with presenters Leila Williams and Christopher Trace.

1964 Explosion of China's first nuclear bomb at the Lop Nor test site, Sinkiang, making China the fifth nation to have a nuclear capability.

1978 Election of the first non-Italian pope since 1542, Polish-born cardinal Karol Wojtyła (1920–2005).

1987 Millions of pounds of damage was caused when southern Britain was hit by hurricane-force winds.

OCTOBER
17

1662 Purchase of Dunkirk by France from Charles II of England for 2.5 million *livres* (£400,000) under the Treaty of Dunkirk.

1727 Birth of John Wilkes in London (d.1797), British politician and journalist, a champion of liberty and upholder of press freedom.

1777 Beginning of the Battle of Saratoga, one of the most important engagements of the American War of Independence.

1849 Death of Frédéric François Chopin (b.1810 in Zelazowa Wola, Poland), composer and pianist.

1854 Patenting of the Bessemer steel-making process by inventor and engineer Sir Henry Bessemer (1813–98).

1860 Prestwick, Scotland, hosted the first professional golf tournament, won by Willie Park.

1906 The first picture was sent by telegraph, revolutionizing the journalism industry.

1915 Birth of Arthur Miller in New York (d.2005), playwright, whose works include *Death of a Salesman* (1949, Pulitzer).

1918 Birth of Rita Hayworth in New York (d.1987), actress, whose films include *The Money Trap* (1966).

1925 Birth of Harry Carpenter in London, British boxing commentator from 1949 to his retirement in the 1990s.

1931 US gangster Al Capone (1899–1947) was given a prison sentence and fined $80,000 for tax evasion.

1938 Birth of Evel Knievel in Butte, Montana, stunt motorcyclist, who became internationally known for his spectacular performances.

1956 Formal opening of Britain's first large-scale atomic energy station, Calder Hall, Cumbria.

1962 Television debut for The Beatles, appearing live on the magazine programme *People and Places*.

1968 At the Mexico Olympics, Tommie Smith and John Carlos, 200 m medallists, gave black power salutes during the victory ceremony.

1978 Greenpeace averted a seal cull with their ship *Rainbow Warrior*.

1979 Mother Teresa of Calcutta (1910–97), Christian missionary in India, was awarded the Nobel Peace Prize.

1980 Queen Elizabeth II made the first state visit to the Vatican by a British monarch, and was received by the pope.

2000 Auction of the piano on which former Beatles member, John Lennon (1940–80), composed *Imagine*; it was bought by UK pop musician George Michael for about £1.5 million.

OCTOBER
18

Feast of St Luke (1st c), patron saint of artists, butchers, doctors, glassworkers, lacemakers, painters, sculptors, and surgeons.

1674 Birth of Richard 'Beau' Nash in Swansea, Wales (d.1762), dandy and gambler, known for his leadership in fashion.

1697 Birth of Canaletto, originally Giovanni Antonio Canal, in Venice, Italy (d.1768), painter, renowned for his series of views of Venice and London.

1842 Laying of the first telegraph cable in New York Harbour by the US inventor of the telegraph and Morse code, Samuel F. B. Morse (1791–1872).

1866 Official transfer of Alaska to the USA by Russia.

1910 Beginning of the trial of Dr Crippen (1862–1910) at the Old Bailey, London, for the murder of his wife.

1922 Inauguration of the BBC, the British Broadcasting Company (became 'Corporation' from 1926).

1926 Birth of Chuck Berry in St Louis, Missouri, rock-and-roll artist, whose hits include 'Johnny B. Goode'.

1931 Death of Thomas Alva Edison (b.1847 in Milan, Ohio), physicist, who invented the phonograph, the carbon-filament light bulb, and motion-picture equipment.

1939 Birth of Lee Harvey Oswald in New Orleans, Louisiana (d.1963), alleged killer of President John F. Kennedy.

1956 Birth of Martina Navratilova in Prague, Czech Republic, tennis player, winner of a record nine singles titles at Wimbledon (1978–9, 1982–7, 1990).

1961 *Le Bateau*, by Henry Matisse, was hung upside down in the Museum of Modern Art, New York; an estimated 116,000 people saw the painting before the error was spotted.

1963 Resignation of Harold Macmillan (1894–1986) as British prime minister through ill health; his successor was Sir Alec Douglas Home.

1968 US athlete Bob Beamon (b.1946) set a new world long-jump record of 8.90 m/29 ft $2\frac{1}{2}$ in during the Mexico Olympic Games.

1977 German anti-terrorist troops stormed a hijacked aircraft at Mogadishu airport, Somalia, killing three of the four Palestinian terrorists and freeing all 86 hostages.

1989 Hungary was proclaimed a free republic, and abandoned the Stalinist constitution.

1989 San Francisco was hit by an earthquake, force 6·9 on the Richter scale.

1995 Death of racehorse Red Rum, three times winner of the Grand National at Aintree, at the age of 30.

OCTOBER

19

1216 Death of King John (b.1167 in Oxford, Oxfordshire), king of England (1199–1216).

1745 Death of Jonathan Swift (b.1667 in Dublin, Ireland), clergyman and writer, best known for *Gulliver's Travels* (1726).

1781 Surrender of Lord Cornwallis to George Washington at Yorktown, Virginia, so ending the American Revolution.

1812 Napoleon Bonaparte's French Army began its retreat from Moscow.

1862 Birth of August Lumière in Besançon, France (d.1954), chemist, who, with his brother Louis, showed the first motion pictures using film projection in 1895.

1872 Mining of the *Holtermann Nugget* at Hill End, New South Wales, Australia; the nugget had a gold content of 99.8 kg/220 lb.

1875 Death of Sir Charles Wheatstone (b.1802 in Gloucester, Gloucestershire), physicist, known for his experiments in sound, who patented an electric telegraph (1837).

1901 Brazilian aviator Alberto Santos-Dumont (1873–1932) circled the Eiffel Tower in his No. 6 dirigible within 30 minutes, winning the 50,000 francs Deutsch Prize.

1937 Death of Ernest Rutherford, 1st Baron Rutherford (b.1871 near Nelson, New Zealand), physicist, who with Frederick Soddy proposed that radioactivity results from the disintegration of atoms (1903).

1940 Birth of Sir Michael Gambon in Dublin, Ireland, actor, whose TV credits include *The Singing Detective* (1986).

1951 Signing of an act by US president Harry S. Truman, officially ending the state of war with Germany.

1954 Conclusion of a treaty on the Suez Canal, ending 72 years of British military occupation; Britain agreed to withdraw its forces by June 1956, and Egypt agreed to maintain freedom of canal navigation.

1970 Announcement of the first major North Sea oil find by British Petroleum.

1987 Black Monday: a major crash on Wall Street wiped out millions on stock markets around the world.

1987 Death of Jacqueline du Pré (b.1945 in Oxford, Oxfordshire), cellist, whose career ended in 1973 when she developed multiple sclerosis.

1995 Announcement by firefighters in China that, after three years' work, they had extinguished a century-old fire in an untapped coal deposit in the Baiyanghe mine.

2003 Beatification of Mother Teresa of Calcutta (1910–97) by Pope John Paul II, before a crowd of 300,000 in St Peter's Square, Rome.

OCTOBER

20

1632 Birth of Sir Christopher Wren in East Knoyle, Wiltshire (d.1723), architect, who designed the new St Paul's Cathedral.

1714 Coronation of George I, king of Great Britain and Ireland (r.1714–27).

1818 Definition of the boundary between Canada and the USA as the 49th parallel by an Anglo-American convention.

1822 First publication of British newspaper *The Sunday Times*.

1827 Destruction of the Turkish and Egyptian fleets by the British, French, and Russians at the Battle of Navarino during the Greek War of Independence (1821–9).

1884 Birth of Bela Lugosi in Lugos, Hungary (d.1956), actor, known especially for his role as Dracula.

1890 Death of Sir Richard Burton (b.1821 in Torquay, Devon), explorer, who set out with Speke on the journey which led to the discovery of Lake Tanganyika.

1934 Birth of Timothy West in Bradford, West Yorkshire, actor and director, whose TV credits include *Churchill and the Generals* (1979).

1960 Penguin Books were taken to court, having been charged under the Obscene Publication Act for publishing D. H. Lawrence's novel *Lady Chatterley's Lover*.

1965 British pop group The Beatles was awarded a gold disc for their record 'Yesterday'.

1968 Marriage of millionaire ship-owner Aristotle Onassis to Jacqueline Kennedy.

1973 Arrival in Britain of Tenzin Gyatso (b.1935), 14th Dalai Lama and spiritual leader of Tibetan Buddhists, for a 10-day tour, his first UK visit.

1973 Public opening of Sydney Opera House.

1988 Death of Sheila Scott (b.1927 in Worcester, Hereford and Worcester), aviator, the first woman to fly solo around the world (1966).

1994 Death of Burt Lancaster (b.1913 in New York), actor, whose films include *Elmer Gantry* (1960, Oscar).

1999 Launch of the entire *Encyclopaedia Britannica* on the Internet, with the addition of archived news updates from current media sources.

2002 Completion in Turkey of Blue Stream, the deepest underwater pipeline in the world, for the transport of natural gas from Russia.

2003 Kirk Jones, of Canton, Michigan, survived a 46-m/150-ft plunge over Niagara Falls with no safety equipment, and was charged with mischief and unlawfully performing a stunt.

OCTOBER

21

1772 Birth of Samuel Taylor Coleridge in Ottery St Mary, Devon (d.1834), poet, whose works include 'The Rime of the Ancient Mariner'.

1797 Launch of US Navy frigate USS *Constitution*, also known as *Old Ironsides*, in Boston harbour; it survived 42 battles undefeated.

1805 Death of Horatio Nelson (b.1758 in Burnham Thorpe, Norfolk), British admiral, mortally wounded on his flagship, HMS *Victory*.

1858 First performance of Offenbach's opera *Orpheus in the Underworld*, at the Théâtre des Bouffes-Parisiens in Paris.

1901 Kodak Brownie cameras could be bought for $1 each.

1912 Birth of Sir Georg Solti in Budapest, Hungary (1997), conductor, who directed orchestras in Munich, Frankfurt, Chicago, and London.

1915 The first direct radio-telephone call was made, from Virginia to Paris.

1918 US typist Margaret Owen set a typing speed record of 170 words per minute on a manual typewriter.

1923 Opening of the first planetarium to the public, at the Deutsche Museum, Munich, Germany.

1926 Birth of Leonard Rossiter in Liverpool (d.1984), actor, whose television series include *Rising Damp* (1974–8).

1940 Introduction of purchase tax in Britain, replaced by value-added tax in 1973.

1950 Birth of John Candy in Toronto, Ontario (d.1994), US actor and writer, whose films include *Planes, Trains and Automobiles* (1987).

1956 Birth of Carrie Fisher in Los Angeles, California, actress, screenwriter, and novelist, best known for her role as Princess Leia in the *Star Wars* films.

1958 Entry of the first women peers to Britain's House of Lords.

1960 Launch of Britain's first nuclear-powered submarine, *Dreadnought*, by Queen Elizabeth II at Barrow-in-Furness, Cumbria.

1961 US songwriter and singer Bob Dylan recorded his first album in a single day, at a cost of $400.

1966 Death of 144 people, including 116 children, when a slag heap at Aberfan, Glamorgan, collapsed and buried a local school.

1996 Nick Park was reunited with his creations, the models Wallace and Gromit, two days after leaving them in a New York taxi.

OCTOBER
22

1797 Aeronaut André-Jacques Garnerin (1769–1823) gave the first public demonstration of a descent by parachute, from a balloon about 1000 m/3200 ft above the Parc Monceau, Paris.

1806 Death of Thomas Sheraton (b.1751 in Stockton-on-Tees, Durham), cabinet-maker and furniture designer.

1811 Birth of Franz Liszt in Raiding, Hungary (d.1886), composer and virtuoso pianist.

1843 Birth of Stephen Babcock near Bridgwater, New York (d.1931), agricultural chemist, the originator of scientific dairying.

1878 The first floodlit rugby match was played, at Broughton, Lancashire.

1883 Opening of New York's Metropolitan Opera House.

1906 Death of Paul Cézanne (b.1839 in Aix-en-Provence, France), Post-Impressionist painter, whose works include *The Card Players* (1890–92).

1909 First solo flight by a woman was made by French aviator Elise Deroche (1886–1919).

1910 Dr Crippen was sentenced to hang for the murder of his wife, Cora.

1938 Chester Carlson (1906–68) and Otto Kornei successfully tested their photocopier in New York, using powdered ink and an electrical charge to create the first photocopy.

1938 Birth of Sir Derek Jacobi in London, actor, whose appearances include the title role in the television drama serial *I, Claudius* (1977).

1943 Birth of Catherine Deneuve in Paris, actress, whose films include *Belle de Jour* (1967).

1952 Birth of Jeff Goldblum in Pittsburgh, Pennsylvania, actor, whose films include *Jurassic Park* (1993).

1962 Nelson Mandela pleaded not guilty to treason in South Africa.

1962 Beginning of the Cuban Missile Crisis, when President Kennedy said he did not want the Russians using missile bases in Cuba.

1979 The exiled shah of Iran, Mohammad Reza Shah Pahlavi (1919–80), was allowed into the USA for medical treatment.

1983 Thousands of people marched to London to support CND (Campaign for Nuclear Disarmament) in their protest about the use of nuclear missiles.

1987 Sale of the first volume of the Gutenberg Bible in New York for $5.39 million/£3.26 million, at the time the largest amount received for a book at auction.

OCTOBER

23

Feast of St John of Capistrano (1386–1456), patron saint of jurists.

4004 BC Creation of the world, at 9 a.m. on Sunday 23 October, according to James Ussher (1581–1656), archbishop of Armagh, and Dr John Lightfoot of Cambridge.

1642 The Battle of Edgehill, first major engagement of the English Civil War (1625–49), was fought inconclusively between King Charles I of England and parliament.

1707 Meeting of the first parliament of Great Britain.

1814 The first plastic surgery in England, a nose operation lasting 37 minutes, was performed by Dr Joseph Constantine Carpue.

1817 Birth of Pierre Larousse in Toucy, France (d.1875), publisher and lexicographer, who wrote several grammars, dictionaries, and other textbooks.

1869 Death of Edward Geoffrey Smith Stanley, 14th Earl of Derby (b.1799 at Knowsley Hall, Lancashire), British prime minister (1852, 1858–9, 1866-8).

1915 Death of W(illiam) G(ilbert) Grace (b.1848 in Downend, Gloucester), cricket player, who became known as 'The Great Cricketer'.

1922 Andrew Bonar Law (1858–1923) became British prime minister, in office for seven months, the shortest term of office in the 20th c.

1925 Birth of Johnny Carson in Corning, Iowa (d.2005), television talk-show host, who starred in *The Tonight Show* (1962–92).

1940 Birth of Pelé in Três Corações, Brazil, footballer, widely held to be the best player in the game's history.

1942 Launch of a huge offensive against German and Italian forces at El Alamein, Egypt, by British and Commonwealth forces during World War 2.

1943 Birth of Anita Roddick in Brighton, retail entrepreneur, who opened her first Body Shop in 1976.

1945 The United Nations was formally established with 51 founder countries.

1950 Death of Al Jolson, originally Asa Yoelson (b.1886 in Srednike, Russia), actor and singer, who became known in the 1920s for such sentimental songs as 'Mammy'.

1956 Beginning of the Hungarian uprising against Soviet leadership, when thousands of demonstrators in Budapest called for the withdrawal of Soviet forces.

1956 Approval of the Statute of the International Atomic Energy Agency by a conference held at the United Nations.

1972 Introduction of Access credit cards in Britain.

OCTOBER
24

National Day, Zambia.
Feast of St Raphael, patron saint of the blind.

1648 Signing of the Peace of Westphalia, ending the Eighty Years' War between Spain and the Dutch, and the German phase of the Thirty Years' War.

1857 Formation of the world's first official football club in Sheffield, South Yorkshire, by William Prest and Nathaniel Creswick, who set up their headquarters in a potting shed and a greenhouse.

1876 Patenting of the wind-up alarm clock by US clockmaker Seth Thomas (1785–1859).

1882 Birth of Dame Sybil Thorndike in Gainsborough, Lincolnshire (d.1976), actress, known for her long stage career.

1901 Retired school teacher Ann Edson Taylor (1838–1921) was the first woman to go over Niagara Falls in a barrel.

1922 Death of George Cadbury (b.1839 in Birmingham, West Midlands), businessman, who established for his workers the model village of Bournville (1879).

1923 Birth of Sir Robin Day in London (d.2000), journalist and broadcaster, who presented BBC television's *Panorama* (1967–72).

1929 Black Thursday: the New York stock market began to fail, marking the onset of the Great Depression.

1936 Birth of Bill Wyman in Penge, London, rock guitarist with The Rolling Stones.

1947 Birth of Kevin Kline in St Louis, Missouri, actor, whose films include *Chaplin* (1992).

1957 Death of Christan Dior (b.1905 in Granville, France), couturier, who founded his own Paris house in 1945.

1964 Northern Rhodesia became the Republic of Zambia, with Kenneth Kaunda as its founder president (1964–91).

1976 British driver James Hunt (1947–93) became Formula 1 world champion after finishing third in the Japanese Grand Prix.

1987 British heavyweight boxing champion Frank Bruno beat Joe Bugner at White Hart Lane, London.

1998 Launch of Deep Space 1 from Cape Canaveral, Florida.

2003 Supersonic aircraft Concorde made its last commercial passenger flight, landing at Heathrow airport, London.

OCTOBER

25

Feast of St Crispin (?–c.287) and Crispinian, patron saints of glovemakers, shoemakers, and weavers.

1400 Death of Chaucer (b.1343 probably in London), poet, whose famous work is the unfinished *Canterbury Tales*.

1415 The Battle of Agincourt was won by Henry V of England.

1759 Birth of William Wyndham Grenville in Wotton House, Buckinghamshire (d.1834), statesman, who formed the coalition 'Government of All the Talents' (1806–7).

1825 Birth of Johann Strauss, known as the Younger, in Vienna, Austria (d.1899), violinist and composer, the 'King of the Waltz'.

1838 Birth of Georges Bizet in Paris (d.1875), composer, whose works include the opera *Carmen* (1875).

1839 Publication of the first national railway timetable in Britain, *Bradshaw's Railway Companion*.

1854 The Charge of the Light Brigade, at the beginning of the Battle of Balaclava, took place during the Crimean War.

1881 Birth of Pablo Picasso in Málaga, Spain (d.1973), painter, whose works include *Guernica* (1937).

1900 Renaming of the Boer Republic as the Transvaal, when Britain's annexation of the republic came into effect; the 1994 constitution divided it into Northern Province and Mpumalanga.

1936 Meeting between Italy and Germany to form the Rome–Berlin Axis, providing mutual assistance and opposition to Communism.

1951 Margaret Thatcher, née Roberts (b.1925), became the youngest candidate to stand at a general election.

1955 First sales of microwave ovens in the USA, with a price tag of $1300, by the Tappan Stove Company.

1961 Publication of the first edition of the British magazine *Private Eye*.

1976 Opening of the National Theatre on the South Bank, London, by Queen Elizabeth II.

1983 Invasion of Grenada by US marines to restore order and protect US citizens after a government coup.

1993 Death of Vincent Price (b.1911 in St Louis, Missouri), actor, whose films include *House of Wax* (1953).

1995 Fans of Cliff Richard gathered outside Buckingham Palace and sang 'Congratulations' after the British singer received his knighthood.

OCTOBER
26

899 Death of Alfred the Great (b.849 in Wantage, Oxfordshire), king of Wessex (871–99).

1685 Birth of Domenico Scarlatti in Naples, Italy (d.1757), composer and harpsichordist, mainly remembered for the 555 sonatas written for this instrument.

1776 Death of William Hogarth (b.1697 in London), painter and engraver, whose works include *A Rake's Progress* (1733–5).

1803 Birth of Joseph Aloysius Hansom, in Micklefield, North Yorkshire (d.1882), inventor and architect, whose inventions include the 'Patent Safety (Hansom) Cab' in 1834.

1825 Opening of the Erie Canal in North America.

1858 Patenting of the rotary motion washing machine by H. E. Smith of Philadelphia.

1863 Formation of the English Football Association.

1881 Gunfight at the OK Corral in Tombstone, Arizona.

1908 Founding of the Territorial Army in Britain.

1917 The October Revolution took place in Russia.

1942 Birth of Bob Hoskins in Bury St Edmunds, Suffolk, actor, whose films include *The Long Good Friday* (1980).

1947 Birth of Hillary Clinton in Park Ridge, Illinois, lawyer, and US first lady (1993–2000).

1950 Opening of the rebuilt chamber of the House of Commons, London, destroyed by bombing in May 1941 during World War 2.

1958 First service flight for America's first jet airliner, the Boeing 707, flying from New York to Paris.

1966 Removal of NATO from Paris to Brussels.

1967 Coronation of Mohammad Reza Shah Pahlavi (1919–80), shah of Iran (1941–79) on his 48th birthday, having deferred his coronation for 26 years.

1987 Opening of London's City airport in the Docklands area.

1994 Signing of a peace treaty by Israel and Jordan on the Israeli–Jordanian border, ending 46 years of war.

2000 Publication of the report into the spread of 'mad cow disease', and its fatal human equivalent vCJD (variant Creutzfeldt-Jakob disease), criticizing officials, scientists, and government ministers.

2002 Russian troops used anaesthetic gas and stormed a Moscow theatre where over 800 hostages were held by rebels demanding withdrawal of Russian forces from Chechnya; all the rebels and over 120 hostages died.

OCTOBER
27

1728 Birth of Captain James Cook in Marton, North Yorkshire (d.1779), navigator, who during three major voyages surveyed areas around North America, the Pacific, and Antarctica.

1775 Establishment of the US Navy.

1782 Birth of Niccolò Paganini in Genoa, Italy (d.1840), violin virtuoso, whose works include *24 Capricci* (1820).

1811 Birth of Isaac Singer in Pittsdown, New York (d.1875), manufacturer, who devised an improved single-thread, chain-stitch sewing machine (1852).

1858 US merchant Rowland Macy (?1822–77) opened Macy's department store in New York.

1879 First publication of Britain's *Liverpool Echo*.

1901 First known use of a getaway car, in Paris, France, when thieves drove off after holding up a shop.

1914 Birth of Dylan Thomas in Swansea, Wales (d.1953), poet, whose works include the radio 'play for voices' *Under Milk Wood* (published 1954).

1920 Relocation of the League of Nations from London to Geneva.

1923 Birth of Roy Lichtenstein in New York (d.1997), painter, best known for his images of American Pop Art.

1925 Patenting of water skis, called Dolphin Akwa-Skees, by Fred Waller (1886–1954), Paramount motion picture engineer who also developed *Cinerama*.

1927 Release of the first newsreel featuring sound, in New York, by Fox MovieTone News.

1932 Birth of Sylvia Plath in Jamaica Plain, Massachusetts (d.1963), poet, novelist, and essayist, whose work includes *The Colossus* (1960).

1936 A decree nisi was granted to US-born Wallis Simpson (1896–1986) from her second husband, Ernest, leaving her free to marry King Edward VIII.

1939 Birth of John Cleese in Weston-super-Mare, Somerset, comic actor, writer, and member of the Monty Python team.

1954 US premiere of Walt Disney's first television programme, *Disneyland*, on ABC Television.

1986 Big Bang day: failure of a computerized share-trading system introduced to London's Stock Exchange, causing a shambles.

1993 The Sultan of Brunei tipped a luxury hotel in Cyprus $170,000 following his stay there of less than a week.

2001 Farm Aid took place at the Millennium Stadium, Cardiff, Wales, a benefit for the farmers and their families who had been badly hit by the foot-and-mouth crisis.

OCTOBER

28

Feast (Western Church) of St Simon and St Jude (1st c), patron saints of fishers and hopeless cases.

1636 Foundation of Harvard University, named after its major benefactor, English-born minister John Harvard (1607–38).

1746 An earthquake magnitude 8.0–8.6, thought to be the biggest in recorded history, destroyed the Peruvian cities of Lima, Callao, and Chanacay, followed by a large tsunami; more than 18,000 people died.

1831 The first dynamo was made by British chemist Michael Faraday (1791–1867).

1886 Unveiling of the bronze Statue of Liberty in New York harbour, designed by French sculptor Auguste Bartholdi (1834–1904); it was designated a national monument on 15 October 1924.

1893 Trialling began of the British Royal Navy's first destroyer, HMS *Havelock*.

1909 Birth of Francis Bacon in Dublin, Ireland (d.1992), Surrealist painter, whose works include *Three Studies for Figures at the Base of a Crucifixion* (1945).

1914 Birth of Jonas E. Salk in New York (d.1995), virologist, who discovered the first vaccine against poliomyelitis (1953–4).

1918 Issue of a proclamation by leaders of the Czechoslovak National Council announcing the formation of an independent Czechoslovakian state.

1927 Birth of Cleo Laine in Southall, London, singer, known for her collaboration with her husband, John Dankworth.

1929 Birth of Joan Plowright in Brigg, Lincolnshire, actress, and third wife of Laurence Olivier; her films include *Tea with Mussolini* (1998).

1938 Birth of David Dimbleby in London, broadcaster, known especially as a presenter of BBC television current-affairs programmes.

1942 Birth of Michael Crichton in Chicago, Illinois, novelist and screenwriter, whose credits include *Jurassic Park* (1993).

1955 Birth of Bill Gates in Seattle, Washington, computer engineer and entrepreneur, who co-founded Microsoft.

1958 First television broadcast of the state opening of Britain's parliament; Richard Dimbleby commentated for the BBC, and Robin Day for ITV.

1962 Opening of Britain's first urban motorway, the M62 around Manchester.

1962 Russia withdrew its missiles, ending the Cuban Missile Crisis.

OCTOBER

29

National Day, Turkey.

1618 Death of Sir Walter Raleigh (b.1552 in Hayes Barton, Devon), courtier, explorer, soldier, and writer.

1787 First performance of Mozart's opera *Don Giovanni* in Prague.

1814 Launch of USS *Fulton*, the first steam-powered warship, in New York.

1863 Foundation of the International Red Cross – at first called the International Committee for Relief to the Wounded – by philanthropist Henri Dunant (1828–1910).

1888 Signing of the Constantinople Convention on Free Navigation of the Suez Canal, allowing the canal to be open to all nations during war as well as peace.

1897 Birth of Joseph Goebbels in Rheydt, Germany (d.1945), minister of propaganda for the German Third Reich under Adolf Hitler.

1911 Death of Joseph Pulitzer (b.1847 in Makó, Hungary), newspaper proprietor, and emigrant to the USA, who established annual Pulitzer Prizes.

1923 Turkey was proclaimed a republic.

1927 Discovery of the tomb of Genghis Khan in China by Russian archaeologist Peter Kozlov.

1929 Black Tuesday: the New York stock market collapse reached its lowest level.

1957 Death of Louis Burt Mayer (b.1885 in Minsk, Belarus), US film producer and distributor.

1960 US boxer Muhammad Ali (b.1942), then called Cassius Clay, won his first professional fight, beating Tunney Hunsaker in Louisville, Kentucky.

1987 US boxer Thomas Hearns (b.1958) won the world middleweight title, becoming the first boxer to win a world title at four different weights.

1989 The African National Congress held its first political rally for nearly 30 years, attended by 70,000 supporters.

1996 An auction of the artwork stolen by the Nazis during the German occupation of Austria during World War 2 was organized by Christie's in Vienna, Austria.

1998 US astronaut John Glenn (b.1921) became the oldest man at 77 to fly in space, on a nine-day mission on the space shuttle *Discovery*.

2001 Introduction of Mr Cheeky, marking the 30th anniversary of the Mr Men and Little Miss characters created by Roger Hargreaves (1935–88).

OCTOBER
30

1485 Establishment of the Yeomen of the Guard by Henry VII.

1580 English seaman Sir Frances Drake (c.1540–96) sailed into Plymouth in the *Golden Hind*, having completed his circumnavigation of the world.

1650 The Society of Friends took the name *Quakers* after a court case when George Fox (1624–91), founder of the society, told the magistrate to 'quake and tremble at the word of God'.

1751 Birth of Richard Brinsley Sheridan in Dublin, Ireland (d.1816), playwright, whose comedies include *The School for Scandal* (1777).

1809 Death of William Henry Cavendish, 3rd Duke of Portland (b.1738 in Bulstrode, Buckinghamshire), British prime minister (1783, 1807–9).

1821 [Old Style calendar, New Style 11 November] Birth of Fyodor Dostoyevsky in Moscow (d.1881), novelist, whose works include *Crime and Punishment* (1866).

1885 Birth of Ezra Pound in Hailey, Idaho (d.1972), experimental poet, regarded as a leading motivating force behind modern poetry.

1893 Birth of Charles Atlas in Acri, Italy (d.1972), US bodybuilder and trainer.

1894 Patenting of the time clock, for recording the arrival and departure time of employees, by Daniel M. Cooper of Rochester, New York.

1905 Aspirin went on sale in Britain.

1910 Death of Henri Dunant (b.1828 in Geneva, Switzerland), philanthropist, who inspired the foundation of the International Red Cross.

1914 Beginning of the first stage of the Battle of Ypres on the Western Front, one of the major battles in World War 1.

1925 Transmission of the first television pictures by John Logie Baird, using the head of a dummy.

1938 The realistic broadcast of Orson Welles' radio play, *The War of the Worlds*, caused panic in the USA.

1956 Birth of Juliet Stevenson in London, actress, whose films include *Truly, Madly, Deeply* (1991).

1960 Birth of Diego Maradona in Lanus, Argentina, footballer, who captained Argentina to their second World Cup in 1986.

1964 US singer and songwriter Roy Orbison (1936–88) was awarded a gold disc for his record 'Oh Pretty Woman'.

1979 Death of Sir Barnes Wallis (b.1887 in Ripley, Derbyshire), aeronautical engineer, whose designs include the R100 airship, the Wellington bomber, and the first swing-wing aircraft.

OCTOBER
31

Halloween, or All Hallows Eve.
Feast of St Wolfgang, patron saint of carpenters.

1485 Coronation of King Henry VII of England.

1517 Religious reformer Martin Luther (1483–1546) posted his 95 Theses on the door of Wittenberg Palace Church, marking the start of the Protestant Reformation in Germany.

1632 Birth of Jan Vermeer in Delft, The Netherlands (d.1675), painter, known for his detailed domestic interiors

1795 Birth of John Keats in London (d.1821), poet, a leading figure of the Romantic movement.

1864 Nevada became the 36th state of the Union.

1888 Patenting of pneumatic bicycle tyres by Scottish inventor John Boyd Dunlop (1840–1921).

1903 Opening of the Hampden Park football ground in Scotland; Queens Park won the inaugural match against Celtic 1–0.

1922 Benito Mussolini (1883–1945) became prime minister of Italy.

1926 Birth of Jimmy Savile in Leeds, West Yorkshire, television and radio personality, who raised huge sums of money for deserving causes.

1941 Completion of the sculptures at Mt Rushmore, South Dakota, after 14 years of work; four presidents (Washington, Jefferson, Lincoln, and Theodore Roosevelt) are represented.

1951 Introduction of zebra crossings in Britain.

1952 Detonation of the first US hydrogen bomb, at Eniwetok Atoll in the Pacific Marshall Islands.

1956 George J. Dufek of Rockford, Illinois, became the first person to land an aeroplane at the South Pole.

1961 Removal of the body of Soviet dictator Josef Stalin (1879–1953) from Lenin's tomb in Red Square to a plot by the Kremlin wall.

1982 First raising of Britain's Thames barrier, a series of 10 movable gates positioned end-to-end across the river.

1984 Assassination of Indira Gandhi (b.1917 in Allahabad, India), prime minister of India, killed by Sikh extremists in her bodyguard.

1993 Death of Frederico Fellini (b.1920 in Rimini, Italy), director, whose films include *La Strada* (1954, Oscar).

1993 Death of River Phoenix (b.1970 in Madras, Oregon), actor, whose films include *Love You to Death* (1990).

NOVEMBER
1

All Saints' Day.
National Day, Algeria.
Feast (Eastern Church) of St Cosmas and St Damian (3rd-c), patron saints of chemists, doctors, hairdressers (men's), midwives, and surgeons.

1695 Foundation of the Bank of Scotland.
1714 Death of John Radcliffe (b.1650 in Wakefield, West Yorkshire), physician, who bequeathed the bulk of his property to form the Radcliffe Library, Infirmary, and Observatory at Oxford.
1755 Death of around 60,000 people in Lisbon, Portugal, during an earthquake and the ensuing tsunami.
1800 John Adams became the first US president to take up residence in the White House.
1848 Opening of the first W. H. Smith bookstall, in Euston Station, London.
1887 Birth of L. S. Lowry in Manchester (d.1976), artist, who produced many pictures of the Lancashire industrial scene.
1923 Birth of Victoria de los Angeles in Barcelona, Spain, lyric soprano, noted for her performances of Spanish songs.
1929 Foundation of the Pony Club in Britain.
1935 Birth of Gary Player in Johannesburg, South Africa, golfer, one of the few players to win each of the four Grand Slam events.

1936 Inauguration of the BBC television service from Alexandra Palace, London; only a few hundred people in the immediate vicinity were able to receive the first programmes.
1956 First sale of Premium Bonds in Britain.
1962 Launch of the first rocket towards Mars by the USSR; communications failed en route, with a last message from the spacecraft in March 1963.
1972 Death of Ezra Pound (b.1885 in Hailey, Idaho), experimental poet, a pioneer of modern poetry.
1985 Death of Phil Silvers (b.1912 in New York), comic actor, whose television series *The Phil Silvers Show* (1955–9) established him as Sergeant Bilko.
1989 East Germany opened its border with Czechoslovakia.
2001 Opening in London of the Tate Britain Centenary Development to the public; the project provided Tate Britain with ten new and five refurbished galleries, and other facilities.

NOVEMBER

2

All Souls' Day, sometimes called the 'Day of the Dead'.
Feast (Eastern Church) of St Eustace, patron saint of hunters.

1734 Birth of Daniel Boone in Berks Co, Pennsylvania (d.1820), legendary pioneer, who made a trail through the Cumberland Gap and became one of the first to explore Kentucky.

1772 First day of publication for the British newspaper *Morning Post*.

1865 Birth of Warren Harding in Corsica (now Blooming Grove), Ohio (d.1923), 29th president of the USA (1921–3).

1889 North Dakota became the 39th state of the Union.

1889 South Dakota became the 40th state of the Union.

1903 Publication of the first issue of the British newspaper *Daily Mirror*, designed as a newspaper for women.

1913 Birth of Burt Lancaster in New York (d.1994), actor, whose films include *Bird Man of Alcatraz* (1962).

1924 The *Sunday Express* published the first crossword to appear in a British newspaper.

1947 US aviator Howard Hughes (1905–76) flew his eight-engine wooden flying boat *Spruce Goose* for a mile off Long Beach, California, its only flight.

1950 Death of George Bernard Shaw (b.1856 in Dublin, Ireland), playwright, essayist, and pamphleteer.

1953 The confidential counselling group, the Samaritans, took their first telephone call on MAN 9000.

1954 First broadcast of the UK comedy series *Hancock's Half Hour* on BBC Radio.

1959 Official opening of Britain's M1 motorway.

1960 The publishers Penguin Books were aquitted of obscenity in the case of *Lady Chatterley's Lover*.

1961 Death of James Thurber (b.1894 in Columbus, Ohio), writer and cartoonist, whose drawings first appeared in *Is Sex Necessary?* (1929).

1962 US President Kennedy reported that all USSR missile bases in Cuba had been destroyed.

1964 Transmission of the first episode of the UK television soap opera *Crossroads* on ITV.

1982 Britain's Channel Four television began broadcasting, at first managed by the Independent Broadcasting Authority; it became a public corporation in 1990.

NOVEMBER

3

National Day, Panama.

Feast of St Hubert (656–727), patron saint of dogs, forestry workers, hunters, and instrument makers.

Feast of St Martin de Porres (1579–1639), patron saint of hairdressers (men's), race relations, beggars, and the poor.

1534 The first Act of Supremacy made King Henry VIII head of the English Church, a role formerly held by the pope.

1718 Birth of John Montagu, 4th Earl of Sandwich (d.1792), British politician, remembered as the inventor of sandwiches.

1801 Birth of Karl Baedeker in Essen, Germany (d.1859), publisher, known for the authoritative travel guidebooks which still bear his name.

1843 The first half of Lord Nelson's statue, executed by Edward Hodges Baily (1788–1867), was sited on top of the column in Trafalgar Square, London.

1900 Opening of the first motor show held in the USA, at Madison Square Garden, New York, under the auspices of the Automobile Club of America.

1903 Independence of Panama from Columbia.

1921 Birth of Charles Bronson in Ehrenfield, Pennsylvania (d.2003), actor, who made his name in such films as *The Magnificent Seven* (1960).

1926 Death of Annie Oakley (b.1860 in Darke Co, Ohio), rodeo star sharpshooter, who with her husband, Frank E. Butler, toured with the Buffalo Bill Wild West Show.

1942 Ending of the Battle of El Alamein during World War 2 with a British victory, the turning point of the war in Africa.

1948 Birth of Lulu (Marie McLaughlin Lawrie) in Glasgow, pop singer and entertainer, whose first hit was 'Shout' (1964).

1952 Birth of Roseanne Barr in Salt Lake City, Utah, actress and former stand-up comic, best known for the television series *Roseanne* (1988–97).

1954 Death of Henri Matisse (b.1869 in Le Cateau, France), painter, leader of the Fauvist movement of the 1900s.

1957 Launch of Sputnik 9 by the USSR, carrying Laika, the first dog in space.

1975 Official opening by Queen Elizabeth II of the North Sea pipeline, the first to be built underwater.

2002 Death of Lonnie Donegan (b.1931 in Glasgow), singer and guitarist, whose hits included 'Rock Island Line' (1956).

NOVEMBER

4

Feast of St Charles Borromeo (1538–84), patron saint of bishops.

1843 The second half of Lord Nelson's statue was placed on top of the column in Trafalgar Square, London.

1846 Patenting of an artificial leg by B. F. Palmer of Meredith, New Hampshire.

1852 Opening of the House of Commons Press Gallery; for the first time in the history of the House, journalists were allowed in to report debates.

1862 Patenting of his machine-gun by US inventor Richard Jordan Gatling (1818–1903).

1873 Patenting of a gold crown for teeth by Dr John Beers of San Francisco, California.

1879 Patenting of the first cash register by James Ritty, saloon owner, of Dayton, Ohio.

1890 Opening of the City branch of the Northern Line, the first electrified underground railway system in London.

1914 The first fashion show, organized by Edna Woodman Chase of *Vogue* magazine, was held at the Ritz-Carlton Hotel, New York.

1916 Birth of Walter Cronkite Jr in St Joseph, Missouri, journalist and broadcaster, who provided vivid eye-witness accounts of World War 2 in Europe.

1918 Death of Wilfred Owen (b.1893 at Plas Wilmot, Shropshire), poet, killed in action on the Western Front one week before the armistice.

1922 The US postmaster-general ordered all homes to get mailboxes or relinquish mail deliveries.

1922 Archaeologist Howard Carter (1874–1939) and Lord Carnarvon (1866–1923) found the first evidence of Tutankhamun's tomb in the Valley of the Kings, Egypt.

1924 Death of Gabriel Fauré (b.1845 in Pamiers, France), organist, and composer of songs, operas, and orchestral pieces.

1946 Inauguration of UNESCO (United Nations Educational, Scientific and Cultural Organization).

1966 Floods in Florence, Italy, killed 113 people, made 30,000 homeless, and destroyed Renaissance artworks and books.

1995 Death of Itzhak Rabin (b.1922 in Jerusalem, Israel), prime minister of Israel, assassinated at a peace rally in Tel Aviv by Yigal Amir, an Israeli law student.

2001 Premiere of the first Harry Potter film, based on *Harry Potter and the Philosopher's Stone* (1997), in London.

NOVEMBER

5

1605 The Gunpowder Plot failed when 36 barrels of gunpowder were found in the cellars under the Houses of Parliament, London.

1854 Defeat of the Russians by the combined British and French armies at the Battle of Inkerman during the Crimean War.

1895 The first US patent for an automobile, granted by patent attorney George B. Selden (1846–1922).

1909 Opening of Britain's first Woolworth's store, in Liverpool.

1912 Birth of Roy Rogers in Cincinnati, Ohio (d.1998), actor, best known as a singing cowboy, usually seen with his horse, Trigger.

1912 Appointment of the British Board of Film Censors.

1913 Birth of Vivien Leigh in Darjeeling, India (d.1967), British actress, best known for her performance in the film *Gone With the Wind* (1939, Oscar).

1914 Britain declared war on Turkey, and annexed Cyprus.

1917 US troops went into action for the first time on the Western Front during World War 1.

1919 Marriage of Rudolph Valentino (Rodolpho Guglielmi), Italian-born US actor and cinema's first male sex symbol, to actress Jean Acker; the marriage lasted less than six hours.

1922 Discovery of Tutankhamun's tomb by British archaeologist Howard Carter (1874–1939).

1927 Installation of Britain's first automatic traffic lights, in Wolverhampton, West Midlands.

1930 US social critic Sinclair Lewis (1885–1951) was awarded the Nobel Prize for Literature, the first American to receive the honour.

1941 Birth of Art Garfunkel in Forest Hills, New York, singer and actor, and half of the duo Simon and Garfunkel.

1956 First broadcast for the British TV programme *What the Papers Say*.

1963 Birth of Tatum O'Neal in Los Angeles, California, actress, whose films include *Paper Moon* (1973).

1991 Death at sea of Robert Maxwell (b.1923 in Slatinske Doly, Czech Republic), British publisher and politician, chairman of the Mirror group of newspapers.

1994 US boxer George Foreman (b.1948) knocked out Michael Moorer to become, at 45, the oldest heavyweight champion in boxing history, regaining the title he had lost 20 years previously.

NOVEMBER

6

Feast of St Leonard, patron saint of black-smiths, captives, coopers, greengrocers, locksmiths, prisoners-of-war, and women in childbirth.

1429 Coronation of King Henry VI of England (r.1422–61, 1470–71).

1814 Birth of Adolf Sax in Dinant, Belgium (d.1894), musician, best known for his invention of the saxophone.

1851 Birth of Charles Henry Dow in Sterling, Connecticut (d.1902), financial journalist, whose name is given to the Dow Jones Index (with Edward D. Jones).

1860 Abraham Lincoln elected 16th president of the USA (1861–5).

1861 Birth of James Naismith in Almonte, Ontario (d.1939), physical education instructor, and originator of basketball in 1891 at the YMCA college, Springfield, Massachusetts.

1869 Discovery of diamonds at Kimberley, Cape Province, South Africa.

1901 Death of Kate Greenaway (b.1846 in London), artist and book-illustrator, who gave her name to the annual *Greenaway Medal* for the best British children's book artist.

1913 Arrest of Mahatma Gandhi (1869–1948) as he led a march of Indian miners in South Africa, including women and children, in a strike against the annual tax on free labourers.

1923 Birth of Donald Houston in Tonypandy, Wales, actor, whose films include *Room at the Top* (1958).

1928 Herbert Hoover was elected 31st president of the USA (1929–33).

1935 Maiden flight for the RAF's first monoplane fighter plane, the Hawker Hurricane, with a 990 hp Rolls Royce Merlin C engine.

1942 Repeal of a Church of England ruling that women should wear hats in church.

1949 Birth of Nigel Havers in London, actor, whose films include *Chariots of Fire* (1981).

1962 A royal decree issued by King Faisal abolished slavery in Saudi Arabia.

1975 The first public performance by British punk rock group The Sex Pistols, at St Martin's College of Art, London, was halted by college authorities after 10 minutes.

1984 The New York Stock Exchange remained open during a presidential election day for the first time in 193 years.

1999 Australian voters rejected proposals to change the Constitution and establish the Commonwealth of Australia as a republic.

NOVEMBER
7

National Day, Russia.
Feast of St Willibrord (c.658–739), patron
saint of The Netherlands.

1783 The last public hanging in Britain took place at Tyburn.

1865 The USA produced the first pocket cigarette-lighter.

1867 Birth of Marie Curie in Warsaw, Poland (d.1934), physicist, who worked in Paris with her French husband Pierre Curie (1859–1906) on magnetism and radioactivity.

1872 Commencement of the last voyage of the brigantine *Marie Celeste*, later found abandoned mid-Atlantic.

1885 Completion of the Canadian Pacific Railway, when the final spike of the transcontinental line was driven into place at Craigellachie, British Columbia.

1897 Birth of Herman J. Mankiewicz in New York (d.1953), screenwriter, who wrote *Citizen Kane* (1941) in collaboration with Orson Welles.

1918 Birth of Billy Graham in Charlotte, North Carolina, charismatic evangelist preacher.

1926 Birth of Dame Joan Sutherland in Sydney, New South Wales, Australia, operatic soprano, who made her debut in 1947.

1929 Britain proposed to ban vehicles with speeds over 60 mph.

1940 Collapse of part of the Tacoma Narrows Bridge, connecting the Olympic Peninsula with Tacoma, Washington, four months after opening.

1943 Birth of Joni Mitchell in McLeod, Alberta, singer and songwriter, whose songs include 'Both Sides Now' (1971).

1953 Birth of Lucinda Green in London, three-day eventer, the only person to win the Badminton Horse Trials six times (1973, 1976–7, 1979, 1983–4).

1962 Nelson Mandela was jailed for five years.

1967 British heavyweight boxing champion Henry Cooper (b.1934) beat Billy Walker (b.1939) to become the only boxer to win three Lonsdale belts outright.

1974 Disappearance of Lord Lucan (Richard John Bingham, b.1934), after nanny Sandra Rivett was battered to death in the family's London home; Lady Lucan escaped with severe head wounds.

1980 Death of Steve McQueen (b.1930 in Slater, Missouri), actor, whose films include *The Magnificent Seven* (1960).

2000 Police posed as cleaners, foiling an attempt to steal £350 million of diamonds from the Millennium Dome, London; the real jewels had been replaced by fakes.

2004 Death of Howard Keel (b.1919 in Gillespie, Illinois), star of MGM musicals.

NOVEMBER
8

1519 Hernán Cortés (1485–1547), conqueror of Mexico, entered Tenochtitlan, the Aztec capital, now Mexico City.

1659 Birth of Edmond Halley in London (d.1742), Astronomer Royal, best known for his discovery of the comet named after him.

1674 Death of John Milton (b.1608 in London), poet, best known for *Paradise Lost* (completed in 1665) and *Paradise Regained* (1671).

1793 Opening of the Louvre, Paris, the national museum of art.

1847 Birth of Bram Stoker in Dublin, Ireland (d.1912), novelist, the creator of *Dracula*.

1889 Montana became the 41st state of the Union.

1895 Discovery of X-rays by German physicist Wilhelm Röntgen (1845–1923), during an experiment at the University of Würzburg, Germany.

1909 Birth of Katharine Hepburn in Hartford, Connecticut (d.2003), actress, whose films include *On Golden Pond* (1981, Oscar).

1910 Patenting of an insect exterminator by William Frost of Spokane, Washington.

1920 The first Rupert bear cartoon appeared in the UK newspaper *Daily Express*.

1923 Attempt by Adolf Hitler to overthrow the Bavarian government in an abortive uprising, the 'Munich beer-hall putsch'.

1927 Birth of Ken Dodd in Liverpool, Merseyside, stand-up comedian, singer, and actor, whose hit songs include 'Happiness'.

1958 Publication of the first British album charts, in UK music magazine *Melody Maker*.

1960 Election of John F. Kennedy (1917–63) as president of the USA, defeating Richard Nixon.

1966 Election of Ronald Reagan (1911–2004), actor and future president of the USA, as governor of California.

1973 Ending of the second 'Cod War' between Britain and Iceland.

1974 Relocation of the Covent Garden fruit and vegetable market from central London to a new site at Nine Elms.

1987 Explosion of an IRA bomb at the cenotaph in Enniskillen, Northern Ireland, just before a Remembrance Day service.

1993 Theft of artwork valued at $52 million, including works by Picasso and Georges Braque, from the Museum of Modern Art in Stockholm, Sweden.

1997 Diversion of the Yangtze R, China, to make way for the Three Gorges Dam.

NOVEMBER
9

National Day, Cambodia.

1837 Moses Montefiore (1784–1885), Italian-born British stockbroker and philanthropist, became the first Jew to be knighted in England.

1841 Birth of Edward VII in London (d.1910), king of the United Kingdom (r.1901–10).

1858 First performance of the New York Symphony Orchestra.

1859 Abolition of flogging as a punishment in the British Army.

1907 Presentation of the Cullinan Diamond, the largest yet found, by the Transvaal government to King Edward VII of Britain on his 66th birthday.

1918 US statesman Herbert Hoover (1874–1964) was sent by President Wilson to Europe to represent the USA in the organization of food relief.

1922 Formation of the SS, Schutzstaffel, in Germany.

1934 Birth of Carl Sagan in New York (d.1996), astronomer and writer, who worked on the physics and chemistry of planetary atmospheres and surfaces.

1953 Death of Dylan Thomas (b.1914 in Swansea, Wales), poet, who also wrote a radio 'play for voices', *Under Milk Wood* (published 1954).

1961 US test pilot Robert White (b.1924) became the first man to fly an aircraft six times faster than the speed of sound, when he flew the X-15 rocket plane at 6587 kph/ 4093 mph.

1961 Birth of Jill Dando in Weston-Super-Mare, Avon (d.1999), television newsreader, who also presented such programmes as BBC's *Holiday* and *Crimewatch*.

1963 Death of over 450 Japanese miners, following an underground coal-dust explosion at the Mitsui Coal Mining Company colliery in Miike, Fukuoka Prefecture, Japan.

1965 Abolition of capital punishment in Britain.

1965 Sections of New York and nine other states were blacked out during the biggest power-cut in American history.

1967 Launch of the first Saturn V rocket, carrying the unmanned Apollo 4 spacecraft, from Kennedy Space Center, Florida.

1970 Death of Charles de Gaulle (b.1890 in Lille, France), French general, and first president of the Fifth Republic (1958–69).

1985 Anatoly Karpov lost the world chess championship title, which he had held for ten years, to Gary Kasparov.

1989 Opening of the Berlin Wall, erected in 1961 by East Germany to separate East Berlin from the part of the city occupied by the three main Western powers.

NOVEMBER

10

1697 Birth of William Hogarth in London (d.1764), painter and engraver, whose works include *Marriage à la Mode* (1743–5).

1728 Birth of Oliver Goldsmith in Kildare, Ireland (d.1774), playwright, novelist, and poet, whose works include 'The Deserted Village' (1770).

1759 Birth of Friedrich Schiller in Marbach, Germany (d.1805), historian, playwright, and poet, whose 'An die Freude' (Ode to Joy) was later set to music by Beethoven in his Choral Symphony.

1871 Explorer and journalist Henry Morton Stanley (1841–1904) found missionary Dr David Livingstone (1813–73) at Ujiji, Africa.

1880 Birth of Sir Jacob Epstein in New York (d.1959), British sculptor, an outstanding modeller of bronze portrait heads of celebrities and children.

1917 Ending of the third stage of the Battle of Ypres, one of the major battles in World War 1, when Canadian infantrymen took Passchendaele after months of trench warfare.

1919 Inauguration of Britain's first civil air-mail service, which operated between Hounslow and Paris.

1925 Birth of Richard Burton in Pontrhydfen, Wales (d.1984), actor, whose early films include *The Robe* (1953), for which he received one of his six Oscar nominations.

1928 Hirohito became emperor of Japan.

1933 The 'Black Blizzard', a huge dust storm, hit South Dakota.

1938 'Kristallnacht', when many Jewish synagogues, shops, and homes in Germany were destroyed or looted by the Nazis.

1944 Birth of Tim Rice in Amersham, Buckinghamshire, lyricist, writer, and broadcaster, whose works include *Jesus Christ Superstar* (1971).

1952 US travel writer Stanton Delaplane (1907–88) introduced Irish coffee to America at the Buena Vista Café, San Francisco, having discovered the drink at Shannon Airport, Ireland.

1954 Dedication of the Iwo Jima Memorial in Arlington, Virginia, based on the Pulitzer Prize-winning photograph 'Raising the Flag on Iwo Jima' by war photographer Joe Rosenthal.

1958 Donald Campbell broke the world water speed record on Lake Coniston, Cumbria, at an average of 400·11 kph/248·62 mph in his jetboat *Bluebird*.

1970 Opening of the Great Wall of China for tourism.

1982 Death of Leonid Brezhnev (b.1906 in Kamenskoye, Ukraine), president of the Supreme Soviet (1977–82).

2004 The Scottish cabinet voted to ban smoking in enclosed public places in Scotland.

NOVEMBER

11

Feast (Western Church) of St Martin of Tours (c.316–c.400), patron saint of France, geese, horse riders, inn-keepers, publicans, soldiers, and tailors.

Feast of St Mennas of Egypt, patron saint of desert caravans, merchants, and pilgrims.

1830 Britain's new Liverpool–Manchester railway line carried the first mail by rail.

1880 Execution of Ned Kelly (b.1855), Australian outlaw, at Melbourne jail, Australia.

1887 Construction began of Britain's Manchester Ship Canal.

1889 Washington became the 42nd state of the Union.

1918 The signing of the armistice, on the 11th hour of the 11th day of the 11th month, marked the end of World War 1.

1920 Burial of an unknown British soldier in Westminster Abbey, London; the grave, containing soil from France and covered by black Belgian marble, is known as the 'Grave of the Unknown Warrior'.

1921 The Royal British Legion held its first Poppy Day.

1925 Birth of June Whitfield in London, actress, whose work includes *Terry and June* (1979–87).

1940 The Willys-Overland Company began production of an all-purpose four-wheel drive jeep for the US Army; the name is derived from the letters GP (general purpose).

1945 Death of Jerome Kern (b.1885 in New York), songwriter, whose

compositions include 'Smoke Gets in Your Eyes' (1933).

1952 First demonstration of a video cassette recorder, in Beverly Hills, California.

1953 First broadcast of *Panorama*, BBC television's current affairs programme.

1964 Birth of Calista Flockhart in Freeport, Illinois, actress, best known for her title role in the television series *Ally McBeal* (1997–2002).

1965 Rhodesian prime minister Ian Smith announced a Unilateral Declaration of Independence (UDI) of Rhodesia from Britain.

1974 Birth of Leonardo DiCaprio in Los Angeles, California, actor, whose films include *William Shakespeare's Romeo & Juliet* (1996).

1987 *Irises*, by Dutch painter Vincent van Gogh (1853–90), was sold for $53.9 million at auction.

2004 Death of Yasser Arafat (b.1929 in Egypt), Palestinian leader, who shared the 1994 Nobel Peace Prize with Itzhak Rabin and Shimon Peres.

NOVEMBER

12

Feast of St Josaphat, patron saint of ecumenists.

Feast (Eastern Church) of St Martin of Tours (c.316–c.400), patron saint of France, geese, horse riders, inn-keepers, publicans, soldiers, and tailors.

1660 John Bunyan was jailed for preaching without a licence.

1840 Birth of Auguste Rodin in Paris, France (d.1917), sculptor, best known for *The Thinker*, in front of the Panthéon in Paris.

1841 First publication of the *Jewish Chronicle*, Britain's first Jewish newspaper.

1859 The first flying-trapeze act was performed by Jules Léotard at the Cirque Napoleon in Paris; the body-hugging costume he wore was later named after him.

1865 Death of Mrs Elizabeth Gaskell (b.1810 in London), novelist, whose works include *Cranford* (1853).

1912 The remains of Captain Scott and his companions were found in the Antarctic.

1919 Australian aviators Ross Macpherson Smith (1892–1922) and his brother, Keith (1890–1955), began the first aeroplane flight from England to Australia, taking 28 days in a Vickers Vimy biplane.

1929 Birth of Grace Kelly in Philadelphia, Pennsylvania (d.1982), actress, who retired from the screen when she married Prince Rainier III of Monaco.

1931 Opening of the Abbey Road recording studios in London by Sir Edward Elgar; the studios were later made famous when used by The Beatles.

1944 Sinking of the *Tirpitz*, last of Germany's fleet of unsinkable battleships, off Håkøy Island, Norway, by Lancaster bombers.

1951 First broadcast of BBC television's *Come Dancing*.

1954 Closure of Ellis Island, New York's main immigration control centre; since its opening in 1892 the centre had admitted c.15 million people into the USA.

1961 Birth of Nadia Comaneci in Onesti, Moldova, athlete, star of the 1976 Olympic Games when, aged 14, she won gold medals for Romania in the beam, vault, and floor disciplines.

1966 Birth of David Schwimmer in Astoria, New York, actor, best known as Ross Geller in the television series *Friends* (1994–2004).

1981 Space-shuttle Columbia became the first reusable spaceship when it made its second trip to low Earth orbit and back again.

1984 British chancellor of the exchequer Nigel Lawson (b.1932) announced withdrawal of the English £1 note.

NOVEMBER
13

Feast (Eastern Church) of St John Chrysostom (c.347–407), patron saint of preachers. Feast of St Homobonus, patron saint of clothworkers, merchants, and tailors.

1687 Death of Nell Gwyn (b.c.1650 probably in London), actress, and mistress of Charles II of England.

1770 Death of George Grenville (b.1712 in London), British prime minister (1763–5).

1831 Birth of James Clerk Maxwell in Edinburgh (d.1879), physicist, known for his theory of electromagnetic radiation.

1850 Birth of Robert Louis Stevenson in Edinburgh (d.1894), writer, whose novels include *Treasure Island* (1883).

1862 Author Lewis Carroll (1832–98) began writing *Alice's Adventures in Wonderland*.

1887 Trafalgar Square, London, became the site of 'Bloody Sunday', when many were injured during riots by the unemployed.

1895 The first shipment of canned pineapple left Hawaii for the USA.

1907 French bicycle-maker Paul Cornu (1881–1944) became the first person to rise vertically in powered free flight, in a helicopter using two counter-rotating rotors to cancel torque.

1914 Patenting of the brassière by US heiress Mary Phelps Jacob, developed from her first attempt using two handkerchiefs and some baby ribbon.

1925 Opening of the inner coffin of Tutankhamun in Luxor, Egypt.

1928 Death of Enrico Cecchetti (b.1850 in Milan, Italy), dancer, teacher, and choreographer, who became ballet master of Diaghilev's Ballet Russes.

1940 Opening of Walt Disney's film *Fantasia* in New York.

1952 US physician Paul Zoll (1911–99) became the first man to use electric shock to treat cardiac arrest.

1955 Birth of Whoopi Goldberg in New York, actress, whose films include *The Color Purple* (1985).

1965 The word 'fuck' was used for the first time on BBC television, by theatre critic Kenneth Tynan (1927–80), during a live debate on censorship.

1971 Mariner 9 went into orbit around Mars.

1973 Death of Elsa Schiaparelli (b.1896 in Rome), fashion designer, noted for her use of colour and traditional fabrics.

1987 BBC television screened its first (unbranded) condom commercial, with a view to encouraging safe sex.

NOVEMBER
14

1666 Report by English diarist Samuel Pepys (1633–1703) of the first recorded blood transfusion, which was between dogs.

1765 Birth of Robert Fulton in Lancaster Co, Pennsylvania (d.1815), engineer, inventor, and artist, whose inventions include the *Nautilus* diving boat (1800).

1840 Birth of Claude Monet in Paris (d.1926), painter, whose painting *Impression: Sunrise* (1872) gave the Impressionist movement its name.

1863 Birth of Leo Baekeland in Ghent, Belgium (d.1944), chemist, a founder of the plastics industry.

1896 Britain no longer required automobiles to be preceded by a man waving a red flag, and the speed limit was raised from 4 mph to 14 mph.

1900 Birth of Aaron Copland in New York (d.1990), composer, whose works include *Appalachian Spring* (1944).

1908 German mathematical physicist Albert Einstein (1879–1955) presented his quantum theory of light.

1910 US navy officer Eugene Ely (1886–1911) was the first person to take off in an aeroplane from a ship deck, flying from USS *Birmingham* at Hampton Roads to Norfolk, Virginia.

1922 Transmission of the BBC's first regular news bulletin.

1932 First sales of book tokens in Britain.

1940 Most of Coventry, including its medieval cathedral, was destroyed by 500 German Luftwaffe bombers during World War 2.

1941 Sinking of Britain's aircraft carrier *Ark Royal*, torpedoed by a German submarine.

1948 Birth of Charles, Prince of Wales, in Buckingham Palace, London.

1952 Publication of Britain's first pop music chart, in the *New Musical Express*.

1969 Launch of Apollo 12, the second mission to the Moon, from Cape Kennedy, Florida.

1969 BBC television began broadcasting in colour.

1973 Marriage of Princess Anne and Captain Mark Phillips.

1973 British footballer Bobby Moore (1941–93) played his final game for England at Wembley, London.

1990 Death of Malcolm Muggeridge (b.1903 in London), journalist, writer, and media personality.

1994 The first paying customers travelled from London to Paris through the Channel Tunnel.

NOVEMBER
15

Feast of St Albertus Magnus (c.1200–1280), known as Doctor Universalis ('Universal Doctor'), patron saint of scientists.

1708 Birth of William Pitt, 1st Earl of Chatham, in Hayes, London (d.1788), statesman, who formed a new ministry in 1766.

1738 Birth of Sir William Herschel in Hanover, Germany (d.1822), astronomer, who built the largest reflecting telescopes of the day.

1805 US explorers Meriwether Lewis (1774–1809) and William Clark (1770–1838) reached the mouth of the Columbia River, completing their trek to the Pacific Ocean.

1806 US military explorer Zebulon Pike (1779–1813) discovered the Colorado peak that now bears his name (Pike's Peak), even though he didn't climb it.

1837 Publication of the shorthand system, *Stenographic Sound Hand*, invented by educationist Sir Isaac Pitman (1813–97).

1891 Birth of Erwin Rommel in Heidenheim, Germany (d.1944), field marshal in World War 2.

1905 Birth of Mantovani in Venice, Italy (d.1980), violinist, composer, and conductor of popular light music.

1918 Victory Day in Britain, following the end of World War 1.

1920 Delegates from 41 nations attended the First Assembly of the League of Nations at Geneva, Switzerland.

1932 Birth of Petula Clark in Epsom, Surrey, singer and actress, best known for hits such as 'Downtown'.

1942 Birth of Daniel Barenboim in Buenos Aires, Argentina, pianist and conductor, the BBC Reith lecturer in 2006.

1956 Premiere of *Love Me Tender*, the first film starring US rock singer Elvis Presley.

1958 Death of Tyrone Power (b.1914 in Cincinnati, Ohio), actor, whose films include *The Mark of Zorro* (1940).

1960 USS *George Washington*, the first submarine with nuclear missiles, sailed from Charleston, South Carolina.

1968 End of the final voyage of the *Queen Elizabeth*, at the time the largest passenger ship ever built.

1972 Announcement of a kidney donor scheme by the British government.

1983 With the arrival of Cruise missiles at the US air-base at Greenham Common, Berkshire, the Women's Peace Movement began its first protest.

2001 Launch of Xbox, the video-game console, in the USA by Microsoft.

NOVEMBER
16

Feast of St Gertrude of Helfta (1256–1302), patron saint of the West Indies.
Feast of St Margaret (c.1046–93), patron saint of Scotland.

1665 First day of publication of the *London Gazette*.

1824 Discovery of the Murray River in Australia by explorer Hamilton Hume (1797–1873).

1841 Patenting of the cork life-preserver (life-jacket) by Napoleon Guerin of New York.

1869 Formal opening of the Suez Canal at Port Said, which shortened the journey from England to India by 6500 km/4000 miles.

1873 Birth of W(illiam) C(hristopher) Handy in Florence, Alabama (d.1958), blues composer, whose works include 'St Louis Blues' (1914).

1902 Start of a Teddy bear craze after a cartoon by Clifford Berryman showed US president Theodore 'Teddy' Roosevelt refusing to shoot a captured bear during a hunting trip.

1907 Oklahoma became the 46th state of the Union.

1920 Introduction in the USA of the first commercial postage meter, designed and developed by inventor Arthur Pitney and entrepreneur Walter H. Bowes.

1933 US president Franklin D. Roosevelt and Soviet people's commissar for foreign affairs Maxim Litvinov exchanged notes to establish the first diplomatic relations between the USA and the USSR.

1953 Birth of Griff Rhys Jones in Cardiff, comic actor and writer, whose television work includes *Not The Nine O'Clock News* (1979–81).

1959 Opening of the stage show *The Sound of Music* on Broadway, New York.

1960 Death of Clark Gable (b.1901 in Cadiz, Ohio), actor, best known for his role as Rhett Butler in *Gone With the Wind* (1939).

1961 Birth of Frank Bruno in London, boxer, and former World, European and British heavyweight champion.

1965 Launch of Soviet spacecraft Venera III towards Venus.

1982 Death of Arthur Askey (b.1900 in Liverpool), comedian, who achieved recognition on radio with *Band Wagon* (from 1938).

1986 Announcement from US company Gerber Products that their baby food would be produced in plastic containers, rather than the traditional glass jars.

2000 British actor Michael Caine (b.1933) was knighted by the queen as Sir Maurice Micklewhite for services to drama.

2004 An unpiloted NASA X-43A jet reached a record speed of 10,460 kph/6500 mph/ (Mach 9·6) using the scramjet engine.

NOVEMBER
17

Feast of St Elizabeth of Hungary (1207–31), patron saint of bakers, charitable societies, and nurses.

1558 Elizabeth Tudor acceded to the English throne as Queen Elizabeth I on the death of Mary I.

1603 English courtier Sir Walter Raleigh (1552–1618) went on trial for treason.

1768 Death of Thomas Pelham, 1st Duke of Newcastle (b.1693), British prime minister (1754–6, 1757–62).

1800 Following ten years in Philadelphia, the US Senate of the Sixth Congress met for the first time at the partially completed Capitol Building in Washington, DC.

1855 Discovery of the Victoria Falls by explorer David Livingstone (1813–73).

1875 Founding of the Theosophical Society in New York by Helena Petrovna Blavatsky (1831–91) and Henry Steel Olcott (1832–1907).

1880 In Britain, the first three women to graduate received Bachelor of Arts degrees from the University of London.

1913 Kaiser Wilhelm of Germany, who disapproved of such contact dances as the waltz and polka, banned the armed forces from dancing the tango.

1937 Birth of Peter Cook in Torquay, Devon (d.1995), comedian and actor, who became known for his collaboration with Dudley Moore in *Not Only … But Also* (1965–71).

1942 Birth of Martin Scorsese in Flushing, Long Island, New York, director, writer, and producer, whose films include *Taxi Driver* (1976).

1944 Birth of Danny De Vito in Neptune, New Jersey, actor, whose films include *Twins* (1988).

1966 Opening of *Don't Drink the Water* on Broadway, the first play written by actor and director Woody Allen (b.1935).

1970 Twenty-year-old German Stephanie Rahn became the *Sun* newspaper's first Page Three girl.

1970 Landing of unmanned Soviet spacecraft Luna 17 on the Moon.

1989 Riot police arrested hundreds of people in Prague taking part in the biggest anti-government demonstrations in Czechoslovakia for 20 years.

1990 Discovery of a mass grave of World War 2 prisoners-of-war near the notorious bridge over the R Kwai, Thailand.

1997 Six gunmen killed over 60 foreign tourists at the Hatshepsut Temple, Luxor, Egypt; the gunmen, members of the Gamaa al-Islamiya, were all killed.

2003 Inauguration of Arnold Schwarzenegger (b.1947), US bodybuilder and actor, as 38th governor of California.

NOVEMBER
18

1477 The first book was printed in England, by printer William Caxton (c.1422–91).

1626 Consecration of the Basilica di San Pietro (St Peter's Cathedral) by Pope Urban VIII in the Vatican, Rome.

1789 Birth of Louis Jacques Mandé Daguerre in Cormeilles, France (d.1851), photographic pioneer, who perfected the photographic process named after him.

1836 Birth of Sir W(illiam) S(chwenck) Gilbert in London (d.1911), parodist and librettist, remembered for his partnership with composer Sir Arthur Sullivan (1842–1900), begun in 1871.

1883 Institution of five standard continental time zones by American and Canadian railroads, ending the confusion of thousands of local times.

1901 Birth of George Gallup in Jefferson, Iowa (d.1984), public opinion expert, who founded the American Institute of Public Opinion (1935).

1903 The Panama Canal strip was granted by treaty to the USA.

1916 Ending of World War 1's Battle of the Somme.

1923 Birth of Alan Shepard in East Derry, New Hampshire (d.1998), the first US astronaut in space.

1928 Premiere of Walt Disney's *Steamboat Willie*, the first Mickey Mouse film, with synchronized sound, in New York.

1935 Members of the League of Nations enforced economic sanctions against Italy, when that country invaded Ethiopia.

1941 Birth of David Hemmings in Guildford, Surrey (d.2003), actor, whose films include *Gladiator* (2000).

1962 Death of Niels Henrik Bohr (b.1885 in Copenhagen, Denmark), physicist, who was awarded the 1922 Nobel Prize for Physics.

1963 Opening of Britain's Dartford tunnel under the Thames, linking Kent and Essex.

1969 Death of Ted Heath (b.1900 in Wandsworth, London), trombonist, and bandleader of his own Big Band.

1978 Over 900 members of the cult 'People's Temple' commited mass suicide in Guyana.

1987 Thirty people died when fire broke out at King's Cross Underground station on the Piccadilly Line, London.

1991 British hostage Terry Waite was freed from the Lebanon.

2000 Marriage of US film star Michael Douglas (b.1944) to Welsh actress Catherine Zeta-Jones (b.1969).

2004 Fox-hunting was outlawed in England and Wales.

NOVEMBER
19

1620 The Pilgrim Fathers anchored off Cape Cod in the *Mayflower*.

1769 Opening of Blackfriars Bridge, across London's R Thames, for carriages.

1794 Conclusion of the Treaty of Amity, Commerce and Navigation between the USA and Britain; it resolved some issues from the Revolutionary War and was the first US extradition treaty.

1798 Death of Theobald Wolfe Tone (b.1763 in Dublin), Irish nationalist, who committed suicide in the Provost's prison, Dublin.

1828 Death of Franz Schubert (b.1797 in Vienna, Austria), composer, whose works include the 'Unfinished' Symphony.

1850 Purchase of the first life-insurance policy issued to a woman by 36-year-old Carolyn Ingraham of Madison, New Jersey.

1850 Appointment of Alfred, Lord Tennyson (1809–92) as British poet laureate by Queen Victoria.

1863 US President Abraham Lincoln delivered the Gettysburg address.

1889 Invention of table tennis by British engineer James Gibb and his family when hitting champagne corks across a table with cigar-box lids; it was first named Gossima, then ping-pong.

1928 *Time* magazine's first colour cover featured a portrait of Japanese Emperor Hirohito.

1942 Birth of Calvin Klein in New York, fashion designer.

1946 The first UNESCO conference opened in Paris, with representatives from 30 governments.

1961 Birth of Meg Ryan in Fairfield, Connecticut, actress, whose films include *When Harry Met Sally* (1989).

1962 Birth of Jodie Foster in New York, actress and director, whose films include *The Silence of the Lambs* (1991).

1969 The US Apollo 12 lunar module, with astronauts Charles Conrad (1930–99) and Alan Bean (b.1932), made the second manned landing on the Moon.

1969 Brazilian footballer Pelé (b.1940) scored his 1000th goal in his 909th professional football match.

1990 The signing of the Treaty of Conventional Armed Forces in Paris ended the 'Cold War'.

1994 Opening of Britain's new National Lottery draw; c.25 million tickets were sold.

1996 Closure of the Channel Tunnel, following a lorry fire in one section.

2002 The oil tanker *Prestige* broke in two and sank in the Atlantic Ocean off NW Spain, at a cost of more than $1·05 billion.

NOVEMBER
20

1752 Birth of Thomas Chatterton in Bristol, Avon (d.1770), poet, who took his own life at seventeen.

1759 Defeat of the French by the British fleet under Admiral Hawke at the Battle of Quiberon Bay off the French coast, thwarting an invasion of England.

1805 Beethoven's *Fidelio* had its first performance in Vienna, Austria.

1818 Independence of Venezuela from Spain.

1866 Patenting of the 'bone shaker' bicycle by Pierre Lallemont in Paris.

1906 Founding of Rolls-Royce Ltd in Britain by C(harles) S(tewart) Rolls (1877–1910) and Sir Henry Royce (1863–1933).

1908 Birth of Alistair Cooke in Manchester (d.2004), US-based broadcaster and journalist, and commentator on current affairs.

1917 Beginning of the Battle of Cambrai in France, in which the British deployed large numbers of tanks (324) for the first time.

1945 Beginning of the Nuremberg War Crimes Trial.

1947 Marriage of Princess Elizabeth to Lieutenant Philip Mountbatten in Westminster Abbey, London.

1954 Death of Clyde Cessna (b.1879 in Hawthorne, Louisiana), aviator, and founder of the Cessna Aircraft Company.

1962 Lifting of the US blockade on Cuba.

1970 The British ten-shilling note ceased to be legal tender.

1975 Death of General Francisco Franco (b.1892 in El Ferrol, Galicia, Spain), Spanish general and dictator.

1992 Twenty watercolours attributed to German dictator Adolf Hitler (1889–1945) failed to attract a single bidder at auction in Trieste, Italy.

1992 Fire at Windsor Castle, Berkshire, damaged or destroyed more than 100 rooms; the castle reopened in 1997 after five years of work costing £37 million.

1995 Diana, Princess of Wales, spoke openly for the first time about her separation from Charles, Prince of Wales, in an interview for BBC Television.

1999 Launch of China's first spacecraft, the unmanned Shenzhou ('Divine Vessel'), from the Jiuquan launch centre, Gansu.

2000 West Londoner Judith Keppel became the first £1 million jackpot winner on the UK television quiz programme *Who Wants To Be a Millionaire?*

2002 German anatomist Gunther von Hagens (b.1945) conducted Britain's first public autopsy in more than 170 years, attended by 500 people at the Atlantis Gallery, London.

NOVEMBER
21

1694 Birth of Voltaire in Paris (d.1778), writer, whose works include the satirical novella, *Candide* (1759).

1783 The first successful manned free flight in a hot-air balloon, when Frenchmen François de Rozier and François Laurent flew for 25 minutes above Paris.

1787 Birth of Sir Samuel Cunard in Halifax, Nova Scotia (d.1865), shipowner, who helped found the British and North American Royal Mail Steam Packet Co, later known as the Cunard Line.

1789 North Carolina became the 12th state of the Union.

1831 Michael Faraday presented his paper on 'Experimental Research into Electricity' to the Royal Society.

1843 Patenting of the vulcanization of rubber in England by Thomas Hancock.

1871 The first 'human cannonball', Emilio Onra, was fired from a cannon.

1898 Birth of René Magritte in Lessines, Belgium (d.1967), Surrealist painter, whose works include *The Wind and the Song* (1928–9).

1904 Motorized omnibuses replaced horse-drawn cars in Paris.

1918 Royal Assent was given to a bill in Britain making women eligible to stand as MPs.

1920 Bloody Sunday: the IRA killed 14 British soldiers, the Black and Tans retaliated, attacking spectators and players at a football match in Croke Park, Dublin, killing 14 and wounding 65.

1936 Britain's first television gardening programme, *In Your Garden with Mr Middleton*, was broadcast by the BBC from a garden outside Alexandra Palace studios.

1945 Birth of Goldie Hawn in Washington, DC, actress, whose films include *The First Wives Club* (1996).

1953 The skull of the 'Piltdown Man', found by Charles Dawson in Sussex, was proved to be a hoax.

1974 Twenty died and 200 were injured by IRA bomb explosions in two public houses in central Birmingham, UK.

1980 An estimated 82 million people in the USA watched the television show *Dallas* to find out who shot JR.

1989 Britain's parliamentary proceedings were televised for the first time.

1994 Death of Telly Savalas (b.1924 in Long Island, New York), Greek-American film and television actor, best known as Kojak, detective in the television series of the same name.

NOVEMBER
22

National Day, Lebanon.
Feast of St Cecilia (2nd c or 3rd c), patron saint of musical instrument makers and musicians.

1497 Portuguese navigator Vasco da Gama (c.1469–1525) became the first person to sail round the Cape of Good Hope, in his search for a sea route to India.

1808 Birth of Thomas Cook in Melbourne, Derbyshire (d.1892), railway excursion and tourist pioneer, who organized his first railway excursion in 1841, from Leicester to Loughborough.

1819 Birth of George Eliot, pseudonym of Mary Ann Evans, at Astley, Warwickshire (d.1880), author, whose novels include *The Mill on the Floss* (1860).

1869 Launch of the sailing ship *Cutty Sark* at Dumbarton on the R Clyde, Scotland.

1906 Adoption of the SOS distress signal at the International Radio Telegraphic Convention in Berlin, replacing CQD.

1910 Patenting by Arthur F. Knight of a tubular steel shaft to replace wooden shafts in golf clubs.

1913 Birth of Edward Benjamin Britten in Lowestoft, Suffolk (d.1976), composer, whose works include the opera *Peter Grimes* (1945).

1930 Birth of Sir Peter Hall in Bury St Edmunds, Suffolk, director, who succeeded Sir Laurence Olivier as head of the National Theatre (1973–88).

1940 Birth of Terry Gilliam in Minneapolis, Michigan, artist and director, who produced the fantasy animations in *Monty Python's Flying Circus* (1969–74).

1946 Ballpoint pens, invented by Hungarian journalist László Bíró (1899–1985), went on sale in Britain at nearly £3.

1956 Opening of the 16th Olympic Games in Melbourne, Australia.

1963 Assassination of President John F. Kennedy in Dallas, Texas.

1963 Death of C(live) S(taples) Lewis (b.1898 in Belfast), academic and writer, whose works include the *Chronicles of Narnia* (from 1950).

1977 Beginning of regular flights to Kennedy Airport, New York, from London and Paris by Concorde.

1980 Death of Mae West (b.1892 in New York), film actress, whose name was given to a pneumatic life jacket.

1986 US boxer Mike Tyson (b.1966) defeated Trevor Berbick and became the youngest-ever world heavyweight champion at 20 years 4 months.

1990 Resignation of Margaret Thatcher (b.1925), British prime minister, who became the first woman party leader in British politics.

NOVEMBER
23

Feast (Western Church) of St Clement I (late 1st c), known as Clemens Romanus or Clement of Rome, patron saint of boatmen, lighthousekeepers, and sick children.

1434 In Britain, the R Thames froze over, with ice stretching from below London Bridge to Gravesend.

1585 Death of Thomas Tallis (b.c.1505), English musician, organist, and composer, 'the father of English cathedral music'.

1804 Birth of Franklin Pierce in Hillsborough, New Hampshire (d.1869), 14th president of the USA (1853–7).

1835 Patenting of a machine to make horseshoes by Henry Burden of Troy, New York.

1852 Installation of Britain's first pillar box, in St Helier, Jersey.

1859 Birth of William H. Bonney, known as Billy the Kid, in New York (d.1881), outlaw and gunfighter.

1887 Birth of Boris Karloff in London (d.1969), film star, who made his name as the monster in *Frankenstein* (1931).

1889 Louis T. Glass and William S. Arnold installed their first coin-operated phonograph in the Palais Royale Saloon, San Francisco.

1910 Hanging of Dr Crippen at Pentonville Prison, London, for the murder of his wife, Cora.

1936 Publication of the first edition of *Life* magazine.

1963 The BBC broadcast the first episode of *Dr Who*; the Doctor was played by William Hartnell (1908–75).

1964 Opening of Manx, Britain's first commercial radio station.

1979 Death of Merle Oberon (b.1911 in Mumbai (Bombay), India), British actress, whose films include *Wuthering Heights* (1939).

1980 Violent earthquakes in southern Italy, measuring up to 6·8, killed over 4800 people and destroyed many villages.

1984 A fire at Oxford Circus, London's busiest underground station, trapped nearly 1000 people in smoke-filled tunnels for three hours.

1990 Death of Roald Dahl (b.1916 in Cardiff), writer, whose children's books include *James and the Giant Peach* (1961).

2002 Removal of the Miss World beauty contest to London from Nigeria, after riots by Muslims opposing the show left 215 people dead and more than 500 injured in Kaduna.

NOVEMBER
24

Feast (Eastern Church) of St Clement I (late 1st c), known as Clemens Romanus or Clement of Rome, patron saint of boatmen, lighthousekeepers, and sick children.

1642 Discovery of Van Dieman's land (now Tasmania) by navigator Abel Tasman (1603–c.59).

1713 Birth of Laurence Sterne in Clonmel, Co Tipperary, Ireland (d.1768), author and clergyman, best known for his comic novel *The Life and Opinions of Tristram Shandy* (1759–67).

1784 Birth of Zachary Taylor in Orange Co, Virginia (d.1850), 12th president of the USA (1849–50).

1849 Birth of Frances Hodgson Burnett in Manchester (d.1924), author, who wrote over 40 novels, including *The Secret Garden* (1911).

1859 Publication of naturalist Charles Darwin's *On the Origin of Species*.

1868 Opening of Smithfield meat market in London.

1874 Patenting of an improved type of barbed wire by US inventor Joseph Glidden (1813–1906).

1914 Ending of the first stage of the Battle of Ypres, one of the major battles in World War 1.

1942 Birth of Billy Connolly in Glasgow, comedian and actor, best known for his one-man comedy performances.

1950 Opening of the musical *Guys and Dolls* in New York.

1955 Birth of Ian Botham in Heswall, Cheshire, cricketer, Worcestershire and England all-rounder.

1962 First broadcast for British television's *That Was The Week That Was*.

1963 Death of Lee Harvey Oswald (b.1939 in New Orleans, Louisiana), alleged killer of President John F. Kennedy; he was shot by nightclub owner Jack Ruby before he could come to trial.

1973 Aborigines in Australia were granted the vote.

1991 Death of Freddie Mercury (b.1946 in Zanzibar, Tanzania), British pop star, who formed the group Queen in 1971.

1993 Sale at Christie's auction of the last 14 bottles of Scotch whisky salvaged from the 1941 wreck of SS *Politician*, inspiration of the book and film *Whisky Galore*.

1995 Voters in Ireland approved a constitutional amendment legalizing divorce (after a 70-year ban) and remarriage by 818,841 votes to 809,731 after a recount.

NOVEMBER
25

Feast of St Catherine of Alexandria (?–307), patron saint of the clergy, girls, knifegrinders, librarians, millers, nurses, old maids, philosophers, spinners, students, tanners, turners, and wheelwrights.

1783 Evacuation of New York by the British, their last military position in America, during the Revolutionary War.

1835 Birth of Andrew Carnegie, in Dunfermline, Fife (d.1919), steel industrialist, who gave millions of dollars to public institutions in the UK and USA.

1837 Patenting of the silk power-loom by William Crompton of Taunton, Massachusetts.

1844 Birth of Karl Benz in Karlsruhe, Germany (d.1929), engineer and car manufacturer, founder of Benz & Co, which merged in 1926 to form Daimler-Benz & Co.

1867 Patenting of dynamite, a mixture of nitroglycerine and silica, by Swedish chemist Alfred Nobel (1833–96).

1882 Premiere of Gilbert and Sullivan's *Iolanthe* in London.

1884 Patenting of evaporated milk by Swiss-born food scientist John B. Meyenberg (1847–1914).

1914 Birth of Joe DiMaggio in Martinez, California (d.1999), baseball player, who spent his entire career as an outfielder for the New York Yankees (1936–51).

1923 First transatlantic radio broadcast from Britain to America.

1937 Death of Lilian Baylis (b.1874 in London), theatrical manager, and founder of the Old Vic Theatre, London.

1949 Death of Bill Robinson, also known as Bojangles (b.1878 in Richmond, Virginia), tapdancer, who starred in the movie *Stormy Weather* (1943).

1952 First performance of Agatha Christie's *The Mousetrap*, which has had the longest continuous run of any theatre show in the world.

1963 The funeral of John F. Kennedy took place.

1969 Ex-Beatle John Lennon (1940–80) returned his MBE, in protest against Britain's involvement in Biafra, and US involvement in Vietnam.

1970 Japanese writer Yukio Mishima (b.1925) committed seppuku (ritual disembowelment) with his sword after making a speech attacking Japan's post-war constitution.

1973 Greek military dictator George Papadopoulos was deposed by rival officers in a bloodless coup.

1974 British home secretary Roy Jenkins announced that the IRA was to be declared illegal in the UK.

1983 Death of Anton Dolin (b.1904 in Slinfold, West Sussex), dancer and choreographer, who co-founded the Markova–Dolin Ballet.

NOVEMBER
26

1379 Foundation of New College, Oxford, by English clergyman William of Wykeham (1324–1404).

1607 Birth of John Harvard in London (d.1638), colonist, who left his wealth to a new school in New Towne, Massachusetts (founded 1636), named Harvard College in 1639.

1703 England was hit by severe gales, known as the 'Great Storm', in which 8000 people died.

1716 The first lion to be exhibited in America went on display in Boston, Massachusetts.

1783 Annapolis, Maryland, became the first peacetime US capital, and the meeting place of the US Congress until 3 June 1784.

1789 The first Thanksgiving Day was held in the USA to commemorate the Pilgrim Fathers' harvest in 1623.

1867 Patenting of a refrigerated railway carriage by US inventor J. B. Sutherland.

1894 Marriage of Nicholas II, last tsar of Russia, to Alexandra Feodorovna at the Winter Palace, St Petersburg.

1905 Birth of Emlyn Williams in Pen-y-ffordd, Flintshire, Wales (d.1987), actor, playwright, and director, whose plays include *Night Must Fall* (1935).

1910 Birth of Cyril Cusack in Durban, South Africa (d.1993), actor, director, and playwright, who toured Ireland with his own theatre company.

1923 Birth of Pat Phoenix in Portnum, Co Galway, Ireland (d.1986), actress, best known as Elsie Tanner in the television soap *Coronation Street* (1960–).

1939 Birth of Tina Turner in Nutbush, Tennessee, pop singer, part of the vocal duo Ike and Tina Turner.

1949 India became an independent republic within the common-wealth.

1956 Death of Tommy Dorsey (b.1905 in Shenandoah, Pennsylvania), trombonist and bandleader, whose big bands were sometimes co-led by his brother Jimmy Dorsey.

1965 France became the third country to enter space, with the launch of a Diamant rocket carrying a satellite into orbit from the Hammaguir test site, Algeria.

1966 Opening of the world's first tidal power-station on the Rance Estuary, St-Malo, in Ille-et-Vilaine department, France.

1979 The International Olympic Committee voted to readmit China after an absence of 21 years.

1983 £25m worth of gold bullion, weighing 3 tons, was stolen from Heathrow airport, London.

1998 Tony Blair became the first British prime minister to address the Irish parliament.

NOVEMBER
27

8 BC Death of Horace (b. 65 BC near Venusia, Italy), Latin poet and satirist, whose greatest work was the three books of *Odes* (19 BC).

1701 Birth of Anders Celsius in Uppsala, Sweden (d.1744), astronomer, who devised the centigrade scale (Celsius scale) of temperature (1742).

1895 Swedish chemist and industrialist Alfred Nobel (1833–96) signed his last will, providing for the establishment of the Nobel Prizes.

1911 First recorded instance of overripe vegetables being thrown at actors in the USA, during *The Playboy in America* by Lady Augusta Gregory, Maxine Elliott Theatre, New York.

1914 First day of duty for Britain's first policewomen, in Grantham, Lincolnshire.

1919 A huge meteor landed in Lake Michigan, USA.

1925 Birth of Ernie Wise in Leeds, West Yorkshire (d.1999), comedian, who teamed up with fellow entertainer Eric Morecambe in 1943 to become Britain's leading comedy double-act.

1926 Jazz trumpeter and singer Louis Armstrong (1901–71) recorded 'You Made Me Love You'.

1938 Birth of Rodney Bewes in Bingley, West Yorkshire, comedy actor, best known for the BBC television series *The Likely Lads* (1964–6).

1940 Birth of Bruce Lee in San Francisco, California (d.1973), martial-arts film star, best known for *Enter the Dragon* (1973).

1942 Birth of Jimi Hendrix in Seattle, Washington (d.1970), rock guitarist, singer, and songwriter, who formed the band The Jimi Hendrix Experience.

1957 Indian prime minister Jawaharlal Nehru made a speech for nuclear disarmament, and appealed to the USA and USSR to end nuclear tests and begin disarmament.

1970 Bolivian artist Benjamin Mendoza, disguised as a priest, attempted to assassinate Pope Paul VI at Manila airport in the Philippines.

1970 First major rally of the UK Gay Liberation Movement, when c.80 members met for a torchlight demonstration on Highbury Fields, Islington, London.

1970 Sotheby's auctioneers, London, sold a Velázquez portrait for £2·3 million.

1975 Death of Ross McWhirter (b.1925 in London), shot on his doorstep by an Irish gunman; he and his twin brother, Norris, compiled *The Guinness Book of Records*.

2002 Daniel Baraniuk of Gdańsk, Poland, set a new pole-sitting world record of 196 days at Heidepark amusement park, Soltau, Germany.

NOVEMBER
28

1520 Portuguese navigator Ferdinand Magellan (c.1480–1521) reached an ocean which he named the 'Pacific', because it was so calm.

1582 Marriage of William Shakespeare (1564–1616) to Anne Hathaway (1556–1623).

1660 Foundation of the Royal Society, London.

1757 Birth of William Blake in London (d.1827), poet, painter, and engraver, best known for *Songs of Innocence* (1789) and *Songs of Experience* (1794).

1820 Birth of Friedrich Engels in Barmen, Germany (d.1895), Socialist philosopher and businessman, who collaborated with Karl Marx and was a founder of 'Scientific Socialism'.

1829 [16 November, Old Style calendar] Birth of Anton Rubinstein in Vykhvatinets, Russia (d.1894), pianist and composer.

1859 Death of Washington Irving (b.1783 in New York), pseudonym of Geoffrey Crayon, author of 'Rip Van Winkle'.

1872 German Wilhelm Reiss and Colombian Angel Maria Escobar became the first climbers to reach the top of Cotopaxi, Ecuador, the world's highest active volcano.

1905 Foundation of the Sinn Féin Irish Party by Irish nationalist politician Arthur Griffith (1872–1922) in Dublin, Ireland.

1909 A law passed in Paris allowed pregnant workers eight weeks' maternity leave.

1919 Viscountess Nancy Astor (1879–1964) became the first woman MP, when she won her husband's former Plymouth seat following his elevation to the peerage.

1942 Beginning of coffee rationing in the USA, which lasted throughout World War 2.

1948 First sales of Polaroid cameras, in Boston, Massachusetts.

1961 Birth of Martin Clunes in London, actor, best known for the television series *Men Behaving Badly* (1992–5).

1963 US president Lyndon B. Johnson announced the renaming of Cape Canaveral as Cape Kennedy, in honour of his assassinated predecessor; the name reverted to Cape Canaveral in 1973.

1964 Launch of US space probe Mariner 4 towards Mars; it passed within 8690 km/5400 miles of the planet in July 1965.

1968 Death of Enid Blyton (b.1897 in London), children's writer, who published over 600 books.

1990 British prime minister Margaret Thatcher (b.1925) tendered her formal resignation to the queen, and left Downing Street.

2000 The Netherlands became the first country to legalize euthanasia, when its parliament approved a bill by a majority of 104 to 40.

NOVEMBER
29

1530 Death of Cardinal Thomas Wolsey (b.1475 in Ipswich, Suffolk), clergyman and statesman, who died on his way to be tried for high treason.

1803 Birth of Christian Johann Doppler in Salzburg, Austria (d.1853), physicist, who described the *Doppler effect*.

1814 *The Times* of London became the first newspaper to be printed on a steam-operated press.

1825 Rossini's *The Barber of Seville* (1816) was the first Italian opera to be performed in the USA, at the Park Theater, New York.

1849 Birth of Sir John Ambrose Fleming in Lancaster, Lancashire (d.1945), physicist, who pioneered the application of electricity to lighting and heating on a large scale.

1895 Birth of Busby Berkeley in Los Angeles, California (d.1976), director, who became one of the cinema's most innovative choreographers.

1907 British nurse Florence Nightingale was the first woman to receive the Order of Merit, presented by King Edward VII for her work during the Crimean War.

1924 Death of Giacomo Puccini in Lucca, Italy (b.1858), operatic composer, whose works include *La Bohème* (1896).

1929 US aviator and explorer Richard Byrd (1888–1957) navigated the first aeroplane flight over the South Pole.

1934 First live radio broadcast of a royal wedding: the marriage of the Duke of Kent to Princess Marina at Westminster Abbey, London.

1947 The UN General Assembly approved Britain's plan to resolve Arab–Jewish conflict in the British mandate of Palestine by partitioning the territory into Jewish and Arab states.

1961 Launch of the US Mercury-Atlas 5 spacecraft with Enos the chimp on board; the spacecraft orbited Earth twice before landing off Puerto Rico.

1962 France and Britain agreed to build Concorde, the first supersonic airliner.

1965 British housewife Mary Whitehouse (1910–2001) began her 'Clean Up TV Campaign', setting up the National Viewers and Listeners Association.

1975 First use of the name Microsoft (originally Micro-soft from 'microcomputer software'), in a letter from Bill Gates (b.1955) to Paul Allen (b.1953).

1986 Death of Cary Grant, originally Alexander Archibald Leach (b.1904 in Bristol, Avon), actor, whose films include *To Catch a Thief* (1955).

2001 Death of George Harrison (b.1943 in Liverpool), musician, who played lead guitar and sang with The Beatles.

NOVEMBER
30

National Day, Scotland.
Feast of St Andrew (d.c.60), patron saint of childless women, fishers, Greece, Russia, and Scotland.

1786 Cities for Life Day, celebrated in 300 cities worldwide to commemorate Tuscany as the first European state to abolish the death penalty.

1872 The first international football (soccer) match was played, between Scotland and England in Glasgow; the match was drawn 0–0.

1886 Introduction of an elaborate revue at the Folies Bergère in Paris, featuring women in sensational costumes.

1901 Death of Edward John Eyre (b.1815 in Hornsea, Yorkshire), explorer, the first European to travel the coastline of the Great Australian Bight and Nullarbor Plain by land.

1924 Birth of Shirley Anita St Hill Chisholm in Brooklyn, New York (d.2005), politician, the first African-American woman elected to Congress.

1936 London's Crystal Palace, designed for the 1851 Great Exhibition, was destroyed by fire.

1937 Birth of Ridley Scott in South Shields, Tyne and Wear, director, whose films include *Alien* (1979).

1939 The Soviet Union attacked Finland over border disputes, triggering the Winter War.

1954 A 3.85-kg/8.5-lb meteorite crashed through the roof of a house in Sylacauga, Alabama, USA, hitting Elizabeth Hodges as she slept, causing extensive abdominal bruising; the first recorded case of an object from outer space hitting a person.

1960 Birth of Gary Lineker in Leicester, Leicestershire, footballer and sports presenter.

1968 The Trade Descriptions Act came into force in the UK, making it a crime for traders to knowingly sell goods with misleading labels or descriptions.

1977 Death of Sir Terence Rattigan (b.1911 in London), playwright, whose works include *The Browning Version* (1948).

1979 Death of Joyce Grenfell (b.1910 in London), writer and entertainer, famous for her comic monologues.

1982 Explosion of a letter bomb at 10 Downing Street, the British prime minister's London residence, injuring a member of staff.

1988 Yasser Arafat, head of the Palestine Liberation Organization, was refused a USA entry visa to address the UN General Assembly in New York.

1996 The Stone of Scone, Scotland's coronation stone, was returned to Scotland and installed in Edinburgh Castle, 700 years after King Edward I took it to England as a war prize.

DECEMBER
1

Feast of St Eloi (Eligius), patron saint of blacksmiths, clockmakers, cutlers, farriers, goldsmiths, jewellers, jockeys, labourers, metalworkers, saddlers, sick horses, tool-makers, veterinary surgeons, and wheel-wrights.

1640 Portugal regained independence from Spain.

1761 Birth of Marie Tussaud in Stras-bourg, France (d.1850), modeller in wax, who toured Britain with her life-size portrait waxworks, and in 1835 set up a permanent exhibition in London.

1887 Publication of Sir Arthur Conan Doyle's *A Study in Scarlet* in Beeton's Christmas Annual, Sherlock Holmes' first appearance in print.

1910 Birth of Dame Alicia Markova in London (d.2004), ballerina, who with Anton Dolin established the Markova–Dolin Company (1935) and the London Festival Ballet.

1913 Introduction by the Ford Motor Company of the first moving assembly line, reducing chassis assembly time from 12·5 hours to 2·66 hours and beginning the era of mass production.

1935 Birth of Woody Allen in Brook-lyn, New York, actor, writer, and director, whose credits include *Hannah and Her Sisters* (1986, Oscar).

1939 The world premiere for the film *Gone With the Wind* was held in New York.

1941 Introduction of points rationing in Britain.

1942 Publication of the Beveridge Report on social insurance, the foundation of the welfare state in Britain, named after economist William Henry Beveridge (1879–1963).

1945 Birth of Bette Midler in Hono-lulu, Hawaii, singer, actress, and comedienne, whose film credits include *The First Wives Club* (1996).

1955 US African-American commu-nity activist Rosa Parks (1913–2005) refused to give up her seat to a white man and was arrested for defying segregation laws; a mile-stone in the civil-rights movement.

1959 Signing of the Antarctic Treaty in Washington, DC, by twelve nations, preserving the area for peaceful purposes and scientific research.

1966 Issue of the first Christmas stamps by post offices in Britain.

1989 Mikhail Gorbachev became the first Soviet leader to visit the Vati-can and meet the pope.

1990 Meeting of British and French engineers working on the Channel Tunnel, when the last dividing rock was removed.

1991 France won its first Davis Cup tennis title in 59 years, defeating the USA.

DECEMBER

2

1697 Opening of London's rebuilt St Paul's Cathedral for worship, although it was not completed until 1910.

1804 Coronation of Napoleon as emperor of France at Notre Dame cathedral, Paris.

1805 Victory for Napoleon Bonaparte at the Battle of Austerlitz, on the first anniversary of his coronation.

1814 Death of the Marquis de Sade (b.1740 in Paris), novelist, whose name provided the language with the word 'sadism'.

1823 Proclamation of the Monroe Doctrine, a major statement of American foreign policy.

1859 Birth of Georges Seurat in Paris, France (d.1891), painter, known for such works as *Bathers at Asnières* (1883–4).

1867 Charles Dickens gave his first US public reading, at a New York theatre.

1901 Patenting of the first safety razor by travelling salesman King C. Gillette (1855–1932), who founded his razor-blade company in 1903.

1923 Birth of Maria Callas in New York (d.1977), operatic soprano.

1926 The Ford Motor Company produced the first new Ford Model A car.

1926 The first aluminium street cars came into use, in Cleveland, Ohio.

1942 The first self-sustaining chain reaction took place at the University of Chicago.

1946 Birth of Gianni Versace in Reggio di Calabria, Italy (d.1997), fashion designer, whose trademark designs were the siren dresses made using innovative materials and techniques.

1952 Broadcasting of the first televised birth when Lillian Kerr had a Caesarean section as part of a US programme, 'March of Medicine'.

1954 The US Senate condemned Senator Joseph R. McCarthy's actions during his investigation of Communism in the USA.

1979 Electors in Iran voted for a new constitution to make Iran an Islamic republic and give absolute power to Ayatollah Khomeini.

1982 Implant of the first permanent artificial heart, in Seattle dentist Barney Clark, by William DeVries at the University of Utah.

1985 Death of Philip Larkin (b.1922 in Coventry, West Midlands), poet, librarian, and jazz critic.

DECEMBER
3

Feast of St Francis Xavier (1506–52), patron saint of missionaries.

1621 Completion of the first telescope by Italian astronomer Galileo Galilei (1564–1642).

1753 Birth of Samuel Crompton in Firwood, Greater Manchester (d.1827), inventor of the spinning-mule.

1818 Illinois became the 21st state of the Union.

1857 Birth of Joseph Conrad (Teodor Józef Konrad Korzeniowski) in Berdichev, Ukraine (d.1924), British novelist, whose books include *Lord Jim* (1900).

1894 Death of Robert Louis Stevenson (b.1850 in Edinburgh), writer, whose books include *Kidnapped* (1886).

1910 First public display for the neon lamp, at the Paris motor show.

1919 Death of Pierre Auguste Renoir (b.1841 in Limoges, France), Impressionist artist.

1931 First sales of Alka Seltzer, antacid and pain relief medicine.

1944 US singer and actor Frank Sinatra (1915–98) recorded 'Old Man River'.

1952 Birth of Mel Smith in Chiswick, London, comic actor and director, whose television work includes *Alas Smith and Jones* (1984–6) with Griff Rhys Jones.

1967 South African surgeon Christiaan Barnard (1922–2001) performed the first successful heart transplant.

1973 US spacecraft Pioneer 10 passed within 130,000 km/81,000 miles of Jupiter's cloud-tops, its closest encounter with the planet.

1984 Leakage of the deadly gas methyl isocyanate began from the Union Carbide plant, Bhopal, India; 20,000 have died to date as a result of their exposure to the gas.

1989 Soviet president Mikhail Gorbachev and US president George Bush declared the Cold War at an end after two days of talks at the Malta summit meeting.

1992 Explosion of two bombs in Manchester city centre, injuring 65 people and causing damage and loss of business of an estimated £10 million.

1993 Announcement by Diana, Princess of Wales, of her intention to step back from the public spotlight, and of her wish for greater privacy and less attention from the tabloid press.

1999 US oarswoman Tori Murden-McClure (b.1963 in Jefferson, Kentucky) became the first woman to row across the Atlantic Ocean.

DECEMBER

4

Feast of St John of Damascus (c.675–c.749), also called St John Damascene.

Feast of St Barbara (?–c.200), patron saint of architects, armourers, brewers, builders, carpenters, those in danger of sudden death, firemen, hatters, masons, mathematicians, miners, soldiers, and tilers.

Feast of St Osmund (?–1099), patron saint of the insane, the paralysed, sufferers from hernias and toothache, and soldiers.

1154 Election of Nicholas Breakspear (c.1100–59) as the first and only English pope, Adrian IV.

1732 Death of John Gay (b.1685 in Barnstaple, Devon), poet and playwright, who wrote *The Beggar's Opera* (1728).

1791 First publication of the *Observer*, Britain's oldest Sunday newspaper.

1798 Introduction of income tax by British prime minister William Pitt (1759–1806).

1812 Patenting of the horse-drawn power mower by Peter Gaillard of Lancaster, Pennsylvania.

1829 Under British rule, suttee, where a widow dies on her husband's funeral pyre, was declared illegal in Bengal Presidency lands in India.

1861 The export of gunpowder, firearms, and materials for their production was forbidden by Queen Victoria of Great Britain.

1930 Birth of Ronnie Corbett in Edinburgh, comedian, best known for his television series with Ronnie Barker, *The Two Ronnies* (1971–87).

1937 First appearance of 'Desperate Dan' in the British comic paper the *Dandy*.

1947 First performance of Tennessee Williams' *A Streetcar Named Desire* on Broadway, New York.

1961 Announcement by health minister Enoch Powell that the female birth control pill would be made available through Britain's National Health Service.

1962 Two British divers set the world record for underwater depth at 300 m/1000 ft.

1965 Launch of US spacecraft Gemini VII to link up with the orbiting Gemini VI.

1976 Death of Edward Benjamin Britten (b.1913 in Lowestoft, Suffolk), composer, whose works include the opera *Peter Grimes* (1945).

1991 Closure of US airline Pan Am, after the failure of a financial rescue bid.

1991 Release of Terry Anderson (b.1947), a US hostage in the Lebanon, after nearly seven years.

1993 Death of Frank Zappa (b.1940 in Baltimore, Maryland), rock musician and composer, who led the satirical 'underground' band The Mothers of Invention.

DECEMBER

5

1766 Auctioneer James Christie (1730–1803) held his first auction sale, in London.

1791 Death of Wolfgang Amadeus Mozart (b.1756 in Salzburg, Austria), composer.

1830 Birth of Christina Rossetti in London (d.1894), poet, influenced by the Pre-Raphaelite artistic movement.

1839 Birth of General George Armstrong Custer in New Rumley, Ohio (d.1876), soldier, best known for 'Custer's Last Stand', when he was defeated at the Battle of Little Big Horn (25 June 1876).

1872 US brigantine *Marie Celeste* was found abandoned with her cargo of alcohol in the mid-Atlantic.

1876 Patenting of the first practical pipe wrench by Daniel Chapman Stillson (1826–90) of Walworth & Co, Massachusetts.

1901 Birth of Walt Disney in Chicago, Illinois (d.1966), artist and film producer.

1926 Death of Claude Monet (b.1840 in Paris), painter, whose 'Impression: Sunrise' (1872) gave the Impressionist movement its name.

1933 End of alcohol prohibition in the USA (in force since 16 January 1920) when Utah became the last state to ratify the 21st Amendment, nullifying an earlier Amendment banning the sale or transportation of liquor.

1935 Birth of Little Richard (Richard Penniman) in Macon, Georgia, rock-and-roll singer and pianist.

1945 Disappearance of five US navy torpedo-bombers from Florida, in the area known as the Bermuda Triangle, while on a routine three-hour training flight.

1946 Birth of José Carreras in Barcelona, Spain, lyric tenor.

1951 Opening of the first push-button Park-O-Mat garage in Washington DC, with no ramps, aisles, or lanes; one attendant could park or return a car in less than a minute.

1958 Opening of Britain's first motorway, a bypass around Preston, Lancashire.

1978 Announcement by the British government that Britain would not join the EEC monetary system.

1991 Administrators were called in an attempt to salvage the business empire of publisher Robert Maxwell, which was more than £1 billion in debt.

2000 Death of Colin Cowdrey (b.1932 in Putumala, India), cricketer, who captained Kent and England.

DECEMBER
6

National Day, Finland.
Feast of St Nicholas (4th c), patron saint of apothecaries, brewers, children, fishers, Greece, merchants, pawnbrokers, perfumiers, Russia, sailors, and unmarried girls.

1492 Discovery of Hispaniola (now Haiti and the Dominican Republic) by Christopher Columbus (1451–1506).

1774 Empress Maria Theresa of Austria laid down General School Regulations, creating the first state education system.

1793 Death of Comtesse du Barry (b.1743 in Vaucouleurs, France), favourite mistress of Louis XV of France, guillotined as a counter-revolutionary.

1865 Ratification of the 13th amendment to the US Constitution, abolishing slavery in the USA.

1877 Demonstration of the first phonograph by US inventor and physicist Thomas Alva Edison (1847–1931).

1884 Completion of the construction of the Washington Monument, Washington, DC, a 169-m/555-ft Egyptian obelisk, over 36 years after the cornerstone was laid on Independence Day, 1848.

1896 Birth of Ira Gershwin in New York (d.1983), songwriter, who worked with his brother George to produce such hits as 'I Got Plenty o' Nothin'' (1935).

1920 Birth of Dave Brubeck in Concord, California, pianist, composer, and bandleader, who formed the Dave Brubeck Quartet in 1951.

1922 Establishment of the Irish Free State.

1938 Signing of the Franco–German Pact, in which France and Germany guaranteed inviolability of current frontiers, and agreed mutual consultation for the peaceful settlement of disputes.

1947 Dedication of Everglades National Park, at Everglades City, Florida, by US president Harry S. Truman.

1964 Martin Luther King (1929–68) gave a sermon in St Paul's Cathedral, London.

1983 Britain's first heart–lung transplant operation was successfully carried out by surgeon Magdi Yacoub and his team on Swedish journalist Lars Ljungberg at Harefield Hospital, London.

1988 Death of Roy Orbison (b.1936 in Vernon, Texas), country pop singer and songwriter, whose hit records include 'Only The Lonely' (1960).

1998 Linking of the first two components of the International Space Station, modules Zarya and Unity, by astronauts from space shuttle Endeavour.

DECEMBER

7

Feast of St Ambrose (c.339–97), patron saint of bee-keepers and bishops.

43 BC Death of Cicero (b.106 BC in Arpinum, Latium), Roman orator, statesman, and philosopher.

1732 Opening of Theatre Royal, Covent Garden, London (now the Royal Opera House).

1783 William Pitt the Younger (1759–1806) became Britain's youngest prime minister, aged 24.

1787 Delaware became the 1st state of the Union.

1842 New York Philharmonic Orchestra's first public concert took place at the Apollo Rooms, Manhattan, New York.

1894 Death of Ferdinand, Vicomte de Lesseps (b.1805 in Versailles, France), French diplomat and entrepreneur who campaigned for the construction of the Suez Canal, completed by his company in 1869.

1907 Eugene Corri became the first referee to officiate from inside a boxing ring, at the National Sporting Club, London.

1915 Birth of Eli Wallach in Brooklyn, New York, actor, whose films include *The Magnificent Seven* (1960).

1926 Patenting of the gas refrigerator by the Electrolux Company of America.

1928 Birth of Noam Chomsky in Philadelphia, Pennsylvania, linguist and political activist, whose *Syntactic Structures* (1957) introduced a theory of language called generative grammar.

1941 Japan attacked the US Pacific Fleet anchored at Pearl Harbor, Hawaii.

1962 Britain made the second of its underground nuclear tests in the Nevada desert.

1963 US television network CBS became the first to show an instant replay, at a football game in Philadelphia, Pennsylvania; the players re-enacted the just-completed play for the cameras.

1972 Launch of Apollo 17 at Cape Canaveral, Florida, the last US Moon mission.

1982 Convicted murderer Charlie Brooks Jr became the first US prisoner to be executed by lethal injection, with sodium pentathol at Fort Worth Prison, Texas.

1985 Death of Robert Graves (b.1895 in London), poet and novelist, whose novels include *I, Claudius* (1934).

1997 Death of Billy Bremner (b.1942 in Stirling, Scotland), soccer player, who captained Leeds United and Scotland.

2004 At Brookfield Zoo, Illinois, gorillas were allowed to mourn the death of Babs, matriarch of their social family, by filing into the room where her body lay.

DECEMBER
8

1733 James Cracker of Fleet, Dorset, reported seeing a polished silver disc in the sky in broad daylight, the first recorded sighting of a UFO (unidentified flying object).

1854 Pope Pius IX declared the dogma of the Immaculate Conception of the Blessed Virgin Mary to be an article of faith.

1864 Opening to traffic of Brunel's Clifton Suspension Bridge, spanning the R Avon near Bristol, Avon.

1894 Birth of James Thurber in Columbus, Ohio (d.1961), writer and cartoonist, whose popular drawings first appeared in *Is Sex Necessary?* (1929).

1914 Ending of the Battle of the Falkland Islands between Britain and Germany in a British victory, with the sinking of four German cruisers.

1925 Birth of Sammy Davis Jr in New York (d.1990), singer, actor, and dancer, whose films include *Porgy and Bess* (1959).

1934 Inauguration of the London-to-Australia air-mail service.

1941 Britain and the USA declared war on Japan.

1943 Birth of Jim Morrison in Melbourne, Florida (d.1971), rock singer with The Doors (1965), who wrote such hit songs as 'Light My Fire' (1967).

1953 Birth of Kim Basinger in Athens, Georgia, actress, who was a top model before making her way in films such as *L.A. Confidential* (1997).

1974 A referendum in Greece resulted in a rejection of the monarchy by over two-thirds of the voters, and support for the establishment of a republic.

1978 Death of Golda Meir (b.1898 in Kiev, Ukraine), Israeli prime minister (1969–74).

1980 Death of John Lennon (b.1940 in Liverpool), pop star and composer, The Beatles' rhythm guitarist, keyboard player, and vocalist, killed by a deranged fan.

1981 British trade unionist Arthur Scargill (b.1938) became leader of the National Union of Mineworkers.

1987 Signing of the Intermediate Nuclear Forces treaty in Washington DC, by US president Reagan, and Soviet president Gorbachev, the first nuclear arms reduction agreement.

1991 Signing of an agreement by the leaders of Russia, Belarus, and the Ukraine, forming the Commonwealth of Independent States following the collapse of the USSR.

1993 Election of Winnie Mandela, estranged wife of Nelson Mandela, as president of the African National Congress Women's League.

DECEMBER
9

National Day, Tanzania.

1608 Birth of John Milton in London (d.1674), poet, whose works include *Paradise Lost* (completed 1665).

1641 Death of Sir Anthony van Dyck (b.1599 in Antwerp, Belgium), Flemish artist, the court painter to King Charles I.

1783 The first executions in Britain took place at Newgate Prison.

1824 Beginning of the Battle of Ayacucho, Peru, in which the Spanish army was defeated and agreed to leave South America.

1854 Publication of Alfred Lord Tennyson's poem 'The Charge of the Light Brigade' in *The Examiner*.

1909 Birth of Douglas Fairbanks Jr in New York (d.2000), actor, writer, producer, and businessman, who made Hollywood movies such as *Sinbad the Sailor* (1947).

1914 The British Admiralty commissioned the first aircraft carrier, HMS *Ark Royal*.

1916 Birth of Kirk Douglas in Amsterdam, New York, actor, whose films include *Spartacus* (1960).

1926 The US Golf Association legalized the use of steel-shafted golf clubs.

1934 Birth of Dame Judi Dench in York, North Yorkshire, actress, whose film credits include *Shakespeare in Love* (1998, Oscar).

1940 The Longines Watch Company signed a contract with W2XOR experimental radio station, New York, becoming the first FM radio advertiser.

1953 Birth of John Malkovich in Benton, Illinois, actor, whose credits include *Empire of the Sun* (1987).

1960 The first episode of the British television series *Coronation Street* was broadcast.

1967 Cunard liner *Queen Mary* docked at Long Beach, California, after her final voyage.

1987 A row between England cricket captain Mike Gatting and umpire Shakoor Rana halted play, and threatened to end the England cricket tour in Pakistan.

1990 Election of Lech Wałęsa, former leader of the trade union Solidarity, as president of Poland.

1992 Official announcement of the separation of the Prince and Princess of Wales.

1993 Completion of five days of repairs to the Hubble Space Telescope by US astronauts aboard space shuttle Endeavour.

1994 The British government and Sinn Féin, the IRA's political wing, held their first formal talks for more than 70 years.

DECEMBER
10

Feast of Our Lady of Loreto, patron saint of aviators.

1520 In Wittenberg, Germany, religious reformer Martin Luther publicly burnt the papal bull issued against him.

1652 The Battle of Dungeness was fought during the first Anglo-Dutch War.

1768 Founding of the Royal Academy of Arts in Britain.

1817 Mississippi became the 20th state of the Union.

1845 Patenting of the first pneumatic tyres by British civil engineer Robert William Thomson.

1851 Birth of Melvil Dewey in Adams Centre, New York (d.1931), librarian, who designed the Dewey system of book classification by decimals in 1876.

1868 First publication of *Whitaker's Almanack*, now a publishing institution.

1868 First day of operation for the world's first traffic lights, near Parliament Square, London; designed by railway signal engineer J. P. Knight, they consisted of two semaphore arms (used in daytime) and red/green gas lights (at night).

1896 Death of Alfred Nobel (b.1833 in Stockholm, Sweden), chemist and industrialist, who endowed the Nobel Prizes awarded since 1901 on the anniversary of his death.

1908 Founding of the National Farmers' Union, in London.

1915 The Ford Motor Company produced its millionth automobile.

1948 The UN General Assembly adopted the Universal Declaration of Human Rights, which states 'All human beings are born with equal and inalienable rights and fundamental freedoms.'

1953 Publication of the first issue of *Playboy* magazine by US entrepreneur Hugh Hefner (b.1926); it was printed undated because of his doubts about a second issue.

1960 Birth of Kenneth Branagh in Belfast, actor and director, whose films include *Hamlet* (1997).

1967 Death of Otis Redding (b.1941 in Dawson, Georgia), soul singer, who died in a plane crash.

1977 Supersonic airliner Concorde flew from London to Singapore, its first scheduled flight.

1979 The Nobel Peace Prize was awarded to Mother Teresa of Calcutta (1910–97).

1998 Completion of the first genetic blueprint for a whole multicellular animal in a joint venture by scientists around the globe; the 97-million-letter code was for a tiny nematode worm, *Caenorhabditis elegans*.

DECEMBER
11

1803 Birth of Hector Berlioz in La Côte-Saint-André, France (d.1869), composer, whose works include the *Symphonie Fantastique* (1830).

1816 Indiana became the 19th state of the Union.

1843 Birth of Robert Koch in Clausthal-Zellerfeld, Germany (d.1910), bacteriologist, who discovered the bacillus of both tuberculosis and cholera.

1844 First dental use of nitrous oxide as an anaesthetic at Hartford, Connecticut, when dentist Horace Wells had a tooth extracted by his friend and former pupil Dr John Riggs.

1882 The Bijou Theater, Boston, New York, became the first US playhouse lit entirely by electricity, when it opened with a production of Gilbert and Sullivan's *Iolanthe*.

1894 Opening of the first motor show, in Paris, with nine exhibitors.

1903 Founding of the world's first wildlife preservation society in Britain, the Society for the Preservation of the Wild Fauna of the Empire.

1918 Birth of Alexander Solzhenitsyn in Kislovodsk, Russia, writer, whose novels include *The First Circle* (1968).

1929 Birth of Sir Kenneth MacMillan in Dunfermline, Fife (d.1992), ballet dancer and choreographer, who became artistic director of the Royal Ballet in 1970.

1936 Abdication of Edward VIII, king of the United Kingdom, over opposition to his proposed marriage to Wallis Simpson, a commoner who had been twice divorced.

1936 Accession of King George VI to the throne.

1941 Germany and Italy declared war on the USA; this was immediately reciprocated by a US declaration of war on Germany and Italy.

1946 Founding of UNICEF, the United Nations International Children's Emergency Fund.

1968 The prototype of the supersonic airliner Concorde was displayed at Toulouse, France.

1972 Landing of Apollo 17 on the Moon.

1981 US boxer Muhammad Ali (b.1942) lost his 61st and last fight, to Trevor Berbick at the Queen Elizabeth Sports Center, Nassau, Bahamas.

1987 Sale of Charlie Chaplin's bowler hat and cane for £82,500 at an auction of Chaplin memorabilia at Christie's in London; his oversized boots sold for £38,000.

1991 Agreement of the Maastricht Treaty, incorporating political and economic measures.

1996 Shipping tycoon Tung Chee-hwa was chosen to be the first chief executive of Hong Kong, following the handover by Britain in 1997.

DECEMBER
12

National Day, Kenya.

1787 Pennsylvania became the 2nd state of the Union.
1800 Washington, DC, officially became the capital city of the USA.
1821 Birth of Gustave Flaubert in Rouen, France (d.1880), novelist, best known for *Madame Bovary* (1857).
1889 Death of Robert Browning (b.1812 in London), poet, the husband of Elizabeth Barrett Browning.
1896 Public demonstration of the wireless in London by Italian physicist and inventor Guglielmo Marconi (1874–1937).
1911 Announcement by King George V during the Imperial Durbar of December 1911 that the capital of British India would be transferred from Calcutta to Delhi.
1913 Recovery of Leonardo da Vinci's *Mona Lisa*, stolen from the Louvre in Paris in 1911.
1915 Birth of Frank Sinatra in Hoboken, New Jersey (d.1998), singer and actor, whose films include *From Here to Eternity* (1953, Oscar).
1915 First flight of the Junkers J1, the first airworthy all-metal aircraft, piloted by Friedrich von Mallinkrodt of the German Air Force.
1917 Roman Catholic priest Father Edward J. Flanagan opened a house for homeless boys in Omaha, Nebraska, that later became known as Boys Town.
1925 Opening of the first motel, the Milestone Motel, in San Luis Obispo, California, by Arthur Heinman; the 55 rooms, each with an adjoining garage, cost $2·50 per night.
1926 Birth of Honor Blackman in London, actress, who became known for her role in the television series *The Avengers* (1960–63).
1929 Birth of John Osborne in London (d.1994), playwright and film producer, whose work includes *The Entertainer* (1957).
1941 Birth of Dionne Warwick in East Orange, New Jersey, pop and soul singer, whose hits include 'Walk On By' (1964).
1955 Patenting of the amphibious hovercraft by British engineer Sir Christopher Cockerell (1910–99).
1963 Independence of Kenya.
1992 Marriage of Princess Anne to Timothy Laurence, the first royal divorcee since Henry VIII of England to remarry.
2003 Mick Jagger (b.1943), of British rock group The Rolling Stones, was knighted for his services to popular music.

DECEMBER
13

Feast of St Lucy (?–303), patron saint of the blind, glassworkers, and writers.

1545 Opening of the Council of Trent, in Trent, Italy, which helped revitalize the Roman Catholic Church in many parts of Europe after the Protestant Reformation.

1577 Sir Francis Drake set sail in the *Golden Hind* from Plymouth, Devon, on his circumnavigation of the world.

1779 The first Smithfield Show, organized by the Smithfield Cattle and Sheep Society, took place at Wooton's Dolphin Yard, London.

1784 Death of Samuel Johnson (b.1709 in Lichfield, Staffordshire), lexicographer, critic, and poet, whose work included the *Dictionary of the English Language* (1755).

1816 Patenting of a dry dock by John Adamson of Boston, Massachusetts.

1862 Victory of the Confederate army, under Robert E. Lee, over the Northern army at the Battle of Fredericksburg, during the American Civil War.

1884 Patenting of the first coin-operated weighing machine by Percy Everitt.

1903 Patenting of the first ice-cream cone by Italo Marcioni, in New Jersey.

1925 Birth of Dick Van Dyke in West Plains, Missouri, actor, whose film credits include *Mary Poppins* (1964).

1927 Birth of Christopher Plummer in Toronto, Ontario, actor, whose credits include *The Sound of Music* (1965).

1937 Japanese forces took the Chinese city of Nanking (Nanjing).

1939 The Battle of the R Plate was fought off the coast of South America, when British cruisers *Exeter*, *Ajax* and *Achilles* engaged German battleship *Admiral Graf Spee*.

1949 Birth of Robert Lindsay in Ilkeston, Derbyshire, actor, who became known for the title role in the television series *Citizen Smith* (1973–7).

1964 US president Johnson and Mexican president Ordaz triggered an explosion at El Paso, Texas, diverting the Rio Grande to reshape the US–Mexico border and end a border dispute.

1973 Following the Arab oil embargo and the British coal miners' strike, the British government ordered a three-day working week, to commence on 31 December 1973.

1998 Death of Baron Lew Grade (b.1906 in Odessa, Ukraine), theatrical impresario, who headed several large British film entertainment and communications companies.

DECEMBER

14

Feast of St John of the Cross (1542–91), originally Juan de Yepes y Alvarez, patron saint of poets, mystics, and mystical theologians.

1503 Birth of Nostradamus, Latin name of Michel de Notredame, in St Rémy, France (d.1566), physician and astrologer, best known for his *Centuries* of predictions.

1546 Birth of Tycho Brahe in Knudstrup, Sweden (d.1601), astronomer and mathematician, who discovered and rectified serious errors in the astronomical tables.

1656 First manufacture of artificial pearls by M. Jacquin, Parisian rosary-bead maker, by coating gypsum pellets with a mixture of fish scales and varnish.

1799 Death of George Washington (b.1732 in Westmoreland Co, Virginia), army leader during the American Revolution, and first president of America (1789–97).

1819 Alabama became the 22nd state of the Union.

1861 Death of Prince Albert (b.1819 at Schloss Rosenau, near Coburg, Germany), Prince Consort to Queen Victoria.

1895 Birth of King George VI at Sandringham, Norfolk, king of the United Kingdom (1936–52).

1900 German physicist Max Planck (1858–1947) presented his quantum theory.

1911 Norwegian explorer Roald Amundsen (1872–1928) reached the South Pole, 35 days before Scott's expedition.

1918 First votes for women over 30 in the British general election.

1920 The first scheduled passenger flight fatalities occurred when an aircraft on a flight from London to Paris crashed into a house in Golders Green, killing the crew and two of the six passengers.

1962 US space probe Mariner 2 sent back the first pictures of Venus.

1970 Ex-Beatle George Harrison was awarded a gold disc for his record 'My Sweet Lord'.

1986 Experimental aircraft Voyager, with pilots Dick Rutan and Jeana Yeager, took off from Edwards Air Force Base, California, on the first non-stop, non-refuelled, flight around the world.

1995 US AIDS patient Jeff Getty received the bone marrow of a baboon, in the first xenotransplant, at San Francisco General Hospital.

2003 Capture of Saddam Hussein (b.1937), former president of Iraq, by US forces at a farmhouse c.16 km/10 miles south of his home town, Takrit.

2004 Opening of the Millau Viaduct, bridging the R Tarn in S France, the world's highest road bridge.

DECEMBER
15

37 Birth of Nero Claudius Caesar (d.68), emperor of Rome (54–68), who was blamed for the Great Fire of Rome (64) and forced to commit suicide.

1654 Meteorological recording was begun for the first time, in Tuscany, Italy.

1675 Death of Jan Vermeer (b.1632 in Delft, The Netherlands), painter, who painted small, detailed domestic interiors, notable for their use of perspective and light.

1891 US physical education instructor James E. Naismith (1861–1939) created basketball in Springfield, Massachusetts; he nailed two peach baskets to opposite ends of a gymnasium balcony.

1906 Opening of the Piccadilly Line in London's underground system.

1962 Death of Charles Laughton (b.1899 in Scarborough, North Yorkshire), actor, whose credits include *Mutiny on the Bounty* (1935).

1964 Adoption of the maple leaf by Canada as the official symbol for the national flag.

1965 US spacecraft Gemini 6 and Gemini 7 accomplished the first-ever space rendezvous.

1966 Death of Walt Disney (b.1901 in Chicago, Illinois), artist and producer, whose films include the first full-length cartoon, *Snow White and the Seven Dwarfs* (1937).

1974 Introduction of new speed limits on Britain's roads to reduce fuel consumption.

1979 Invention of the board game *Trivial Pursuit* by Canadians Chris Harvey and Scott Abbott.

1982 After 13 years, the gates isolating the people of Gibraltar were opened to pedestrians, by Spain's new Socialist government.

1993 Fashion designer Yves Saint-Laurent (b.1936) was refused permission by a Paris court to give the name 'Champagne' to his new perfume ($120 per bottle).

1995 The proposed European single currency was named the Euro.

2000 Official closure of the last remaining nuclear reactor at the Chernobyl nuclear power station, Ukraine, site of the world's worst nuclear accident in 1986.

2001 Reopening of the Leaning Tower of Pisa, Italy, to the public after a £15 million realignment operation lasting over a decade.

DECEMBER
16

1485 Birth of Catherine of Aragon in Alcalá de Henares, Spain (d.1536), queen of England, the first wife of Henry VIII (1509–33).

1653 Oliver Cromwell (1599–1658) was declared Lord Protector of England.

1773 Chests of dutied tea were destroyed in Boston harbour during the Boston Tea Party, the climax of resistance to British attempts at direct taxation during the American Revolution.

1775 Birth of Jane Austen in Steventon, Hampshire (d.1817), novelist, whose works include *Sense and Sensibility* (1811).

1899 Birth of Noel Coward in London (d.1973), playwright, composer, and actor, whose plays include *Blithe Spirit* (1941).

1904 The first female ushers in the USA began work, at the Majestic Theater, New York; despite gloom-and-doom predictions of moral turpitude, nothing untoward occurred.

1905 Publication of the first issue of *Variety* magazine in New York; it had just 16 pages, cost 5 cents, and had no mention of film.

1913 British actor Charlie Chaplin began work at Keystone studios for his first film, *Making a Living*, released later in the year.

1917 Birth of Arthur C(harles) Clarke in Minehead, Somerset, writer of science fiction, especially known for *2001: a Space Odyssey* (1968).

1921 Death of Charles-Camille Saint-Saëns (b.1835 in Paris), composer, whose works include *The Carnival of the Animals* (1886).

1925 Work began on Britain's Mersey Tunnel, Liverpool.

1929 Release of the first British-made all-talking feature film, *The Clue of the New Pin*, made by British Lion and British Photophone at Beaconsfield Studios, with a cast including John Gielgud.

1944 Beginning of the Battle of the Bulge, the German offensive in the Ardennes.

1954 Production of the first synthetic diamonds, by Professor H. T. Hall, at the US GEC Laboratories.

1965 Death of William Somerset Maugham (b.1874 in Paris), English novelist and playwright, whose works include the novel *Of Human Bondage* (1915).

1977 Opening of the Piccadilly Line underground extension to Heathrow airport, London.

1991 Dame Stella Rimington (b.1935) became the first female director-general of Britain's MI5.

1996 Announcement of a £28 billion merger between Boeing and McDonnell Douglas.

DECEMBER
17

1770 Birth of Ludwig van Beethoven in Bonn, Germany (d.1827), composer.

1778 Birth of Sir Humphry Davy in Penzance, Cornwall (d.1829), chemist, who invented the miner's safety lamp (1815).

1791 Opening of the first one-way street for traffic, in New York.

1828 William Burke (1792–1829), charged with grave robbery, went on trial in Edinburgh.

1834 Opening of Ireland's first railway-line between Dublin and Kingstown (Dun Laoghaire); the world's first suburban railway.

1843 Publication of 'A Christmas Carol' by Charles Dickens (1812–70).

1849 London hatmakers Thomas and William Bowler sold their first bowler hat.

1857 Death of Rear Admiral Sir Francis Beaufort (b.1774 in Navan, Co Meath, Ireland), naval officer and hydrographer, who devised the *Beaufort scale* of wind force in 1805.

1888 Opening of the Lyric Theatre in Shaftesbury Avenue, London.

1892 The Russian Imperial Ballet gave the first performance of Tchaikovsky's *The Nutcracker* in St Petersburg.

1902 The first radio message travelled across the Atlantic.

1903 First recorded powered flight, by US aviation pioneers and brothers Orville (1871–1948) and Wilbur Wright (1867–1912).

1907 Death of Lord Kelvin (b.1824 in Belfast), mathematician and physicist, known for his research into thermodynamics and the absolute temperature scale (measured in kelvin).

1956 Imposition of petrol rationing in Britain, following the closure of the Suez Canal.

1957 First completely successful flight of Missile 12-A, the third Atlas flight missile, from Cape Canaveral, Florida, to its full range of 1100 km/684 miles.

1969 Closure of the Project Blue Book by the US Air Force, following the investigation of 12,618 UFO (unidentified flying object) reports, of which 701 remained unidentified.

1973 Birth of Paula Radcliffe in Northwich, Cheshire, cross-country and marathon athlete.

1983 Explosion of a car bomb planted by the IRA outside Harrods, central London, killing six people.

1986 The first heart, lung, and liver transplant took place, in an operation on Davina Thompson, at Papworth Hospital, Cambridge, Cambridgeshire.

DECEMBER
18

Feast of St Adjutor, patron saint of yachtsmen.

Feast (Eastern Church) of St Sebastian (?–288), patron saint of archers, athletes, and soldiers.

1737 Death of Stradivari (b.1644 in Cremona, Italy), violin maker, who perfected the Cremona type of violin.

1787 New Jersey became the 3rd state of the Union.

1792 Trial for treason of radical British political writer Thomas Paine (1737–1809), for his publication in support of the French Revolution and the abolition of the British Monarchy.

1862 Establishment of the USA's first orthopaedic hospital, the Hospital for the Ruptured and Crippled, in New York.

1865 Slavery was abolished in the USA in the 13th Amendment to the Constitution.

1898 Gaston de Chasseloup-Laubat set the world's first official automobile land-speed record, of 63 kph/ 39 mph, near Paris.

1912 Announcement of the discovery of fossil remains of 'Piltdown Man', an extinct human species, at a meeting of the Geological Society, London; the remains proved to be a fraud.

1936 Arrival in San Francisco of Su-Lin, the first giant panda to come to the USA.

1943 Birth of Keith Richards in Dart-ford, Kent, guitarist, and member of The Rolling Stones rock group.

1944 First day of publication for the French newspaper *Le Monde*.

1947 Birth of Steven Spielberg in Cincinnati, Ohio, director, whose films include *Schindler's List* (1993, 2 Oscars).

1956 Admission of Japan to membership of the UN.

1963 Birth of Brad Pitt in Shawnee, Oklahoma, actor, whose films include *Troy* (2004).

1969 Abolition of the death penalty for murder in Britain.

1974 The British government agreed to pay £42,000 compensation to relatives of the 13 men killed in the 1972 Bloody Sunday riots in Londonderry, Northern Ireland.

1979 First breaking of the sound barrier on land, by Stanley Barrett, driving *Budweiser Rocket* at 1190 kph/739·6 mph at Edwards Air Force Base, California.

1984 Appointment of Ted Hughes (1930–98) as poet laureate, succeeding John Betjeman (1906–84).

DECEMBER
19

Feast of St Adam, patron saint of gardeners.

1154 Henry II became king of England.

1562 Beginning of the French Wars of Religion, with the Battle of Dreux between the Huguenots and the Catholics.

1848 Death of Emily Brontë (b.1818 in Thornton, West Yorkshire), writer, whose works include the novel *Wuthering Heights* (1847).

1851 Death of J. M. W. Turner (b.1775 in London), landscape artist and watercolourist.

1871 Patenting in the US of corrugated paper for packaging, by inventor Albert L. Jones, of New York.

1884 Birth of Sir Stanley Unwin in London (d.1968), publisher, chairman of the firm of George Allen and Unwin (founded 1914).

1887 A boxing match in Paris between Jake Kilrain (USA) and Jem Smith (UK) was declared a draw when night fell; it went to 106 rounds and lasted 2 hours 31 minutes.

1902 Birth of Sir Ralph Richardson in Cheltenham, Gloucestershire (d.1983), actor, whose films include *The Fallen Idol* (1948).

1906 Birth of Leonid Brezhnev in Kamenskoye, Ukraine (d.1982), president of the Supreme Soviet (1977–82).

1910 First commercial production of rayon (known then as artificial silk), in Marcus Hook, Pennsylvania, by the American Viscose Company.

1915 Birth of Edith Piaf in Paris (d.1963), singer, remembered for her husky, powerful delivery of such songs as 'Non, Je ne Regrette Rien'.

1923 Birth of Gordon Jackson in Glasgow (d.1990), actor, who became a household name as Hudson, in the television series *Upstairs, Downstairs* (1971).

1932 Transmission of the first international BBC broadcast, from the Empire Service, later the World Service; it was broadcast to Australia and New Zealand, and lasted two hours.

1957 Inauguration of the air service between London and Moscow.

1974 Beginning of the personal computer revolution, with an offer in *Popular Electronics* magazine for a $397 microcomputer kit, the MITS Altair 8800, based on the new Intel 8080A microprocessor.

1984 Britain and China signed an agreement for the return of Hong Kong to China in 1997.

1989 Death of Stella Gibbons (b.1902 in London), novelist and journalist, whose works include the satirical novel *Cold Comfort Farm* (1932).

DECEMBER

20

1699 Announcement by Peter the Great of a reorganization of the Russian calendar, with the new year moving from 1 September to 1 January.

1803 France sold the USA an area of land between the Mississippi R and the Rocky Mts for $15 million; the Louisiana Purchase.

1880 Broadway, New York, was lit by electricity for the first time, earning it the name the 'Great White Way'.

1920 Comedian Bob Hope, originally Leslie Towne Hope (1903–2003), and his six brothers became US citizens by virtue of their father's naturalization.

1926 Birth of Sir Geoffrey Howe in Port Talbot, Wales, British chancellor of the exchequer (1979–1983), foreign secretary (1983–9), and deputy prime minister (1989–90).

1928 Introduction of postal deliveries by dog sledge in Lewiston, Maine.

1928 Opening of Harry Ramsden's first fish-and-chip shop near Bradford, West Yorkshire.

1946 Birth of Uri Geller in Tel Aviv, Israel, psychic, known for his performances of metal bending and telepathy.

1952 Birth of Jenny Agutter in Taunton, Somerset, actress, whose films include *The Railway Children* (1970).

1954 Death of James Hilton (b.1900 in Leigh, Lancashire), novelist, many of whose works were filmed, such as *Lost Horizon* (1933).

1957 US rock singer Elvis Presley received his call-up papers.

1968 Death of John Steinbeck (b.1902 in Salinas, California), novelist, who won the 1962 Nobel Prize for Literature.

1973 Death of Luis Carrero Blanco (b.1903), prime minister of Spain, killed in a car bomb attack in Madrid.

1973 In a tennis match billed as the 'Battle of the Sexes' Billie Jean King (b.1943) defeated former Wimbledon champion Bobby Riggs (1918–95) in the Houston Astrodome, Texas.

1982 Death of Artur Rubinstein (b.1887 in Łódź, Poland), pianist, who became a US citizen in 1946, making over 200 recordings.

1985 Appointment of Robert Penn Warren (1905–89) as US poet laureate.

1996 Death of Carl Sagan (b.1934 in New York), astronomer and writer, who was involved in the Mariner, Viking, and Voyager spacecraft missions.

DECEMBER
21

Feast of St Thomas the Apostle (1st c), patron saint of architects, the blind, builders, and Portugal (also 3 July).

1620 The Pilgrim Fathers landed, in the *Mayflower*, at Plymouth Rock, Massachusetts.

1804 Birth of Benjamin Disraeli, 1st Earl of Beaconsfield, in London (d.1881), British prime minister (1868, 1874–80).

1844 Opening of the first successful cooperative store, by the Rochdale Pioneers, in Toad Lane, Rochdale, Greater Manchester.

1846 Anaesthetic was used in Britain for the first time during an operation by Robert Liston.

1849 Founding of the first ice-skating club in the USA, Philadelphia, Pennsylvania.

1879 Birth of Josef Stalin in Gori, Georgia (d.1953), dictator of the Soviet Union (1928–53).

1879 First performance of Henrik Ibsen's *A Doll's House*, at Det Kongelige Teater, Copenhagen; the play was so controversial that Ibsen was forced to write a second ending he termed 'a barbaric outrage'.

1913 Publication of the first crossword puzzle, compiled by British-born Arthur Wynne, in the *New York World*.

1933 Dried human blood serum was first prepared in the USA, at the University of Pennsylvania, by Dr Earl W. Flosdorf and Dr Stuart Mudd.

1937 Premiere of Walt Disney's *Snow White and the Seven Dwarfs* in Los Angeles, the first full-length animated talking picture.

1940 Birth of Frank Zappa in Baltimore, Maryland (d.1993), rock musician and composer, who led the satirical 'underground' band The Mothers of Invention.

1958 Charles de Gaulle became president of France (1958–69).

1964 The British government voted against the death penalty.

1966 Birth of Kiefer Sutherland in London, actor, whose films include *Flatliners* (1990).

1968 Launch of Apollo 8 in the USA.

1988 Explosion of a Pan Am Boeing 747 over Lockerbie, Scotland, on a flight from London to New York, killing 270 people, including residents of the town.

1990 Cricketers and twins Mark and Steve Waugh shared an unbroken partnership of 464 for the fifth wicket of New South Wales v. Western Australia; a record for any wicket in Australian interstate four-day matches.

DECEMBER

22

Winter Solstice.
Feast of St Francesca Xavier Cabrini (1850–1917), patron saint of immigrants, the first US saint.

1135 Coronation of King Stephen of England (r.1135–54).

1583 Adoption of the Gregorian calendar by Switzerland and Germany.

1858 Birth of Giacomo Puccini in Lucca, Italy (d.1924), operatic composer, whose works include *La Bohème* (1896).

1879 Announcement of the liquefaction of oxygen by Swiss chemist and physicist Raoul Pierre Pictet (1846–1929), in a telegram to the French Academy.

1882 Edward Johnson strung 28 bulbs on a tree in his home, creating the first electrically lit Christmas tree; he lived in the first part of New York to be wired for electricity.

1895 Physicist Wilhelm Konrad von Röntgen (1845–1923) made the first X-ray, of his wife's hand.

1907 Birth of Peggy Ashcroft in London (d.1991), actress, whose films include *A Passage to India* (1984, Oscar).

1916 Establishment of the Ministry of Pensions in Britain.

1943 Death of Beatrix Potter (b.1866 in London), writer and illustrator of children's books, who created such popular characters as *Benjamin Bunny* (1904).

1949 Birth of Maurice (d.2003) and Robin Gibb in Douglas, Isle of Man, rock musicians, who with their elder brother, Barry (b.1946), formed The Bee Gees.

1956 Birth of Colo at Columbus Zoo, Ohio, the first gorilla to be born in captivity.

1961 Death of James T. Davis, US Army cryptologist, the first American to die in the Vietnam War; his is the first name to appear on the Vietnam War Memorial in Washington, DC.

1962 Birth of Ralph Fiennes in Ipswich, Suffolk, actor, whose film credits include *The Constant Gardener* (2005).

1965 Introduction of the 70 mph speed limit in Britain.

1965 Death of Richard Dimbleby (b.1913 in Richmond-on-Thames, London), broadcaster, who became the BBC's first foreign correspondent.

1989 Opening of the Brandenburg Gate, Berlin, for the first time in almost three decades, effectively ending the division of East and West Germany.

1989 Death of Samuel Beckett (b.1906 in Dublin, Ireland), writer and playwright, whose works include *Waiting for Godot* (1954).

2000 Marriage of US singer Madonna (b.1958) to British film director Guy Ritchie (b.1968).

DECEMBER
23

1732 Birth of Richard Arkwright in Preston, Lancashire (d.1792), inventor of mechanical cotton-spinning, who set up his celebrated spinning-frame in Preston in 1768.

1787 HMS *Bounty* set sail for the South Seas, under the command of William Bligh.

1790 Birth of Jean-François Champollion in Figeac, France (d.1832), Egyptologist, who used the Rosetta Stone to decipher Egyptian hieroglyphics.

1805 Birth of Joseph Smith in Sharon, Vermont (d.1844), founder of the Church of Jesus Christ of Latter-day Saints (the Mormons).

1812 Birth of Samuel Smiles in Haddington, Lothian (d.1904), writer and social reformer.

1834 Patenting of the 'Patent Safety (Hansom) Cab' by British inventor and architect Joseph Aloysius Hansom (1803–82).

1888 Following a quarrel with Gauguin, Dutch painter Vincent van Gogh (1853–90) cut off part of his own ear.

1905 Britain's first beauty contest took place at the Olympia Theatre, Newcastle-upon-Tyne.

1913 Foundation of the USA Central Bank, the Federal Reserve System (known as 'The Fed').

1922 Commencement of the BBC's daily radio news broadcasts.

1938 A Coelacanth, a prehistoric fish thought to be extinct, was caught off the South African coast.

1947 Demonstration of the first working solid-state transistor, at Bell Laboratories, New Jersey.

1948 Execution of Hideki Tojo (1885–1948) and six other Japanese military leaders, found guilty of crimes against humanity.

1954 Dr Joseph E. Murray performed the first kidney transplant, at the Peter Bent Brigham Hospital, Boston, Massachusetts, between identical twins Ronald and Richard Herrick.

1968 Release of eighty-two crewmen from USS *Pueblo* by North Korea after 11 months in captivity; they claimed the US Navy intelligence ship had crossed into their waters.

1970 *The Mousetrap* by Agatha Christie (1890–1976) reached its 7511th consecutive performance in London, breaking the world record for the longest-running play.

1972 Rescue of survivors from a plane that crashed in the Andes (13 Oct 1972), a story which became the subject of the book and film *Alive* (1992).

1973 Arab oil producers doubled the price of oil.

1992 The *Sun* newspaper published the queen's Christmas speech two days ahead of its scheduled BBC broadcast, leading to an investigation into the leak.

DECEMBER

24

Christmas Eve.

1508 Water was piped to houses in London for the first time.

1814 Signing of the Treaty of Ghent in Belgium, ending the War of 1812 between Great Britain and the USA.

1818 'Silent Night' was first performed, at Obertsdorf, Bavaria.

1865 Founding of the Ku Klux Klan by six former Confederate officers in Pulaski, Tennessee.

1894 Death of Frances Mary Buss (b.1827 in London), pioneer in women's education, who founded the North London Collegiate School for Ladies age 23, and became the first woman to call herself a headmistress.

1904 Opening of the London Coliseum.

1905 Birth of Howard Hughes in Houston, Texas (d.1976), millionaire businessman, film producer and director, and aviator, who eventually became a recluse.

1914 First air raid on Britain during World War 1; a German aeroplane dropped a single bomb in the grounds of a rectory in Dover, Kent.

1920 Final public appearance of Enrico Caruso (1873–1921), who sang Eléazar in Halévy's *La Juive* at the Metropolitan Opera House, New York.

1922 BBC transmission of the first British radio play, *The Truth about Father Christmas*.

1936 First use of nuclear medicine, when a woman with chronic leukaemia was treated using a radioactive isotope of phosphorus-32, in Berkeley, California.

1948 The first completely solar-heated house, designed by architect Eleanor Raymond (1888–1989), was occupied in Dover, Massachusetts.

1963 Birth of Caroline Aherne in Manchester, actress and writer, whose roles include her chat-show persona Mrs Merton.

1965 A shower of meteorites fell on Barwell, Leicestershire, after a fireball was seen; breaking on impact, the main mass weighed 4·7 kg/ 10·36 lb.

1968 The Apollo 8 spacecraft with three astronauts on board became the first manned space mission to orbit the Moon.

1974 The British pop group The Beatles was legally dissolved.

1974 British politician John Stonehouse (1925–88) was found living as Donald Clive Mildoon in Australia, after faking his own death by drowning in Miami, Florida.

1979 Launch of the first European-built rocket, Ariane 1, from the Kourou Space Centre, French Guiana.

1997 Death of Toshirô Mifune (b.1920 in Tsingtao, China), Japanese actor, known for his portrayals of samurai characters.

DECEMBER

25

Christmas Day.

1066 Coronation of William I, known as the Conquerer, first Norman king of England (r.1066–87), in Westminster Abbey, London.

1771 Birth of Dorothy Wordsworth in Cockermouth, Cumbria (d.1855), sister of poet William Wordsworth, famous for her diaries.

1800 Erection of the first Christmas tree in Britain at Windsor Castle by Queen Charlotte, wife of George III.

1843 The first US theatre matinee was held at the Olympic Theater, New York.

1899 Birth of Humphrey Bogart in New York (d.1957), actor, whose films include *Casablanca* (1942).

1906 Birth of Ernst Ruska in Heidelberg, Germany (d.1988), scientist, who developed the electron microscope.

1914 British and German troops facing each other in Flanders staged an impromptu Christmas Day truce, in the first year of World War 1.

1914 First isolation of the thyroid hormone thyroxine, by Edward Kendall (1886–1972) of the Mayo Clinic, Rochester, Minnesota.

1946 Death of W. C. Fields (b.1879 as William Claude Dukenfield in Philadelphia, Pennsylvania), actor, famous for his distinctive voice.

1950 Four Scottish students broke into Westminster Abbey, London, removed the Coronation Stone, or Stone of Scone, and took it to Scotland.

1952 Millions of BBC radio listeners heard Elizabeth II make her first Christmas Day speech, following the tradition begun by George V in 1932.

1957 Elizabeth II's Christmas Day speech was shown on television for the first time.

1959 Ringo Starr (b.1940), who became the drummer with The Beatles, received his first drum set as a Christmas present.

1974 Cyclone 'Tracy' swept through Darwin in Australia's Northern Territory, destroying much of the city.

1977 Death of Charlie Chaplin (b.1889 in London), actor and director, best known for his character in a bowler hat, with out-turned feet, moustache, and walking-cane.

1991 Soviet president Mikhail Gorbachev (b.1931) appeared on television to announce his resignation.

1995 Death of Dean Martin (b.1917 in Steubenville, Ohio), actor and singer, whose songs include 'Memories Are Made of This' (1955).

2004 Alain Robert (b.1962), the 'French Spiderman', climbed the world's tallest skyscraper, TAIPEI 101 (512 m/1680 ft), in Taipei, capital of Taiwan.

DECEMBER
26

Feast (Western Church) of St Stephen (1st c), patron saint of bricklayers, deacons, headache sufferers, smelters, and stonecutters.

1716 Birth of Thomas Gray in London (d.1771), poet, whose works include the 'Elegy Written in a Country Churchyard' (1751).

1791 Birth of Charles Babbage in London (d.1871), mathematician and inventor, known for his designs of calculating machines.

1890 Death of Heinrich Schliemann (b.1822 in Neubukow, Germany), archaeologist, who discovered and excavated the legendary cities of Troy and Mycenae.

1893 Birth of Mao Zedong, in Shaoshan, Hunan Province, China (d.1976), leading theorist of the Chinese Communist revolution.

1906 Premier of *The Story of the Kelly Gang*, the first continuous narrative film of any real length, in Melbourne, Victoria, Australia.

1908 Jack Johnson (1878–1946) became the first African-American to win the world heavyweight boxing title, when he knocked out Canadian Tommy Burns in Sydney, Australia.

1924 Show business debut for Judy Garland, during a Christmas show at her parents' theatre in Grand Rapids, Michigan; aged $2\frac{1}{2}$, she appeared as Baby Frances.

1928 A world record cricket partnership of 307 for the tenth wicket was set by A. F. Kippax (260 not out) and J. E. H. Hooker (62) during a match between New South Wales and Victoria, Australia.

1944 First performance of *The Glass Menagerie*, by Tennessee Williams, at the Civic Theatre, Chicago, Illinois.

1957 Death of Charles Pathé (b.1863 in Paris), film pioneer, who founded Société Pathé Frères (1896) with his brothers Emile, Théophile, and Jacques.

1959 The first charity walk took place along the Icknield Way, England; monies raised were donated to the World Refugee Fund.

1982 *Time* magazine's 'Man of the Year' was a non-human for the first time; a computer was honoured as 1982's 'greatest influence for good or evil'.

1991 Sale of the ·38 Colt Cobra revolver used by Jack Ruby in 1963 to kill Lee Harvey Oswald; it raised $220,000 at auction in New York.

2004 An earthquake in the Indian Ocean triggered a tsunami that hit Indonesia and eight other Asian countries; the death toll was estimated at 300,000.

DECEMBER
27

Feast of St John the Apostle (1st c), also known as John son of Zebedee and John the Evangelist, patron saint of publishers, writers, and theologians.

Feast (Eastern Church) of St Stephen (1st c), patron saint of bricklayers, deacons, headache sufferers, smelters, and stonecutters.

1571 Birth of Johannes Kepler in Weilder-Stadt, Germany (d.1630), astronomer, who formulated three laws of planetary motion.

1822 Birth of Louis Pasteur in Dôle, France (d.1895), chemist and microbiologist, who established the pasteurization process for milk.

1831 British naturalist Charles Darwin (1809–82) set sail, in HMS *Beagle*, on a five-year scientific voyage.

1834 Death of Charles Lamb (b.1775 in London), essayist and poet, whose works include the essays he wrote under the pen name of Elia.

1845 First use of anaesthesia for childbirth, when Dr Crawford Williamson Long administered ether during the birth of his own baby in Jefferson, Georgia.

1901 Birth of Marlene Dietrich in Berlin, Germany (d.1992), actress, who became famous for her role in the German film *The Blue Angel* (1930).

1904 First performance of J. M. Barrie's play *Peter Pan*.

1904 Opening of the Abbey Theatre, Dublin.

1911 Birth of Grote Reber in Wheaton, Illinois (2002), radio astronomer; intrigued by reports of Karl Jansky's 'cosmic static', he built a parabolic dish, the first radio telescope.

1934 Opening of the first US youth hostel, in Northfield, Massachusetts, by Isabel and Monroe Smith.

1945 Formation of the International Monetary Fund, a financial agency affiliated to the UN, located in Washington, DC.

1948 Birth of Gérard Dépardieu in Châteauroux, France, actor, whose films include *Cyrano de Bergerac* (1990).

1965 Capsize of the 5600-tonne oil rig *Sea Gem* in the North Sea, killing 13 people.

1975 Introduction of the Sex Discrimination and Equal Pay Acts in Britain.

1979 Invasion of Afghanistan by Russia.

1981 Death of Howard Hoagland (Hoagy) Carmichael (b.1899 in Bloomington, Indiana), jazz pianist, who composed such classics as 'Stardust' (1927).

2003 Death of Sir Alan Bates (b.1934 in Allestree, Derbyshire), actor, whose films include *A Kind of Loving* (1962).

DECEMBER
28

Holy Innocents' Day.

1065 Consecration of Westminster Abbey, London, in the reign of Edward the Confessor, whose remains are entombed in front of the High Altar.

1598 The Lord Chamberlain's Men pulled down The Theatre in London, and took the materials across the R Thames to build a new theatre, The Globe, on Bankside.

1612 First observation of Neptune was made by Italian astronomer and mathematician Galileo Galilei (1564–1642); he recorded the planet as an 8th-magnitude star.

1694 Death of Mary II (b.1662 in St James's Palace, London), queen of Britain and Ireland from 1689.

1734 Death of Rob Roy (b.1671 in Buchanan, Stirling), Highland outlaw, whose life was romanticized in the novel by Sir Walter Scott.

1846 Iowa became the 29th state of the Union.

1879 Collapse of the Tay railway bridge, Scotland.

1895 First public demonstration of the Lumière brothers' Cinématographe at the Grand Café, Paris.

1897 First performance of *Cyrano de Bergerac* by Edmond Rostand, at the Théâtre de la Porte Saint-Martin, Paris.

1923 Death of Gustave Eiffel (b.1832 in Dijon, France), civil engineer, who designed the Eiffel Tower, Paris.

1926 The highest first-class cricket innings score of 1107 runs was made by Victoria against New South Wales, in Melbourne, Australia.

1934 Birth of Dame Maggie Smith in Ilford, London, actress, whose films include *The Prime of Miss Jean Brodie* (1969).

1937 Death of Maurice Ravel (b.1875 in Ciboure, France), composer, whose works include *Boléro* (1928).

1954 Birth of Denzel Washington in Mount Vernon, New York, actor, who became known for his role in the television medical drama *St Elsewhere* (1982–8).

1956 Birth of Nigel Kennedy in Brighton, East Sussex, violinist, noted for his unconventional style of dress as well as for his remarkable playing ability.

1981 Birth of Elizabeth Jordan Carr, first baby born from in-vitro fertilization in the USA, at Norfolk General Hospital, Virginia.

1984 Death of Sam Peckinpah (b.1925 in Fresno, California), director, whose films include *The Wild Bunch* (1969).

2004 Death of Susan Sontag (b.1933 in New York), critic and writer, whose books include *In America* (1999).

DECEMBER
29

1170 Death of Thomas Becket (b.1118 in London), archbishop of Canterbury, murdered in Canterbury Cathedral, Kent.

1675 Issue of a proclamation by the British parliament ordering the closure of all coffee houses, believing they were centres of malicious gossip about the government; it was later reduced to a warning.

1809 Birth of W(illiam) E(wart) Gladstone in Liverpool (d.1898), British prime minister (1868–74, 1880–85, 1886, 1892–4).

1845 Texas became the 28th state of the Union.

1848 The first gaslight was turned on in the White House, during the administration of President James Knox Polk (1795–1849).

1860 Launch of HMS *Warrior*, the first iron-hulled warship, and at the time the longest and largest ever built.

1890 The Battle of Wounded Knee, South Dakota, the final defeat of the Sioux Indians by US forces.

1918 First publication of Britain's *Sunday Express* newspaper.

1930 Radio Luxembourg began broadcasting.

1936 Birth of Mary Tyler Moore in New York, actress, whose television credits include *The Mary Tyler Moore Show* (1970–77).

1937 The Constitution of Ireland came into force; adopted in a referendum on 1 July 1937, it legislated for two Houses: Dáil Éireann and Seanad Éireann.

1938 Birth of Jon Voight in Yonkers, New York, actor, whose films include *Midnight Cowboy* (1969).

1940 London suffered its most devastating air raid, when German bombers dropped 24,000 incendiary bombs and 120 tons of high explosives on the city, killing 163 people and causing much fire damage.

1946 Birth of Marianne Faithful in London, singer and actress, who had a much-publicized relationship with Mick Jagger in the 1960s.

1952 First sales of the transistor hearing-aid, in the USA.

1972 Birth of Jude Law in London, actor, whose films include *A.I.* (2001).

1987 Russian cosmonaut Yuri Romanenko (b.1944) returned to earth from Soviet space station Mir, having spent a record 326 days, 11 hours, and 37 minutes in space.

1989 Václav Havel (b.1936) became president of Czechoslovakia, on a huge wave of popular support.

1997 Hong Kong began killing its entire chicken population of up to 1·4 million birds, to stem the spread of avian flu, which had already killed four people.

DECEMBER
30

1460 Death of Richard, Duke of York (b.1411), defeated and killed by the Lancastrians at the Battle of Wakefield.

1865 Birth of Rudyard Kipling in Mumbai (Bombay), India (d.1936), writer, whose works include the *Jungle Books* (1894–5).

1879 First performance of *The Pirates of Penzance* by Gilbert and Sullivan, at the Bijou Theatre, Paignton, Devon.

1887 More than a million women petitioned Britain's Queen Victoria for the closure of pubs on Sundays.

1894 Death of Amelia Bloomer (b.1818 in Homer, New York), champion of women's rights and dress reform, which included her own version of trousers for women, later called 'bloomers'.

1903 A fire at the Iroquois Theater, Chicago, Illinois, killed 602 of the audience of 1900 who had come to see Eddie Foy in the musical comedy *Mr Bluebeard, Jr.*

1916 Death of Rasputin (b.1871 in Pokrovskoye, Russia), religious sectarian, who gained the confidence of the Russian emperor and empress, but whose political influence led to his murder.

1922 Russia became the USSR, the Union of Soviet Socialist Republics.

1924 US astronomer Edwin Hubble (1889–1953) established the existence of galaxies other than the Milky Way.

1932 Completion of the electrification of the London-to-Brighton railway line.

1953 First US sales of colour television sets that worked independently (without a converter or adapter), made by Admiral, priced $1175.

1959 Birth of Tracey Ullman in Slough, Berkshire, actress and singer, who became known as an impressionist in the comedy television show *Three of a Kind*.

1970 Death of 'Sonny' Liston (b.1917 in St Francis Co, Arkansas), boxer, who defeated Floyd Patterson to become world heavyweight champion in 1962.

1979 Death of Richard Rodgers (b.1902 in New York), composer, and collaborator with lyricists Lorenz Hart and Oscar Hammerstein II in many hit musicals.

1982 Eclipse of the second full moon of the month, known as a 'blue moon'; the only total eclipse of a blue moon in the twentieth century.

1999 George Harrison (1943–2001), former member of The Beatles, was stabbed in the chest at his home in Henley, Oxfordshire, by an intruder.

DECEMBER
31

1600 Queen Elizabeth I granted a Royal Charter establishing the London-based East India Company.

1695 Imposition of window tax in Britain.

1719 Death of John Flamsteed (b.1646 in Denby, Derbyshire), Britain's first Astronomer Royal.

1720 Birth of Charles Edward Stuart in Rome (d.1788), claimant to the British crown, known as 'Bonnie Prince Charlie'.

1857 Queen Victoria named Ottawa as capital of the British colonial Province of Canada.

1869 Birth of Henri Matisse in Le Cateau, France (d.1954), painter, leader of the Fauvist movement of the 1900s.

1890 Opening of Ellis Island, New York, as the new immigration depot.

1900 A storm felled an upright and its lintel at Stonehenge, Wiltshire, the first stones to fall since 1797; they were raised again in 1958, approximately restoring the monument to its appearance during Roman occupation.

1917 Sugar rationing began in Britain during World War 1.

1923 First broadcast of the chimes of Big Ben by the BBC; a microphone connected to Broadcasting House was placed in the clock tower of the Houses of Parliament, London.

1935 Patenting of the board game *Monopoly* by its inventor, US game designer Charles Darrow (1889–1967).

1938 Introduction of Dr Rolla N. Harger's 'drunkometer', the first alcohol breath-testing device, by the Indianapolis police department in the USA.

1941 Birth of Sir Alex Ferguson in Glasgow, former footballer, who managed Aberdeen and Manchester United football clubs.

1943 Birth of Ben Kingsley in Snainton, North Yorkshire, actor, who received an Oscar for his title role in the film *Gandhi* (1980).

1948 Death of Sir Malcolm Campbell (b.1885 in Chislehurst, Kent), land and water speed-record contestant, who called all his cars and boats *Bluebird*.

1960 Last day as legal tender for the British farthing.

1964 British land and water speed-record contestant Donald Campbell (1921–67) set the world speed record on water at 276·33 mph on Lake Dumbleyung, Australia.

1973 Introduction of the three-day working week in Britain to conserve fuel during a miners' strike.

know more

PENGUIN POCKET REFERENCE

THE PENGUIN POCKET DICTIONARY OF QUOTATIONS
EDITED BY DAVID CRYSTAL

The Penguin Pocket Dictionary of Quotations is essential reading for
anyone searching for the perfect quotation – whether you need a
snappy one-liner for a speech or a remark of brilliant insight for your
written work. With this pithy and provocative selection of wit and
wisdom, you will never be lost for words again.

– Includes quotations from a vast range of people, from film stars to
  politicians

– Arranged alphabetically by name of person quoted, with the original
  source for each quotation given

– Provides a full index of key words to help you find each quotation
  quickly and easily

www.penguin.com

PENGUIN POCKET REFERENCE

THE PENGUIN POCKET DICTIONARY OF BABIES' NAMES
DAVID PICKERING

The Penguin Pocket Dictionary of Babies' Names is essential reading
for all expectant parents wishing to choose the perfect name for their
child. It gives the meanings and stories behind thousands of names
from all parts of the world – ranging from the most well-known choices
to more unusual names.

- Gives variations and shortened forms for each name

- Highlights names popularized by books, films and celebrities

- Lists the most popular girls' and boys' names from 1700 to the
  present

- Shows how tastes for names have changed in the twenty-first century

know more ⬤

PENGUIN POCKET REFERENCE

THE PENGUIN POCKET BOOK OF FACTS
EDITED BY DAVID CRYSTAL

The Penguin Pocket Book of Facts is a goldmine of information, figures and statistics on every conceivable subject – from the world's highest mountains and longest rivers to the gods of mythology, and from time zones to Nobel Prize winners. The ultimate one-stop factfinder, this is the essential book for browsers, crossword and trivia addicts, and for anyone who needs to check facts at home or at work.

- Up-to-date information about everything from astronomy to zoology

- Easy to use

- Illustrated throughout with maps and diagrams

www.penguin.com

Penguin Pocket Reference

THE PENGUIN POCKET ENGLISH DICTIONARY

This pocket edition of the bestselling *Penguin English Dictionary* is the perfect reference book for everyday use. Compiled by Britain's foremost lexicographers, up to date and easy to use, it is the ideal portable companion for quick reference.

- Includes a wealth of words, phrases and clear definitions, with more information than other comparable dictionaries

- Covers standard and formal English, as well as specialist terms, slang and jargon

- Provides invaluable guidance on correct usage, commonly confused words and grammar and spelling

---

know more

PENGUIN POCKET REFERENCE

POCKET ROGET'S® THESAURUS
GEORGE DAVIDSON

Roget's Thesaurus is the world's most trusted wordfinder and a writer's best friend, and this Pocket edition is ideal for helping you to find the exact words you need for all your written work. It will help improve your knowledge and use of the English language, build up your vocabulary and provide the key to stimulating and creative writing.

– Contains over 880 sections, covering objects, activities and abstract words and phrases

– Includes formal English, technical language, slang and jargon

– Provides full cross-referencing

'The indispensable guide to the English language' *Daily Express*

www.penguin.com

He just wanted a decent book to read ...

Not too much to ask, is it? It was in 1935 when Allen Lane, Managing Director of Bodley Head Publishers, stood on a platform at Exeter railway station looking for something good to read on his journey back to London. His choice was limited to popular magazines and poor-quality paperbacks – the same choice faced every day by the vast majority of readers, few of whom could afford hardbacks. Lane's disappointment and subsequent anger at the range of books generally available led him to found a company – and change the world.

'We believed in the existence in this country of a vast reading public for intelligent books at a low price, and staked everything on it'
Sir Allen Lane, 1902–1970, founder of Penguin Books

The quality paperback had arrived – and not just in bookshops. Lane was adamant that his Penguins should appear in chain stores and tobacconists, and should cost no more than a packet of cigarettes.

Reading habits (and cigarette prices) have changed since 1935, but Penguin still believes in publishing the best books for everybody to enjoy. We still believe that good design costs no more than bad design, and we still believe that quality books published passionately and responsibly make the world a better place.

So wherever you see the little bird – whether it's on a piece of prize-winning literary fiction or a celebrity autobiography, political tour de force or historical masterpiece, a serial-killer thriller, reference book, world classic or a piece of pure escapism – you can bet that it represents the very best that the genre has to offer.

Whatever you like to read – trust Penguin.

read more
www.penguin.co.uk